Public Administration

Public Administration

Agencies, Policies, and Politics

Ira Sharkansky

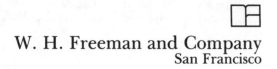

W. H. Freeman and Company
San Francisco

Project Editor: Pearl C. Vapnek
Manuscript Editor: Robyn Brode
Designer: Nancy Warner
Production Coordinator: Valerie Swanson
Illustration Coordinator: Cheryl Nufer
Compositor: Graphic Typesetting Service
Printer and Binder: The Maple-Vail Book Manufacturing Group

Library of Congress Cataloging in Publication Data

Sharkansky, Ira.
   Public administration.

   Bibliography: p.
   Includes index.
   1. Public administration.   I. Title.
JF1351.S463   1982   350   81-22220
ISBN 0-7167-1321-7   AACR2

Printed in the United States of America

1 2 3 4 5 6 7 8 9 0   MP   0 8 9 8 7 6 5 4 3 2

For my mother,
Beatrice Mines Sharkansky

Contents

Preface

Public administration is a rich and varied field. Instructors differ vastly in their approaches. Some focus on the politics of administration, while others concentrate on the techniques of management. Some are explicitly comparative, while others prefer to emphasize the United States—the federal government, their home state, or local authorities. Some concentrate on organizational theory, while others rely heavily on case studies or workshop exercises. Some instructors purvey a distinctive point of view: the importance of institutions, organizational development, employee-centered management, issues of political accountability, or a cynical view of snafu-laden bureaucracy.

In light of the wide variety among courses in public administration, I have tried to prevent any narrow perspective from dominating this book. I want to introduce the student to the whole field. Moreover, I have written the book both for the student who wishes to understand the functions of administration in the larger worlds of politics and policy-making and for the prospective administrator.

The book descends from my earlier *Public Administration: Policy-Making in Government Agencies*. It is, however, entirely new in structure and in most of the substance. Its roots remain in academic political science, for it seeks to outline and explain—from the vantage points of political disputes and pressures—the nature of public administration. More than its predecessor, *Public Administration: Agencies, Policies, and Politics* attempts to acquaint prospective administrators with the range of skills that contribute to a career in government. There are chapters on agency management, budgeting, personnel, administrative law and regulation, and program evaluation. Other chapters describe policy-making, implementation, and the accountability of administrators to the institutions of democratic government. The systems framework, which was a feature of the earlier book, does not appear here.

While the focus remains on American materials, I hope that its comparative statements have been enriched by the years I have spent outside the United States. Thus, most of the book deals with public administration in the United States, especially in the federal government. However, one chapter compares administrative behavior between and within other countries. Another chapter describes intergovernmental relations within the American federal system, and another deals with the increasingly important, but often overlooked, growth of public administration via contractors operating on the margins of government.

Two introductory chapters explain basic concepts, outline the structure of public administration in the United States, and relate the structure to theories of organization that are relevant to the public sector. The first chapter emphasizes the ever-present nature of public administration in modern society and clarifies such key terms as "administration" and "public policy." Chapter 2 charts the fundamental terrain of departments and other entities included in the scope of public administration. It outlines general ideas about organization, especially those that have guided the development of public administration in the United States.

A group of three chapters treats the topic of accountability from the perspectives of various political institutions, the elected branches of government, and administrators themselves. Chapters 3 and 4 deal with controls over administrators that come from public opinion, elections, political parties, and interest groups, plus the elected officials in the executive and legislative branches. Chapter 5 explores the issue of political accountability from the perspective of agency managers and personnel.

Four chapters discuss the tools of administration. The question *How to do it?* in areas of concern to prospective administrators is the subject of Chapters 6–9: agency management, budgeting, personnel, and program evaluation. Administrators are regarded as active participants in shaping the mechanisms perceived by politicians and managers as ways to control administrators. These chapters also stress the larger political issues that affect choices of administrative techniques.

Chapters 10 and 11 deal with the formulation of public policy and its implementation. Both describe idealized expectations, but concentrate on how policy-makers work to formulate and implement policies under various conditions that are less than ideal.

A final group of five chapters treats several topics that warrant special consideration: the instructive role of comparison between U.S. states and among other nations, intergovernmental relations in the United States, the operation of regulatory agencies, the use of private contractors as extensions of government departments, and the perspective on public administration of citizen clients.

Each chapter approaches public administration from multiple perspectives. In the bulk of the book, the perspectives of observers and practitioners are emphasized more often than is the perspective of the citizen client. Chapter 16 closes the book with an overview that stresses the client's perspective. Several recurrent themes are developed into operating principles and handy rules that may help clients in their dealings with public administrative units.

Many people have contributed to this book. Conversations with numerous students and colleagues sensitized me to their needs in a public administration textbook. In moving from draft outline to final manuscript, I benefited from the critiques of Roger E. Durand, University of Colorado, Colorado Springs; Nicholas P. Lovrich, Jr., Washington State University; James P. Pfiffner, California State University at Fullerton; Roby D. Robertson, Texas A & M University; and James A. Thurber, Battelle Human Affairs Research Centers, Washington Operations. I am especially indebted to James J. Kloss for his many excellent suggestions. Deanna Gervasi was a prompt and proficient typist on this project, as she was on many others. My thanks are due Robyn Brode. I found her grasp of the material to be exceptional, and her suggestions well thought out. Her editing has added greatly to the book. Varda Horn contributed much in the final stages of production. My mother has done a great deal to deserve my love and the dedication of this book.

January 1982   *Ira Sharkansky*

PART I

Introduction

Administration is at the heart of modern government. It is the citizen's most frequent contact with government, and often the focus of complaints. Part I introduces key concepts in public administration. Chapter 1 identifies the variety of people who work as public administrators, offers a working definition of public policy, and describes various perspectives on the study of public administration. Chapter 2 outlines the structures of public administration in the United States and describes key theories that are used to explain the character of public administration.

1

Historical Survey
and Contemporary Overview

Public administration affects your life many times each day. By reading this book, you indicate an interest in administration as a topic of study or as a career. You may already be working for government and be attending school part-time. Chances are your school is state-supported. Your instructor is more likely than not to be a government employee. Even if your school claims to be private, it—or many of its students—probably receives sizable amounts of government aid and feels the constant scrutiny of government officials. Is the university's athletic budget divided between male and female athletes in a way that satisfies the U.S. Department of Education? If not, the university may find itself on a blacklist, unable to qualify for federal aid. You travel on public roads in vehicles built according to government standards for safety, pollution, and fuel economy, or on public transportation that is operated or subsidized and regulated by government.

Neither your food nor your clothing escapes the concern of public administrators. There are programs for farming, marketing, and labeling food and fiber, plus controls on the amounts of food and clothing imported from overseas. Your insurance and bank account come under public control. Housing is taxed; its construction is regulated and perhaps subsidized. Your pursuit of leisure may depend on public libraries or parks, or on vehicles and toys that meet government standards for safety. Should there be an accident, you will almost surely enter a hospital that enjoys a public subsidy and—along with its physicians—must comply with numerous controls. Your religious denomination may operate social welfare agencies that have become contractors with government agencies, thus receiving more funds from government budgets than from church collections. The quality of your retirement may largely depend on the Social Security Administration. And alas, when you die, there will be a final social security payment for burial expenses, including the services of an undertaker who is licensed and regulated for reasons of professional standards and consumer protection.

This book is about people who do the work of government. Public administrators design programs, deal with the public, and manage the many persons who perform these tasks. They are men and women who sit at desks and examine papers that authorize other people to spend money, recruit employees, and offer clients a service. Others inspect factories or schoolrooms, visit farmers, and audit tax returns. Still others evaluate the work of program administrators or argue the merits of agency proposals in the many settings in which officials must decide the course of government activity.

Many kinds of government employees affect our lives. Physicians in government hospitals and professors at state universities, for example, have a great deal of freedom in choosing how to cure and educate their clients. Administrators who manage government hospitals and state universities recognize the status of their professional employees and generally respect their rights to make decisions about their patients or students.

In contrast, welfare counselors, police officers, and tax auditors are dealt with much differently. Typically they work in hierarchical agencies, are accountable to bosses for the details of each job, and work according to rules that specify how to deal with each situation. When these employees of government use discretion, it often may be in an informal or extralegal manner. For example, welfare department rules generally indicate that a grant is to be given to each client according to such traits as age, income, and family status. However, the case worker can choose to report or overlook a live-in companion or a part-time job that would trigger a reduction in the monthly payment. Tax auditors are trained to demand payments or grant exceptions according to the agency manual. However, the laws and the court decisions that lie behind the manuals are complex enough to require discretion. How to treat certain income or expenses is partly a contest between the taxpayer and the government auditor, and the quality of the taxpayer's argument at least partly determines whether the auditor grants the taxpayer's interpretation, draws a clear line with respect to agency rules, or sends the case upstairs to a more senior auditor.

The job of the public administrators—*whether professional, paraprofessional, or clerical*—in public life has grown immensely. The character and reasons for that great growth are necessary subjects of our attention.

THE HISTORICAL GROWTH
OF PUBLIC ADMINISTRATION

Government was not always a behemoth. In the early years of the United States, government was a tiny fragment of its present self, concerned almost exclusively with tax collection, land surveys, defense, delivering the mail, and operating the courts. Government-operated schools were a rarity, and public health and welfare depended on the whims of private charity and personal fortune.

Growth in public services has come about as a result of increasing population and social technology, public demands for services and tolerance for taxation, and one crisis after another that has given politicians the courage and the excuse to establish new activities. War and economic depression have been especially prominent in the periods of rapid growth of American government at national, state, and local levels, while a steadily growing population has accounted for constant growth between the spurts. Table 1-1 offers some public work-force data with which to gauge the growth of American public administration. The number of government employees is listed in representative years by federal and state and local governments.

In more recent years the size of the national government administration has been stable or declining in size, especially when viewed in relation to an increasing population. State and local administrations, in contrast, have grown rapidly (see Box 1-1). Also increasing has been the number contractors who work for national, state, and local agencies. By some estimates, they alone may employ up to 12 million people.

The character as well as the size of public administration has changed over the years. New programs reflect contemporary experiences. Early in the twentieth century the society was predominantly rural and the federal government created programs to benefit agriculture. Welfare programs began in the 1930s, brought on by the Great Depression and the political coalitions of President Franklin D. Roosevelt (see Table 1-2). In the climate of Cold War competition with the Soviet Union during the 1950s, new programs carried a defense label even if they were primarily domestic in nature; such as the Interstate and *Defense* Highway Program and the National *Defense* Education Act. The 1960s and 1970s saw new programs focused on poverty, the cities, the environment, and energy.

Other changes have come about in the techniques of managing public administration. Years ago, it was the style to view administration in hierarchical terms, with superiors assumed to control subordinates. "Scientific management" was the label for this approach to administration. It was thought to be scientific to define the workload that each employee could handle, as well as the combination of inducements, such as salary and discipline, that would produce the most work. Later generations of adminis-

Table 1-1 Historical Changes in Government
Employment (in thousands of employees),
1830–1978

Year	Federal	State and local
1978	2,888	12,743
1976	2,879	12,169
1970	2,928	10,147
1965	2,539	8,001
1960	2,430	6,387
1955	2,402	5,054
1950	2,117	4,285
1945	3,770	
1940	1,614	
1935	719	
1930	580	
1925	533	
1920	691	
1915	476	
1910	384	
1905	301	
1900	230	
1890	160	
1880	100	
1870	53	
1860	49	
1850	33	
1840	23	
1830	19	

SOURCES: U.S. Bureau of the Census. *The Statistical Abstract of
the United States, 1979* (Washington, D.C.: U.S. Government
Printing Office, 1980) and *Historical Statistics of the United States:
Colonial Times to 1970* (Washington, D.C.: U.S. Government
Printing Office, 1972).

trators began to see the benefits of a "human-relations approach." Hierarchical structures with clear demarcations between superiors and subordinates
came under fire, and employees in all ranks were encouraged to participate
in defining their tasks.

The politics of administration also change. Early in American history,
employees won their jobs because of party activity. The political party that
won an election rewarded its supporters with government jobs. Criteria of
personal merit first emerged for the federal government when reformers
enacted the Pendleton Act of 1883, and later when similar legislation was

adopted by states and localities. Job candidates were to be chosen according to skill rather than political favor. This trend had moved so far by the 1960s that several governors were unable to appoint persons committed to their political philosophy to key administrative posts, in order to assure the proper implementation of their programs. The pendulum has recently begun to swing back to giving chief executives more control over "policy-level appointments." Even so, the vast bulk of civil servants comes under routine selection procedures that take into account skills, preferential treatment of veterans, and affirmative action on behalf of women, certain minorities, and the handicapped.

WHO ARE PUBLIC ADMINISTRATORS?

In one view, all the people working for government are public administrators and should be the subjects of this book. In another view, administrators are only those who administer or manage what other employees do. These two groups are given attention in this book.

A direct connection to government is common to public administrators, however different their status or hierarchical standing may be. They work for administrative departments or agencies that carry out the missions of government. Public administrators receive their salaries from the government budget, and they work according to laws passed by the legislature. Like the elected officials they take direction from, public administrators often have the special attention of the public, the press, and the electronic media, which have a stake in assuring the accountability of government to its people.

Administrators vary in prestige and power, from junior clerks and janitors in government buildings to senior professionals and officers who direct the work of many subordinates. Some administrators draft policy statements for the President or write the regulations that determine how their agencies will carry out the intent of legislation. This book considers all employees of administrative units to be public administrators. However, it focuses mostly on those personnel involved in the formulation or execution of public policy. Chapter 15 goes beyond government employees, per se, and deals with private organizations that do the work of government agencies under contract.

WHAT IS PUBLIC POLICY?

Public policies are the important things that government makes. This statement is more the start of a discussion than a complete definition. Each key term requires further comment.

The rate of governmental growth may be tapering off.

BOX 1-1   The Great Transformation—Growth to No Growth

After growing almost twice as fast as the economy for a quarter of a century (1949–1975), aggregate state and local spending has lagged the nominal growth in Gross National Product since 1975. What we have is the great transformation of the state and local sector from a fast growth to a no growth industry.

State and Local Expenditures, Including Federal Aid, Selected Years 1949–1980

Calendar years	As percent of GNP	Per capita (constant dollars)
1949	7.8%	$189
1959	9.6	302
1969	12.5	528
1975	15.1	670
1976	14.6	682
1977	14.3	691
1978	14.3	710
1979	13.9	688
1980[a]	13.7	656

[a]Estimate

The no growth character of the state and local sector is also dramatically underscored when per capita expenditures are adjusted for inflation. For the

Important is defined in terms of the financial value of an activity, the number of people affected, or the intensity of feeling that an activity arouses. Things are more or less important according to the magnitude of these values. When a clerk in the Social Security Administration punches the computer buttons that result in one check going to one senior citizen, that is not an action that is policy-making. However, when an analyst in the Social Security Administration argues for an increase in social security taxes or benefits that amounts to a great deal of money spread over many people, that is an activity with policy significance.

Things range from the tangible to the symbolic. Some administrators deal with the concrete features of buildings, equipment, or the delivery of social services. Others deal mainly in the symbols that have importance to many people, such as the words used for program goals or the expressions of government concern for a troublesome issue. Some policy statements have great social impact, while others have no immediate impact on the goods or services received by the population. President Gerald Ford once sought an calendar year 1980, we estimate that per capita state and local expenditures will total $656 (constant dollars)—somewhat less than the $670 figure registered five years earlier.

UNDERLYING CAUSES

Much of this striking change in recent state and local fiscal behavior can be attributed to fundamental changes in our society.

Public opinion change—from support, or at least toleration, of fast growth to a demand for slower growth. Many of the recent lids imposed on state and local spenders are designed so as to prevent state and local taxes from growing at a faster rate than the income of the taxpayers.

Economic change—from that characterized by significant real growth to that marked by slow or no real growth and high rates of inflation. Among other things, inflation injects high octane fuel into the fires of local property tax discontent. The recent explosion in California serves as the most dramatic case in point. It also shows portents of sparking an indexation fire among income taxing governments.

Demographic change—during most of the post World War II era, steadily rising school enrollments exerted enormous upward pressure on state and local fiscs. Now declining enrollments have tended to stabilize the pressure on this important expenditure front.

SOURCE: U.S. Advisory Commission on Intergovernmental Relations, *Intergovernmental Perspective*, 6 (Spring 1980).

easy way to cope with a surge of inflation by publicly urging ("jawboning," as the press calls it) business and labor to temper their price and wage increases. Virtually the only concrete action taken by the President was the distribution of buttons with the acronym WIN (Whip Inflation Now) brightly displayed for public consumption. Another example of a policy with relatively little impact was the statements issued by the Carter Administration in behalf of human rights elsewhere in the world.

Makes is another word in the statement about public policy that requires comment. Often government stops with an expression of concern or a hint of future action, and does not actually implement a program to deal with a problem. Sometimes government announces a policy *not* to do something, such as not to regulate wages or prices, or not to interfere in the internal affairs of a friendly country. Some of the policies government makes are not decided overtly but are apparent only by inference, after the fact. An aggregate of actions may benefit one class of people more than another, without any explicit decision having been made to benefit that class. One

Government benefits are growing. More of us rely on government for more of what is important to us. This reliance increases our demands on policy-makers for more and better benefits, and leads them to increase their own resources for better decision-making.

Table 1-2 The Steady Growth of the Welfare State
(in thousands of beneficiaries), 1945–1990

Benefit	1945	1950	1960	1970	1979	1985	1990
Social security							
Retirement	691	2,326	10,599	17,076	22,496	25,977	28,702
Disability	—	—	687	2,665	4,792	6,356	7,311
Survivors	579	1,152	3,558	6,468	7,595	10,209	7,149
Medicare	—	—	—	19,312	26,317	30,572	NA
Medicaid	—	—	—	14,507	21,378	NA	NA
Supplemental security income	2,100	3,000	2,800	3,100	4,200	NA	NA
Veterans retirement[a]	2,232	3,376	4,457	5,511	5,164	4,911	4,792
Civil service retirement[a]	85	172	512	959	1,617	1,932	2,099
Military retirement	NA	138	243	750	1,287	1,373	1,464
Railroad retirement	177	398	809	979	1,026	NA	NA
Aid to families with dependent children[b]	1,450	3,099	4,317	10,715	11,203	NA	NA
Food stamps	—	—	—	4,340	17,700	19,000	NA
School lunch	—	8,600	14,100	23,100	27,000	NA	NA
Housing[c]	—	—	426	932	3,007	3,800	NA
Unemployment aid	—	1,600	2,100	2,100	2,400	NA	NA

[a]Includes disability and survivors' benefits.
[b]Includes general assistance.
[c]Number of housing units.

SOURCE: *National Journal*, January 19, 1980. Reprinted with permission.

group of researchers has found that the sum total of national, state, and local taxes weigh most heavily on lower-income groups. These may all be "policy," but they are different kinds of policies from those made in an explicit fashion that lead to tangible steps.

Government may be the trickiest part of the statement about public policy. Governments in the United States and in many other countries have assumed responsibility for many activities that they handle by means of instrumentalities that are not part of government. Government agencies contract with private organizations to construct facilities; supply equipment; and design, administer, and evaluate social services. Some public administrators arrange and supervise these contracts. In recent years, much, if not most, of the work done by government has been administered through bodies that are not formally part of government. A lawyer may be able to provide a legal definition of what is and is not part of government. For a political scientist, however, the task is elusive. In this book, those activities undertaken by private contractors acting as agents of public agencies are viewed as fully within the scope of public policy analysis.

As a result of the examples portrayed in this book, you may come to understand the great varieties of public policies and the many roles that administrators play in policy formulation and implementation. To begin with, however, you must recognize that many kinds of public policies do not lend themselves to a simple definition.

WHY STUDY PUBLIC ADMINISTRATION?

There are four answers to this question, depending primarily on your perspective.

Academic Specialists

For academic specialists in political science and public administration, the study of public administration provides an opportunity to integrate their interests in government and politics with the study of how public policy is formulated and public services delivered. As social scientists interested in the specific realm of public administration, we must take into account not only administrative departments, but also the most salient influences on them—namely, public opinion, elections, political parties, interest groups, legislatures, chief executives, and the courts.

> *How do these forces influence administrative personnel and the character of policy?*
>
> *How are these political forces influenced by administrators?*

These and related questions are the special concern of academic specialists in political science.

A complete view of politics must include public administration. There is little formulation of policy goals and virtually no implementation of policy without administrators. There can be no complete study of classical issues in political theory without a concern for administration. *Equity, justice,* and *freedom* can be defined fully only in terms of the benefits and costs associated with concrete public programs.

How much in taxes actually is paid by different classes of citizens?

How do the police, prosecutors, and courts actually treat different kinds of people?

How do welfare counselors treat their clients, and what sums do the needy receive?

What health services are offered in different communities?

Which students receive high-quality education and vocational training?

Which schools have the smallest classes, the most equipment, and the best-trained teachers?

Are there patterns in the distribution of services that challenge obvious standards of equity?

Who pays? and *Who gets what?* are simple expressions of profound questions.

Accountability is another issue of concern to academic specialists in political science and public administration. Accountability gets at the question of control, or *Who rules?* According to conventional notions of democratic theory, the people should rule. But how do they do it when so much of what government does is actually designed and delivered by nonelected professional administrators? Studies of accountability look at the links between the political process—public opinion, voting behavior, parties, interest groups, and elected officials—and the departments of government. Administrators do not simply follow the orders that come from elected officials. Much discretion for administrators is written into the laws meant to govern them. Some administrators exercise more discretion than the politicians intend. Open conflict and much covert maneuvering are common. There is no simple answer to the question *Who rules?* just as there are no simple answers to the other questions of classical political theory.

Among their other tasks, academics seek to describe variations in public administration as they appear in different times and places, and to explain these variations with reference to the contexts in which they develop. Countries differ in the way they organize their governments, in the styles of their politics and administration. Especially in those countries that are large and diverse, conditions may vary from one locale to another. Diversity is firmly rooted in U.S. political traditions. The special needs of groups and individuals are expressed in our concern for liberty and freedom. More than other people, Americans find themselves in a schizoid ambivalence between a commitment to big public programs and a passion for individuality and free enterprise. What passes for proper activity in Mississippi, moreover, may not find acceptance in Minnesota.

Professional political scientists and academic specialists in public administration seek to understand in an orderly fashion what most citizens do haphazardly: why the agencies of government work as they do. The key questions are the same for everyone; the professionals simply muse about them in a more explicit fashion. From deceptively simple questions like these, all else follows:

> ***What are government agencies doing?***
> ***Why do government agencies do what they do?***
> ***What are they going to do next?***
> ***Who gets what as a result of their activities?***
> ***How can we get them to do what we want?***

Administrators

For prospective and present administrators, the study of public administration offers both training in the mechanics of "how to do it" and an understanding of the larger context in which they operate. The elements of agency management, budgeting, personnel selection, and program evaluation concern almost all administrators during their careers—either as they practice them or as they are affected by the way other administrators practice them. Codes of ethical conduct, regulations on conflict of interest, and rules governing political activities come to administrators from legislatures and chief executives. These rules and regulations define how administrators should deal with clients who receive their services, how to do business with firms that sell to the government, and what limits exist for the role that administrators can play in election campaigns. Administrators must also learn much about the methods available for the analysis of social problems and program options.

Not all of these activities can be encompassed within a single book. Budgeting, personnel administration, management, and program evaluation all warrant specialized treatment. Skills of policy analysis divide according to fields of service, such as education, taxation, health, police, and defense. This book seeks to provide you both with an introduction to the various fields that should be mastered by a public administrator, as well as with an overview of how administration fits into the larger context of American politics. The ultimate test of this effort will be if you are prompted to look further into specialized texts.

Politicians

For politicians, it is essential to appreciate the roles administrators play in shaping public policy. The individual campaigner can make public promises, but, once elected, cannot deliver them alone. Not only must other politicians be considered in a democratic government with several centers of power, but also, even if all politicians acted in concert, they would still have to take professional administrators into account. While the law and constitutional tradition assign great power to elected officials, reality often favors administrators.

Individual legislators depend on administrators and may value their advice more highly than that of other legislators. For a program to succeed in the legislature, it may need the active support of the administrators who will implement it. Once programs are passed by the legislature and signed by the chief executive, they depend on administrators. For example, in 1979 it was the National Transportation Safety Board, not an elected official, that first decertified then recertified the DC–10. An American Airlines DC–10 dropped an engine and crashed during take-off from Chicago's O'Hare Airport. When all DC–10s were grounded for a period of several weeks at the beginning of the summer travel season, airlines lost a major part of their fleets. Millions of passengers felt the shock waves in canceled flights, airport confusion, and deferred plans.

Similarly, it is professionals in the Food and Drug Administration who approve or ban the sale of new drugs. In their hands rest the safety of consumers who might be harmed by dangerous substances, the hopes of patients who suffer disease and wish the speedy processing of new drugs that might help them, as well as the profits of corporations that wish to market their new products.

Elected officials have built a system of policy implementation that puts key decisions in the hands of administrators. If politicians want to maximize their influence with respect to public policy, they must understand administration. To do this, they must master the existing laws and regulations that define policies in the program field they wish to shape, and know the key institutions and individuals that generate program advice and implement services. This can be a humbling experience for the politician excited by the prospect of turning a bright idea into public policy.

Citizens

For citizens, it is important to know that administration makes up the vast bulk of government. Almost all of the people on the payrolls of national, state, and local governments in the United States work for administrative departments. Typically, over 95 percent of these governments' budgets funnel through administrative departments. Remaining funds support the office of the Chief Executive, the legislature, and the courts. Moreover, administrators do much of what we think of as "making public policy." To be sure, members of the legislative and judicial branches and the Chief Executive make the prominent decisions and pronouncements. However, they usually depend heavily on professional administrators to provide advice and draft legislation, and almost always an administrator's workaday activities determine how a program will be implemented. The park ranger, school teacher, welfare case worker, police officer, and tax auditor who come into contact with citizens at the points where programs are delivered determine what citizens receive from government.

We all spend our lives as students of public administration. We must, for we are all clients—willingly or unwillingly—of government agencies. More-over, many of us are or will be employees of government. Either implicitly or explicitly, we must spend a great deal of time figuring out how govern-ment agencies work and how we can get what we want from them. There is an emphasis throughout this book on the controversies that are explicit or latent in administrative agencies, the pressures on administrators that come from other political arenas, and the implications of administrators' activities for public policy. The book will be successful if you do better at the end of it what you have been doing in an unorganized fashion since youth—seeking to understand government agencies.

SUMMARY

Government, and therefore its administration, affect our lives daily. Along with government's growth have come changes in character, managerial style, and political philosophy. Employees of administrative units are the focus of this book, particularly those who are involved with the formulation and implementation of public policy (loosely defined as the important things that government makes). There are many ways to look at public adminis-tration: academically, administratively, politically, and as citizens. This book is intended to help you understand better the relationships and complexities of public administration.

2

The Organization
of Government Departments
and Agencies

There is much variety in public administration. The national government of the United States employs roughly 2.8 million civil servants in 13 cabinet departments, several dozen independent officials, and boards and commissions. Beyond this, untold numbers of business firms and other private organizations work for the national government under contract. This chapter deals with three crucial questions; their answers will help to guide you through the remaining chapters dealing with various aspects of public administration. The key questions are:

What are the departments and agencies of the U.S. goverment?
How are they organized?
Why are they organized in those ways?

THE ORGANIZATION OF THE U.S. GOVERNMENT

The simple description of the U.S. government begins with the official organization chart, reproduced in Figure 2-1. It is formally a hierarchy, although space prohibits the display of each bureau, organization, and office within the major departments and independent offices. The independent offices report directly to the President, as do the cabinet departments.

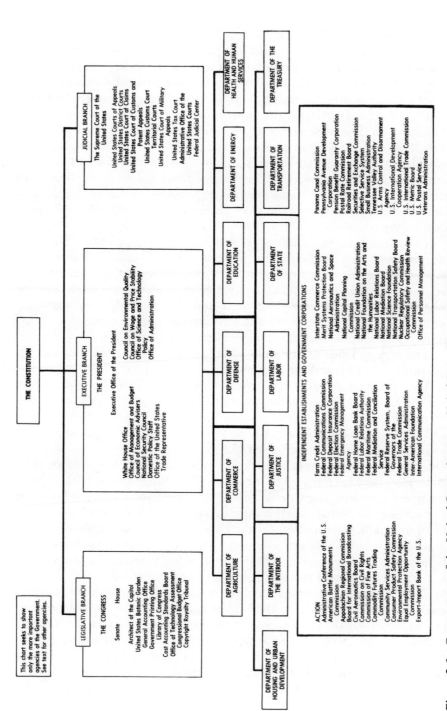

Figure 2-1 Government of the United States. [SOURCE: *United States Government Manual, 1980–1981* (Washington, D.C.: U.S. Government Printing Office, 1980.)]

Cabinet Departments and Independent Offices

The cabinet departments and independent offices are the principal doers of governmental work. They deal in agriculture, education, defense, economic regulation, and other important national activities, usually as indicated by their titles. Some titles, however, are not particularly illuminating. The General Services Administration (GSA) operates government buildings and is the central purchase and supply arm for most other agencies. The International Communications Agency seeks to show the cultural and intellectual sides of the United States to foreign audiences by arranging tours of artists, writers, and performers. It also operates the Voice of America international radio network to disseminate news and views to all parts of the world. The Interior Department is responsible for conservation activities and manages millions of acres of government-owned land in the "interior" of the country.

The administrative departments and agencies that provide services are the *line* units of government. In the vocabulary of public administration, line units operate the principal services of government, such as defense, education, health, and pollution control. *Staff* units are responsible for serving or controlling the line units. Staff units handle budgeting, planning, staffing, and such other matters as advising the Chief Executive on issues of policy development or the management of the line units.

The various kinds of line units differ in their status, their place in the organization chart, and the manner of their operations.

The most prominent in the organization chart of the U.S. government are the 13 cabinet departments. Among the line units, the cabinet departments are generally the oldest and most prestigious, with the largest budgets and work forces. Historically, the secretaries of cabinet departments met with the President and counseled him on crucial matters. They were the inner circle of government. In recent years, however, the roles of chief counselors have been played by members of the White House staff. Cabinet members may even have trouble getting an appointment with the President to discuss matters that concern their departments. A White House aide is likely to handle these matters for the President. There are few actual meetings of the cabinet; those that do occur are largely ceremonial. Some independent offices have grown to rival cabinet departments in size, even if they have not been granted the prestige of cabinet designation.

Table 2-1 ranks the cabinet departments and major independent offices according to their budgets in 1980. The table shows that a few independent offices are among the major actors on the administrative scene: the National Aeronautics and Space Administration (NASA), the Postal Service, the Veterans Administration (VA), and the Environmental Protection Agency (EPA). The functions of the VA are every bit as broad in scope as those of most cabinet departments. Its units deal with services in the fields of edu-

Table 2-1 Cabinet Departments and Independent Agencies by Order of Spending (in billions of dollars), 1980

Department/Agency	Amount
Health and Human Services	$195.4
Defense	141.5
Treasury	94.1
Housing and Urban Development	35.7
Labor	28.1
Agriculture	24.7
Veterans Administration[a]	21.2
Transportation	17.8
Education	13.9
Energy	10.5
National Aeronautics and Space Administration[a]	5.3
Environmental Protection Agency[a]	4.7
Interior	4.6
Commerce	3.7
Justice	2.5
State	2.1

Note: Because of separate budgeting and accounting procedures, the Postal Service is not listed here.

[a]Independent agency.

SOURCE: Fiscal 1981 Budget of the U.S. Government.

cation, research, health care, real estate, insurance, and pensions. The agency's principal clientele are veterans of the armed services, plus their dependents, widows, and orphans who qualify for special services. If periodic wars continue, the VA will probably remain in business as an important segment of the national government, even if it never attains cabinet rank (see the organization chart of the VA in Figure 2-2).

With the exception of those few units that were already established at the time of the Constitutional Convention in 1787 (the Departments of State, War, and Treasury),[1] all of the cabinet departments began their organizational lives as independent offices or as components of other cabinet departments. When they became cabinet departments in their own right, it signified a victory for themselves, for clientele groups, and for other

---

[1]The Department of War was reorganized and merged with the Department of the Navy in 1947 to form the Department of Defense.

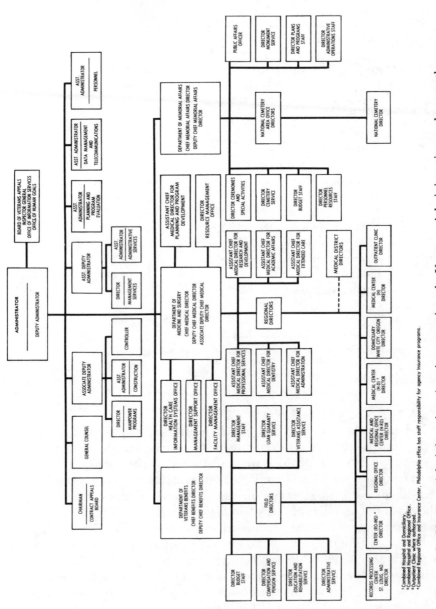

Figure 2-2 Veterans Administration. A major operation, the Veterans Administration ranks seventh among federal administrative units in budget and third in size of work force. It displays an elaborate organization; yet it remains an independent agency outside the cabinet. [SOURCE: *United States Government Manual, 1980–1981* (Washington, D.C.: U.S. Government Printing Office, 1980).]

supporters who sought to increase their prestige. The increased visibility of a cabinet department may gain more support from the White House, Congress, and citizens' groups. This may help the department obtain more legal authority, personnel, and funds.

The elevation of some units to cabinet status has been opposed by some members of Congress or interest groups who were apprehensive about the growth of certain programs. Conservatives opposed the elevation of the Federal Security Agency to the Department of Health, Education and Welfare (HEW), and the elevation of the Housing and Home Finance Administration to the Department of Housing and Urban Development (HUD). The Housing and Home Finance Administration faced an additional hurdle when President Kennedy proposed it for cabinet rank: Its administrator, Robert Weaver, seemed likely to become the first black in the cabinet.

Major cabinet alterations have increased since World War II. Table 2-2 records the amalgamation of separate war and navy departments into the

Table 2-2 Chronology of Major Alterations in the President's Cabinet, 1789–1980

Year	Alteration
1789	Departments of State, Treasury, and War created
1798	Department of Navy created
1814	Office of Attorney General given cabinet rank
1829	Postmaster General acquired cabinet rank, although Post Office remained in Treasury Department
1849	Department of the Interior created
1870	Department of Justice created
1872	Post Office Department separated from Treasury Department
1889	Department of Agriculture acquired cabinet rank
1903	Department of Commerce and Labor created
1913	Departments of Commerce and Labor each given separate cabinet rank
1947	Department of Defense emerged from amalgam of War and Navy Departments
1953	Department of Health, Education and Welfare created
1965	Department of Housing and Urban Development created
1967	Department of Transportation created
1970	Postal Service created; Post Office Department lost cabinet rank
1977	Department of Energy created
1980	Department of Health, Education and Welfare divided into Department of Education and Department of Health and Human Services

SOURCE: Adapted from *Congressional Quarterly Weekly Report*, 28 (June 19, 1970).

Department of Defense, and the creation of the Departments of Health, Education and Welfare (1953), Housing and Urban Development (1965), Transportation (1967), Energy (1977), and most recently the division of Health, Education and Welfare into the Department of Education and the Department of Health and Human Services (1980). In 1970, Congress approved President Nixon's proposal for the transformation of the Post Office Department into the Postal Service; this marks the first instance of a department's departure from the cabinet.

Within both cabinet departments and independent offices additional controversies have arisen over the placement of programs and units in one organization or another, or over their status in the hierarchy of a certain organization. For example, conservation-minded friends of the Forest Service managed to have that agency transferred from the Interior Department to the Department of Agriculture. They argued that the Interior Department was less interested in conservation than in providing resources to commercial foresters and livestock ranchers. Similarly, friends of the Children's Bureau sought to have it shifted from a unit of the Social Security Administration, which was one level below the top leadership in the Federal Security Agency, to a position of its own directly below the top leadership. They wanted it in a position of greater prominence, where it would be more visible, more likely to attract congressional and presidential support, and more able to develop its programs without having them limited by administrative superiors.[2]

Aside from cabinet departments and independent offices, several other kinds of organizations enjoy peculiar relationships with the President and Congress. They include independent regulatory commissions, government corporations, government contractors, plus several additional hybrids that defy even a general label.

Independent Regulatory Commissions

The independent regulatory commissions include units in charge of setting rules and regulating activities in several fields of commerce, transportation, finance, communications, and labor relations.[3] They differ from "normal" departments and offices in several ways. Each of them is headed by a board of several members instead of by one secretary or agency head. Further-

---

[2]See "The Transfer of the Children's Bureau," in H. Stein, ed., *Public Administration and Policy Development: A Case Book* (New York: Harcourt, Brace, 1951), pp. 15–30.

[3]The major commissions are Civil Aeronautics Board, Federal Communications Commission, Federal Energy Regulatory Commission, Federal Reserve Board, Federal Trade Commission, Interstate Commerce Commission, National Labor Relations Board, Nuclear Regulatory Commission, Securities and Exchange Commission, U.S. Maritime Board, and U.S. Tariff Commission.

more, fixed terms of commissioners, bipartisanship, and vague guarantees of job protection promise some independence from the President. Commissioners are appointed for terms ranging up to 14 years. Their terms overlap in a way that makes it unlikely that any one President can appoint all the members of a commission. The members of each commission must include a balance of members with different party affiliations. Members of several commissions cannot be removed by the President, except for certain causes, which include inefficiency, neglect of duty, or malfeasance.

The peculiar structure of the commissions seems to fit their often-delicate assignments. They make rules within the broad grants of authority provided by their enabling statutes, apply their own rules to specific cases, and adjudicate cases where parties appeal the commission's first decision. Because they seem to be more independent of the Chief Executive than are other agencies, the regulatory commissions take on some of the characteristics of judicial bodies. This quasi-judicial style of operation is in good part designed to win the acceptance of business firms and public-interest groups that must endure adverse decisions. The commissions' independence of the President can also lessen the President's concern with their budgets and program development. Thus, they often become more subject to legislative control than to presidential guidance. This increases the appeal of regulatory commissions to members of Congress who might otherwise object to government regulation of private industry. What these explanations overlook, however, are agencies that have important regulatory functions but are part of cabinet departments without independent status. Examples include the Food and Drug Administration (FDA) and the Occupational Safety and Health Administration (OSHA). (Chapter 14 probes further into the character of regulatory agencies.)

Government Corporations

Several corporations are wholly owned by the federal government. They are subject to budget and basic policy controls of the President and Congress, but they also enjoy some of the freedom of private firms. Their activities include banking, insurance, scientific research, electric power generation, land development, and the delivery of mail.[4] Their boards of directors are appointed by the President with approval by the Senate, and they are subject to the formal budget controls of the President and Congress. However, much of their income comes from the sale of products or services

---

[4]They include Commodity Credit Corporation, Export-Import Bank of Washington, Federal Crop Insurance Corporation, Federal Deposit Insurance Corporation, Federal National Mortgage Association, Federal Prison Industries, Federal Savings and Loan Insurance Corporation, Panama Canal Corporation, Postal Service, Smithsonian Institution, and Tennessee Valley Authority.

in the private sector. The corporate format is said to permit them to use economic as opposed to political criteria in setting pricing policies and in determining the nature of products and services.

The businesslike status of government corporations does not protect them from political controversy. For example, the Tennessee Valley Authority (TVA) has undertaken comprehensive programs for conservation, flood control, navigation, and electric power generation throughout the seven-state area that is drained by the Tennessee River and its many tributaries. It has engaged in numerous controversies with individual landowners whose land would, or would not, be taken for a TVA project, with producers of electricity and fertilizer who felt the TVA would move into their market with an unfair price advantage, and with local governments who felt their tax base was eroded by tax-free TVA facilities or by the flooding caused by the TVA dams.

Government Contractors

Government contractors are business firms and other private bodies that serve important functions for government agencies. They build weapons for the military, construct post offices and other buildings to lease to the government, provide janitorial and protection services for government installations, conduct research in numerous fields of social and natural sciences, operate halfway houses for convicts or the mentally ill, manage health-care clinics, and evaluate the work of government agencies and other contractors. What some agencies do for themselves, others hire out to a contractor. Some decisions to contract are motivated by the agency's desire not to tie up its funds in capital construction. It takes less of an outlay for the Postal Service to lease a building than to build one itself. At times, the temporary nature of a program will lead an agency to contract for services rather than to enlarge its own staff. Contractors have some freedom from federal standards that offer them flexibility in certain aspects of personnel, budgeting, and pricing. Contractors can pay higher wages for scientific or technical jobs, and thus more easily attract talent. In other areas, however, they are subject to official procedures. Contractors must accept equal-opportunity provisions in hiring and may not segregate their employees on the basis of race. They are also subject to audits by the General Accounting Office (GAO) and may have details of their expenditures and profits made public by the GAO.[5] (Chapter 15 looks at the benefits and the problems of government contracting.)

---

[5]See I. Sharkansky, *Wither the State? Politics and Public Enterprise in Three Countries* (Chatham, N.J.: Chatham, 1979).

their major work during the first two decades of this century. Both men sought to describe and explain important general tendencies in human organizations, and the work of both scholars has survived the test of time.

Michels' Oligarchy

Roberto Michels was an Italian Swiss. His major idea—that there is an iron law of oligarchy—is relatively simple, but it goes a long way toward explaining a central factor in human organization. Michels observed that the members of organizations do not wield equal power. Some of them inevitably have more time to devote to the organization, and are more skillful in obtaining and using information and persuading colleagues to accept them as leaders. In explaining why oligarchy—the rule of the many by the few—is inevitable, Michels explains why organizations with formal hierarchical structures and leadership abound, while autonomous individuals are rarely found. Michels' actual studies dealt with trade unions—groups whose common interests lead them to associate with one another. Michels found that even these groups cannot run themselves along the lines of pure democracy. Some figures eventually dominate, and then structure the organization to perpetuate their own control. If Michels were alive today, he might marvel at the career of George Meany as an embodiment of his theory. Meany retired as the active president of the AFL–CIO when he was well into his 80s, after dominating the nation's largest labor union for five decades.

Weber's Types of Organization

While we can thank Roberto Michels for making the basic explanation of why organization and leadership are inevitable, we look to another European sociologist, Max Weber, for helping us understand the variety in organization. It is not enough to know why there are organizations. We are driven by the obvious variety to identify the principal types, and to know why each pattern develops as it does.

Weber was a prolific writer, whose essays cover an enormous scope of historical time and geography, from ancient China to his contemporary Germany. We are concerned primarily with two of his contributions: the description of the *major patterns of authority* that prevail in organizations and his outline for the *ideal type of bureaucracy*.[6]

---

[6]H. H. Gerth and C. W. Mills, trs., *From Max Weber: Essays in Sociology* (New York: Oxford University Press, 1946).

Patterns of Authority

Weber found three different patterns of authority in the organizations he surveyed: *charismatic, traditional,* and *legal-rational.*

Charisma is what aspiring leaders crave and what other persons fear. The magic of a person's appeal to the masses can lead to great and sudden changes in society. Moses and Jesus were endowed with charisma. After Weber's time, writers have used the concept of charisma to explain the special appeal of such figures as Adolph Hitler, Mao Tse-tung, Franklin Roosevelt, and John Kennedy. Some leaders have used their magnetism to help them alter established social or political frameworks. Modern leaders may be aided by charisma, but typically need other kinds of authority to assure control over administrative bodies. With organizations defined in laws and regulations, the simple appeal of a person can seldom ensure success in leadership.

Tradition is the basis for the authority of monarchs, the leaders of churches, and family patriarchs or matriarchs. The authority is based on a formal position that has deep roots in history and relies on a people's feeling that the occupant of a position has an inherent right to lead. Today tradition provides the authority of the British monarch and the Pope. However, both of these figures are more constricted than their predecessors by legal-rational authority held by other leaders with whom they must deal.

Weber saw *legal-rational authority* as the basis for organizations in the modern world. This means rule by explicit laws or regulations that are themselves defined by determining the actions most likely to accomplish stated goals. Rule of this kind is appropriate in a cultural setting dominated by rational and secular values. The mass of the population is literate and comfortable with behaviors that are purposive and chosen according to self-interest.

It is most often the case in the United States and other western democracies that rules and orderly procedure govern a leader's selection and a leader's control over an organization. A leader may be helped greatly by charisma, if so blessed by personality, or even by tradition in the case of a long-distinguished family. Even when heads of state have such advantages, the large number of specialized organizations needed to operate a modern society relies heavily on legal-rational authority.

Ideal Bureaucracy

Max Weber's second major contribution to the study of public administration is his description of the ideal bureaucracy. By ideal, Weber did not mean desirable. For him, an ideal type was the archetypal or pure manifestation of bureaucracy. Such an ideal type is a useful component of theory that can guide research in real bureaucracies. The ideal is a base point from which departures can be noted and explained.

Weber's conception of legal-rational authority fits closely with his ideal type of bureaucracy and the concept of *hierarchy*. Legal-rational authority is at the heart of bureaucracy, which is marked by:

1. Specialized positions described with respect to fixed duties and according to explicit laws or regulations.
2. Clear lines of control from superiors to subordinates through a system of hierarchy.
3. Selection of employees according to their demonstrated skills in filling specific positions.
4. Decisions made within the framework of law and regulation, as opposed to individual, family, or ethnic loyalties.

Weber's model of bureaucracy has shaped much of what has been written about organizations since his time. It is an image of specialized personnel, each working in a narrow segment of an organization's affairs, making decisions according to detailed manuals of procedure, and communicating with colleagues only according to the formal chains of command. The pyramidal organization chart of a typical hierarchy is the graphic embodiment of Weber's ideal type. The Roman Catholic Church and military organizations often serve as examples of Weber's bureaucracy. Each is governed by leaders who occupy designated ranks and who govern subordinates according to formal rules that are promulgated according to known procedures. In the Church, the Pope is superior to cardinals, who govern the bishops within their domain, who in turn govern the parish priests. At the bottom of the organization are the faithful, who depend on priests for the administration of sacraments. The U.S. Army is a secular bureaucracy. At the top are, in descending order, the President, the Secretary of Defense, the Joint Chiefs of Staff, and the commanding general. Arrayed beneath this pinnacle are successive generals of lower rank, colonels, lieutenant colonels, majors, captains, lieutenants, noncommissioned officers, and lower-ranking enlisted personnel. Each layer is entrusted to command the one below it, and obligated to accept orders from above.

One type of behavior resembles what is formally expected in a bureaucracy, but does so to such an extreme that it threatens the smooth working of the organization. It has been labeled *bureaupathic* to signify its counterproductive character.[7] Bureaucracies *require* a degree of informal behavior; they cannot function well if their members take the rules too seriously. Bureaupathic behaviors are such things as: excessive effort by leaders to

---

[7] V. A. Thompson, *Modern Organization: A General Theory* (New York: Knopf, 1964).

maintain aloofness from their subordinates, ritualistic attachment to formal procedures, petty insistence on the rights of one's status within the organization, insensitivity to the needs of subordinates or clients resulting from preoccupation with one's own duties, and obsessive resistance to change procedures that one knows well and is used to dealing with. Some measure of this conduct is required in organizations: the need to have persons in positions of authority, the use of standard procedures for making certain kinds of decisions and a stability of these procedures, and the need to make some decisions about subordinates or clients that run counter to the feelings produced by personal relations. However, the pathological variants of these activities greatly hinder communications within an organization. These pathologies often create distrust and threaten the kind of rapport necessary for reasonable discussions.

Informal Organization

Weber recognized that in actuality bureaucracies depart from the abstract ideal model. The leaders of churches and armies depend for their authority partly on tradition, and partly on charisma, and a great deal on the structure of command and on formal rules. Employees will always take short cuts; they will communicate outside the formal chains of command and continually employ criteria other than technical merit for assessing the character of others. A sergeant may contact a captain directly, to skirt a lieutenant who seems uncooperative. Individuals exercise discretion in treating some cases differently than the rules suggest. Some members of organizations acquire status higher than that indicated by their formal positions, and find that others look to them for leadership. Some members are downright crooked in accepting payments from people who want special benefits. All of this can be lumped under the heading of *informal organization,* or how things really work, despite what the formal rules indicate.

Physicians in a hospital and professors in a university may be generous or stingy in dealing with their clients. One physician may refer a patient to a specialist or recommend an operation much more readily than another. One may perform an abortion on request, contrary to the formal rules, merely reporting the reasons for the operation in such a way that the rules appear to be complied with. Patients often trade information among themselves about the physicians who are more or less liberal in their adaptation of the rules. Students, in their concern to find professors who are cooperative in their interpretation of university rules, will likewise exchange this kind of information. Employees also seek informal ways around the procedures that govern their work. Which clerk in the financial office will probably approve a disbursement of funds for an equipment purchase, and which one will demand elaborate justification for each dollar to be spent? This information, which is crucial to getting things done in an organization, is seldom if ever stated in the formal rules and regulations available to organization members.

The complexities of informal organization combine with many differences in formal procedures to frustrate any simple answers to the question *How are public agencies organized?* To learn one's way around an organization may require intimate knowledge of the organization chart and the official manual, plus a great sense of the nuances in officials' treatment of one another and their clients.

Frank Serpico almost paid with his life for his organizational naiveté. He tried to be a good police officer in New York City, living according to formal rules and lectures at the Police Academy. His first shock came when he found senior officers working according to their own norms, which often required overlooking or disobeying official departmental rules. These informal norms indicated which kinds of crimes should attract the police officer's concern and established bribery as an extra form of compensation outside the official paycheck. Serpico's greater shock came when he sought to report violations of the formal rules. The senior officers and municipal authorities showed either indifference or outright hostility to his complaints. And coworkers decided to discipline Serpico so that he would behave "properly." Their techniques ranged from subtle coaxing in how police officers should "get along by going along" to violent measures meant to rid the police department—permanently—of an officer who took the formal rules too seriously.[8]

Informal behavior is not always threatening to decency or human life. Often it is possible to accomplish good things, speedily, through informal means. "Cutting through red tape" is what we call informal behavior that we like, in which favored results are sought outside of formal procedures that would require more time or might preclude the accomplishment altogether.

The political environment that surrounds an organization can shape the informal behavior of its members. Several writers have commented on the amount of attention directed at organizations and on how this feature changes with time. There seems to be a life cycle of organizations. At the beginning, hopes are high that an organization will accomplish its mission. Politicians and citizens pay it much attention, it has a generous budget to work with, and the organization's staff exudes great enthusiasm. All this may reflect a recent victory in the legislative chambers, where the organization was created to solve a problem that had caught the public's attention.[9] With

---

[8]P. Maas, *Serpico* (New York: Viking, 1973).

[9]M. Bernstein, *Regulating Business by Independent Commissions* (Princeton, N.J.: Princeton University Press, 1955); and A. Downs, "Up and Down with Ecology," *Public Interest* (Summer 1972): 38–50.

time, however, things change. Often the problem that was the reason for the organization's creation proves difficult to solve. Politicians turn their attention elsewhere. Organization members feel a lessening of support. The excitement of program innovation is less apparent in the unit. Mostly there are a routine application of established procedures and a recognition that the procedures cope with only some of the problems in the organization's jurisdiction. Eventually, pressure may build for another wave of reform, resulting in new legislation, a special boost in the budget, and a change in key staff members.

ORGANIZATIONAL THEORIES FOR PUBLIC ADMINISTRATION

The realities of administrative behavior create headaches for organizational theorists who try to summarize their activities. Officials who design the departments of government are guided only partly by theories about the kinds of organizations that should be created. For the most part, officials respond pragmatically to the pressures of the day. They select names for organizations that currently have wide appeal, and they assign powers to offices and individuals according to many considerations. Important in these matters is the influence of an interest group or a key individual, and what that group or individual thinks will happen if certain powers are assigned to certain administrators.

To describe the principal theories of public organizations, it is appropriate to begin with the hierarchy and other features of Weber's ideal type of bureaucracy. It is also necessary—as with organizational theory generally—to recognize the importance of informal organization. What is distinctive about public organizational theory, however, is the addition of explicitly *political* norms and expectations. Moreover, the politics that are relevant must be seen in their geographical and historical contexts. U.S. federal organizations bear the imprint of American political history, especially the fascination with the separation of powers and checks and balances. Much that Americans have created seems strange to the citizens of just about every other country, whether democratic or authoritarian. American public administration is an oddity to people familiar with parliamentary forms of government or with the integration of national, regional, and local government into a single framework.[10]

---

[10]V. Ostrom, *The Intellectual Crisis in American Public Administration* (University: University of Alabama Press, 1974).

"Programs" cut across the boundaries of departments and agencies. Different units may deal with programs that relate closely to each other. One result may be problems in communication and coordination. Civil rights is one field of programs that is affected by the work of several departments and agencies. This special budget analysis indicates how much is being spent by various units on civil rights programs.

Table 2-3 Civil Rights Outlays (in millions of dollars), 1979–1981

Department / Agency	1979 actual	1980 est.	1981 est.
Agriculture	$ 6.5	$ 7.4	$ 7.7
Commerce	.1	1.8	2.1
Defense	47.0	49.4	50.9
Education[a]	—	18.5	41.8
Health, Education and Welfare[a]	50.4	32.1	—
Health and Human Services	—	13.6	26.8
Housing and Urban Development	5.2	5.8	6.3
Justice	32.2	36.8	39.1
Labor	47.0	56.8	59.3
Transportation	2.0	2.2	2.7
Office of Personnel Management	9.0	8.2	8.0
State	d	d	d
Commission on Civil Rights	10.2	11.4	11.9
Equal Employment Opportunity Commission[b]	255.0	290.5	322.1
Postal Service[c]	(17.4)	(19.3)	(21.5)
Small Business Administration	1.1	1.2	1.8
All other	3.4	4.7	4.5
Total	$469.1	$540.4	$585.0

[a]Assumes transfer from HEW to the Department of Education.
[b]Includes outlays for all federal service equal employment opportunity, including Upward Mobility.
[c]Postal Service outlays for memorandum purposes only.
[d]Less than $100,000.

SOURCE: *Congressional Quarterly*, February 2, 1980.

Organizational Design as Political Controversy

Important issues in the design of government organizations concern the links between administrative bodies and the elected branches of government, as well as the internal structure of the administrative organizations. Ideas come partly from theories that claim to have general application and partly from the politics surrounding individual programs and the interest groups that either support or oppose them. Debates about administrative organization erupt over the creation of new government agencies, over the elevation of existing units to cabinet rank, over the transfer of a program from one agency to another, over powers that will strengthen or weaken the ability of the Chief Executive or the legislature to control agencies, and over the alteration of budgeting or other devices used to govern administrative units.

Hierarchical Management and Its Problems

The model used often in U.S. administrative organizations is the hierarchy. The typical organization chart shows several department heads who are directly responsible to the chief executive and whose own departments fan out beneath them to include several layers of leadership and, ultimately, the personnel who actually provide the services or impose the regulations that are the department's major tasks. The pinnacle of the hierarchy is the chief executive. He or she controls the department heads and, through them, all administrative personnel.

The hierarchy corresponds closely to some management theory principles for managing large private firms and to Weber's ideal type of bureaucracy. Its proponents see it as "the one best way" to organize administrative personnel to maintain control over subordinates and to maximize the efficiency of their performance. The key principles of a hierarchy are:

1. Activities should be grouped by purpose, process, clientele, place, or time, and should be the responsibility of small units under the direct control of a supervisor.

2. Work units should be organized hierarchically, so that several units are grouped under the control of a single supervising unit (or supervisor) that is subsequently grouped with other supervisors under the control of a yet higher supervisor.

3. There should be a narrow "span of control," with a limited number of subordinates under each supervisor. In this way, supervisory personnel can give sufficient attention to each subordinate unit or person.

4. There should be a clear "chain of command" and "communications through channels," so that superiors will have full information about the activities of subordinates and be assured that their directives will control their subordinates.

5. Executives should have sufficient authority to appoint and remove their subordinates.

6. Personnel appointments and promotions should be made on the basis of competence, with no interference from politicians seeking to reward fellow partisans.

7. Executives should control the expenditures of administrative units.

8. There should be sufficient staff services to provide executives with the information necessary to understand and control the activities of subordinates.[11]

These principles have enjoyed strong support in such prestigious commissions charged with proposing administrative reforms as: President Taft's Commission on Economy and Efficiency, President Franklin Roosevelt's Committee on Administrative Management, and the two Hoover Commissions set up by Presidents Truman and Eisenhower. Hierarchical principles were also implicit in President Johnson's budget reforms, labeled Planning-Programming-Budgeting (PPB), and in President Carter's Zero-Based Budgeting (ZBB). During his first months in office, President Reagan expressed interest in clarifying the hierarchy of the federal government.

The simple hierarchy is so often violated in practice that it hardly qualifies as *the* model of public administration. It is comprised of several features that weaken the chief executive's control over department heads and make department heads, as well as their own subordinates, responsible to numerous people besides the chief executive. Those wanting to have a say in the policy-making of administrative units—and willing to violate hierarchical principles—include legislators, the clients of agencies, interest groups, administrators, and even the President himself.

The framers of the Constitution created two devices that compromise hierarchical control of the federal administration: senatorial confirmation of key appointees and congressional control of the budget. Later in American history, Congress had professional or political criteria in mind when enacting legislation on administration staffing. Each of these features represents congressional competition with the President for control of the Administration. As a result, the Administration is not a hierarchy with a single head. It is, rather, a collection of organizations that is permeated by efforts at control from the White House, the Congress, and numerous other power centers that have leverage in Congress. The organization of the Department of Agriculture provides an example of administrative hierarchy made complicated by the addition of many programs with friends in Congress (see Figure 2-3).

Legislators are not content to write general policies and then let the Chief Executive and his subordinates administer their departments accordingly.

---

[11]A. Lepawsky, *Administration: The Art and Science of Organization and Management* (New York: Knopf, 1948).

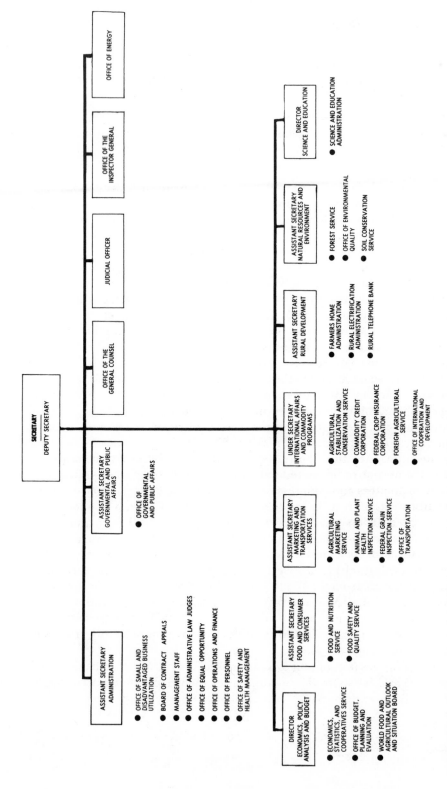

Figure 2-3 Department of Agriculture. A departmental hierarchy. [SOURCE: *United States Government Manual, 1980–1981* (Washington, D.C.: U.S. Government Printing Office, 1980).]

The history of legislative-executive-administrative interaction has seen countless devices employed by legislators to retain control over those aspects of program administration that interest them. These devices include specific recommendations in committee reports that administrators are expected to follow, detailed questioning during annual budget hearings on the minutiae of program administration, special investigations into the operation of agency field installations, and statutory amendments designed to prohibit certain practices that legislators have found distasteful. Congress has established the General Accounting Office under its own auspices in order to supervise the expenditures of administrative agencies. This institution—employing over 5,000 persons—is a staff arm of the legislature with the power to question and to disallow individual items of agency expenditure.

Another factor that compromises administrative hierarchy is the disinclination of some Chief Executives to operate in a hierarchical manner. President Franklin Roosevelt often ignored the niceties of hierarchical etiquette. He dealt directly with bureau chiefs without going through their department heads. He guaranteed conflict in the Administration by appointing antagonists to positions in which they had to deal with one another. He also divided what appeared to be single jobs into multiple positions, so that different officials would contend with one another in their operations. Each of these devices was designed to create noise, thus informing the President of important debates in the lower reaches of government.

Another device that Roosevelt used to infiltrate the hierarchy was a freewheeling personal assistant. Harry Hopkins had several formal positions in the Roosevelt Administration, but his most important tasks were ad hoc assignments that permitted Roosevelt direct information about significant decisions that were made deep within the hierarchy. A more recent counterpart of Harry Hopkins was Robert F. Kennedy. In his brother's Administration, his formal position was attorney general. But he served beyond the boundaries of the Justice Department and was an analyst and adviser in matters of defense, international relations, and domestic politics.

A new problem that has emerged in the hierarchy of the U.S. government concerns the roles of the Chief Executive, major staff aides in the White House, and the cabinet secretaries. Too many subordinates serve directly below the President for personal control. In the words of hierarchical principle 3, the *span of control* is too broad for effective supervision. As a result, White House aides who do some of the President's work can stand between the Chief Executive and the heads of major departments. The President deals with a small number of personal aides in the White House, and they deal with cabinet secretaries and heads of the independent offices. Both Presidents Richard Nixon and Jimmy Carter had difficulties with cabinet members because of this. The secretaries asserted that the language of the Constitution and the ritual of presidential appointment meant that they should have direct access to the Oval Office. President Nixon's cabinet had problems dealing with the abrasive personality of Chief of Staff Robert Haldeman. When President Carter's secretaries of the Treasury, HEW, Transportation, and Energy were fired or quit during two hectic days in July 1979, their reasons included their inability to get along with the White House staff.

The plurality of governments that join together to formulate and implement policies also confounds hierarchical principles. "Government" in the United States is actually some 78,000 separate entities: the nation, the states, and numerous categories of local authorities, plus countless business firms, nonprofit organizations, and private individuals that work for government on a contract basis. When different bodies produce services in education, highways, or welfare, no one is clearly the superior or subordinate of another. Relationships among them do not work like a smooth chain of command. A great deal of haggling and compromise exist among persons who feel that they have a right to stand up for the distinct interests of their organizations.

The hierarchical model is no longer in vogue among organizational theorists who are concerned with interpersonal relations in the workplace. Among the major shortcomings of a hierarchy in both private and public organizations are: its failure to account for complex motivations of employees, the executive's inability to master all the information necessary to control subordinates, and informal behaviors. For a hierarchy to operate according to design, subordinates must accept their superior's definition of organizational goals. However, employees come to their jobs with a variety of personal and professional interests, and it is no easy task to win their loyalties for any common goal. Indeed, it is often difficult to define the common goal. Department heads themselves may not agree with their superiors on the proper tasks of their organizations. Conflict within a hierarchy may reflect the imperfect knowledge of the executive about the department head and the department head's need to compromise with subordinates. Although the theory of managerial hierarchy prescribes strict adherence to the decisions of a superior, that is a difficult standard to obtain. Different goals, different levels of motivation, and different loyalties are often symptoms of an organization's inability to articulate its goals clearly. It may be easier to muddle through on the strength of approximate agreement about specific programs, without raising the specter of long-range goals. One result is the lack of clear normative standards against which executives can screen prospective subordinates or can test their loyalty once they are employed.[12]

If the hierarchy is not the perfect model for public administrative orga-

---

[12]J. March and H. Simon, *Organizations* (New York: Wiley, 1958). C. E. Lindblom, *The Policy-Making Process* (Englewood Cliffs, N.J.: Prentice-Hall, 1978).

nizations, no other single model serves better. The official charts portray hierarchical lines of authority within and between units at each level of government. Thus, the hierarchy is a useful model—like Weber's ideal type of bureaucracy—even if we begin with the knowledge that it distorts reality.

Political Concerns in Organizational Design

In the United States, the appeal of the hierarchy has had to compete with three other considerations that have deep roots in political thinking and that are apparent in administrative structures. If nothing else existed to invite controversy into the construction of administrative institutions, the attempts to obtain some benefits from each of these would guarantee that conflict. These concerns are:

1. The desire to maintain political control over public administration.
2. The desire to maintain the traditional equilibrium among the three constitutional branches of government via the separation of powers and checks and balances.
3. The desire to ensure that professional and technical skills are brought to bear on relevant matters of policy formulation and implementation.

Political Control by Elected Officials

The political control of public administration is a principle that draws upon notions of democracy and the relation of the people to their public servants. (The discussion that follows is related to the issue of political accountability, which is treated more fully in Chapters 3–5.)

Two distinct varieties of political control appear in American government. One approach, which can be termed *traditional* by virtue of its historical basis, maintains that elected officials should have the final say over the activities of administrative agencies. This means that agency programs are defined by laws that are subject to the approval of the legislature and a Chief Executive. Moreover, annual budget requests are subject to similar law-making procedures and also require the approval of the legislature and the Chief Executive.

An aspect of traditional political control is executive and legislative choice of agency personnel. At the extreme, this has meant control over individual appointments by the political branches and the insistence that all administrators be contributing members of the party in power. These excesses of "Jacksonian" patronage are no longer evident at the federal level and are decreasingly apparent in state and local governments. Yet, for many years public bureaucracies experienced mass turnover with a change in executive party control.

Jacksonianism is often equated with patronage for the sake of maintaining party strength. However, it was presented to the country as an integral component of democratic political theory. President Andrew Jackson felt that the administration had become the possession of an elite class, and he sought to bring it within reach of the common person. He said:

> Office is considered as a species of property and as a means of promoting individual interests [rather] than as an instrument created solely for the service of the people. Corruption in some and in others a perversion of correct feelings and principles divert government from its legitimate ends and make it an engine for the support of the few at the expense of the many.
>
> The duties of all public officers are, or at least admit of being made, so plain and simple that men of intelligence may readily qualify themselves for their performance; and I cannot but believe that more is lost by the long continuance of men in office than is generally to be gained by their experience.[13]

By now, a series of administrative reforms has all but eliminated party patronage in the federal civil service and has curtailed it sharply in most state and local governments. Recent Supreme Court decisions (for example, *Branti* v. *Finkel*)[14] have barred the dismissal of personnel from some state and local government positions that had been filled on a patronage basis, simply because the employees are not members of the party currently in power. Yet several features still testify to the remaining strength of this element in administrative organizations. Senior positions in many public agencies are filled by the chief executive's appointment of "outsiders" brought in from private life, rather than by people who have devoted their careers to the agency. Prominent exceptions are the military and the police, but even in these cases, top policy-makers are "civilians" (in other words, nonprofessionals) appointed by a popularly elected chief executive or by a commission that is itself appointed by the chief executive. In this way, administration is thought to remain responsive to the wishes of the people, either because the elected chief executive makes the top appointment or because the appointees are citizens rather than professional bureaucrats.

Political Control by the People

The second major approach to political control is direct client participation in agency decisions. This idea attracted much public attention when it was given a boost by the community action programs begun by President John-

---

[13]Quoted in P. Van Riper, *History of the United States Civil Service* (Evanston, Ill.: Row, Peterson, 1958), pp. 36–37.

[14]*Branti* v. *Finkel*, 445 U.S. 507 (1980).

son's Office of Economic Opportunity. A direct clash between the two principal forms of political control ensued. Elected officials, especially state governors and local mayors, felt that their own control over administrative activities would be undercut by selecting citizens for policy-making councils and by citizen control over the selection of agency personnel. This was a clear instance of intense political conflict over the design of administrative structures. Elected officials charged that the "extreme" device of citizen participation would not only threaten their own capacity to supervise and control government activities, but also put untrained and irresponsible persons in control of government resources. They predicted that huge sums would be siphoned off for the support of new "political organizations"; that untrained supervisors would waste resources in poorly conceived and poorly managed programs; and that cadres of new revolutionaries would gain control of these programs and use them to challenge established norms. From the other side, those speaking for citizen participation said that existing programs for welfare, health, and education were poorly conceived to assist those people who were most in need, and the recipients were the best qualified to formulate policies for their own benefit.

The uproar over citizen participation in administrative systems suggests that it is a new kind of structure. But, in fact, several old programs include client control. State commissions to regulate the professions and trades usually include members of the regulated group on the policy-making boards. A board of physicians typically oversees the regulation of the medical profession, and boards of barbers, plumbers, and electricians supervise the regulation of their trades. Several of the federal agricultural programs established in the 1930s include boards of farmers that make the crucial decisions about local operations. County committees for agricultural stabilization and conservation, for example, pass on farmers' applications for acreage allotments and for federally assisted conservation activities.

Checks and Balances in the Separation of Powers

Another theoretical root of administrative organization seeks to maintain a separation of powers. The framers of the U.S. Constitution implemented this mode of organization and established it as a tradition to be followed by the builders of state and local governments. The separation of powers takes the form of a bicameral legislature, a separately elected Chief Executive, an independent judiciary, and a further division of powers between national and state governments. Along with these divisions, each branch was given some tools with which to protect itself against the others: the Chief Executive was given a veto; the legislature was given the opportunity to override the veto with an extraordinary majority, and the opportunity—in the Senate—to review major presidential appointments; the judiciary was given a vague grant of authority that it interpreted (in *Marbury* v. *Madison*) as the right to review the actions of other branches for their constitutionality. Finally, the personnel of each branch faced the threat of impeachment if they violated certain prohibitions on their own behavior. The checks and balances, inherent in the separation of powers, is a special way of expressing political control over administration.

The attachment that American constitution-makers had to the separation of powers has implications for administrative organizations:

1. Control of administrative units is not given entirely to any one of the constitutional branches.

2. The concern to divide the leadership of administration precludes the use of a simple administrative hierarchy under the control of one executive. The Chief Executive must share prerogatives over administration with an independent legislature and judiciary. The legislature has many opportunities to affect the structure, procedures, and programs of administration. These powers include review of new program proposals, periodic review of agency budgets, the approval of key personnel appointments, special legislative investigations into the operation of certain programs, the ability to initiate (and to pass, over Chief Executive veto) new programs or to make changes in existing ones, and informal arrangements in which administrators seek the approval of key legislators for certain kinds of decisions. The judiciary hears cases that aggrieved citizens bring against administrators, and may void or restrict certain powers that the administrator had exercised.

3. Each administrative unit may be subject to demands from competing superiors. A committee in the upper or lower house of the legislature and the Chief Executive may send conflicting directives to the administrator. At times this may benefit the administrator. An agency head can plead the excuse of conflicting instructions to explain a lack of compliance with any one of them. However, each potential superior may have an advocate within an agency, and the agency may be split by internal conflict over the choice of superiors. Multiple loyalties can upset the agency head's control at the same time that they inhibit clear control by either the Chief Executive or the legislature.

Professional Expertise

Another approach to administrative organization emphasizes the professional and technical competence in each agency. This approach generates severe conflicts with advocates of political accountability. The concern for expertise draws upon both Weber's ideal type of bureaucracy and the hierarchical model. However, the emphasis on expertise in American writing on administration is also a reaction against the older emphasis on party patronage. Those who advocate hiring experts often pose as reformers against politicians who would use public employment as the spoils of electoral victory.

The civil service movement is an expression of expertise being used to protect government employees from political control. Its most prominent success was the Pendleton Act, passed by Congress in 1883 and amended numerous times since then. Over 90 percent of the positions in the federal administration are now covered by merit provisions. This has not been an easy process, since each major extension has removed patronage appointments from the control of the legislative and executive branches.

Early merit programs sought only to remove the criteria of partisanship from personnel decisions. More recently, they have been concerned with increasing the level of technical competence in administrative agencies by well-designed procedures of recruitment, selection, and training. Administrative agencies increasingly require highly trained specialists in the natural or social sciences and other professions. Yet, this concern with professionalism has its opponents. Some advocates of citizen participation in welfare and education administration feel that established professions are insensitive to clients' needs. Advocates of affirmative action for women and minorities often criticize such concerns for professionalism as excessive "credentialism." Advocates of hierarchical organization are often pitted against those who want program professionals to head their own administrative structures. When this happens in a university, it is called faculty versus administration. In a hospital, it is called physicians against administration.

Program professionals may not like to think of themselves as beholden to their clients or as subordinates of hierarchical managers. Hierarchical managers may emphasize cost savings and program changes that fit the policy statements of the chief executive or the legislature. Program professionals are more inclined to support values from their academic, scientific, or medical training. Physicians, for example, want to decide on procedures of treatment without interference from hospital administrators. Professors want to decide on degree requirements and the content of their courses without control from the dean or the registrar. Some professors prefer that university administrators limit themselves to raising funds, caring for buildings and grounds, and keeping records. Professionals express the sentiment that administrators should serve the professionals by seeing to the "housekeeping" tasks of finding money and hiring secretaries, janitors, and other nonprofessional staff.

The designers of public organizations have been motivated by a combination of political accountability, separation of powers and checks and balances, professional competence, and principles of hierarchical management. At different times and in different minds, each of these roots has seemed more or less important. There is no prevailing mode apparent in the organizational schemes of administrative systems in the United States. If the basic outline is a hierarchy, that outline is frequently compromised.

A Caveat: Organizational Design from the Bottom Up

At this point, you may perceive that administrators are passive in the face of organizational theories that designate schemes of control. This passivity is consistent with the classical works of Max Weber. American manifestations of hierarchy are explicit in their assumption of the passive administrators. Schemes built according to the separation of powers likewise expect that administrators will accept the rules of the executive or legislative branch.

However, an assertive role for administrators appears in organizational models based on professional expertise. Writers who recognize the importance of informal behaviors in organizations use as an example administrators who carve out for themselves a more active role than what is allowed by the official rules. Administrative entrepreneurs, who have the creativity and hard-driving ambition that stimulate some programs, may also shock agency managers who are wedded to conventional procedures.

Administrative *discretion* is an inevitable feature of contemporary administration, no matter how well it fits with other models of hierarchy. Discretion occurs when an official is "free to make a choice among possible courses of action or inaction."[15] Legislative, executive, and judicial branches have left many issues in the hands of operating administrators—and the contractors with whom they deal—rather than spelling out all possible conditions that should govern their actions. A prosecutor exercises discretion when plea bargaining with a defendant to plead guilty to a misdemeanor in order to escape prosecution on a felony charge. A police officer exercises discretion when encountering someone who seems intoxicated. The officer can drive the person home and make no record of the occurrence, take the person to a hospital, or make an arrest and put the person in jail. A social worker can choose to be strict or lenient in supervising welfare recipients. The case worker can overlook or enforce regulations when a client earns a bit of money on a part-time job or when an unwed mother begins living with a man.

Administrative discretion can be good or bad. It may be good to introduce flexibility into a bureaucracy that would otherwise be unyielding in handling the varied needs of its clients. If everyone were ticketed for driving over the speed limit, there might be more work than the authorities could handle, unhealthy public attitudes toward the law would develop, and no opportunities would exist to combat rush-hour congestion by urging drivers to go faster. The problem with discretion, however, lies in opportunities for discrimination. The prosperous drunk is likely to be sent home in a taxi, while the skid-row character goes to jail. Plea bargaining is thought to favor the white or the wealthy rather than the black or the poor. Administrative

---

[15]K. C. Davis, *Discretionary Justice: A Preliminary Inquiry* (Urbana: University of Illinois Press, 1971), p. 4.

flexibility is more acceptable for welfare recipients who deal with lenient social workers than for those who deal with strict moralists. For one commentator, the largest problem of discretion is its exercise at the lowest levels of administration by personnel who are the least educated and the most narrow in their understanding of the implications of their actions.[16]

SUMMARY

In the search to describe or explain the structures of public administration, no single theory of organization predominates. Rather, there are *theories* to accommodate different concerns: for political control via elected officials or clients, for the separation of powers, for professional expertise, or for control and efficiency via the formal hierarchy. Most of these perspectives treat administrators themselves as passive objects of organizational design. However, we cannot overlook the potential activism of administrators or the importance of informal organization. No single description of public organizations can claim to reflect more than a portion of the total. Max Weber remains a prominent figure in the literature about administration. His description of the ideal bureaucracy is the implicit standard of comparison. By viewing other forms of public organization as departures from Weber's ideal, the student gains an insight into the commonalities in administrative form and purpose, without losing sight of the important differences.

---

[16]Ibid., p. 88.

PART II

Accountability

Accountability is an essential feature of democracy and one of the major themes considered in this book. A government is accountable to the people to the extent that it pursues policies that are consistent with public desires. Accountability can be expressed in a number of ways, through several kinds of connections between the people and government officers. Part II deals with some of the most important connections. Chapter 3 deals with expressions of public opinion and the mechanisms that link the public with policy-makers. Chapter 4 treats the elected branches of government and the various ways in which the President and Congress define policy and oversee its implementation by the administrative agencies. Chapter 5 raises some general issues of accountability, especially from the perspective of administrators. Part III, "The Tools of Administration," is an extension of the discussion of accountability, only in a more detailed manner. It treats the techniques of agency management, budgeting, personnel administration, and program evaluation.

3

The People

Since the Revolution of 1776, Americans have indicated their suspicion of government; California's Proposition 13 is the Boston Tea Party of our generation. When the voters of the nation's most populous state approved Proposition 13, they limited the growth of local property taxes and signaled their suspicion of government. One result was the spread to other states of the kind of antigovernment campaign that Howard Jarvis conducted in California. In California, local authorities are scrambling to replace property-tax revenues with other funds.

The people are the ultimate reference point of government in a democracy. The U.S. Constitution begins with the assertion that "We the People of the United States . . . do ordain and establish this Constitution . . . ." The referenda considered by the voters in California and many other states are prominent expressions of popular government. Another expression is the attention paid to the President's standing in public opinion surveys, which continually seek to measure general support for his presidency or support for particular presidential actions. Yet another message comes from the silent citizens, those 40–50 percent of the population who do not participate in presidential elections, and the many survey respondents who indicate that they do not care about politics.

Democratic political theory assigns a crucial role to the people, and American political institutions provide many ways for the people to express their preferences. Nevertheless, there is no absolute assurance that government policies will correspond with the popular will. Events in Iran and Nicaragua in 1979–1980 provide two examples of what can happen when the people become really angry about the difference between what they

want and what they get from government. In 1979 and 1980 the people of
these countries overthrew the established governments with force, and
installed new regimes. In neither case, however, was democracy more than
a slogan expressed by cunning politicians. In the United States there are
many mechanisms for popular expression: opinion surveys, a mass media,
elections, interest groups, and political parties. Some of these mechanisms,
like elections, formally link the people with government. Until now, these
mechanisms have seemed sufficient to keep government accountable to the
people. The American record of only one civil war, won by the establishment, is quite enviable on the world scene.

Even if the large picture of the United States shows substantial opportunities for citizen influence with government, the detailed view is much
more uneven. Amidst all the noise of a free press, countless surveys, active
interest groups, and a continuous stream of campaigns and elections, the
signs are disturbing. Take, for example, the large number of people who
indicate no interest in, or alienation from, politics and government. Or the
frustration expressed by activists (for example, environmentalists, consumers, minorities) that their efforts in influencing policy-making are ineffective and that government continues to do much that is against the popular will.

This chapter does not place to rest all of these problems; however, it
outlines the important channels that connect the people of the United States
with public administrators, and inquires about their operation. The key
questions of interest are:

> *How do policy-makers know what the people want?*
>
> *How effective are the mechanisms in connecting the people with public
> administrators?*
>
> *How do the people know whether administrators are carrying out their
> wishes?*

DETERMINING THE POPULAR WILL

Public Opinion

To a casual observer, Americans are saturated with public opinion polls.
Despite the large number of public opinion surveys that are reported each
month, however, they are not a perfect mechanism for judging the congruence between public opinion and government policy. For one thing, the
mechanics of policy do not match the mechanics of policy-making. Pollsters
ask simple questions: Do you favor or oppose—

The death penalty?

Busing school children for racial integration?

Legalized abortion?

Decreased spending for social programs?

Policy-makers deal in more details that expose the subtle character of issues:

The death penalty *under which conditions?*

Busing *over what distance? at whose expense?*

Abortion *under what conditions? at public or private expense?*

A decrease *of how much in which social programs?*

For another thing, most opinion polling does not match the geographical perspective of policy-makers. Members of Congress think in terms of their constituents from a state or congressional district, while polls tend to be national in scope. A legislator might argue that "hometown folks don't think that way." Also, the precise wording of a question or its timing can influence the answers received. Surveys taken in 1968–1970 showed marked variations in attitudes toward American involvement in Vietnam, depending partly on how the questions were worded and what was occurring in Vietnam at the time of the survey.[1]

Because of these problems, public opinion surveys only gauge the congruence between the people's desires and the government's performance. As might be expected from such imperfect sources, the indications are mixed. One comparison of survey results with existing policies showed that opinions matched national policies on only 6 out of 14 issues.[2] Another study estimated state-by-state opinions and state government policies, and found a match one-half to two-thirds of the time.[3] Table 3-1 shows the opinion-policy match for 14 issues in 1974.

While some surveys try to pinpoint attitudes toward concrete issues, others search for underlying currents. Nationwide surveys taken since the 1950s find a marked increase in a sense of alienation from government. Expressions of distrust for the government, individual feelings of powerlessness, and feelings of the meaningless nature of political activity have shown a steady increase in the last decade (see Table 3-2). Such attitudes are heavily represented in all social groups and all regions of the country, but they appear most frequently among the poor, the black, and the least

[1]M. J. Rosenberg, S. Verba, and P. E. Converse, *Vietnam and the Silent Majority* (New York: Harper, 1970).

[2]G. C. Edwards III and I. Sharkansky, *The Policy Predicament: Making and Implementing Public Policy* (San Francisco: W. H. Freeman and Company, 1978), Chapter 2.

[3]F. Munger, "Opinions, Elections, Parties, and Policies: A Cross-State Analysis" (paper presented at meeting of American Political Science Association, New York, 1969).

Table 3-1   Correlation Between Public Support for 14 National Policies
and Actual Policies Adopted by the Government, 1974

Policy	Percentage of respondents supporting policy	Majority opinion congruent with existing policy?
Decreased defense spending	56%	No
Wage and price controls	62	No
Busing school children for racial integration	32	No
Gun registration	71	No
Aid to parochial schools	52	No
Establishment of diplomatic relations with Cuba	63	No
Unconditional amnesty	41	Yes
Legalization of marijuana	26	Yes
Equal Rights Amendment	79	Yes[a]
Federal financing of congressional elections	72	No
Death penalty	63	No
5 percent income surtax	46	Yes
Decreased spending for social programs	34	Yes
Legalized abortions	52	Yes

[a]Congress passed the amendment although it has not yet been ratified by the requisite 38 states.

SOURCE: George C. Edwards III and Ira Sharkansky, *The Policy Predicament: Making and Implementing Public Policy* (San Francisco: W. H. Freeman and Company. Copyright © 1978). Compiled from Gallup Poll data reported in "Election Mandates Economic Actions," *New Orleans Times–Picayune*, November 4, 1974.

educated. At the same time, there is an increasing dissatisfaction with the major political parties, although there is as yet no evidence that large numbers of voters prefer a nondemocratic alternative to the American political process.[4]

What has produced this alienation? Typically cited as the causes of this public disaffection are the war in Southeast Asia, the unsettling domestic events of the 1960s, Watergate, and the sense of drift in the Carter Administration on such issues as energy and inflation. It is difficult to chart a simple course between the nature of public policy and the alienation of the body politic. Consider the improvements in civil rights and social welfare

[4]N. H. Nie, S. Verba, and J. R. Petrocik, *The Changing American Voter* (Cambridge, Mass.: Harvard University Press, 1976).

Congress and the executive branch were lower in public esteem during 1979 than during 1966, but their lowest point may have been in 1976. Other institutions have also suffered.

Table 3-2 A Crisis of Confidence in Institutions, 1966–1979

Institution	1966	1971	1973	1974	1975	1976	1977	1978	1979
Television news	25%		41%	31%	35%	28%	28%	35%	37%
Medicine	73	61%	57	50	43	42	43	42	30
Military	62	27	40	33	24	23	27	29	29
Press	29	18	30	25	26	20	18	28	28
Organized religion	41	27	36	32	32	24	29	34	20
Major companies	55	27	29	21	19	16	20	22	28
Congress	42	19	29	18	13	9	17	10	18
Executive branch	41	23	19	28	13	11	23	14	17
Organized labor	22	14	20	18	14	10	14	15	10
Average	43	27	33	28	24	20	24	25	23

Note: Since 1966, Louis Harris and Associates Inc. has been asking the public whether it has "a great deal of confidence, only some confidence, or hardly any confidence at all" in the leaders of nine major institutions. This table shows the percentage of respondents who expressed "a great deal of confidence."
SOURCE: *Public Opinion,* October–November 1979.

policies undertaken in the late 1960s. Many whites feel that such programs went too far, were too costly or wasteful, and caused a breakdown in respect for hard work and law and order. On the other hand, many blacks find that the programs were not ambitious enough, were not administered in a way to deliver the benefits promised by the political rhetoric, and then were weakened or curtailed under the pressure of the white establishment. In his controversial study of American cities, Banfield describes how living conditions of the urban poor improved according to objective measures, even while the level of satisfaction deteriorated in poor neighborhoods.[5]

Elections

Elections are the official device for citizens to enforce their will on public officials. The campaigns that precede elections are an opportunity for the voters to learn about government activities. Good and bad news about pro-

---

[5]E. C. Banfield, *The Unheavenly City Revisited* (Boston: Little, Brown, 1974).

grams—their successes and failures, benefits and costs—are highlighted by opposing candidates in their pursuit of voter support. For this reason, the election is superior to the public opinion poll as a connection between the people and the government. Public opinion polls merely inform government about the public's wants. The election campaign helps to inform the people about the government, and the election itself provides some indication of what the people want.

The chief executives and members of the legislatures at all levels of U.S. government are subject to periodic election. Even those localities that employ city managers as chief executive officers make them subordinate to an elected council. In state governments, election procedures often extend to the heads of major administrative units. Presumably, elected officials control administrative agencies to produce the kinds of policies desired by the electorate. However, the character of elections, as well as the imperfect mechanisms that elected officials use to control administrators, limit the usefulness of elections as a means of control over administrative agencies. In most cases, citizens are limited to voting for a person, but without indicating to that person which policies to support. Important exceptions are to be found in the initiative and referendum procedures available to many states and localities. Through the use of these forms of direct legislation, the voters can signal their support for or opposition to specific revenue issues, constitutional amendments, and advisory questions.

Part of the voters' problem lies in the political parties. Voters cannot be sure by a party label alone which policies a candidate will support once in office. Individual candidates for election typically support a range of programs. But their election does not necessarily mean popular approval of those programs. The presidential campaign of 1964 provides a good example. The policy choices presented to the voters were unusually clear. The voters could choose between Johnson and Goldwater on the issues of civil rights, the war in Vietnam, and welfare policies. Most observers agree that Johnson took more liberal positions than his opponent on civil rights and welfare issues, and that he took a more restrained position with respect to extending the war in Vietnam. The problem came when pundits had to determine which policies were supported by the majority.

Despite President Johnson's clear victory in 1964, the election results alone did not indicate which positions the electorate supported. It is possible that only a minority of Johnson's supporters agreed with his civil rights platform. Most citizens might have agreed with Goldwater on this, or any other, issue, but voted for Johnson because they felt he represented their position on the war issue, which they felt to be the most important. In a presidential election, observers can usually compare a large volume of poll results with the election outcome. These results are not available for most state and local elections; the newly elected official can read into a victory any combination of policy preferences, and the loser cannot present substantial evidence to the contrary.

Even when election results are compared with opinion surveys, little citizen control may result over the policies of the winning candidate. The statements of the campaign may not stay relevant beyond the first crisis of the new government. Again, the Johnson–Goldwater campaign provides an example. Although Johnson indicated his own opposition to expanded American participation in Vietnam, he claimed a release from his campaign statements after the election. Although some observers felt that Johnson had gone beyond his presidential mandate, others felt that conditions justified subsequent war policies. Moreover, no control mechanisms operated to keep Johnson and his administrative subordinates from pursuing policies that ran counter to campaign promises.[6]

The 1972 presidential election also showed the weakness of voter control over policies. The magnitude of the Nixon–Agnew victory was outstanding at 60.7 percent of the vote. There were sharp policy differences between the Republican and Democratic tickets. Richard Nixon promised a different kind of withdrawal from Vietnam and different approaches to welfare and school integration than George McGovern. It is not clear, however, whether voters provided Richard Nixon with a mandate for his policies. Much of the Nixon vote was anti-McGovern, reflecting a lack of confidence in the Democratic candidate. Later, when the Nixon–Agnew Administration became mired in the scandals of Agnew's acceptance of bribes to influence the awarding of government contracts and of Nixon's involvement in the cover-up of the Watergate break-in and several lesser issues, the election landslide dwindled in importance. President Nixon's popularity in the polls dropped to such a degree that only 25 percent of the population approved of his actions. With the resignations of Agnew and Nixon less than halfway through their four-year term, only the most contorted argument could claim that Ford could read any directives from the election mandate of 1972.

Political Parties

In order to understand the problems of elections in failing to link the American people with the government, it is necessary to consider the nature of political parties in the United States. Where parties are strong and disciplined, citizens can vote for their candidate with an expectation that their programs will—if the party is victorious—be enacted into policy. However, American parties lack procedures with which to discipline their mem-

---

[6]R. A. Dahl, *A Preface to Democratic Theory* (Chicago: University of Chicago Press, 1956).

bers on policy issues. There are no central controls of party financing and nominations, no assurances that state and local organizations will support the positions of national party leaders, and no guarantee of unity between party members in the White House and Congress.[7]

The decentralized structure of the American parties is largely responsible for their lack of discipline. Party candidates or incumbents owe their obligations to a variety of state and local party divisions, each of which has its own constituency of voters' attitudes, beliefs, and policy preferences. Nominations for state, local, and congressional campaigns come from state and local organizations, which may be nothing more than personal organizations focused on the career of one politician. The nomination of presidential candidates also depends on decisions made in state and local organizations. No national officers control the resources necessary to state organizations, and none can issue policy directives to party nominees. Some members of Congress and governors campaign openly against the presidential nominee of their own party. At one time, this was solely a Democratic problem, when liberal presidential nominees like Harry Truman and Adlai Stevenson were expected to write off the support of conservative southerners. But the 1964 presidential campaign saw Republican governors Nelson Rockefeller and George Romney, Senator Jacob Javits, and Mayor John Lindsay refusing to endorse Barry Goldwater's candidacy.

Some party members view their ideological diversity as an asset. Candidates cast a broad appeal when they have ambiguous platforms. American parties are led by pragmatic office seekers who cherish flexibility and the capacity to adjust policy positions for electoral success. The parties have not developed permanent staffs to maintain a coherent set of principles.

The parties have declined. The voters who identified themselves as *independents* increased from 23 percent in 1952 to 38 percent in 1974. In the same period, the voters who identified themselves as strongly partisan declined from 37 to 26 percent.[8] Voters have shown more familiarity with issues and more consistency in their feelings about issues in such fields as welfare, taxation, defense, and foreign policy. Yet, the parties themselves have not become more consistent on these policy issues. Each party has both distinctive liberals and conservatives among its leading members, who blunt each party's capacity to offer clearly different alternatives to the voters, and then the promise, with victory, to implement the voters' mandate into policy.

Despite the barriers to strong political parties, elected chief executives assume the role of party leader. They call on party loyalty to win votes in Congress and to improve their control over the agencies. When executives make high-level appointments, they typically appoint members of their own

---

[7]J. M. Burns, *The Deadlock of Democracy: Four-Party Politics in America* (Englewood Cliffs, N.J.: Spectrum, 1963).

[8]Nie, Verba, and Petrocik, op. cit.; also E. C. Ladd, Jr., *Where Have All the Voters Gone? The Fracturing of America's Political Parties* (New York: Norton, 1978).

party. Appointing partisans to administrative jobs is justified with the claim that the practice improves government. Presumably, a chief executive is more able to count on subordinates who have party ties. Partisans are more likely to share the executive's policy orientation and to help compile a record of administrative accomplishments that will appeal to the voters at the next election. Such sentiments did not protect Secretary Joseph Califano of the Department of Health, Education and Welfare in 1979. He was dismissed by President Carter, partly because of his loyalty to the wrong faction of the Democratic Party. Richard Nixon and his White House aides were also choosy about which kinds of Republicans were appointed. An established membership in the party seemed less important than personal loyalty to the President.[9]

The appointment power that remains in the hands of chief executives is only a vestige of what they formerly had. Several changes in government programs and the public's distrust of partisanship have limited an executive's freedom. Nonpartisan criteria are now required for over 90 percent of the civilian positions in the federal government and for many positions in state and local governments. Government services are increasingly technical and require professional expertise in many administrative positions. A chief executive must often weigh professional competence above partisanship in selecting department heads, even when the law permits the use of partisan criteria. In many instances, the only feasible partisan standard holds that the "right person" not be uncompromisingly in support of the opposition. A politically neutral person or a bland member of the opposition party may be selected over a party member if the position calls for special competence.

The weakening of party patronage seems good to those concerned with professional expertise in administrative agencies. To the extent that a decline in patronage reflects a general weakening of political parties, however, it also weakens one of the links between the people and their government. The decentralized and undisciplined political parties of the United States are not as effective as their British and European counterparts in connecting the voters to government. American parties in opposition are less able to present the voters with clear criticisms of the party in power. American parties in power are less able to transform their election platforms into government programs.

Interest Groups

Much of the writing about interest groups concerns their relations with legislators. The common name for interest-group representatives—lobbyists—derives from the tradition of speaking with elected representatives in

---

[9]H. Heclo, *Government of Strangers* (Washington, D.C.: Brookings Institution, 1977).

the lobbies off the legislative chambers. Lobbyists seek to influence the character of public policy. They inform policy-makers about the features that interest-group members wish to add to government activities and about those proposals that threaten interest-group members with undesirable consequences. They make presentations at formal hearings of congressional committees and contact individual legislators with an eye toward their roles in committees or in floor votes. Lobbyists also deal with administrative agencies. Even if interest groups are successful in the legislature, they must work further to assure favorable treatment in the agencies.

Legislatures do not expect to provide for all possible situations by their statutes, and they permit administrators to operate within established standards. Some legislation provides narrow grants of authority that administrators can exercise within clear limits. Other legislation offers great leeway. The basic statute establishing the National Aeronautics and Space Administration (NASA), for example, authorized the agency to:

1. Research the solutions of problems of flight within and outside the earth's atmosphere, and develop, construct, test, and operate aeronautical and space vehicles.
2. Conduct activities required for the exploration of space with manned and unmanned vehicles.
3. Arrange for the most effective utilization of the scientific and engineering resources of the United States and for cooperation by the United States with other nations engaged in aeronautical and space activities for peaceful purposes.
4. Provide for the widest practicable and appropriate dissemination of information concerning NASA's activities and their results.[10]

The NASA administrators have read the law in such a way as to permit significant programs that are, at most, tangential to the exploration of space. They have subsidized research to measure changes in the quality of lifestyles in the United States[11] and have supported university curricula to train public administrators, as well as natural scientists and engineers.

The values and attitudes of administrators can shape the ways in which agency powers are employed, and these values may differ from those that prevail in the legislature. Because of these possible differences, the constellation of groups that influences the legislature does not necessarily influence administrative units. Studies of regulatory policy suggest that even though consumer groups may win strong statutory controls over business

---

[10]*U.S. Government Organization Manual, 1965–66* (Washington, D.C.: U.S. Government Printing Office, 1965), p. 462.

[11]See, e.g., R. Bauer, ed., *Social Indicators* (Cambridge, Mass.: MIT Press, 1966).

firms, the lobbyists of business may gain enough influence in the administration to weaken the regulation that actually occurs.[12]

Interest groups can express their desires at various points in the federal administration. They may seek access to the White House, so that they can have an opportunity to shape presidential proposals on their way to Congress, executive orders, and key decisions about staff appointments and budgets. They may convey their desires to cabinet secretaries and the personnel who are close to them. They may also be active at the working levels of agencies. They may make presentations at public hearings and may maintain contacts with the people who affect their interests.

Interest groups thrive in a climate like the United States. There is great diversity in public opinion. On most issues no clear majority opinion prevails; instead, many shades of support exist that can justify a group's claim to represent the public interest. There are constitutional guarantees of free expression and the right to petition government. Government itself is divided into separate executive and legislative branches—as well as national, state, and local arenas—thus giving interest groups the chance to succeed in one arena if they fail in another. Also, the parties are decentralized and undisciplined, and cannot claim a mandate to govern according to their programs. In this setting, interest groups claim the role of informing policymakers and administrators of the public's wants and the public of the government's pursuit of its interests.

Many kinds of interest groups present their claims to government:

1. Economic groups that represent various segments of industry, commerce, banking, and labor.
2. Consumer groups.
3. Government groups, such as those representing state or local officials in their pursuit of federal aid.
4. Single-interest groups, on various sides of such issues as abortion, gay rights, and nuclear power.
5. Agency-clientele groups, such as organizations that pursue a better deal for welfare recipients or handicapped students.
6. Unions of government employees that seek better wages and working conditions.

Many agencies welcome the appearance of groups that represent agency clientele or other interested segments of the population. Sometimes out of respect for the democratic norms of popular access, and sometimes because

---

[12]M. Edelman, *The Symbolic Uses of Politics* (Urbana: University of Illinois Press, 1964), especially Chapter 2. See also M. Bernstein, *Regulating Business by Independent Commissions* (Princeton, N.J.: Princeton University Press, 1955).

Table 3-3 Tax Freedom Day,
1930–1980

Year	Date
1930	February 13
1940	March 8
1950	April 4
1960	April 18
1970	April 30
1975[a]	April 30
1976[a]	May 3
1977[a]	May 5
1978[a]	May 6
1979[b]	May 8
1980[c]	May 11

[a]Revised.
[b]Preliminary.
[c]Forecast.

SOURCE: *Monthly Tax Features*, 24 (April 1980). Reprinted with permission of Tax Foundation, Incorporated.

Tax Freedom Day is the point in the calendar when the mythical average American can say, "Now I've stopped working for the government." It represents a calculation by the Tax Foundation of how much of each working year is needed to earn the money to pay national, state, and local taxes. As the table indicates, Tax Freedom Day is getting later each year, meaning that taxes are increasing as a percentage of average income. The calculation of Tax Freedom Day is also an expression of political views. The implied statement of the Tax Foundation is: "Taxes are too high and they are continuing to increase."

legislation requires it, administrators establish formal procedures for interest groups to express their preferences. These procedures include opportunities to petition the agency and to explain one's desires at an informal conference or a formal hearing, and advanced notice of impending changes in policy. Some agencies establish advisory bodies to represent various segments of their clientele. One author has written that interest groups are offered the most generous opportunities to express themselves when the following conditions prevail:

1. When a large number of people or a great magnitude of resources will be affected by an administrator's policy.

2. When an administrator can delay the implementation of policy without causing substantial harm.

3. When interests are given the status of legal recognition, in other words, when provisions in a statute require the consultation of certain groups.

4. When an impending policy decision will have the effect of finally disposing of an issue, without affected parties having the opportunity to prevent the loss or recoup their losses at a later hearing.[13]

---

[13]W. W. Boyer, *Bureaucracy on Trial: Policy-Making by Government Agencies* (Indianapolis: Bobbs-Merrill, 1964).

Interest-Group Allies

Administrators need not wait passively for interest-group allies. They can keep the mass media informed about activities that may win public support, and they can maintain contacts with interest groups.

An allied interest group can help an agency by taking a position that an administrator cannot take publicly, because it might offend the President or important members of Congress. An interest group can support an agency's requests for funds or statutory authority, or help an agency resist undesirable directives. An interest group can build public support for an administrator who is currently the target of hostile politicians.

Some agencies are so well endowed with the support of interest groups and private citizens that they seem virtually impervious to the President or Congress. The Federal Bureau of Investigation built up a great reservoir of goodwill among associations of local police departments (whose members are trained at FBI academies and whose analyses are done in FBI laboratories) and with many private citizens (long accustomed to watching the FBI capture society's offenders on television shows produced with bureau cooperation). One sign of the FBI's power was the tenure of its former director. J. Edgar Hoover held the post of director from the time of the Coolidge Administration until his death in 1972. Presidents kept him in the office beyond the "mandatory" retirement age for federal personnel. Yet agency reputations are not immortal. This truth became apparent when the FBI's status plummeted after the discovery that extralegal activities occurred under J. Edgar Hoover and during the interim directorship of L. Patrick Gray.

Agencies run a risk when they maintain close relations with interest groups. In exchange for political support, a group might win control of an agency program. The agricultural education programs of some state universities seem tailored to the demands of certain groups that are important in state politics. These programs may be thought of as "loss leaders"—effective control of programs that a university is willing to lose to farm groups in order to receive these groups' support for the university's total program. One study of the early years of the Tennessee Valley Authority also suggests that the TVA gave control over some of its programs to interest groups that provided it with general support. There appear to have been effective vetoes by those interest groups over agency programs that threatened their interests.[14]

Some alliances between administrative agencies, interest groups, and other organs of government are so strong that they are labeled *subgovernments*. The subgovernment for elementary and secondary education, for

---

[14]P. Selznick, *TVA and the Grass Roots* (Berkeley: University of California Press, 1949).

example, includes professionals in federal and state departments of education, legislators who serve on education committees of Congress and state legislatures, and interest groups like the National Education Association and the American Federation of Teachers. A subgovernment develops a tight network of members who rely on one another for advice about what is good for the field. Outsiders have trouble penetrating the circle. Ranking politicians, such as state governors and legislators from outside the education committees, feel helpless in the face of education-oriented legislators, administrators, and their interest-group allies. Elected chief executives have difficulty imposing government-wide perspectives—like the need for economy—on persons who try to put their own field's needs above all else.

One subgovernment that has received much public attention is the military–industrial complex: a network of military and civilian personnel in the Department of Defense, defense contractors and the interest groups that represent them, and members of Congress. They are allied partly by the economic incentives of defense contracts that appeal to industry and to the members of Congress whose districts will benefit, and partly by promised improvements in U.S. military posture. Some commentators accuse this conglomerate of applying irresistible pressure on the President and Congress. These pressures have implications not only for the size of the military budget, but also for the flexibility of U.S. foreign policy. It has been said that the State Department is hard-pressed to negotiate far-reaching arms control with the Soviet Union when domestic American incentives are so great for continued arms buildup. It is difficult to assess the accuracy of these allegations. The economic-political incentives in arms escalation have bothered officials at the highest levels of government. One of the surprising features of President Eisenhower's farewell address was his warning of the "acquisition of unwarranted influence . . . by the military–industrial complex."[15] After the U.S. withdrawal from Vietnam, there was a decline in the size of the defense budget relative to the budgets of civilian agencies. In 1981, Ronald Reagan came to the White House with a commitment to increase sharply defense preparedness. Because of that commitment antidefense interest groups are likely to raise again the specter of the military–industrial complex.

Any effort to assess the roles of interest groups must reckon with several factors that limit their influence. Policy-makers themselves seem to dominate the relationships. The status of interest groups is ambiguous. They carry the image of selfish lobbyists ready to gratify their own interests at the expense of the public. There have been episodes of deceit on the part of interest groups, heavily financed campaigns designed to defeat politicians who have opposed group demands, and overt attempts to bribe government officials. Policy-makers are sensitive to these interest-group traditions. If

---

[15] D. Carter, *Power in Washington* (New York: Vintage Books, 1964), Chapter 2.

"undesirable pressures" are perceived, an official may terminate the access a group has enjoyed and frustrate its campaign to influence policy.

Lobbyists themselves admit their secondary status in their relations with government officials. In response to a question about the influence of various participants in federal policy-making, more than one-half of 114 lobbyists surveyed named the President or agency administrators as the most important actors, about 20 percent named the voters as most important, 10 percent named Congress, and only one of the respondents gave the lobbyists first rank.[16]

Mass Media

The mass media can add to the information citizens have about public affairs and thereby enhance the people's influence on administrators. The mass media—including newspapers, popular journals, radio, and television—also have their own influence on administrators. They help to shape the agenda of public debate by emphasizing some issues and making them important. They originate some issues by campaigns against social problems, the failure of government programs, or the malfeasance of certain officials. The operators of newspapers and broadcasting networks liken themselves to other muckrakers who have been responsible for major innovations in public policies.[17] Some officials watch the media for signs of the public's wants. Letters to the editors, editorials, and the character of news stories may convey messages about the character of the public's interests.

The events surrounding one television documentary illustrate the role of the media—along with other influences—in helping to shape public policy. In May of 1968, CBS broadcast "Hunger in America." It illustrated in powerful detail the horrors of starving children and the inadequacies of existing government programs. The television program had an immediate effect on some administrators, if only to force some defensive public statements. The secretary of agriculture identified some factual errors in the telecast and condemned it as "a biased, onesided, dishonest presentation of a serious national problem."[18] Over the succeeding months, however, the Department of Agriculture took several steps to increase the flow of food to the poor.

---

[16]L. W. Milbrath, *The Washington Lobbyists* (Chicago: Rand McNally, 1963).

[17]Classic examples of muckraking literature include these books: Upton Sinclair's *The Jungle* (Cambridge, Mass.: Robert Bentley, 1971, reprint of 1906 ed.), which aided the campaign to begin the regulation of food processing by the federal government; Michael Harrington's *The Other America* (New York: Macmillan, 1970), which informed and aroused readers about the condition below the "poverty line" in the United States and helped in the development of the programs of the Office of Economic Opportunity; and Ralph Nader's *Unsafe At Any Speed* (New York: Grossman, 1972), which provided much of the evidence—and passion—for federal auto safety regulations.

[18]E. B. Drew, "Going Hungry in America," *Atlantic* (December 1968): 53–61.

Coming as it did in the midst of numerous other expressions about the same social problem, "Hunger in America" probably added some pressure on Congress, the President, and the Department of Agriculture. Yet, the media joined an attack that was already under way. In the preceding year, a private foundation sponsored a survey by several prominent physicians and local practitioners in the delta counties of northwestern Mississippi. Their report to the Senate Subcommittee on Employment, Manpower, and Poverty then provoked other prominent groups and individuals. The subcommittee attracted a great deal of press coverage, partly because Robert F. Kennedy was a member of the subcommittee and, at the time, a potential candidate for the presidency. The food problem was made a target of the "Poor People's Campaign," which itself was stimulated by public reaction to the assassination of Dr. Martin Luther King. Labor unions also joined the issue. The Citizens' Crusade Against Poverty (with support from the United Auto Workers) published a critical assessment of the federal government's food programs entitled *Hunger, U.S.A.*[19] Undoubtedly, the media did increase grass-roots interest in the food problem by popularizing an issue that had been raised by others.

The media also illuminated some details about the limited effectiveness of the Agriculture Department's policies. Food programs were developed to relieve the surplus food problems of farmers as well as the hunger of poor people; administrators and legislators seemed more concerned about agricultural than social considerations. CBS also showed some of the controversy between the House and Senate Agriculture Committees, which included Mississippians Jamie Whitten and James Eastland (frequently accused of being short on social conscience), and the more liberal Senate Labor and Public Welfare Subcommittee on Employment, Manpower, and Poverty, chaired by Joseph S. Clark and including Robert F. Kennedy.

Several factors keep the media from exercising continuing control over either the public or administrative agencies. The media do not have a captive audience. Citizens are involved in many relationships that provide different kinds of information. For many people, political discussions with friends, family members, or coworkers are better sources of political information than the media. Some people distrust the political messages in the media. The phenomenon of selective perception leads individuals to overlook items of fact or opinion that challenge their own views.

Many newspapers and broadcasting stations provide little information about administrative agencies or other practical aspects of politics. Most of the media are organized for commercial rather than political purposes. Local newspapers and television stations carry wire-service copy on national and international news, usually in small proportion to the space or time devoted to sports and advertising. News about administrative agencies may

---

[19]Citizens' Board of Inquiry, *Hunger, U.S.A.* (Boston, Mass.: Beacon, 1968).

be especially thin. Without the excitement of election campaigns or the involvement of prominent personalities, the media are not likely to view administrative events as newsworthy.

Administrators and other policy-makers do credit the mass media with a powerful role. At times, they seem obsessed with the media's influence on their reputations or policies. Presidents Johnson and Nixon, Vice-President Agnew, and Secretary of State Kissinger sought to manage the media with selective handouts of vital information. They occasionally vilified those reporters and commentators who described their activities in uncomplimentary terms. President Carter began his presidency with kind words for the press, but was sharply critical of the Washington news corps by the summer of 1979. He made a point of holding news conferences in small towns in order to reach the non-Washington media. Numerous figures throughout the bureaucracies of national, state, and local governments repeat these patterns on their own smaller stages. They seek to put the best face on their activities for the benefit of the media. Occasionally, they become preoccupied with the potential adversarial character of reporters.

CITIZENS AS CLIENTS AND PARTICIPANTS

Many citizens are not concerned with influencing policy-making at the highest levels, but with service and delivery at the street level. In other words, their concern is not so much with top policy-makers in Washington or the state capital, but with personal encounters close to home. For many people, government does not work well. Complaints range from modest to extreme and from matters prosaic to profound. Some problems center on bureaus that are oppressive in their dealings with the people: police who are callous or brutal, schoolteachers who are nasty, welfare workers who harass, factory inspectors who are arbitrary. Other problems focus on the difficulties in penetrating the maze of service-providing agencies in order to receive benefits.

Some complaints reflect the incoherence of social-service delivery to citizens in need. Social services have developed in a piecemeal fashion, without any inherent logic in the way that programs are attached to a particular office. With state and local governments contracting out various services to private agencies (counseling, job training, health care, child care, halfway houses for mental patients and criminal offenders, sheltered workshops for the handicapped), the number of service providers multiplies further. Some administrators—whether governmental or contractual—are ignorant of other service providers from related sources, while other administrators take a proprietary interest in their own terrain and refuse to guide clients elsewhere. As a result, many clients end up wandering aimlessly from one office to another.

"Power to the People" is a cry heard with some frequency. Like other slogans, its meaning is not always clear, but it is seldom a sign of support for established bureaucracies. The inner neighborhoods of large cities offer numerous experiments in citizen involvement in policy-making and administration. They give us an opportunity to see some of the problems involved in self-government, as well as to experience the intensity of feeling that certain opponents have about established agencies.

Various kinds of citizen participation have appeared. Some—like block associations—are self-help bodies established by neighborhood residents that have little or no contact with municipal authorities. They focus on cleaning-up, fixing-up, and painting-up campaigns and block parties. Other—like "little city halls"—may be the establishment's effort to decentralize some decision-making authority to the bureaucrats working in the neighborhoods, with little or no consultation between officials and neighborhood residents. Often there is a combination of citizen initiative and official responses. Some cities have neighborhood school boards with certain controls over budgetary and personnel matters. These school boards still may have to work with city-hall bureaucrats. The goals and styles of participation vary, often from one neighborhood to another in the same city. The prominent characteristics of some neighborhoods may be intense protest, inflamed rhetoric, and only grudging cooperation with the authorities. An official board run by citizens that reviews complaints against the police has been a popular demand of inner-city groups, and has been established in several places. Some neighborhoods mobilize around prosaic concerns for clean streets and improved upkeep of private property, and some make pragmatic efforts to channel citizen complaints to the proper office in the city's bureaucracy.

In judging the success of citizen participation, it is necessary first to establish the viewpoint from which the participation is judged—from the established bureaucrat's, mayor's, or city council member's or from an abstract standard of political theory. We can judge experiments according to their contributions to citizen involvement in public affairs, the substantive improvement of certain local services, or the citizens' sense of satisfaction.

Citizen trust in local government has increased in places that have mechanisms for participation. On the other hand, the record of actual citizen involvement is not impressive. Turnout rates for neighborhood elections have ranged between 1 and 5 percent. Residents have not scored well in surveys designed to test their knowledge of what neighborhood programs actually exist. And members of citizen boards are preoccupied with petty issues and have poor records of follow up. Indeed, neighborhood bodies may have some inherent weaknesses in dealing with major policies. Projects in education, welfare, policy, housing, and jobs may depend on resources or statutory powers that neighborhood bodies do not control. The fragmented nature of metropolitan government defies coordination by neighborhood bodies with limited authority and political leverage. The political support for neighborhood autonomy is not dependable. In some communities, the enthusiasm of black elites for home rule at the neighborhood level has evaporated as they gained control of the mayor's office and acquired an appreciation of authority centralized in city hall.[20]

PUBLIC ADMINISTRATORS
AND PUBLIC RELATIONS

Administrators are not passive recipients of public demands. They are active both in collecting information that serves agency needs and in disseminating information that creates a favorable climate of opinion. Some agencies invest in public-opinion surveys in order to gauge the thinking of relevant publics or to learn what clients know about agency programs. Many agencies clip newspaper and magazine stories about their activities, and analyze client complaints. Federal agencies sometimes hold full-blown inquiries into public attitudes about certain programs. These inquiries can include the rituals of presidential appointments for prestigious citizens to serve on blue-ribbon panels, the taking of testimony in numerous locales, and well-publicized reports that suggest new program developments. A prominent example was the Kerner Commission, the National Advisory Commission on Civil Disorders, which was chaired by Otto Kerner, the former Governor of Illinois, and formed to look into urban riots in the late 1960s. Its report alleged that "white racism" was prevalent in society, and urged sweeping changes based on community-oriented programs by the police and other agencies of local government. Local police departments and officers' unions responded with their own contrary public relations efforts, and there was quite a squabble.

Administrators' efforts to shape public opinion have sparked much controversy. Administrators' public relations activities pit them against the mass media and individuals who want to be opinion leaders. "Managing the news" is a frequent criticism that journalists direct at public administrators. Administrators are accused of withholding information that might embarrass themselves or their organizations. Related to this is the charge that administrators play favorites among journalists, giving important information to those journalists most likely to treat it favorably.

A serious charge directed against administrators who try to influence public opinion is that they distort information to put themselves in a better light. Put simply, some administrators lie. Governmental lying may be the

---

[20]R. L. Cole, *Citizen Participation and the Urban Policy Process* (Lexington, Mass.: Heath, 1974); D. Yates, *Neighborhood Democracy* (Lexington, Mass.: Heath, 1973).

most prevalent in foreign and military affairs. Officials in these fields may be tempted to stretch or invent truth because American journalists cannot easily ferret out the truth miles from their home base, and because of the secrecy that prevails in such matters. Some lies are meant to hide blunders both from international adversaries and domestic critics. Among the more spectacular lies of American officials are the following:

1. The U–2 plane shot down over the Soviet Union in 1960 was a weather plane that drifted off course. President Eisenhower later admitted the plane was on a spy mission over the heart of the Soviet Union.

2. The United States was not involved in fighting in Cambodia during 1969–1970. In fact, numerous bombing strikes were made.

3. Civilian deaths at My Lai did not occur. The military first reported that there was a justifiable fire fight between U.S. Army personnel and Viet Cong combatants. Subsequent investigations and a military court martial revealed a massacre of civilians.

The ombudsman is an institution that was created in Scandinavia and has been adopted by various government agencies in the United States in order to improve the chances of citizens in dealings with government. The task of the ombudsman is to investigate complaints against administrators and to support those complaints that are found to be justified. Ombudsmen deal mostly with individual cases of poor treatment and refrain from questions of general policy. For this reason, the topic is treated along with other aspects of client services in Chapter 16.

Government Interest Groups

Administrators and other officials create their own interest groups to represent their views before the public and in policy-making arenas. These groups may have an advantage in the policy process, insofar as their members understand both the formal and the informal aspects of the process. Government interest groups make several kinds of demands:

1. Demands for personal benefits, such as the wage and working condition demands made by unions of government employees.

2. Demands for agency benefits, such as budgetary requests lobbied in the legislature by the lobbyists who work for administrative agencies.

3. Demands for benefits that accrue to governments, per se, such as the requests for more funds spent on intergovernmental assistance lobbied by the U.S. Conference of Mayors and the Governors' Conference.

4. Demands for changes in the substance of policy, which are lobbied
   by associations of professionals employed by government.

SUMMARY

In a democracy, the people are the ultimate reference point for administrative activity. For the people to be more than an empty symbol of legitimacy, however, there must be effective means to reveal public demands and
to hold administrators accountable. American administrators face a great
array of information about the public and several mechanisms for obtaining
accountability. The quality of information that administrators have about
the public and the effectiveness of the public's mechanisms for holding
administrators accountable are questionable. It is certain, however, that public opinion motivates action and influences the direction of policy in administrative departments.

The connections between the public and public administration include
survey research, elections, political parties, interest groups, the mass media,
various kinds of citizen participation, and the ombudsman. This scope may
seem to leave little chance for administrators to escape from the public's
net. However, each mechanism that links citizens with the government has
faults. Elections and political parties, for example, are effective ways of
selecting officeholders, but they are not very effective in signaling the people's demands for public policy.

Administrators are not simply inert in the face of these several mechanisms for transmitting popular demands. Many administrators have their
own ideas of proper policy, and are not averse to using techniques of their
own influence to the public. Administrators seek support for their programs
at the same time that they receive demands from the public. They employ
the mass media and their own interest groups to make their arguments in
public or before the executive and legislative branches. Administrators
argue the importance of their program needs and compete with other opin-
ion-makers in interpreting support for their programs from the complex
indications of public opinion.

4

The Chief Executive and the Legislature

> He'll sit here, and he'll say, 'Do this! Do that!' And nothing will happen. Poor
> Ike—It won't be a bit like the Army. He'll find it very frustrating.
>
> *Harry S Truman*[1]

President Truman was reflecting his own experience. His desk carried a
sign that read "The Buck Stops Here." Such words may have helped the
President feel heroic, but they did not signal his command over the government. President Truman's cute shot at Ike also exaggerated the new
President's expectations about what it would be like to be President. Eisenhower may have been new to electoral politics, but he was an old hand at
administration. He climbed to the top of the army by learning how to work
with ornery subordinates and how to accept less than he demanded.

This chapter continues the theme of accountability. It focuses on elite
policy-makers at the head of the U.S. national government, and inquires
into their capacity to serve as links between the people and government
administration. To do this well, elected officials must be able to comprehend
and control the work of administrators. Accordingly, the key questions to
be answered are:

> *What controls do the elected Chief Executive and legislators exercise over
> the administration?*
>
> *How do these controls operate?*

---

[1]T. Bailey, *Presidential Greatness* (New York: Appleton-Century-Crofts, 1966), p. 78.

The U.S. President has great power as well as many problems. One of the President's problems is the enormous range of his power. Another problem is Congress. More than any other legislature in the world, the U.S. Congress has the independence and the resources to be a significant force in shaping public policy. Just as Congress is a problem for the President, however, the President is a problem for Congress. Each benefits from and suffers under the separation of powers. There are frequent standoffs between the two, with the result that neither can dominate the administrators.

Not only does the jostling between political leaders leave much in the hands of administrators, but also much of the power that the President and Congress wield is managed by their staffs. The Executive Office of the President exercises much of the policy control that is identified formally with the President's name. On the congressional side, much of the work is done by staff aides of individual members and committees, plus organizations like the Congressional Budget Office and the General Accounting Office. Thus, much of what passes for political control *of* professional administrators is really managed *by* professional administrators.

It would be a mistake to assume that administrators sit idly by and wait for instructions from on high. Key reports go from the agencies upward through the "chain of command" to the White House and Congress. Departmental liaison personnel prowl the corridors of Congress and visit the White House to present their organizations' interests. As noted in Chapter 3, ranking officers of the departments belong to organizations that lobby their interests with elected officials and with target public groups.

Most of the material in this chapter deals with top-level policy matters. For the most part, the President and Congress concern themselves only with the most important policy issues—those involving the most resources, of interest to many people, or considered to have major implications. Their direct contacts with departments and agencies tend to be with administrators at the top—the formal heads, or key personnel chosen to aid or represent the heads in contacts with the White House or Capitol Hill. The typical bureaucrat may come into direct contact with the President or a member of Congress no more often than a typical citizen. For issues of accountability, however, the contact between elected officials and administrative chiefs remains an important concern. Without effective supervision and control at these junctures, administrative chiefs and employees cannot fully claim to be carrying out the will of the people.

THE PRESIDENT AS CHIEF ADMINISTRATOR

The President is at the top of the official administrative organization chart, with nominal control over the departments and agencies. This formal authority includes the following actions that have relevance for administrative departments and agencies:

1. Appointment—and removal—of department heads and other key figures.
2. Review of administrators' budget requests and the preparation of a President's budget that becomes the focus of congressional deliberation.
3. Review of existing programs and new proposals, and submission of legislative proposals for congressional deliberation.
4. Review of congressional legislation, with a right to cast a veto that can be overriden only with an extraordinary majority in both the House of Representatives and the Senate.
5. Promulgation of certain regulations as defined by law (for example, awarding international air routes to airlines and deciding on the initiation of certain military actions).

Within these general areas of power, a number of formal exceptions, as well as some political deficiencies, weaken the President's influence. Most civil servants are now appointed by routine procedures, wthout provision for presidential input. Some formal exceptions limit the President's ability to appoint or remove key administrators. Members of independent regulatory commissions have fixed terms and can be dismissed only for certain causes. The President also shares the roles of policy initiation and supervision with the legislature. An uncooperative committee in either house can keep a President's bill from being considered on the floor. A committee can also support an administrator who challenges the Chief Executive.

The President's necessity of sharing policy-making with the legislature is only one part of a more general problem: the need to take account of various constituencies when making decisions. A classic study of the presidency has identified six constituencies: the legislature, the administration, the political party, the citizens and the organizations that represent them, state and local authorities, and foreign governments.[2] Another study of the presidency identifies ten roles: chief of state, chief executive, chief diplomat, commander in chief, chief legislator, party chief, chief moral leader, chief keeper of domestic peace and tranquillity, chief guardian of the economy, and leader of an international coalition.[3] Each of these constituencies and roles represents a portion of the President's status. But each, too, represents the diverse sets of interests that must be taken into consideration when important decisions are made. A decision made as chief legislator, for example, must not clash so much with a President's needs as chief executive that the President will lose the support of agency personnel on another occasion.

---

[2] R. Neustadt, *Presidential Power: The Politics of Leadership* (New York: Wiley, 1976).

[3] C. Rossiter, *The American Presidency* (New York: Signet, 1966).

The President is hemmed in by the office's vast power. Because so many decisions affect different constituencies, the President is typically constrained from acting from several sides at once. The President has a great deal of power with which to manipulate others, but this power is tenuous, and depends on the President's ability to persuade the members of different constituencies that presidential decisions have important benefits with only minimal costs to their interests.

Administrators can either openly dispute the Chief Executive's position, or they can covertly supply information to interest groups or legislators, who, in turn, oppose the position. If the Chief Executive's proposals threaten the established activities of administrative agencies, the President may be drawn into a squabble that drains away his public standing.

The President's weapons include his informal power to persuade administrators, plus his roles in formulating the budget, asking Congress for substantive legislation, and issuing executive orders that administrators need to operate their programs. There is also the President's public position, the claim to represent "all of the people," and the technical arguments provided by aides. Yet, the weaknesses of using all this clout are the time it consumes and the publicity that dispute gives to the President's problems. The Chief Executive can win confrontations with administrators, but the time and political costs involved may lead him to concede all but his most vital concerns to the administration.

The President suffers from a short time horizon in relation to administrators. The President wants program results during his time in office, and during the first term, wants results before the next election. Administrators have a perspective that is career-long. If they disagree with a White House initiative, they may delay or dilute their responses until the President loses interest or leaves office.

The lofty position of the Chief Executive can mean isolation from many administrative arenas where important decisions are made. The Chief Executive may have direct access to department heads, but the operating bureaus are submerged within the departments. These bureaus—such as the Food and Drug Administration, the Urban Mass Transportation Administration, the Internal Revenue Service, and the Federal Bureau of Investigation—carry the burden of filling in the big picture of presidential policy. They define the regulations called for in executive messages or congressional legislation, and are entirely responsible for putting the words into practice through program implementation.

Unless the Chief Executive is willing to break through the hierarchical lines on the organization chart, the Executive is separated from most policymakers in the administration. A study of 20 bureau heads found that they had served a total of 170 years, but had met with the President only 79 times. This averaged to one meeting every two years for each bureau head. If meetings with the Internal Revenue commissioner were excluded (25 visits in about 4 years), the average fell to 1 meeting every 3 years. These meetings included ceremonial and social functions as well as policy sessions. Except for social and ceremonial occasions, 7 out of the 20 bureau heads had no contacts with the President. Two had no contacts with the President at all.[4]

The record of the Nixon Administration demonstrates the capacity of the Chief Executive to develop the strengths of the Executive Office. Between 1970 and 1974, staff aides in the White House Office grew from 311 to 583, and the total staff of the Executive Office grew from 1,945 to 4,626. While the Executive Office grew by 137 percent, the total civilian staff of the federal government declined by 1 percent. President Nixon added to the powers of the Office of Management and Budget, created the Domestic Council to advise him on internal policies, and sought to broaden his control by holding back (impounding) unprecedented amounts of the funds appropriated by Congress. Many teachers of political science and public administration approved these additions to the President's powers in principle, even though, being mostly Democrats and not enamored of Nixon personally, they were reserved in their public praise.[5] To these observers, the presidency was the one opportunity for focused authority, leadership, and political accountability in an otherwise divided government. Those who wanted government to do something saw their best chances for success in a strong presidency. Yet, President Nixon seemed to be indulging in too much of a good thing. Cabinet members found it impossible to penetrate Nixon's staff and get time on his calendar. Along with all the other particulars grouped under the general label of Watergate, here was a presidential office that had ballooned to such an uncontrollable size that it contributed to the separation of the President from the administration.

Richard Neustadt authored the most influential book of the 1960s calling for a strong presidency. In a new edition in 1976, he continued to see a strong presidency as the best chance for integrated policy-making in a government with too many centers of power. Yet, he also saw great danger in his own prescriptions. In his view, Presidents Johnson and Nixon were preoccupied to the point of obsession with their own power, and

> set themselves on disastrous courses, leading one to premature retirement, the other forced resignation, and in the process either damaged or demolished (history will tell) their dearest policy objectives: Johnson's Great Society at home, Nixon's balance-of-power in the world.[6]

---

[4]D. S. Brown, "The President and the Bureaus: Time for a Renewal of Relationship?" *Public Administration Review*, 26 (September 1966): 174–182.

[5]J. L. Sunquist, "Reflections on Watergate: Lessons for Public Administration," *Public Administration Review*, 34 (September–October 1974): 453–461.

[6]Neustadt, op. cit., preface.

Reactions to Watergate reverberated throughout government. At the national level, President Ford read with sensitivity the mood toward an outsized presidential institution and reduced the size of the Executive Office staff by two-thirds during his first year in office. In the states, several governors tried to extend their powers of appointment and removal to more department heads, but were thwarted by legislatures sensitive to the threat of too much executive power.

The President Versus the Congress:
The Case of Impoundment

The actions of the President and Congress with respect to administrative departments may be explicitly political. The elected branches are rivals for the control of policy, especially when they are held by different parties. President Nixon in particular squabbled with Congress over the control of policy. A prominent example concerned the impoundment of budgeted funds. Ultimately, the issue concerned who would control spending.

In the spring of 1971, the Nixon Administration announced it was withholding from the agencies some $12 billion in appropriated funds, most of which had been designated by Congress for highways and urban programs. Members of the White House staff argued that the programs in question were scheduled for termination, and that it was pointless to pour more money into programs with little or no future. Congressional critics charged that the executive branch could not alone determine program termination, and that impoundments of this kind threatened the constitutional separation of powers.[7]

Executive impoundment of funds did not originate with the Nixon Administration, however. In 1803, President Jefferson informed Congress of his refusal to spend $50,000 that had been appropriated for gunboats to patrol the Mississippi River. Impoundment also became a major presidential tool in the early years of World War II. President Roosevelt withheld funds from several programs not related to the war effort in order to control inflation.

After the war, major presidential impoundments went beyond the control of inflation. In 1948, President Truman withheld $735 million that would have increased the air force from 48 to 58 groups, on the ground that the additional groups were unnecessary. President Eisenhower impounded $137 million that had been appropriated for the development of the Nike–Zeus antimissile system, using the argument that additional tests

---

[7]L. Fisher, *Presidential Spending Power* (Princeton, N.J.: Princeton University Press, 1975); J. P. Pfiffner, *The President, the Budget, and Congress: Impoundment and the 1974 Budget Act* (Boulder: Westview, 1979).

should precede further action. A major executive–legislative squabble occurred in 1961 when President Kennedy refused to spend $180 million that Congress had allocated to the B–70 bomber. He argued that added funding was not justified, because the United States already had an advantage over the Soviet Union in bombers and missiles. In an attempt to curb the inflationary pressures generated by the military escalation in Vietnam, President Johnson withheld $5.3 billion from domestic programs during 1966 alone.

The Nixon Administration did introduce two new elements to the impoundment issue. First, President Nixon impounded more funds than his predecessors: at least $12 billion in 1971 and 1972. Second, President Nixon used impoundment to promote his domestic priorities over those of Congress. This preferential treatment occurred first when the President reduced grants for health research, the Model Cities Program, and urban renewal. During that same period, he allowed spending to proceed for programs he particularly liked, such as the supersonic transport, a new manned bomber, a larger merchant marine fleet, and the Safeguard Anti-Ballistic Missile (ABM) system.

The impoundment controversy between the Nixon Administration and Congress did not occur in a political vacuum. It paralleled a growing sense of outrage over the revelations of executive involvements in wiretaps and bugging and the cover-up of the White House role in the Watergate break-in. At the same time, members of Congress suffered a long-standing malaise over their declined status in budget-making. In July 1974—just one month before Nixon's resignation—the large Democratic majorities in the House and Senate passed the Congressional Budget and Impoundments Control Act of 1974. This act fashioned major reforms in the budget process, and included new constraints against presidential impoundments of funds appropriated by the Congress. (Chapter 7 returns to this topic in its treatment of budgeting.)

CONGRESSIONAL ROLES IN ADMINISTRATION

To Americans, the story of impoundment is not surprising. It reveals Congress as a major competitor of the President's in dealing with administrative departments. To observers of just about all other democratic governments, however, the sight of a major legislative victory over the Chief Executive is strange indeed. In parliamentary forms of government, the executive (Prime Minister) is chosen from the leading party in the legislature. One branch of government depends on the other. If they cannot get along on a major issue, both the government and parliament usually fall—either to be replaced by new leaders of parliament or to be chosen by a new parliament after a popular election. We need not comment at length about the

A budget proposed is not a budget enacted.

Table 4-1 Far from a Carbon Copy of President's Budget Proposals
(in billions of dollars), 1970–1981

Year	Presidential proposals			Actual outcomes		
	Outlays	Revenue	Surplus/ Deficit	Outlays	Revenue	Surplus/ Deficit
1970	$195.3	$198.7	$ 3.4	$196.6	$193.7	$− 2.8
1971	200.8	202.1	1.3	211.4	188.4	−23.0
1972	229.2	217.6	−11.6	232.0	208.6	−23.4
1973	246.3	220.8	−25.5	247.1	232.2	−14.8
1974	268.7	256.0	−12.7	269.6	264.9	− 4.7
1975	304.4	295.0	− 9.4	326.2	281.0	−45.2
1976	349.4	297.5	−51.9	366.4	300.0	−66.4
1977	394.2	351.3	−43.0	402.7	357.8	−45.0
1978	440.0	393.0	−47.0	450.8	402.0	−48.8
1979	500.2	439.6	−60.6	493.7	465.9	−27.7
1980	531.6	502.6	−29.0	563.6[a]	523.8[a]	−39.8[a]
1981	615.8	600.0	−15.8	?	?	?

Note: Because of congressional action and changing economic conditions, actual spending and revenue totals for the federal government often turn out very different from presidential proposals, as this table shows.

[a]Estimate.

SOURCE: *Congressional Quarterly,* January 19, 1980.

legislatures of authoritarian countries. They are usually rubber stamps for a strong chief executive on issues of major policy, although they may be useful in transmitting popular feelings to the center of government and in adjusting details of law or administration to help their constituents. The separation of powers written into the U.S. Constitution makes the Congress independent of the President. When the two branches of the American government disagree, they must tolerate one another at least until the next scheduled election.

The U.S. Congress has a formidable role. Its members organize themselves into committees that permit them to specialize in selected areas of policy, thus acquiring expertise that is useful in judging the requests of program administrators, interest groups, and the White House. Each member and committee has resources to hire professional staff assistance. The House and Senate employ about 18,000 people. Figure 4-1 illustrates the continuing congressional staff growth. Along with staff are the impressive

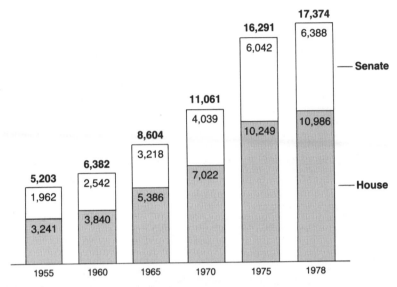

Figure 4-1 Congressional Staff Growth: Up and Up. Congress has hired some help. [SOURCE: *Congressional Quarterly,* November 24, 1979.]

resources and reference services of the Library of Congress, plus the General Accounting Office.

The actions that Congress may take to shape the activities of administrative agencies include:

1. Enacting statutes that authorize agencies to engage in certain activities and that forbid others.
2. Defining the budget, including precise upper and lower limits in the sums to be spent for each activity.
3. Granting some powers to administrators, but holding in reserve a legislative veto whereby an action can be curtailed within a certain period of time by a resolution that is passed by one or both houses.
4. Limiting the number and types of employees to be hired.
5. Issuing instructions to administrators as part of committee reports, during hearings, or in conversation; while lacking the force of law, these instructions provide administrators with indicators of what certain legislators desire and what to expect in the future when seeking additional funds or program authority.

The Congress, like the President, can be its own worst enemy. Its powers entail built-in limitations. The 535 representatives and senators have diverse interests. Their political parties are not strong enough to weld Republicans or Democrats into unified blocs. The legislators are free-wheeling politicians, whose interests include:[8]

1. National policy, especially in the fields covered by their committee memberships.
2. The policy needs of their states or districts.
3. Individual problems brought to their attention by voters, business firms, and organizations.
4. Political obligations, such as party fund-raising activities and campaign appearances in behalf of other candidates.
5. Their own political future, entailing meetings with campaign aides and personal appearances for fund raising and campaigning.
6. Personal matters, such as investments, lectures, nonpolitical occupational activities, families, friends, hobbies.

This list is not ordered according to rank. For some senators and representatives, first priority goes to committee work in behalf of national policy. For others, constituency service is most important. For many, tending to their political needs is important enough to compete with all other concerns. In the aggregate, the conflicting preferences of all legislators add to the problems of discipline. Without strong parties, it is a continuing struggle for Congress to marshal its resources for a concerted campaign against the White House or the departments.

Congress is more effectual in saying "No" or "Yes" than in formulating proposals from scratch and steering them through the maze of policy-making. Congress's agenda features issues that come to it from the White House.

The diverse interests of Congress appeared in the process of considering President Carter's proposal for a new cabinet post for the Department of Education. After the measure was approved in the Senate, it became a vehicle for numerous amendments in the House. The amendments dealt with school prayers, busing for purposes of racial integration, quotas of race and sex to be used in selecting students, abortion rights, and numerical staff limits for the proposed department. Some of these topics were the most controversial in American politics and were related indirectly, if at all, to the organization of a separate Department of Education. The success of these amendments in the House indicates something about the gamesmanship that occurs in the legislature and the many dimensions that can be part of each legislative decision.

---

[8]See, e.g., R. Ripley and G. A. Franklin, *Congress, the Bureaucracy and Public Policy* (Homewood, Ill.: Dorsey, 1980); and M. P. Fiorina, *Congress: Keystone of the Washington Establishment* (New Haven: Yale University Press, 1977).

Most of the time, legislators, the Chief Executive, and key administrators need each other's cooperation. Virtually no major new ventures that are opposed by department heads pass the legislature. However, administrators must also lobby heavily to win favorable treatment for their proposals. Administrators try to anticipate and accommodate the wishes of the legislators. No administrator knows when a legislative committee will begin a prolonged inquiry into agency affairs and decide to concentrate its energies on controlling the agency.

Some administrative units receive exhaustive reviews. Congress once compiled 5,371 pages of published testimony on NASA's budget for one year, resulting in a budget cut of $600 million. "A thorough reading of the hearings, reports, and floor debates . . . indicates that the agency was not being given just an across-the-board cut. Rather, it was being explicitly told to absorb the cut by dropping, postponing, diminishing, or not expanding various activities or construction projects." During a 4-year period, NASA was called before 12 different committees and many more subcommittees. Besides the appropriations committees in the House and Senate, they included the space, government operations, and armed services committees in both houses, plus the Senate Small Business Committee, Senate Judiciary Committee, Senate Committee on Foreign Relations, and Joint Committee on Atomic Energy.[9]

ORGANIZATIONS UNDER THE PRESIDENT AND THE CONGRESS

The presidency and Congress are more than the individuals elected by the populace. Each has its organizations that pyramid under the elected figures. The Executive Office of the President normally claims 1,800 employees, and the Congress 18,000. While the organizations make a show of acting for the elected leaders, much of their dealing with administrators is routinized. The transactions pass between professional employees in one office— labeled presidential or congressional—and professional employees in another office—labeled administrative.

The Executive Office of the President

The Executive Office developed from recommendations of President Franklin Roosevelt's Committee on Administrative Management. According to that committee, the President needed help in administering the sprawling collection of departments and independent offices that had grown up in

[9]T. P. Jahnige, "The Congressional Committee System and the Oversight Process: Congress and NASA," *Western Political Quarterly*, 21 (June 1968): 227–239.

the Great Depression. Now, the Executive Office of the President is a major influence on the policy scene. The units that figure most prominently are the White House Office, the Office of Management and Budget, the Council of Economic Advisers, and the National Security Council. Their status in the organization chart of the U.S. government is shown in Figure 2-1.

The Executive Office came into great public prominence as a result of Watergate and related events. Depending on one's interpretation of those activities, Watergate represents the zenith or nadir of Executive Office growth, perhaps beyond the range of the Chief Executive's capacity to control (or to know) what transpired in this domain.

White House Office

This office includes the most intimate of the presidential aides: the press and appointment secretaries for the President and First Lady, the President's physician, and other members of his personal staff. More important from a policy-making point of view, the White House Office includes several key individuals, whose formal titles are unrevealing—such as special assistant, legislative counsel, special consultant, special counsel, or administrative assistant—but whose duties involve them in drafting bills; writing speeches; or negotiating with legislators, administrative agencies, business firms, and foreign governments. The responsibilities of these assistants are not prescribed in any formal document. The White House Office is a flexible mechanism that permits the President to assign trusted individuals to major tasks. Figure 4-2 shows how part of one White House staff was organized. Before the White House Office was established, the President was forced to do without some of these services or to employ private citizens, often without compensation, as his informal representatives. Private citizens, or government employees hired in other capacities, still advise the President and perform other services for him. However, the opportunities provided by the White House Office have lessened the President's need for auxiliary helpers.

As a special assistant for foreign policy during 1968–1973, Henry Kissinger rivaled Secretary of State William Rogers in influencing major issues. When Kissinger replaced Rogers as secretary of state in 1973, the promotion ratified what many had already perceived as Kissinger's role. President Carter signaled the importance of his White House Office in mid-1979 when he dismissed several cabinet secretaries, partly because they could not get along with White House aides.

Office of Management and Budget

The Office of Management and Budget (OMB) was created by President Nixon. As presented to Congress, it was an expanded version of the Bureau of the Budget, long a major element in the Executive Office. The powers

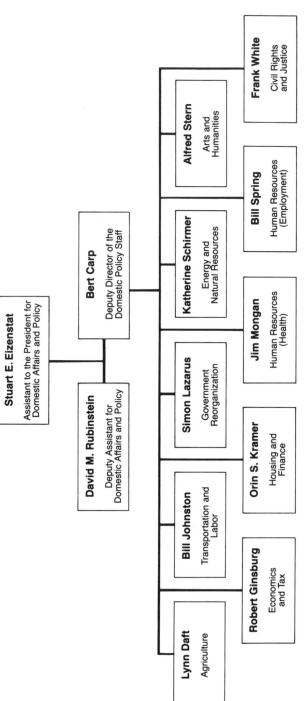

Figure 4-2 White House Domestic Policy Staff During the Carter Administration. Beneath one assistant to the President is an entire organization. [SOURCE: *Congressional Quarterly*, October 6, 1979.]

inherited by the OMB were primarily financial, but they also included controls over the substance of departmental programs that reinforce the OMB's financial roles. During the annual budget cycle, the OMB screens administrative requests before they are transmitted to Congress. The OMB's recommendations are what the Congress considers. The rules of procedure prohibit any administrator from making a financial request of Congress that has not been cleared through the OMB. Congress is not prohibited from granting more funds to a unit than has been requested by the OMB, so it sometimes happens that an administrator's budget will be larger after the congressional phase. Under certain conditions the OMB can prevent an agency from spending funds after they are appropriated by Congress.

Outside the financial area, the OMB has certain controls over the statutory authority of each department. Before any agency can formally initiate a request for new legislation, or even reply formally to a member of Congress's inquiry about new legislation, the communication must be cleared through the OMB. One of its units circulates the proposed communication to other agencies whose programs might be affected by the proposal. It then cumulates opinions and defines the implications of the proposal for the "President's program." Without a favorable evaluation from the OMB, a government agency cannot formally support a measure being considered in Congress. The Office of Management and Budget cannot stop Congress from granting powers to departments the OMB has not initially approved. However, the OMB has an opportunity to act again after Congress has acted. While a measure is awaiting presidential action, the OMB circulates it to relevant agencies, gathers their opinions, and then prepares a recommendation for the President's veto or approval.

The personnel of the OMB are mostly career officers who carry over from one presidential term to another. The President appoints such officers as the director and deputy director of the OMB. The President also appoints associate directors and thus can influence the middle levels of the office. Most of the contacts between the OMB and the agencies take the form of inquiries by career budget examiners who specialize in the activities of certain programs. Of all the components in the Executive Office, these budget examinations approach most closely the image of one group of bureaucrats supervising another group of bureaucrats.

Council of Economic Advisers

The Council of Economic Advisers (CEA) consists of three professional economists, plus a staff of assistants. The three professionals are appointed by the President with the consent of the Senate. The CEA traces its origin to the Employment Act of 1946 and is one of the instruments established by that act to give the federal government responsibility for supervising and, it was hoped, controlling the nation's economy.[10] The most prominent activity of the CEA is the annual Economic Report of the President, which is submitted to Congress early each January. In this and other reports, the CEA assesses the current state of economic growth and stability, balance of payments, and other international matters; appraises likely impacts on the economy from certain policy proposals; and recommends corrective measures for economic distress. The CEA has no direct role in the implementation of policy. However, its advice on the economic implications of activities affects decisions of the President and the OMB, and through them the administrative agencies.

National Security Council

The National Security Council (NSC) is the Chief Executive's most prominent organization for rendering advice on military and international affairs. Formal members of the council are the President, Vice-President, and secretaries of state and defense. They sit with whoever else is invited by the President to deliberate about the prominent crises of world affairs. A major input to the NSC's deliberations comes from the Central Intelligence Agency, which is organized under the NSC on the official charts.

The Congress

Congress has not been content to watch the President overpower it with organizations. It has also increased its own staff aide system (see Table 4-2). Established in 1800, the Library of Congress is interesting, historically and structurally, as a major arm of Congress. More interesting from the perspectives of policy control and Congress's struggle to make administrative agencies accountable to it are two bodies created in the twentieth century: the Congressional Budget Office and the General Accounting Office.

Congressional Budget Office

As part of its Congressional Budget and Impoundments Control Act of 1974, Congress created the Congressional Budget Office (CBO) to provide analyses independent of the President's Council of Economic Advisers and Office of Management and Budget. The CBO produces macroeconomic studies that feed into congressional deliberation on the total size of govern-

---

[10]W. W. Heller, *New Dimensions of Political Economy* (New York: Norton, 1967).

1970	1975	1980[a]
$ 54,837,660	$111,135,870	$ 206,884,000
104,813,635	185,546,445	312,903,900
13,233,322	45,789,324	60,152,500
171,849,200	422,350,500	578,045,000
$344,733,817	$764,822,139	$1,157,985,400

During 1980 the GAO undertook reports on such topics as:

1. The reliability of a new tank being designed for the military.
2. The equity of criteria used by the military in selecting personnel for early discharge.
3. Deficiencies in the information on costs supplied to Congress by the National Aeronautics and Space Administration.
4. The adequacy of home-heating oil supplies in the Washington, D.C., area.
5. Variations in the prices paid by hospitals in the same city for comparable supplies.
6. Problems faced by federal government agencies in collecting the debts owed to them.

In recent years the GAO has served Congress as an adviser when prospective programs are under consideration for enactment. This use of the GAO's program expertise is controversial. In one view, the audit agency compromises its independence when it advises the Congress about a program before it is enacted. After enactment, the GAO must take pains to avoid bias in reviewing a program's performance.

Relations between the GAO and administrative departments are generally cooperative. Reports of illegal or inefficient operations are welcomed by the President, the Office of Management and Budget, and administrative superiors who are interested in credible information about their subordinates' activities. Yet, there are times when the GAO runs into the barrier of strict administrative formality. Some information about agency programs is denied to the GAO by officials who cite "executive privileges" and the need to keep certain business within the administration. To the administrators who cite these protections, the GAO is an arm of Congress that—with certain information at its disposal—could help legislators gain undesirable advantages in their relations with agencies.

CONFLICTS BETWEEN CENTERS OF POWER

Several of the GAO's inquiries into program costs and operations provide us with opportunities both to illustrate the activities of the GAO and to explore the continuing battle between a congressional organ, the executive branch, and administrators over issues of public policy. Tension has been exhibited between the separate branches of powers since the adoption of the Constitution. One crisis or near-crisis after another has surfaced over the years to demonstrate the persistence of conflict within the government. The resolution of each crisis has defined the powers of each branch in relation to the others. Here, we consider two conflicts between the GAO and certain legislators on one side and the Chief Executive and administrative personnel on the other side.

The GAO is a major tool of Congress in trying to hold administrative agencies accountable to its members. It is symptomatic of American politics, however, that the GAO is not the tool of a united legislature. In its dealings with the Defense Department and with the Philadelphia Plan in the examples that follow, the GAO found both supporters and antagonists in the Congress. Some members of Congress wanted the GAO to be more aggressive in controlling administrative departments, and some felt the GAO had already done too much in limiting administrators. The case of the Defense Department suggests that an aroused Congress can use one of its arms—in this case, the GAO—to impose its will on the executive branch and an agency, at least to the point of squeezing previously withheld information from the agency. However, the case of the Philadelphia Plan suggests that an aroused administration can beat back the demands of Congress and the GAO.

Department of Defense Claims of Privilege

Disputes between the GAO and administrators have occurred predominantly in connection with the Defense Department's programs of research, development, and procurement. The Defense Department is especially concerned that GAO inquiries do not open courses of action that are alternative to those already chosen by the department. The department does not release to GAO detailed information about its alternatives to current policy. In the department's official view, Congress should review the department's recommendations directly, without independent policy analyses by the GAO. By making separate program assessments and recommendations, the of strong parties, there is continuing struggle within Congress about how it should deal with the President or the agencies.

Each political branch is more than its key elected members. The presidency goes beyond the Oval Office to encompass many hundreds of employees of the White House Office, the Office of Management and Budget, the Council of Economic Advisers, the National Security Council, and other bodies. Congress will not be outdone in constructing agencies of its own to help its members deal with the presidency and the administration. Beyond many thousands of staff aides of individual members and their committees, there are the central institutions of the Library of Congress, the Congressional Budget Office, and the General Accounting Office.

5

The Administrators

If you become an administrator, you might sit in your office and ponder your masters. There are The People, enshrined in the preamble to the Constitution and inscribed at the top of official charts of the government organization. Which people? Some people claim special attention because they are clients of your program. Some of them sit on your panel of advisers or claim to be advisers to the President or Congress. Then there is the President himself. As the executive power—again, in the words of the Constitution—the President claims to be the chief officer of the administration. Organization charts usually put him at the top of the bureaucratic hierarchy. But there is also Congress; it, too, has a position at the top of the organization chart, and the Constitution gives it authority to make the nation's laws and provide the funds for all government activities. However, the President and Congress have both assigned a great deal of authority to senior department administrators. What is more, officials do not act alone; of necessity, they must depend on the Office of Management and Budget and the staffs of congressional committees to formulate much of what goes over their signatures to the departments. This model of authority is initiated to some extent in state and local governments. Ultimately, perhaps you will be responsible to yourself. You may have to choose your primary points of reference from among different masters, each claiming to be legitimate. You will filter their instructions and hints through your own sense of what ought to be done. That sense of propriety will come partly from your professional training and partly from your personal experiences in your family and the community.

The essence of accountability is an administrator's subordination to laws, rules, and the instructions of higher officers that have been defined in a proper manner. In a democracy like the United States, the people and the Constitution are at the base of government. Elections, the President, Congress, and the heads of administrative departments and agencies serve to link the people with their public servants. Most of the time the vast majority of administrators work routinely, according to an agency manual or rule book that identifies the procedures to be followed in each case. When a case does not clearly fit into the rules, it is usually resolved by consultations with higher-ranking officers, who make judgments about the most reasonable course of action. In making such judgments, they rely on their knowledge of general policy statements that have come from the department head, the President, members of Congress, or the decisions of courts in related cases.

While most administrators follow explicit laws and regulations most of the time, some cases are difficult to resolve. Chapters 3 and 4 showed the ambiguities that can develop in the messages received from public opinion polls, elections, and the actions of the President and Congress. Courts, too, may add to the confusion. Decisions in different cases may suggest alternate lines of treatment for the case at hand.

The idea of accountability is a seemingly simple one. Administrators are essential for the work of government, but they must work according to rules or policies that are widely viewed as legitimate. To achieve this legitimacy, policies must have the support of the highest authorities charged by the Constitution with proclaiming the policies of government. In a democracy, policies need at least the tacit support of the people in order to be legitimate. If administrators lose touch with their political roots, they run the risk of bringing down the government of the day, or perhaps the entire political regime.

Legitimacy depends partly on political fashion and partly on the perceived strength of a leader. Groups may accept some policies as legitimate only as long as they feel the head of state has enough strength to protect his friends and punish his enemies. The regime of Iran underwent a far-reaching revolution in 1979. New principles of government were proclaimed, and the new authorities began to execute their predecessors. Some of the factors contributing to the revolution were the "illegitimate" policies of the deposed Shah, and what were widely perceived as the excesses of his secret police agency, SAVAK.

The Iranian case was extreme. Most governments—especially among the established democracies—do not face the prospect of revolution. A loss at the polls is a possibility, however, which generally makes elected leaders and their subordinates in the administration sensitive to the people's demands and the limits of popular tolerance.

Here is another extreme case to ponder. At the Nuremburg trials of persons accused of war crimes during the Nazi regime, the international tribunal in which the United States participated ruled that higher laws of morality were superior to orders issued by administrative superiors. In other words, the claim of "following orders" was not acceptable as an excuse for all of an administrator's actions. There are some orders an administrator should not follow: those that violate explicit laws or regulations or that violate widely held codes of human conduct. Fortunately, most administrators in democratic settings never face such extreme prospects as a potential revolution or instructions that violate deeply held moral values. However, these extremes do warrant mention in a chapter on accountability, in order to set the outer parameters.

This chapter explores the issue of accountability from the perspective of administrators who are held accountable. Its key questions are:

> ***Accountability to whom?***
> ***Accountability to what?***

The answers to such questions require the definition of authority in a society, and an understanding of the philosophical values that are held most dear. Such questions invite lengthy discussion and no sure conclusions. The United States has a plurality of power centers written into its Constitution, as well as a great proliferation of groupings and value preferences in its population. Another issue of accountability is:

> ***Accountability by what means?***

Some of the means of administrative control are discussed briefly in this chapter (and are explored more fully in Chapters 6–10).

ACCOUNTABILITY TO WHOM?

The administrator working at the street level of government has several potential reference points for accountability: Public opinion in general, the particular groups of people who assert their interest in the agency's program, members of the legislature, the chief executive, superiors in the administrative department, professional peers, and personal values all have some legitimate claim on the individual administrator. The vast majority of street-level administrators work for local governments, but with some funds and program controls from national and state governments. While most of these administrators have relatively simple careers—applying the rules to cases that are generally simple—some receive contrary directives from two or more sources to which they are accountable. For example, should they be particularly attuned to public opinion as a reference point for accountability, they may often find contrary messages coming from national, regional, and local groups.

It was not so long ago that local school administrators in the southern states were affected by explicit opposing directives from national and state authorities with respect to racial integration; demands to integrate from Washington, D.C., were accompanied by commitments to remain segregated from the state capital. Today, with the disappearance of *de jure* segregation (segregation *required* by state law), these contrary messages are less explicit. However, the persistence of *de facto* segregation continues throughout the country as a product of housing patterns, the location of neighborhood schools, and the widespread opposition to programs that would overcome these factors through busing.

Local school administrators now must decipher the subtle messages from local officials and citizens. Their task is to figure out who is saying what, at which level of intensity, and what is likely to happen in the face of various policies they might pursue. In the old days it was easier for local administrators. School superintendents could select an explicit instruction and stand in company with the attorneys hired by the school district. Today few politicians endorse segregation explicitly, but many speak in code. They allude to the virtues of neighborhood schools—one code for continued segregation—while they support quality education for all of the people—a code for integration. A mixture of support and opposition may come from school board members. Financial resources are limited, and there are other claims for the resources that would have to be spent on busing. At the same time, superintendents receive explicit pressure for greater integration from the U.S. Department of Education and perhaps the State Department of Public Instruction.

Administrators who work in the upper echelons of the national government are at the interface of national politics and routine administration. These figures deal in policy matters and issue directives to be followed by numerous subordinates. Their work is delicate, involving careful reading of the messages received from elected officials. Communications from the White House do not usually come from the Chief Executive personally. They come from aides, who speak or write ambiguously in the name of the Chief. "This is the White House calling" is a powerful prefix to a telephone call. Yet the recipient of a directive from an executive staff aide should mull over several questions: Does the Chief Executive really know about this directive? Has the Chief Executive considered this matter seriously, or has the aide inferred this directive from some general language of the Chief Executive? Is the aide pursuing a private interest, and using the name of the executive office as a prestige cover for the operation? What will happen if I stall, or comply with the directive halfheartedly?

It is not easy for a high-ranking administrator to check these suspicions with the President directly. The Chief Executive protects himself with aides who screen requests for appointments and telephone conversations. Sometimes the President uses an aide to transmit a message that the President does not want to be identified with directly. On various counts, an agency head may not want to probe the inner workings of the Chief Executive's office. The President develops loyalty to individual members of his staff, and may not like others to challenge their authority.

The problem of obtaining clear messages from above is also serious when high-ranking administrators consider the wishes of Congress. There are 535 elected members of the U.S. House and Senate, each with his own motives for urging administrators to pursue general lines of policy or for making certain decisions in behalf of a client. The chairpersons of committees speak with great authority, although not always with the active support of other committee members. Yet, a program head in the field of agriculture would think twice about ignoring a request from the head of the House or Senate Agriculture Committee, or from the head of the House or Senate Appropriations Subcommittee that funds the Department of Agriculture. If contrary messages come from the heads of different committees, then the administrator has a problem in selecting the key reference points for accountability or in deciding how to satisfy all the contending reference points.

One member of Congress devised a color code to help administrators understand the different responses required by circumstances. Like other legislators, he felt badgered by constituents for both good and bad causes. As an elected representative, he felt compelled to write a letter in their behalf. Often, however, he wrote the letter only to demonstrate some action to the constituent, and not as a serious request that a certain person be hired or that a certain project be undertaken. How to signal the recipient of the letter that it contained a serious request or simply a show of support for a constituent? This Congressman advised administrators that he would sign in blue ink those letters he considered important, and in black ink those that were written only to satisfy constituents. As long as administrators could tell the difference between blue and black, and remember what each one meant, the Congressman's letters would bring responses that were appropriately cursory or intensive.

Legislative dealings are not only with elected members and their committee heads, but also with professional staff aides. The U.S. Congress employs many persons to assist individual members and their committees. Some of them operate like the aides to the President by suggesting to administrators that they are actually speaking for the elected members.

Within an administrative organization, subordinates who are accountable to their superiors must face other problems. Messages of diverse kinds come from department heads and their deputies to employees at the working levels. They range from explicit memos on official stationery to vague allusions about particular clients voiced on the way to the water cooler. Is the superior being serious in signaling an important change in policy, or just giving vent to a cunning personal observation that should not be implemented, or going through the ritual of passing on an unwanted directive received from somewhere else in executive or legislative circles? Sometimes, there is an explicit message that a directive is not to be taken at its face value. At other times, such a message is implied by means of code words, a tone of voice, or a facial expression.

On rare occasions, the issue of *Accountability to whom?* emerges explicitly, at the highest levels, and with stark implications for government. Such was the case in the final hours of the Nixon Administration. For the first time in American history, a President was under severe pressure to resign. In other countries, a President might forestall such pressure by recourse to his role as commander in chief of the armed forces, using the army to keep himself in power. According to a story that has circulated about the final hours of the Nixon Administration, then White House Chief of Staff General Alexander Haig—later President Reagan's Secretary of State—sought to head off such a possibility. General Haig reminded the military commanders in the Washington, D.C., area about the formal chain of command. Although the President is commander in chief, he does not have routine control over troops in the field. Procedures call for him to work through the chairman of the Joint Chiefs of Staff, who in turn puts the machinery of the Pentagon and the field commands into operation. Haig reminded the generals that they were not to respond to direct orders from the President, but to wait upon their superiors in the military. Although President Nixon did not use his military role to perpetuate his presidency, General Haig was counting on sane heads at the top of the military establishment to avoid an irregular perpetuation of the President's rule. According to the report, Haig was asking generals to buck a hypothetical order from the President, thus clarifying a point of reference for their accountability.

ACCOUNTABILITY TO WHAT?

When administrators choose reference points for accountability, they may have more in mind than the person or office that transmits instructions. Often it is not so much whether the President or some other officer issues instructions, but the nature of the instructions. *What is expected?* as well as *Who expects it?* triggers sentiments about accountability. Thus, President Nixon ordered his helicopter and *Air Force One* for a journey to California on his final day in office, and he received unquestioned compliance. Had he ordered the Washington garrison to surround the White House or to arrest his congressional antagonists, that would have been another story.

Administrators who consider themselves members of an independent profession have special problems in choosing reference points for accountability. A physician, a lawyer, an accountant, or an engineer who is serious about professional norms does not sell his or her soul to an administrative agency. The professional offers skills and judgment to an employer, with the implied provision that a professional code of conduct may be contrary to the stated wishes of government superiors. Issues of *Accountability to whom?* are conditioned by *what* a superior is asking an employee to perform. A government physician should not mistreat patients or ignore their symptoms, even to accommodate the needs of an administrative superior who might wish to report an absence of health problems in certain industries. A government accountant should not slight professional canons in order to put a good face on departmental records. A government lawyer should not encourage fellow workers to give false testimony. John Dean and several other attorneys in the Nixon White House paid for their lapses while on the government payroll with disbarment from the legal profession.[1]

The questions of *Accountability to whom?* and *Accountability to what?* may arise in subtle ways, and not be apparent to the administrator who deals with them. Welfare counselors are charged with monitoring the incomes and spending patterns of clients in order to avoid giving aid to persons with substantial resources of their own. The manuals of most welfare offices impose harsh taxes on recipients. Often for every dollar that recipients earn, they must forego a dollar of aid. That amounts to a tax of 100 percent! Not only is that a higher rate than ordinary taxpayers face, but it cannot help but discourage job seeking among welfare recipients. Because of this problem, some welfare counselors do not oversee their clients too carefully, being inclined to overlook any signs that clients have occasional income from part-time jobs. Some administrators may not define this behavior as an issue of accountability to the welfare rules or to superior officers, but as being reasonable and humane.

Accountability to what? involves ideals that are widely shared by administrators, even if they are not made explicit in laws or regulations. Some of the loftiest ideals in political history serve as reference points for accountability: justice, equality, freedom, democracy. Others that are more recent in their development may not evoke strong emotions: the quality of public services, home rule, conflict of interest. Such concepts are rooted in the language of the U.S. Constitution, enactments of federal and state laws, and state constitutions. While these words appear widely in the comments of administrators, they do not always mean the same thing. Each of these ideals has many volumes of political thought devoted to their abstract definition and detailed application. The analyses are lengthy, partly because the disagreements are many. The synopses that follow would not pass muster in a course on political theory. They are meant only to give a feeling for the hard choices that public administrators must encounter in choosing reference points for accountability.

Justice is the most abstract of political values. It summarizes many of the

---

[1] J. Dean, *Blind Ambition: The White House Years* (New York: Simon & Schuster, 1976).

virtues sought in public figures. Virtually no one would oppose justice. Yet the word eludes clear definition. It has to do with being right, or fair, or using appropriate criteria to make decisions, and ultimately of giving to people what they deserve.[2] But one person's justice may be another's crime. Historically, Robin Hood was good for the poor but bad for the rich. (If we believe the favorable legends. To his detractors, Robin Hood was a simple thief with a good sense of public relations.) A modern public administrator can use the label of justice to describe a wide range of official policies or evasions of official policy in behalf of higher ideals. When Daniel Ellsberg took the step of distributing an official analysis of the Vietnam War (*The Pentagon Papers*) to the *New York Times,* he violated laws and regulations pertaining to government secrecy, as well as his own oaths as a former participant in making the analysis. Yet he defended his actions by referring to the higher ideal of justice. In a subsequent event, officials of the national government likewise referred to higher ideals when they broke the law and stole Ellsberg's medical records from his psychiatrist's files, hoping to discredit Ellsberg in the public's eyes.

The ideal of *equality* can mean using identical procedures in treating all clients or distributing benefits equally to all persons. It can also be cited to explain treating certain people *unequally* in order to make up for misfortunes they—or their ancestors—suffered in the past. "All persons are created equal" is a statement more able to generate emotion than to instruct administrators in proper behavior. Affirmative action programs in job placement and education give preferential treatment to women, certain ethnic minorities, and the handicapped in order to compensate for the feeling that such people have been disfavored in the past.[3] However, assertions of equality are used by persons who oppose as well as support affirmative action. American public administrators of southern and eastern European extraction and whites from southern Appalachia have been known to drag their feet in implementing present requirements of affirmative action, considering themselves accountable to higher standards of equality. People of their own background are not demonstrably better off in the American economy than people of Chinese or Japanese extraction. Because of the wording of legislation and administrative rules, the Chinese and Japanese benefit from affirmative action programs, while males from backgrounds in southern and eastern Europe or the southern highlands of the United States do not.

Freedom can also serve different masters. It justifies social programs that promise freedom from need, police actions described as assuring freedom from fear, restraints against censorship as assuring freedom to express, and

---

[2]J. Rawls, *A Theory of Justice* (Cambridge, Mass.: Belknap, 1971).

[3]S. Krislov, *Representative Bureaucracy* (Englewood Cliffs, N.J.: Prentice-Hall, 1974).

sometimes suppressions of dissent in order to give the citizenry freedom from what the government labels as misinformation.[4] A local police officer may explain that one person's freedom ends where his or her neighbor's begins. The exact point of demarcation may be easy when a neighbor wants to erect a fence: He or she can do so only within the property line. The issue is stickier if the fence will be so high that it will block the neighbor's view of the sea or his enjoyment of fresh breezes. Likewise, one neighbor's view of freedom—to play a stereo at full volume—is not easily distinguishable from another neighbor's freedom to enjoy peace and quiet.

Public administrators have their own quarrels about freedom. Many of them claim the same freedoms as other citizens to speak publicly in behalf of public issues or political candidates. In doing so, they may be asserting the superiority of unwritten ideals in behalf of free expression, contrary to explicit rules that forbid government employees from involving themselves in partisan election campaigns and from publicly criticizing government policies.[5]

Democracy is another tricky ideal. It means popular control of government, the just and equal treatment of all citizens, and freedom of expression. Yet each of these sentiments can mean different things to different people.[6] When administrators cite the principles of democracy in behalf of their own freedom of expression as citizens, others may cite the citizens' needs to be free of domination by their public servants. In one argument, a democratic government can be accountable only when administrators do what they are told and follow the policies established by elected officials. This view returns us to fundamental questions about accountability. In tough cases, how can public administrators discern the right point of reference for accountability when there are so many reference points? Included in the collection of reference points is the very notion of democracy that some citizens use to silence the free expression of their civil servants.

Justice, equality, freedom, and democracy are not the only ideals that are points of reference for administrators' accountability. More prosaic values of *service quality* also intrude. What is high-quality service? Just about anything that a person with self-perceived expertise claims it to be.[7] School administrators have excused themselves from affirmative action guidelines by stating their commitment to hire the best teachers, no matter what their ethnic characteristics. School administrators, with the support of local clergy, have insisted that high-quality education includes prayers and bible

---

[4]F. C. Mosher, *Democracy and the Public Service* (New York: Oxford University Press, 1968).

[5]F. Marini, ed., *Toward a New Public Administration* (San Francisco: Chandler, 1971).

[6]H. Pitkin, *The Concept of Representation* (Berkeley: University of California Press, 1976).

[7]L. I. Langhein, *Discovering Whether Programs Work: A Guide to Statistical Methods for Program Evaluation* (Santa Monica, Calif.: Goodyear, 1980); D. Nachmias, ed., *The Practice of Policy Evaluation* (New York: St. Martin's, 1980).

reading, despite what the Supreme Court has ruled in opposition to the practice. Health administrators explain their opposition to hospital cost-containment policies, designed to limit health-care costs by allocating expensive facilities between hospitals, by insisting that their hospitals must have the most sophisticated equipment, sometimes despite the presence of the same equipment with unused capacity at a competing hospital only a short distance away. Police officers have persisted with traditional techniques of search and interrogation, despite contrary rulings from the courts, arguing that they know the "only way" to learn about criminal behavior. Some welfare case workers have justified the loose supervision of their clients' living and working patterns on the basis of good program values, while other case workers have used the same assertions of program quality to justify close scrutiny.

Local autonomy or *home rule* is a value that appears frequently in discussions of American public administration and in the legislation of national and state governments. Many of us would allow local citizens and their officials wide latitude in defining government activities. It is a sentiment that Alexis de Tocqueville observed when he toured the United States in the 1830s, and that more recent surveys of national and state administrators have confirmed.[8] National and state officials often cite this ideal as the reason they do not push local authorities for strict compliance with the rules laid down by higher authorities. Such behavior is praiseworthy for those who respect local autonomy, but is an annoyance for those who prefer the uniform administration of nationwide programs. Local autonomy is the first line of defense for those who oppose nationally mandated programs of integration. It is also used by those who prefer local economic growth to national standards of industrial safety or pollution control, or those who prefer to drive at 70 miles per hour rather than to hold to the national standard of 55 miles per hour. Norms in behalf of local preferences may have their impact on countless issues that are decided in administrative offices, hidden from public notice. Federal and state officials do tolerate local deviations from their rules, especially when the deviations are not flagrant or announced publicly by officials who boast about their independence.[9]

NEW PUBLIC ADMINISTRATION

With a lack of clarity in the reference points for *Accountability to whom?* and *Accountability to what?* it is tempting for administrators to define accountability in terms of their own values. At the end of the 1960s, a conference of

---

[8] A. de Tocqueville, *Democracy in America* (New York: Vintage, 1959). E. W. Weidner, "Decision-Making in a Federal System," in A. Wildavsky, ed., *American Federalism in Perspective* (Boston: Little, Brown, 1967).

[9] V. O. Key, Jr., *The Administration of Federal Grants to the States* (Chicago: Public Administration Service, 1939).

young academics who taught public administration developed a standard of accountability and labeled it the new public administration.

The historical setting of the conference made itself felt. The initial papers were written in 1968 amid considerable upheaval in American politics and administration. The influences ranged from the assassination of John Kennedy, the first years of the Johnson Administration, riots in Watts and other urban ghettos, the development of community action and concern for "maximum feasible participation," Vietnam, the assassinations of Martin Luther King and Robert Kennedy, plus the confrontations at the Democratic convention in Chicago.

Most participants at the conference seemed to share certain points of view.[10]

1. A perception of revolutionary ferment and change.
2. A perception of government being repressive and unresponsive to demands from racial and low-income minorities.
3. Claims for the maturity of young people.
4. Demands that social science, including public administration, adopt explicit value orientations, identify with the interests of powerless minorities, and promote equity in income and power.
5. The need for overt political roles for public administrators.
6. A political process of confrontation rather than negotiation and compromise.

In their concern to promote policy-making by administrators, participants criticized hierarchical controls and offered "confrontation" and "consociated" models of administration. An important concern was the freedom of administrators to express and pursue their political goals. Writers saw administrators as likely to speak for disadvantaged minorities, while elected officials are likely to speak for the majority or for the privileged.

It is clear that ideas of accountability are complex. They do not offer to administrators clear guidance among the several reference points for accountability. The answers to *Accountability to whom?* and *Accountability to what?* are ambiguous. There are competing masters and clients who would have administrators accountable to them. The ideals that might serve as reference points, like equality or justice, are too abstract and vague to be helpful when tough decisions must be made. With all of these problems, however, the various reference points for *Accountability to whom?* and *Accountability to what?* do offer other-than-personal reference points. Provided that certain bureaucratic mechanisms have the effect of monitoring an administrator's compliance, these reference points offer more of a prospect of

---

[10]Marini, op. cit.

accountability to widely held values than to assertions that administrators act solely according to their own values.

CODES OF CONDUCT
AND CONFLICTS OF INTEREST

Leading administrators, the Chief Executive, and members of Congress have sought to influence the behaviors and morals of administrators by setting rules that describe codes of conduct. Some provisions seek to define proper conduct for all government employees, while others pertain to employees with particular duties or who work in certain agencies. All government employees may be required to swear or affirm that they will be loyal citizens and will uphold the Constitution and laws.

Many administrators come within *conflict-of-interest* provisions. In general terms, a conflict of interest occurs when officials might be led by personal interests to form or approve an action related to their official duties. Administrators who decide about contracts may be prohibited from taking part in the ownership or management of companies that do business with their agencies. Accountants and lawyers who work for the Internal Revenue Service are barred from engaging in private practice on tax matters, not only while they are employees of the IRS, but for some time after they leave the tax agency. Personnel who deal in sensitive matters regarding national security—in the military, the State Department, and the CIA—commit themselves to guarding the secrecy of their agencies' procedures and documents, under penalty of criminal prosecution. As is apparent in the rash of CIA agents who have quit "The Company" and published exposés, however, the threat of punishment may differ from the reality.

Elected officials do not refrain from imposing high-sounding ethics on public service. However, they may not help administrators decide exactly what to do when faced with a difficult problem. The following statement, delivered by President Nixon in 1968, conjures up mirth rather than respect:

> And let us begin by committing ourselves to the truth, to see it like it is, to tell it like it is—to find the truth, to speak the truth, and to live the truth—and that's what we will do.

MECHANISMS TO KEEP
ADMINISTRATORS ACCOUNTABLE

Officers who serve as reference points for administrative accountability are not content to accept whatever choices the administrators want to make about their accountability. The Chief Executive, Congress, and leading administrators assert themselves in a struggle for accountability, and design techniques to assure that they get what they demand from the agencies. The techniques employed include:

1. Training and indoctrination.
2. Control over the funding of programs.
3. Control over the selection and promotion of personnel.
4. Control over the laws and regulations that govern departmental activities.
5. Extensive systems of reporting designed to elicit detailed information about administrators' activities.
6. Some independent watchdog agencies, directly accountable to senior executive and legislative branch personnel, who keep track of administrators' compliance with instructions.

The mechanisms that seek to control administrators are introduced below, in order to show their contributions to the process of accountability. (Chapters 6–9 describe several mechanisms of control, and how administrators struggle within each context to maximize their own discretion.)

Training and Management

The discussion of abstract ideals, like justice, equality, freedom, and democracy suggested that the personal values of administrators affect their feelings of accountability. Senior officers recognize the inevitability of intense personal feelings by some administrators in sensitive positions. Nevertheless, extensive and continuous programs of training emphasize compliance with official procedures, norms, and chains of command. Much of this training deals with the details of budgeting, the selection and placement of personnel, and the program manuals that govern the treatment of clients. Training programs may indicate an administrator's rights and privileges; often they stress the need for judgment. However, the emphasis lies on the official interpretation of how an individual should exercise personal judgment.

Some people claim that management is a science; others assert that it is an art. In either case, there are management techniques of telling people what to do. How people are managed depends on such features as the structure of government and the laws that define superiors and subordinates, the culture that permeates government, and shifting styles of management techniques.

Managers depend heavily on reports to keep them informed of program administration. Much of what is ridiculed as paperwork or red tape consists of the information that superior officers use to monitor their subordinates.

Budgeting and personnel procedures, for example, require a flow of requests, workload reports, and personnel evaluations. Not every piece of paper is scrutinized; much, perhaps most of it, is filed and forgotten. Even if filed in the first place, however, this information remains available for review if someone feels the need to scrutinize it. Administrators recognize that they leave tracks of their daily activities throughout the files of government. For this reason, they often ponder how they will complete a report in order to leave the best tracks possible.

Accountability does not depend entirely on formal reports. There is also an administrative grapevine, plus the mass media and interest groups, with which to convey information on administrative activities. Department heads, legislators, and chief executives can pick up signals of trouble before they appear in the official networks. The media have news as an incentive for spotting problems. Some of this "news" is routinized through "action columns" in newspapers that solicit citizen complaints. Other news comes from a journalist's incentive to write a spectacular story and earn recognition as an investigative reporter.

Control Over Resources

In the day-to-day work of administration, superiors employ their control over essential resources to assure themselves of compliance with official norms. At stated intervals, administrators must justify their activities so that they can get the resources they need to continue their work. The most continuous control over resources is money. Other controls concern personnel.

Money is not everything, as the old saying has it, but it does buy most things. Officers of the executive and legislative branches have long recognized the value of money as a control over their subordinates, and they have developed elaborate procedures to regulate the flow of funds. Administrators must justify their funds in an annual budget exercise, and again at quarterly periods throughout the year. Each department makes an initial review of the budget requests coming from its agencies. The President's Office of Management and Budget reviews and monitors administrators' use of funds. Congress has its own staffs to provide independent expertise for checking figures from administrators and the President.

People are as important to administration as money. However, personnel resources are not as adjustable as money and are not as adaptable to continued monitoring. People tend to be hired on a permanent basis and an agency's supply of people is not reviewed as routinely as its stock of money. However, requests for new positions or promotions do provide opportunities for reviews of agency activities. These reviews are shared in the executive branch by a personnel office in each department, the Office of Personnel Management, and the Office of Management and Budget. They may be joined in the legislative branch by the committees concerned with a department's programs and its budget.

Schemes of *program evaluation* feed into procedures for controlling administrators through budgets and personnel. Evaluators seek to learn what agencies are doing and how their work compares with the goals of policy-makers. Much evaluation is implicit and impressionistic. Increasingly, however, Congress and the Chief Executive require explicit periodic reviews of agency activity. A new profession of civil servants and private contractors is emerging to do the work, and the language of evaluators appears more frequently in discussions of budget and personnel reviews.

SUMMARY

This discussion of accountability summarizes much of what is fascinating about public administration. A number of superiors can claim an administrator's loyalty. Several abstract ideals can command an administrator's attention, with each abstraction lending itself to widely different interpretations. The essence of accountability is an administrator's subordination to higher-ranking officers and ultimately to the foundations of the political system. In the national government of the United States the pinnacles of accountability are the President, the Congress, the Constitution, and the people. Most of the time, most administrators hold themselves accountable by following the explicit rules in their agency manuals. Yet, there are numerous tough cases in which the channels and principles of accountability must be used and weighed with great discretion. Then, much depends on the administrators' choices of reference points, and the behaviors they follow in maintaining accountability to the *whom* or to the *what* they select.

PART III

The Tools of Administration

Instructions from the people and from elected officials do not administer themselves. Nor is government populated by angels. A host of formal procedures clarify the intentions of elected officials and provide supervision and control over administrative departments. These mechanisms provide the links between the people's expressions of preference in elections and the actions taken at the street level of program administration, where clients receive services and feel the impact of regulation.

Part III deals with several devices that connect the elected branches of government to the heads of administrative units, as well as with devices that work within departments and agencies to link the upper levels of management to the working levels where programs are implemented. Each chapter looks at supervision and control from the perspectives of a potential administrator who wants to know "How to do it?" and a political scientist interested in the political issues that surround each device.

Chapter 6 examines the issues pertaining to leadership within agencies and describes the principal approaches to management. Chapter 7 introduces the concepts, vocabulary, and techniques of government budgeting. Chapter 8 describes various traits of government employees and the tasks of personnel administration. Chapter 9 looks at the emerging field of program evaluation.

Agency Management

Persons in charge at all levels of government deal with the techniques and policies of management. The President and his aides not only make policy, but also must seek to persuade department heads to implement programs according to their interpretation. Department heads deal with bureau chiefs and seek to align bureau priorities with overall departmental policy. Bureau chiefs deal with the heads of regional offices and directors of major programs, seeking consistent policies from one site to another and the smooth implementation of policy changes. Further down the line, office or depot managers supervise workers at the lowest levels of organizations. At all levels, it is seldom sufficient to issue instructions and expect their ready compliance. Getting others to do what you want them to do calls for being sensitive to those on the receiving side of the instructions. No simple recipe for successful management serves in all contexts.

The key questions of this chapter are:

What are the major ingredients of administrative management?
What are the major approaches or attitudes toward management?
What are some of the management issues peculiar to public agencies?

THE INGREDIENTS OF MANAGEMENT

Subordinates respond to numerous stimuli, some of which may run counter to the instructions received from the head office. Administrators are motivated by economic, social, psychological, philosophical, and political influences. Because of different orientations, two administrators may interpret and respond to a given set of instructions in contrary ways. At times, personnel may not be conscious that they have received information. Administrative superiors seek the compliance of their subordinates in several ways: through authority, communication, incentives, and leadership.

Authority

Authority delineates the sources of influence within administrative organizations. It answers the question "Why does x control the behavior of y?" Many factors give some people a measure of control over others. The aspects of authority that are the most relevant to government agencies are formal power, wealth, expertise, respect, and affection.

Formal Power

Formal power is described in the provisions of constitutions, statutes, or regulations and permits one person to control others. In each administrative unit, certain officers have the formal power to appoint new members to the organization, promote or increase the salaries of those who are already in the organization, authorize the expenditure of funds, and approve the provision of certain services to certain clients. The chief officer of an administrative organization is likely to possess some of these powers. However, others may exercise control only over budgetary or personnel matters, or the agency's services to clients. In federal hospitals, for example, it is the physicians and not the head administrators who control the character of medical treatment. Many agencies have a budget or personnel officer who must certify that fiscal or personnel actions are proper.

An officer's possession of formal power may directly influence the behavior of other people in the organization. Budgetary officers may allow or prevent the spending of funds by other officers. An official with the power to approve the hiring, promotion, or assignment of personnel can influence certain programs by the staff allocated to them. At times, formal power permits an officer to exercise indirect influence over matters that are technically outside that officer's domain. "Logrolling" occurs—trading favors along the lines of "I'll help roll your log if you'll help roll mine"—in agencies as well as in the legislature. Individuals with different powers cooperate in administrative agencies, with each obtaining some measure of authority over the other because of decisions they may render at another time or for a different purpose. These relationships may persist over such a long time and may become so embedded with personal feelings that an officer's authority can depend on respect and affection as much as it does on formal powers.

Physicians who serve together on committees to review the need for surgery may accept the judgment of the colleague who has worked closest with a patient, without each of them making an intensive review of the case. When this occurs, one person has obtained indirect influence over others, and calls upon their exercise of a formal power to approve his or her recommendations. Some professionals are affronted when their judgments are not routinely accepted by colleagues. However, logrolling of this kind can undo the benefits received from committee reviews. Informal norms may lead colleagues to accept the recommendations of some colleagues, but to look seriously at the recommendations of others who are thought to be careless.

Wealth

In administrative agencies, as elsewhere, the person who controls the money is important. In a government agency, this means a budget officer. A budget officer has formal authority over financial matters. A budget officer may accept or reject a program officer's recommendations for next year's budget or may refuse to release some budgeted funds for spending. Like others who possess authority, the budget officer may use resources in ways that maximize or minimize control over others. The officer may be "hard-nosed" and measure expenditures carefully. He or she may examine program plans in detail and may pare down requested amounts. Or the budget officer may ignore program content and focus only on the bare legal requirements of financial accountability: Is the money being spent according to the most obvious statutory requirements?

Expertise

Expertise is the source of the specialist's authority. Sometimes this authority is bolstered with formal powers. Only physicians may prescribe for a hospital's patients. Only an engineer may approve plans for construction. Usually, the title of expert is bestowed as a result of formal training and a professional license. Sometimes, however, the designation comes gradually to a person who demonstrates an understanding of a particular problem more thoroughly than others. One tax auditor, for example, may demonstrate a special knowledge of foreign tax laws that impinge on U.S. taxpayers. As news of this expertise filters through the office, other auditors, and even the office manager, may consult with this person about files that pertain to this issue. An agency manager who wishes to maintain the loyalty of subordinates should be sensitive to their expertise. The manager can consult with acknowledged experts, and try to avoid issuing instructions that appear naive to the staff.

Managers are also concerned about their own professional expertise. The professionalism of administrators is a common topic of concern among agency personnel and academics in university departments of political science and public administration. Several professional organizations seek to unite the perspectives of administrators and teacher–scholars in order to improve the understanding, teaching, and practice of administration. Prominent among professional organizations are the American Society for Public Administration, the National Association of Schools of Public Affairs and Administration, the National Academy of Public Administration, and the International City Managers' Association.

Respect and Affection

Respect and affection can be intertwined with the bases of formal power, wealth, and expertise in providing the foundation of a person's authority. Especially in small or closely knit organizations, personal attachments may combine with work relationships.[1] Managers may win respect simply because of their age or seniority in an agency. Others may benefit from their demonstrated skill in handling a certain kind of problem. For some, their most polished skills are those of gracious manners or conviviality; such people may gain authority in an agency simply because their personalities are well liked. Personal feelings can be negative as well as positive. They can generate discord and produce managerial problems for an agency head who is not liked.

Communication

Communication links the members of an administrative organization together. Instructions are communicated from superiors to subordinates; reports and recommendations are communicated from subordinates to superiors. Communication downward serves to link headquarters with a scattered staff and to keep work within the policy guidelines determined by the agency head. Communication upward informs the agency head of problems in the field, and provides subordinates with opportunities of urging changes in policy.

A great deal of communication is routine in character. Assignments or work schedules may come weekly from a central office. Reports of budgeted funds that have been spent and those remaining may arrive monthly, with a major budget summary coming every three months. Reports of workloads

---

[1]G. Homans, *The Human Group* (New York: Harcourt, Brace, 1950).

for each employee may flow upward each week, with detailed comments about new cases or those presenting special characteristics. Inquiries may go upward and responses travel downward with respect to unusual expenditures, vacation schedules, overtime work, or the treatment of certain clients.

As is known by any listener or purveyor of rumors, communication can do its job poorly or well. In order to control what gets said or written to whom, government agencies devise formal rules of communication.

> If everyone in the organization communicated with everyone else: the organization would be Babel . . . each communicator communicates with a defined and usually limited number of others. . . . A low-level employee may do little more than communicate with fellow employees and his immediate superior, and any communications he has with more senior persons in the organization is likely to be indirect and carried out by his superior.[2]

This passage describes proper communication in a pure hierarchy. As noted in Chapter 2, however, the hierarchy does not always perform as designed. Even when an agency's communication operates by rules that define appropriate "channels," several pitfalls can block transmission. The targets of the communication may not perceive the message as its sender intended, or they may not comply with the instructions received. People can avoid seeing messages that are sent to them, especially if the messages threaten a preferred course of action. At times, the failure to see may be intentional; but, at other times, it reflects the selective perception that keeps an unpleasant message below the threshold of awareness. An employee may see but not recognize a hostile message, or may simply forget it.

Related to selective perception is the administrator's capacity to read a preferred message in an ambiguous communication. Some messages are intentionally vague, because the policy-makers who originated them cannot agree about the details of a precise formulation. When superiors allow the "technical details" to be ironed out by subordinates, they invite their subordinates to define important phases of the operation. If it is a controversial issue, subordinates may disagree among themselves and continue the chain of ambigious communication. They will pass discretion further down the line to operating officers. This procedure may produce inconsistent agency services to different clients.

Many organizations suffer from an information overload—more communication than their members can handle. A harried manager may receive too many messages about office problems. Some messages may simply be overlooked in the confusion. Even a unit that is skilled in information processing—like a library—may not know all that it contains. The agency

---

[2]J. W. Davis, Jr., *The National Executive Branch* (New York: Free Press, 1970), pp. 99–100.

library may contain information relevant to a current problem, but the staff may be unaware of the information and not have time to make a detailed search. If personnel do not know about the available information, an agency may initiate new research on a subject already investigated in an earlier project.

Pitfalls in the communications network of an agency can put a burden on both superior and subordinate officers. In order to maintain control over their organizations, leaders must recognize which subordinates are tempted to exploit an ambiguous policy statement. Agency heads may attempt to guard themselves against insubordination by making sure a document has no loopholes that are likely to be exploited. Yet communicaton alone will not guarantee a superior's control when dealing with subordinates who wish to act in a contrary manner. In anticipation of conflict, the leader must be certain that a communication is unambiguous and must couple the communication with auxiliary kinds of authority. The leader must be certain that formal powers provide the means to insist on compliance, and the leader must be sure that the instructions are "legitimate." Legitimacy—the widespread acknowledgment of proper action—allows a leader to discipline an errant subordinate without loss of the leader's own reputation.[3]

Subordinates also have problems with sending communication upward. Some superiors discourage candid reports from the field. The classic tale of the king who executes messengers bringing bad news has its analogs in modern administration. Managers may signal their lack of interest in negative messages and threaten the standing of subordinates who report bad news. Under these conditions, all but the most dedicated employees may do what they can to put a good face on bad news, and thereby mislead agency managers.

Bad feelings can also distort the candor of communication that passes laterally among peers in an organization. Committees of peers depend on honest reports and frank discussion. Yet members' attitudes can become known and can color the discussion. The animosity that prevails within a committee can be a strong negative factor in the larger organization. Members can use their places in a committee to bait or score points against colleagues they distrust or dislike.

Not all of an organization's communications are formal. Office grapevines can be crucial in transmitting details that escape formal channels. Comments about the personal lives of colleagues help to explain their formal communiqués. An informal report may supply details that could embarrass an agency if they appeared in the formal record. Conversation

---

[3] R. Neustadt, *Presidential Power: The Politics of Leadership* (New York: Wiley, 1976). See also K. W. Deutsch, *The Nerves of Government* (New York: Free Press, 1963); and H. Kaufman, *Administrative Feedback: Monitoring Subordinates' Behavior* (Washington, D.C.: Brookings Institution, 1973).

at lunch or chitchat between administrators' spouses can provide information that does not emerge in official documents—such as how important a request really is to the person who signed it, or whether there is something in the background of a report that a recipient should ponder with care.

Incentives

Incentives are the rewards offered by an organization to elicit the cooperation of its members. The most obvious incentive is an attractive salary with periodic increments. Other incentives include the provision of material benefits an employee would otherwise acquire with personal funds: an agency car, housing, insurance, and other fringe benefits. Some incentives have appeal mainly because of the status they confer on the person who receives them; these include a chauffeur for the agency car, a desirable title, and various accoutrements that go with an elevated position in the agency.

In private firms, a superior may use incentives in a flexible manner to reward or stimulate certain individuals: a well-timed raise in pay, a subsidized vacation, or rapid promotion. In the public sector, such incentives are seldom available. Most pay incentives are standardized by regulations or statutes. Such documents generally define the salaries for certain positions, criteria for awarding promotions, kinds of transportation used by government employees, and amounts allowable for hotel rooms and meals while traveling on official business. Likewise, regulations govern status symbols for persons in each rank: the size and nature of one's desk (wood is more desirable than metal or plastic), the size of one's office, whether the carpeting merely surrounds one's desk or is wall to wall and extends to the secretary's antechamber, the presence of flags behind one's desk, whether one has a conference table and its size.

Due to the political character of public administration, the most visible incentives—salary and fringe benefits—are the subject of public controversy. Employees with the most clout in the legislature seem to be offered the greatest incentives. More election votes occur among lower-level employees than among middle- and upper-level employees. Also, employees at the bottom of the hierarchy are more often organized into unions or employee associations that are aggressive on bread-and-butter issues. The salaries and fringe benefits of lower-level employees are generally better— relative to comparable levels in the private sector—than those of middle- and upper-level employees.

The codification of incentives does not mean that the head of a government agency is entirely without discretion in the distribution of rewards. The agency head can offer a choice assignment either in a short-term effort to reward an employee for a job well done or in a long-term strategy to groom a promising subordinate for promotion. A patron can help protégés build an impressive set of credentials by giving them opportunities to prove themselves in challenging (but not impossible) assignments or by rotating them among various units so that they can become familiar with the full range of agency operations. Conversely, the head can block the careers of subordinates who might otherwise be scheduled for assignments that would advance their standing. The agency head can approve or reject an employee's request for a subsidized trip to a professional convention at an attractive resort; the response he or she gets to such a request often indicates what kind of favor he or she is in.

"Merit pay" is a controversial subject in personnel administration. Typically, civil servants are paid according to fixed scales, with a seniority increment and an across-the-board salary increase according to whatever increase comes from one period to the next. It is widely felt that the lack of special increments limits the capacity of managers to reward special talents, and removes an incentive for hard work or innovation among workers. Unions typically resist merit pay. They distrust the discretion that it provides to management, and they dislike the prospect that most of their dues-paying members may go without a special increment, while a few are singled out. Where there are provisions for merit pay, they are often distorted by pressures on management to pass out small increments to a large number of employees. Often the amount of money that can be awarded as merit increments does not justify the efforts needed by managers to identify appropriate employees for benefit and the acrimony received from employees who are not selected. When almost everyone receives a merit award, almost no one achieves recognition, either in dollar terms or in the rewards offered for outstanding performance. The Civil Service Reform Act of 1978 includes a provision that may improve merit pay awards in the federal government. It limits the granting of merit pay increases to a certain percentage of the work force.

The incentives a leader can offer are limited by their compatibility with the desires of other subordinates. To be of use to the leader, an incentive must offer a desired commodity. Employees who are *job-oriented* may be pleased by inducements that are job-related: the opportunity to participate in agency planning or an assignment to a challenging task. For some employees, the willingness of the boss to consult with them on important decisions is sufficient incentive to maintain their agency loyalty. Employees who are *consumption-oriented* view their jobs as a means to an end. Salary may be the key to their loyalty. Yet other employees may appreciate *symbols of prestige:* a choice office, a change in title, or access to the executive dining room. Certain incentives may influence people at one point in their career, but these same incentives may have no effect at a later time. As a person's salary increases, for example, there may be diminishing incentives attached to each additional dollar. Once a person occupies an executive suite and feels the first ulcer pain, the prospect of further promotion may lose its

There are many rewards for serving in government, money being prominent among them. Many civil servants carry cards in their wallets with a calendar on one side and the civil service salary schedule on the other side. Here is the schedule that prevailed in October 1979. It shows the principal grades GS–1 to GS–18, with 10 salary steps in most of the grades. This card does not show the opportunities for merit pay increases that were written into the Civil Service Reform Act of 1978. However, note the caveat at the bottom of the card. Congress had frozen the top civil service salary at $50,112.50. As a result, every worker at GS–15, Step 8 and higher, received this maximum salary.

Table 6-1 Civil Service General Salary Schedule, 1979

Grade (GS number)	Salary step									
	1	2	3	4	5	6	7	8	9	10
1	$ 7,210	$ 7,450	$ 7,690	$ 7,930	$ 8,170	$ 8,410	$ 8,650	$ 8,890	$ 8,902	$ 9,126
2	8,128	8,399	8,670	8,902	9,002	9,267	9,532	9,797	10,062	10,327
3	8,952	9,250	9,548	9,846	10,144	10,442	10,740	11,038	11,336	11,634
4	10,049	10,354	10,719	11,054	11,389	11,724	12,059	12,394	12,729	13,064
5	11,243	11,618	11,993	12,368	12,743	13,118	13,493	13,868	14,243	14,618
6	12,531	12,949	13,367	13,785	14,203	14,621	15,039	15,457	15,873	16,293
7	13,925	14,389	14,853	15,317	15,781	16,245	16,709	17,173	17,637	18,101
8	15,423	15,937	16,451	16,965	17,479	17,993	18,507	19,021	19,535	20,049
9	17,035	17,603	18,171	18,739	19,307	19,875	20,443	21,011	21,579	22,147
10	18,760	19,385	20,010	20,635	21,260	21,885	22,510	23,135	23,760	24,385
11	20,611	21,298	21,985	22,672	23,359	24,046	24,733	25,420	26,107	26,794
12	24,703	25,526	26,349	27,172	27,995	28,818	29,641	30,464	31,287	32,110
13	29,375	30,354	31,333	32,312	33,291	34,270	35,249	36,228	37,207	38,184
14	34,713	35,870	37,027	38,184	39,341	40,498	41,655	42,812	43,969	45,124
15	40,832	42,193	43,554	44,915	46,276	47,637	48,998	50,359	51,720	53,081
16	47,889	49,485	51,081	52,677	54,273	55,869	57,465	59,061	60,657	
17	56,099	57,969	59,839							
18	65,750									

The statutory level on federal pay is $50,112.50.

SOURCE: U.S. Office of Personnel Management.

appeal. As with communication, the successful use of incentives depends on the skill of the agency head. The better the agency head understands the desires of subordinates, the better the agency head will be able to tailor the incentives to fulfill those desires.

Incentives can also emanate from an administrator's colleagues or from subordinates. Respect, conviviality, or social rejection may result if an administrator meets or fails to meet the informal norms of a work group. These norms may compete with those of superiors in regulating the amount of work to be done, the treatment extended to clients, and the acceptance of other agency policies.[4]

Maslow's Hierarchy of Needs

Abraham Maslow's theory about the incentives offered to employees is widely cited. By means of his *hierarchy of needs,* Maslow described the ranked importance of human requirements. Presented in order of presumed importance, the hierarchy is:[5]

1. Physiological needs (food, sleep, and other basic requirements).
2. Safety needs (protection from danger and a stable and orderly environment).
3. Belongingness and love needs (family, friends, contacts, and intimacy).
4. Esteem needs (self-esteem and the respect of others, competence, reputation, status).
5. Need for self-actualization (able to develop talents and use one's potential fully).

Maslow's hierarchy is a useful reminder that employees have many needs, and might be induced to cooperate by rewards that appeal to different needs. However, no firm information exists about the percentage or kind of workers who are actually motivated by these needs, in this order of preference. For managers who are not accustomed to thinking beyond salary and other material rewards, Maslow's work may lead them to see that some employees can be encouraged by greater attention to their needs for belongingness, esteem, or self-actualization. To go along with Maslow's hierarchy, a management training course should also suggest to the manager how Maslow's theory might be used in an organizational setting that

---

[4]See, e.g., F. J. Roethlisberger, *Man-in-Organization* (Cambridge, Mass.: Harvard University Press, 1968).

[5]A. A. Maslow, *Motivation and Personality* (New York: Harper, 1970).

is constrained by unattractive salary scales, and how the incentives offered by the official management may compete with those offered by the informal organization.

Leadership

Leadership is a label for all the material discussed so far in this chapter. The effective leader of an administrative unit uses authority, resources, communication, and incentives to guide and control subordinates. The leader puts it all together. It is already evident, however, that good leadership is not a simple process. There are various kinds of authority, plus different kinds of incentives and communication. Authority may be questioned; communication can go astray; available incentives may not satisfy the desires of subordinates. There is no assurance that the holder of a formal position is an effective leader.

The leader's role is ambiguous. A leader cannot expect that orders will be obeyed on the basis of words alone. At the very least, the leader must be sensitive to the complex nature of an organization and of the larger environment in which it operates. An agency head in the national government, for example, must recognize that subordinates respond to their own sense of proper action; to professional standards acquired in their training or previous experience; to the demands of clients; and to the propensities of those involved in federal, state, and local legislatives and in numerous interest groups. As stated in a classic study of leadership:

> All leaders are also led; in innumerable cases, the master is the slave of his slaves. Said one of the greatest German party leaders referring to his followers: "I am their leader, therefore I must follow them."[6]

And a recent study of a man with a reputation for strong leadership described his tactics with the terms "compromise," "bargain," "cajole," "swap," "bend," "plead," "amend," "coax," and "unite."[7]

The leader of an administrative agency must contend not only with the sensitivities of subordinates and personnel in other bodies that the agency deals with, but also with established procedures and previous commitments that minimize discretion. Although such factors limit the leader's options, they do not reduce the leader to an automaton with no options. However, they do put a premium on the leader's capacity to identify opportunities and to pursue effective strategies.

---

[6]G. Simmel, "On Superordination and Subordination," quoted in J. Manley, "Wilber D. Mills: A Study in Congressional Influence," *American Political Science Review*, 63 (June 1969): 442–464.

[7]Manley, op. cit.

Styles and Traits

The operating styles of administrative leaders differ considerably. An influential study of leadership has described three distinctive types.[8]

1. An *authoritarian* leader determines policy alone, specifies in detail the steps to be taken in order to implement the policy, and assigns tasks to each member of the organization.

2. A *democratic* leader encourages group discussion, group selection of policies, and steps to be taken in the process of implementation, including the parceling out of assignments to group members. The democratic leader suggests alternative courses of action, but avoids dominating the discussions or final choices.

3. A *laissez-faire* leader allows a maximum of group freedom with a minimum of leader participation.

Research done with these contrasting styles has shown some advantages for the democratic style. It is associated with greater contentment among workers than authoritarian leadership, and with less hostility and scapegoating behavior. Work output is higher in the democratic style, especially when the leader is absent from the scene. The democratic style performs better than either authoritarian or laissez-faire style in showing evidence of group behavior that is creative and practical. In thinking about such findings, however, the reader should recognize that results of studies vary from one setting to another, and that some of the research occurred in laboratory situations that were quite different from a government office. Some of the basic research that was responsible for describing the authoritarian, democratic, and laissez-faire styles of leadership, for example, was done in a laboratory setting at the University of Iowa, and its subjects were adults who were assigned as leaders of ten-year-old boys.

Some research has sought to identify the traits of successful leaders. One scholar has grouped the traits tested into the following categories:[9]

1. Capacity (intelligence, verbal facility).
2. Achievements (in school, athletics, profession).
3. Responsibility (dependability, persistence).
4. Participation (activity, sociability).
5. Status (economic position, popularity).

This line of research has not gone forward in recent years. In general, it appears that the answer to the question "What makes a good leader?" is, "It depends." It is not so much a single trait as it is a mixture of traits and

[8]R. White and R. Lippitt, "Leader Behavior and Member Reaction in Three Social Climates," in D. Cartwright and A. Zander, eds., *Group Dynamics, Research and Theory* (New York: Harper, 1960).

[9]R. M. Stogdill, *Handbook of Leadership: A Survey of Theory and Research* (New York: Free Press, 1974).

how they fit the *situation* of an organization at a particular time. Some relevant factors in any organizational situation are the traits of the organization's employees, including their skills, motivations, degree of harmony, and the kinds of leadership they are inclined to accept. Also important to a situation are the external demands and constraints felt by the organization. Is the organization being pressed to make difficult decisions quickly? Does it have adequate financial resources?

Many factors seem relevant to the development of effective leadership. Researchers have not reached agreement on the traits or styles that assure effective leadership. Given this fact, it is probably safe to conclude that leadership entails as much art as it does science.

MODES OF ORGANIZATIONAL CONTROL

Agency heads can choose how to deal with their subordinates. Choices depend partly on the sources available and partly on their opinions of what will effectively shape workers' performance. Some assessments about useful techniques are both personal and haphazard. Most governments, however, do not allow their administrators to operate with complete freedom. Proper techniques of agency management are the subject matter of executive manuals and training sessions and are often reduced to statements of do's and don'ts. Over the course of the twentieth century, the prescriptions offered to agency managers, and the assumptions about employee motivation and behavior on which those prescriptions are based, have changed. The changes did not occur in government alone, but have reflected widespread attitudes about the control of people in public and private organizations. Indeed, much of the impetus for public management theory has come from prior developments in large business firms. Research into employee performance on the industrial assembly line and in the management sectors of large merchandising operations, investment banking units, and insurance companies has found its secondary influence in the management manuals of national, state, and local governments.

Scientific Management

The first major approach in twentieth-century management theory carries three distinct labels: *classical theory,* due to its seniority; *scientific management,* based on its pretentions at precise measurement and prescription; and *Taylorism,* in honor of its creator and most prominent advocate.[10] Advocates of this approach assume that employees are motivated primarily by economic incentives, that the performances desired by an organization can be defined

---

[10] The dominant early work in this field was Frederick Taylor's *Scientific Management* (New York: Harper, 1960).

in precise terms and taught to employees, and that physical fatigue is the most important limit on employee compliance. Scientific management had its most direct applications to the highly repetitious work of the industrial assembly line. The clipboard and the stopwatch were its most famous symbols. "Time-and-motion studies" were designed to measure how quickly employees could perform each of the tasks that comprised their particular job, how heavy a load they might be able to carry, and how physical fatigue diminished their productivity. By watching employees and testing various procedures for each of their tasks, Frederick Taylor's "human engineers" produced such findings as:[11]

1. The two hands should begin and complete their motion simultaneously.
2. Smooth, continuous motions of the hands are preferable to zigzag or straight-line motions involving sudden and sharp changes in direction.
3. Proper illumination increases productivity.
4. There should be a definite and fixed place for all the tools and materials.

After the "one best way" of doing a job was defined, engineers would scale incentives to the procedure and schedule of work they had established. Piecework was the preferred incentive: An employee would be compensated in direct relation to the work actually produced. If piecework was not possible because of the nature of an employee's job or objections by the union, then payment by the hour was preferred to payment by the week or month. Work was clearly scheduled and payment was offered in response to closely monitored activities. Money was considered the primary motivation:

> The principal objectives of the employee are to secure maximum earnings commensurate with the effort expended, while working insofar as conditions will permit, in a healthful and agreeable environment.[12]

In a widely cited article, Douglas McGregor caricatured scientific management with an approach he called "Theory X." According to this theory, management views a worker as

> indolent—he works as little as possible. He lacks ambition, dislikes responsibility, prefers to be led. He is inherently self-centered, indifferent to organizational needs. . . . He is gullible [and] not very bright. . . .[13]

---

[11]See A. Etzioni, *Modern Organizations* (Englewood Cliffs, N.J.: Prentice-Hall, 1964), p. 22.

[12]Quoted in J. March and H. Simon, *Organizations* (New York: Wiley, 1958), pp. 18–19.

[13]D. McGregor, "The Human Side of Enterprise," *Management Review* (November 1957).

With this view of employees, managers feel they must run things with close supervision and control. They set the norms, check on subordinates continuously, and seek to mold errant employees to the needs of the organization.

In Government

What importance does scientific management have for public administration? Some agencies have applied its principles to mail sorting and other repetitive tasks. Thus, the time-and-motion study has entered the portfolio of the public manager. In more subtle ways, the widespread adoption of "human engineering" in private industry has spread to the public sector and influenced the ways in which organizations have been designed and managers trained. The principle of hierarchical management and the consequent design of government departments into neat pyramids with precise chains of command have drawn on the precepts of scientific management.

There has been much acceptance of Taylor's view of an organization's members as pliable instruments, who will, when given appropriate material inducements, perform the assigned tasks. Employees are not seen as variable personalities having needs, preferences, attitudes, and commitments, all of which much be considered by an organization's leaders. Those who have designed government departments and trained their managers have been concerned with "span of control" (how many subordinates a manager can supervise) and with other principles of the "one best way" for management: Each subordinate should have a single superior; there should be no division of responsibility; there should be no responsibility without commensurate authority.[14]

"Economy" and "efficiency" are the prime goals of public management experts who rely on the precepts of Taylor's scientific management. Their emphasis on saving money in the production of government services reflects the industrial origins of their organizational theory and the fiscal conservatism that has prevailed among government reformers.[15] President Taft appointed a commission on economy and efficiency to advise him on management reform in the national government. Similar reform groups were appointed by several Presidents, culminating in the second Hoover Commission established in the early 1950s. Like the Taft Commission, they concentrated on budgetary and personnel instruments that would both increase the President's control over the sprawling administration and save money.

---

[14]March and Simon, op. cit., p. 22. Also L. H. Gulick et al., *Papers on the Science of Administration* (New York: Institute of Public Administration, 1937).

[15]See R. Hofstatder, *The Age of Reform* (New York: Knopf, 1955).

POSDCORB *"Principles"*

A recurrent theme in the literature of scientific management is that a manager should learn every management-related task. Academic texts and courses in public administration offer POSDCORB as an acronym that represents each major component of management science: *p*lanning, *o*rganizing, *s*taffing, *d*irecting, *c*oordinating, *r*eporting, and *b*udgeting. These are procedures that superiors use to control subordinates. In discussing these procedures, some textbooks and manuals minimize any concern with the leader's sensitivity toward the goals, motivations, or norms of employees, or with the problems involved in maintaining efficient communication, designing effective incentives, or providing leadership to a diverse and demanding organization.

Herbert Simon led an attack against the POSDCORB "principles" of scientific management.[16] He railed against some of them for their ambiguity. The idea that workers should be grouped either according to function, work process, clientele, or geography, for example, does not clarify which one should be chosen. Simon criticized other principles for contradicting each other. One principle, for example, ordains that no superior officer should have too wide a span of control (too many subordinates under direct supervision). One way to avoid this is to add layers to an organization (by placing a supervisor in charge of 3 people instead of 12, with responsibilities arranged so that each of the 3 deals with 4 intermediate supervisors below them, who themselves each deal with various work centers. However, another principle of scientific management urges a "flat" organization, with a minimum number of layers between chief officers and line workers.

In fact, the principles of scientific management are too simple to support precise recommendations. Reading some of the theoretical writing and actual recommendations identified as scientific management makes one wonder how helpful the theory really is to those who use it—and to some of those who wrote about it.

Human Relations Theory

The excessive simplicity in the assumptions of scientific management spawned an opposing body of management literature. Its most common name—*human relations*—highlights its crucial distinction from scientific management. This newer school of thought views employees as complex human beings whose personal motives, goals, and cultures have to be considered by leaders who want effective control over their organizations.

---

[16]H. Simon, *Administrative Behavior* (New York: Free Press, 1976).

Figure 6-1 Average Annual Rate of Change in Output per Employee-Year by Functional Groups and Total Measured Sample, Fiscal Year 1977–1978. Despite popular feeling to the contrary, civil servants are concerned about efficiency. Here is a scale showing relative increases and decreases in worker output, by field, during 1977–1978. Some 2,660 performance indicators were used in the calculations. [SOURCE: U.S. Office of Personnel Management and U.S. Bureau of Labor Statistics, *The Annual Productivity Report for Fiscal Year 1978* (Washington, D.C.: U.S. Government Printing Office, 1979).]

According to proponents of the human relations theory, there can be no "one best way" of management, because an organization's members are not pliable enough to fit precast molds. Nor is money alone a sufficient inducement to ensure the cooperative effort of employees. Maslow's hierarchy of needs is important to those who prescribe a human relations approach to management. The proponents stress that employees want status, security, respect, freedom to define their working situations, and opportunities for the work group to help set the organization's norms.

The human relations challenge to scientific management originated in the late 1920s. As a result of research that examined the performance of industrial workers under a variety of conditions, it was found that several of Taylor's principles do not work as expected. Economic incentives do not assure rates of production that utilize employees' full physical capacity. Moreover, it was discovered that formal leaders compete with informal leaders who are recognized as such by the workers themselves. The employees who are the most influential in defining work norms are not necessarily the supervisors or managers. Informal sanctions are imposed when output goes too high or falls too far below the work group's norms. Informal sanctions include the threat of withdrawn affection or respect by one's peers and, under extreme provocation, damage to one's tools or personal property.

The human relations approach emphasizes that work output depends on the quality of relationships among employees and their leaders. The prior concern with "chain of command" and "span of control" was replaced by an accent on effective communication, attentiveness to employees' motives and morale, consultations between formal leaders and organization members, and employee participation in the definition of their working conditions: production norms, coffee breaks, parking privileges, vacation schedules, and the promotion of workers to supervisory positions.

McGregor's "Theory Y" pertains to this human relations category of management:

> The motivation, the potential for development, the capacity for assuming responsibility, the readiness to direct behavior toward organizational goals are all present in people. ... It is the responsibility of management to make it possible for people to recognize and develop these human characteristics for themselves.[17]

For many of the hypotheses of human relations literature, there was a ready market in public, as well as private, organizations. The advice to consult with employees, to recognize the existence of employee groups that set informal norms, and to provide a variety of noneconomic incentives fit

---

[17] McGregor, op. cit.

the needs of government service departments that employ large numbers of highly trained professionals. While much of the writing stressed the contribution of human relations to increased output and efficiency, a substantial portion of the literature went beyond the needs of the organization, per se, to relate them to issues of ethics, morality, and theology. The writing has its saccharine qualities:

> The way to make the organization fully rational was to increase by deliberate efforts the happiness of the workers. There are many almost lyric pages in Human Relations writing which depict the worker as anxious not to miss a day at the factory or to come too late lest he miss spending some time with his friends, and even as anxious not to disappoint his foreman. . . .[18]

Contemporary Theories

At the present time, there is dissatisfaction with both the scientific management and the human relations approaches to administrative control. The problems with scientific management are those cited by the human relations school. Critics of the human relations literature recognize that it has produced an important awareness of the social and psychological needs of organizational members. However, the principles of human relations are now considered to overlook several problems and to be overly simple. Three criticisms directed at the human relations approach are:

1. It substitutes employee happiness for the production of goods and services as the dominant task of leadership.
2. It deemphasizes the use of material incentives to obtain compliance with organizational goals.
3. It fails to perceive and cope with persistent conflicts between goals of the organization and goals of the employees.

The human relations literature abounds in oversimplification. In much of it there are implicit recommendations that the "one best way" to run an organization is to maximize the members' happiness. In the fascination with social and psychological incentives, minimum attention has been paid to economic incentives. This is doubly unfortunate, for not only does it overlook the employees who are motivated by considerations of salary and other tangible rewards, but it also places too much emphasis on a kind of incentive that organizations can provide only with great difficulty. Decisions about salary and fringe benefits can be made with clarity, and the rewards can be precisely allocated to employees. If an organization seeks to control its mem-

---

[18]Etzioni, op. cit., p. 40.

bers by intangible rewards, however, it enters a domain where managers and supervisors may not be able to supply the necessary incentives. Top management can oversee the distribution of material rewards far more easily than it can monitor the distribution of psychological and social gratifications.

Both scientific management and human relations have been considered manipulative, in that both seek to exploit employees for the benefit of an organization. Just as time-and-motion studies exploit the fatigue of industrial workers, the human relations expert uses the personal needs of employees to profit the employer. Human relations, according to this view, touts happiness but means increased productivity. Its concern is not with the employees' emotional and social well-being, except as they produce more output.

Akin to the criticism of being manipulative is a denunciation of the human relations tendency to equate the interests of employee and organization, as if each were bound to the other. The one-happy-family image is misleading. The organization has its own needs, which change at different times and for different reasons than do employees' needs. The one-happy-family image may harm the organization by inhibiting changes that would be in its own best interest. If changes are made, this image may frustrate employees who view change as a fracture in their organizational family. To critics, the notion of an organizational family is insulting and unfair to employees. An overdose of human relations resembles the paternalism of an older-style company town. It can discourage employees from nurturing their separate interests and make them excessively vulnerable, both economically and emotionally, to the fortunes of their organization.

At this time, it does not appear as if any one approach has become dominant in the field of administrative management. Several distinct orientations are popular. As might be expected in any literature that has seen two full generations, present-day writers are borrowing in an eclectic fashion from all of their major predecessors, as well as from intellectual currents that have pased through other branches of social science.

Chris Argyris is a contemporary figure whose writing continues an important theme of the human relations school. He describes the psychological energy of employees that organizations can either bottle up and frustrate or release for creative outlets. Both an organization and an individual can benefit to the extent that the organization permits the individual to do work that is attractive and rewarding according to the individual's own perception. When an organization thwarts its employees' desires, it risks their frustration. Often, the risk is minimal. But the organization suffers the lack of the individual's most creative talents and may receive only routine compliance with instructions. On occasion, employee frustration may find outlets in counterorganizational behaviors, such as stirring up resentments among other employees, doing work that is intentionally substandard, and even embezzlement or sabotage.[19]

One writer describes a *structuralist* approach that seeks to "take everything into consideration."[20] Its proponents view the organization as a system, having an environment and internal components that depend on one another. By this reasoning, every organization may be unique; each may require separate efforts to identify features of environment, employees' traits, and leaders' characteristics, all of which influence one another. Under some conditions a leader might pursue a human relations concern with maximizing worker satisfaction, while elsewhere the leader might profit from a more classical interest in tying wages to production.

Another school of thought views employee conflict as a constant element. Persons thrive on competition and will compete for targets defined by their informal groups if the agency does not provide its own targets.[21] The workplace is seen as a tough setting where one employee is pitted against others. This competitive approach would be difficult to implement where unions are strong and seek to cushion their members from harsh demands. However, annual salary increments that depend on some reasonable standard of performance may add life to an organization made bland by too much of a human relations emphasis.

There is almost an infinite menu from which to choose in the literature of organizational control. If some writers fault leaders for soothing the workers only in an effort to benefit managers, others write that there is actually a common interest between the organization and its members. One widely read author argues that organizations can pursue their own needs while preserving the dignity of their employees. He recommends management techniques that draw heavily on the human relations literature, but that are said to pay off for the employer while they respect employees' personal drives.

> Most people ideally prefer to be and actually can be self-controlling in the attainment of organizational objectives, given the proper organization of work. . . . Such assumptions—and they seem generally realistic—underlie the structural arrangements and managerial techniques consistent with the Judaeo-Christian Ethic.[22]

Much writing about contemporary organizations stresses the variety of employees, and the mixture of personal goals and patterns of behavior that

---

[19]C. Argyris, *Integrating the Individual and the Organization* (New York: Wiley, 1964).

[20]Etzioni, op. cit., especially Chapter 4.

[21]M. Crozier, *The Bureaucratic Phenomenon* (Chicago: University of Chicago Press, 1964).

[22]R. T. Golembiewski, *Men, Management, and Morality: Toward a New Organizational Ethic* (New York: McGraw-Hill, 1965).

Employees and supervisors agree on some of the motivators that spur work. To both groups, personal goals, interesting work, feelings of achievement, and the perceived importance of work are effective motivators. Also, both employees and supervisors do not rate highly the effectiveness of disciplinary action as a motivator.

Table 6-2 Motivators of Work Performance

Motivator	Employees' rating		Supervisors' rating		Contrast
	Rank	Percent selecting	Rank	Percent selecting	Percentage difference
1. The ratings on your next performance appraisal	9	49	9	59	+10
2. Your possibility of an award	16	32	14	37	+5
3. Your personal work-related goals	4	83	5	72	−11
4. Good physical working conditions	15	34	15	33	−1
5. Your feelings of loyalty and friendship for your supervisor	18	18	16	31	+13
6. Your doing interesting work	5	78	8	60	−18
7. The possibility of higher salary	8	51	13	41	−10
8. Your not wanting to let the group down	13	38	10	53	+15
9. Recognition by your peers	12	40	2	79	+39
10. The possibility of promotion	6	71	4	73	+2
11. Feelings of achievement from doing challenging work well	1	96	6	69	−27
12. The possibility of disciplinary action by your supervisor	20	3	17	23	+20
13. Being part of a team	16	32	11	52	+20
14. Your inner need to always try to do a good job	2	94	7	68	−26
15. Strong job security	14	36	18	20	−16
16. Appreciation and recognition from your supervisor	10	42	2	79	+37
17. Your doing work you feel is important	3	88	1	81	−7
18. Your desire to help the agency attain its goals	7	57	20	7	−50
19. The possibility of increased freedom on the job	11	41	12	48	+7
20. Being appointed the leader of a work group	19	10	19	11	+1

SOURCE: Richard E. Wasiniak, "What Really Motivates Workers?" *Management*, 1 (Summer 1980): 15–17. (A publication of the U.S. Office of Personnel Management.)

managers have to recognize. One author lists *company men* (women), *gamesmen* (gameswomen), and *jungle fighters* as common organizational types.[23] Company men are loyal, hard-working, careful with respect to their own future, and adhere to the organization's rules. Gamesmen are opportunists who seek to advance themselves and perhaps their program units by exploiting advantages of money, talents, information. The gamesman is more expansion-oriented than the company man, but is not as unbounded as the jungle fighter, an unchecked entrepreneur who views others as hostile. While the jungle fighter has some resemblance to the bureaupath described in Chapter 2, the gamesman looks like the budget strategist of Chapter 7 or the cunning program implementer of Chapter 11.

Some leaders are concerned primarily with smooth-running organizations, and take pains to nurture effective communication and a sharing of values among staff members. Other leaders are concerned with little more than maximum production. To them, employees are more easily replaced than nurtured. What is important is getting the work done, according to standards that are clear if not always popular with the workers.[24]

Contingency theory is a label for management techniques that recognize the likely varieties in organizational settings. Some settings, such as routine mail sorting, invite scientific management or Theory X. Others, such as those requiring professional judgment and delicate interpersonal relations, may succeed only with permissive human relations or Theory Y. Indeed, some research has found that in an industrial setting greater efficiency could be obtained when a scientific management approach was applied to routine worker tasks, while a research institute with mostly professional employees who are likely to be self-motivated had better results with a more permissive, employee-oriented style of management.[25]

ORGANIZATIONAL DEVELOPMENT

How to change management techniques? is a separate issue from *How to manage an organization?* Neither employees nor managers are pliable stuff to be molded easily by human engineers. All the writing about the diverse interests of employees has a message for those who would make changes in management techniques. In this and other textbooks on administration, the label *OD* stands for *organizational development*. This is the term used by those who seek to understand the climate of particular organizations, to prescribe

---

[23]M. Maccoby, *The Gamesman* (New York: Simon & Schuster, 1971).

[24]R. R. Blake and J. Mouton, *The Managerial Grid* (Houston: Gulf, 1964).

[25]J. J. Morse and J. N. Lorsch, "Beyond Theory Y," in H. J. Leavitt and L. R. Pondy, eds., *Readings in Managerial Psychology* (Chicago: University of Chicago Press, 1973).

change, and to chart the procedures for bringing about the desired changes. The techniques of OD range from personnel surgery—dismissing or reassigning managerial and supervisory staff—to formal presentations of the changes to be made in an organization's structure, to designing training programs for the personnel to be affected by changes.

Training techniques draw upon the full range of management materials. They must inform employees of new patterns of authority, clarify channels and techniques of communication, and teach styles of leadership that are appropriate to the needs of the organization and its employees. The tools of training include pamphlets and conventional lectures that explain the changes to be made, as well as training groups (T-groups) and sensitivity sessions, which are intensive meetings designed to probe employees' innermost feelings. If conducted well, they can clarify the basic dynamics of organizational interaction and pave the way for more effective behavior.

POLITICS

The political environment of government makes itself felt in the workplaces of administrators. Agency managers must be sensitive to employees' claims of their political rights, especially in an era when government employees are increasingly articulate and organized in behalf of their own interests. Among the issues that affect the management techniques that are feasible in government are:

> *Should administrators abandon their own professionally determined manner of providing services when their "political" superiors establish contrary policies?*

> *To what extent can superiors deny to administrators opportunities to express their professional opinions about agency policy?*

> *Can administrators be stripped of political rights enjoyed by other citizens, for example, to campaign actively for candidates seeking public office or for the passage of certain bills in the legislature?*

Effective management is only one of the things that troubles policy-makers. Devices that claim to bring harmony into a government office cannot be viewed independently from citizens' demands to deliver services in a convenient manner, or from administrators' demands that government recognize their rights as citizens. An agency manager is faced with diagnosing problems like this:

> When does a problem in service delivery raise the issue of adequate resources, of incompetence or insubordination, and when does it raise the issue of employees' rights? (There is a difference between police officers who sleep when they are supposed to be on patrol

and staff physicians who refuse to perform abortions as a matter of conscience.)

Some problems of management require the lungs of a football coach and the conviction that yelling louder will produce more results. Other problems require the wisdom of Solomon and the finesse of a poet.

This chapter has focused on techniques of agency management. In closing, however, you should keep in mind those issues of politics that intrude on managers. (Chapter 8 on personnel management will return to them.)

SUMMARY

Authority, communications, incentives, and leadership reflect various aspects of administrative management. These elements also represent extensive fields of inquiry in their own right. Major disputes appear among three approaches to management that have become prominent in this century: scientific management, human relations, and now an amalgam of several views that are united only in their feeling that earlier approaches are inadequate.

The initial impetus for changes in management technique often comes from the private sector. When each new approach achieves distinction in public administration, however, it is combined with other controversies to make the management of public agencies a subject of political dispute.

How much should we pay employees?

Should we recognize their rights to bargain collectively, to participate in policy-making for their agencies, or to refuse certain directives as a matter of conscience?

Issues like these clothe themselves in the provocative labels of "freedom to bargain collectively," "professional self-determination," "faculty rights," and "patient–physician relationships." With claims of this sort, public administrators assert their independence from their organizations. If agency heads do not succeed in maintaining communication and providing appropriate incentives, organizational conflicts may spill over into confrontations that involve not only public employees and their administrative superiors, but also the agency's clients, other members of the public, and other branches of government.

7

Budgeting

While money is not everything, it buys a great deal. Money is a pervasive instrument of control in government. It is a prime tool of elected officials who seek to define what government does. Money measures the support given to individual agencies, and within agencies, to each of their programs. Administrators demand money and measure their success by how much of it they receive. Much of the communication that passes from one government office to another concerns money. Budget requests and spending reports provide much of the accountability that the line agencies of administration owe to elected officials.

Budgeting is not simply a tool of government; it has a life of its own. It is voracious in its use of time and personnel. Its stages of planning, compilation, and review in the executive and legislative branches, and its implementation stretch routinely over 28 months for each fiscal year! If post-spending audits are counted as part of the budgetary process, it ranges indefinitely beyond that span of time. At any one time, personnel in the operating agencies are spending money in the current fiscal year, defending their estimates to the Office of Management and Budget or to Congress for the coming fiscal year, and planning their estimates for the fiscal year after that.

Budgeting has attracted its own cadre of professionals in government, as well as academics in university departments of political science, public administration, and management.[1] Academics chart the activities of gov-

---

[1] A. Wildavsky, *The Politics of the Budgetary Process* (Boston: Little, Brown, 1979); and J. Wanat, *Introduction to Budgeting* (North Scituate, Mass.: Duxbury, 1978).

ernment budgeters, teach aspiring budgeters, invent new techniques of budgeting, and criticize the inventions of their colleagues. Budgeting has been a lively field for both practitioners and academics throughout this century. The period since World War II, in particular, has seen a continuous series of reform proposals, with several of them ballyhooed as essential to the proper functioning of government. In the 1960s and 1970s, an alphabet soup of PPB (planning-programming-budgeting), MBO (management by objectives), and ZBB (zero-based budgeting) has won official endorsement by one or another President, and each has had its day in the sun of public administration textbooks, official government pamphlets, and short courses for working administrators. This chapter deals with each of these techniques, partly from the persepective of "how to do it" and partly to show how each fits into ongoing efforts to use budgeting to bring order to the complicated tasks of policy-making and administration. The key questions of this chapter should lead first to an understanding about the role of budgeting in the larger picture of public administration, and second to an appreciation of the major activities involved in budgeting. The key questions are:

> ***Why budget?***
> ***How to budget?***

WHY BUDGET?

The question *Why budget?* is a simple query that provokes numerous answers. First, it is necessary to answer another question: *Who's asking?* Several perspectives are possible in budgeting. The purpose of the budget exercise depends on the players. The most prominent types of budgeters are those in the line agencies (for example, the Food and Drug Administration), their departmental superiors (for the FDA, the Department of Health and Human Services); the Office of Management and Budget; the President; various committees and their staffs in Congress, including House and Senate budget committees, the Congressional Budget Office, and House and Senate appropriations committees; and the General Accounting Office. More participants would be counted if we treated the budget in its larger conception to include revenue as well as expenditure decisions. For purposes of simplicity, this chapter treats revenue policy as fixed, and focuses only on expenditures.

In seeking answers to *Why budget?* several perspectives can be considered. An economist might say that we budget in order to economize, or to conserve scarce resources by allocating them according to plan. Since there is not enough money to do everything that is desirable, it is necessary to choose

among competing programs. A political scientist might accept the economist's statement with some skepticism. Appreciating the struggles for power
that always rage within and around government, the political scientist might
say that we budget in order to keep score, or to show which interests have
won and which have lost in the latest round. Political scientists think more
in terms of conflict than in terms of rational planning, and are therefore
likely to see conflict in budgeting. An academic specialist in public administration might defer somewhat to both the political scientist and the economist, but would add the perspective of organizational integration and
accountability. To this academician, budgeting is done in order to tie the
various parts of administration to one another, to assure that resources flow
in accordance with the program needs that have been decided on, and to
make an accountability framework with which to judge the work of administrators.

The participants in administration also express different perspectives on
budgeting. For personnel in operating agencies, budgeting is an opportunity to assert their demands for resources, and to claim which programs
will (or will not) be produced in exchange for specified amounts. Note
carefully the words used. Agency personnel make demands and claims
about their monetary needs. But there may be so much puffery in their
statements that their real intentions are difficult to ascertain. Administrators may offer rarified estimates about what they need to operate at desired
levels of service, or they may target their requests for sums they consider
obtainable (for example, an amount equivalent to last year's budget, plus a
figure to cover inflation), which then become the frameworks for rational-
ized budget presentations.

An element of simple gamesmanship may also apply in agency budget
presentations. For example, administrators often compare their budget
increments with those of their colleagues in other agencies. Administrators
want signs of budgetary success that can bring standing and respect among
organizational powers. Alternatively, an entrepreneurial administrator may
want budget success for its own sake, no matter what it means for the
character of agency programs. For these and related reasons, it is important
to do as well in budgeting as other agencies in a reference group. Success
may be defined in simple dollars of increment, in holding one's base against
a general sweep of budget cutting, or moving ahead in percentage terms
against last year's budget.

Contrary perspectives are heard from budget reviewers in the executive
branch and the legislature. Among these people, there are incentives for
holding the line against agencies that are perceived to be overly inclined to
growth. Guarding the treasury, conserving resources, or implementing
national economic policies are among the answers to *Why budget?* that come
out of these offices. While many agencies are acquisitive, some are not. They
take a modest posture toward budget growth, and their employees express

a conservationist answer to the question *Why budget?* When dealing with agencies that want to save money, the Office of Management and Budget and congressional committees might take activist postures. The OMB and Congress might explain a budget increase beyond inflation as a way of prodding lethargic administrators into accepting the resources needed to move forward in important programs.

Perhaps it is incorrect to overrationalize the perspectives on budgeting. Many of the people who do budgeting would answer our question simply by stating that laws and regulations require the various steps in the budget process, or that "It's a job." Among other things, budgeting is a continuous ebb and flow of paper, with many tasks required to keep the tides on schedule. Clerks who compile workload projections in the agencies or who review agency paperwork in the OMB or the congressional committees can be swept up by details without comprehending how they fit into the larger scheme of government. The details are complex enough for all but the most introspective of participants to lose sight of the larger issues.

The political elite does not lose sight of the issues involved in budgeting. Quite the opposite. The President and members of Congress leave most of the details to staff aides. The President is personally involved in only the most dramatic issues, involving the big sums or those problems not resolved directly by the OMB, the congressional committees, and the agencies. Members of Congress likewise leave much to the professional staffs of the Congressional Budget Office and the appropriations committees, and pick on items they consider to be relevant to major policies or their personal interests. For the politicians, budgeting is an opportunity to define the big picture of how much government will do and to protect the important details of that picture by occasional personal involvement.

Each year features squabbles between the White House and Congress on funding issues:

1. How much to allow for defense or social services?
2. Which programs to boost or protect against their adversaries?
3. Which programs to trim in order to shift resources elsewhere?

Budgeting is an opportunity for politicians to send signals to their protagonists: more money for the programs that are valued highly and less for those favored by the opposition.

Conflict in budgeting centers not only on the allocated sums for each program, but also on the powers to be granted each participant in budgeting. If money is the blood of government, then budgeting is its heart. Within the continuing process of budget-making reform during this century, two important themes keep recurring: Congress seeks to enhance its own role, while the President seeks to enhance his role at the expense of Congress. Presidential–congressional competition over budgetary powers has been

Spending is up, but the amount of growth depends on how it is measured. And growth is not equal across all fields or levels of government.

Table 7-1   A Half Century of Government Spending
(in billions of dollars and share of gross national product, calendar years)

Government	1929		1949		1959	
	Amount	Share	Amount	Share	Amount	Share
Federal	$ 2.6	2.5%	$41.3	16.0%	$ 91.0	18.7%
Defense	1.1	1.1	22.0	8.5	53.6	11.0
Domestic	1.5	1.5	19.3	7.5	37.4	7.7
State and local	7.8	7.5	20.2	7.8	46.9	9.6
State	1.7	1.6	7.7	3.0	17.5	3.6
Local	6.1	5.9	12.5	4.8	29.4	6.0
Total[a]	$10.2	9.9%	$59.3	23.0%	$131.0	26.9%

[a]Totals are greater than the individual categories because federal grants to state and local governments are counted as both federal and state–local funds.

SOURCE: *National Journal*, January 19, 1980.

prominent during periods of sharp conflict on other matters. When Richard Nixon was in the White House and the Democrats controlled large majorities in the House and Senate, there was a donnybrook over who should control spending after the budget had been written into law.

HOW TO BUDGET?

There are as many answers to the question *How to budget?* as there are governments or as there are experts with ideas for budget reform. While there is no one best way to budget, there are several major approaches, along with the variety of nuances that distinguish one government's way of doing a budget from another's. Here we focus on the principal dimensions of budgeting in the national government of the United States. Our concern is with the most important of the explicit rules and informal procedures, and with the most prominent of the recent proposals to improve the system. Even with this focus, however, it is necessary to note differences in budgeting. The roles of agency personnel differ from those of departmental superiors, the Office of Management and Budget, and the congressional committees. Moreover, styles differ from one agency to another, as well as from one congressional unit to another. Undoubtedly, further dif-

	1969		1979	
Amount	Share	Amount	Share
$188.4	20.1%	$507.0	21.6%
495.1	10.2	155.0	6.6
93.3	10.0	352.0	15.0
117.5	12.5	335.5	14.3
44.4	4.7	137.9	5.9
73.1	7.8	197.6	8.4
$285.6	30.5%	$764.5	32.6%

ferences exist within each of these bodies, but we will not delve to such a level of detail.

Budgeting proceeds according to jargon. In order to understand what budgeters say and write, it is necessary to be familiar with the most important of their terms:[2]

1. *Appropriation.* A congressional act allowing agencies to incur obligations and make payments from the Treasury for specified purposes.

2. *Authorization.* Legislation that establishes a program; such legislation typically is required before enactment of an appropriation, which sets a limit on the money that can be spent on the program.

3. *Base.* The amount of money appropriated the preceding year and available for agency spending the current year; typically the starting point that participants use to calculate what an agency should ask for or receive in the coming year.

4. *Budget authority.* Authority for agencies to incur financial obligations; appropriations, contract authority, and authority to spend receipts are three different kinds of budget authority that may be granted by Congress.

[2]Adapted from "Budget in Brief" (Washington, D.C.: U.S. Government Printing Office, 1980).

5. *Contract authority.* Permission for an agency to incur specified obligations in advance of appropriations; this must be followed by an appropriation to pay for the obligation.

6. *Fiscal year.* The period for which budgeting and other financial accounting is usually designated; the fiscal year of the U.S. government runs from October 1 through September 30; fiscal year 1983 began October 1, 1982, and will end September 30, 1983.

7. *Functional classification.* A presentation of budgetary information in terms of the major purposes being served; current U.S. government budgets classify information according to the functions of: national defense; international affairs; general science, space, and technology; energy; natural resources and environment; agriculture; commerce and housing credit; transportation; community and regional development; education, training, employment, and social services; health; income security; veterans' benefits and services; administration of justice; general government; general-purpose fiscal assistance (to state and local governments); interest; allowances (for government pay increases and other contingencies); and undistributed offsetting receipts (from various special funds).

8. *Object classification.* A presentation of budgetary information in terms of the nature of goods or services purchased; current U.S. government budgets classify information according to the following objects: personnel compensation; personnel benefits; benefits for former personnel; travel and transportation of persons; transportation of things; rent, communications, and utilities; other services; supplies and materials; and equipment.

9. *Obligations.* Contracts or other commitments to pay out money for products or services; obligations may not be larger than budget authority.

10. *Outlays.* Checks issued, interest accrued on the public debt, or other payments made, as offset by reimbursements or refunds.

11. *Supplemental appropriations.* Appropriations made by Congress, after passing the initial budget, to cover expenditures beyond earlier estimates.

The Executive Phase

Budget Formulation

Budget-makers have their own calendar as well as their own language. First on the agenda is the formulation of the budget in the executive branch. This involves high-level discussions between the Office of Management and Budget (OMB), the Council of Economic Advisers, the Treasury, and the President. The result is a general statement of likely economic events, and a directive about program emphases that is supposed to reach the operating agencies while they are doing their own study of current programs and future plans.

President Reagan sought to put his stamp on the federal budget during his first months in the White House. Together with senior members of his Administration and allies in Congress, he spoke about the themes of his presidency as they would be applied in spending: reducing allocations for certain social services and programs to regulate industry, and putting increased emphasis on defense preparedness.

Departmental budget officers also have a role in the formulation phase, acting between each operating agency and the OMB. A department budget office compiles requests from all of its agencies, then seeks to reconcile them with the department secretary's priorities and with the program directives that come out of the White House and the OMB. Between March and January, several exchanges occur between agencies, departments, the OMB, and—in some cases—the President. In January, the President's budget is printed, bound, and sent to Congress. Agencies have an opportunity to present their demands before their department budget offices, and then to support what their departments have recommended for them before the Office of Management and Budget. Note the change in wording. The only opportunity an agency has formally to push its *own* proposal is at the lowest stage of review. By the time a department budget office has prepared a consolidated statement of all its agencies' requests, agency personnel are expected to remain within that framework and not to revert to earlier requests. Chances are that a department will recommend sums lower than the original agencies' requests. At a later stage a similar rule applies: When the OMB has prepared a consolidated request for all departments and agencies, each agency has an opportunity to testify in its own behalf before Congress. At that stage, however, it is supposed to testify within the framework of the OMB's request. This is likely to be for a sum even *lower* than that recommended by a department budget office. To ask for an amount beyond this, however, would be to break rank with the "President's team." Some agencies do break these rules and push their own cases aggressively. However, this action may involve the subterfuge of arranging with a friendly member of the appropriations committee to ask explicitly, "How much do you *really* need?"

Impoundment

Until the second Nixon Administration, Presidents had been able to exercise control over allotments from the Treasury, *after* Congress had acted. Usually the President would allow agencies to spend up to the ceilings appropriated by Congress. Occasionally, however, the President would impound monies from the sums appropriated. The practice goes back at least to the Administration of Thomas Jefferson. Nixon, more than any President before him, leveled impoundments against programs favored by Congress. As noted in Chapter 4, the result was the Congressional Budget

President Carter's budget for 1982 as submitted to Congress and as revised by President Reagan. Note that Congress votes "budget authority" to the agencies. This sets a ceiling within which the agencies may commit the government to expenditures. "Outlays" represents the sums actually spent or expected to be spent.

Table 7-2 President Reagan's Fiscal 1982 Budget Revisions (in billions of dollars)

Budget by function	Budget authority					Outlays				
	Actual 1980	Fiscal 1981 Carter	Fiscal 1981 Reagan	Fiscal 1982 Carter	Fiscal 1982 Reagan	Actual 1980	Fiscal 1981 Carter	Fiscal 1981 Reagan	Fiscal 1982 Carter	Fiscal 1982 Reagan
National defense	$145.8	$173.9	$180.7	$200.3	$226.3	$135.9	$161.1	$162.1	$184.4	$188.8
International affairs	15.5	25.2	23.7	19.6	17.9	10.7	11.3	11.3	12.2	11.2
General science, space, and technology	6.1	6.6	6.5	8.1	7.2	5.7	6.3	6.2	7.6	6.9
Energy	36.4	8.3	5.8	12.1	9.0	6.3	8.7	9.3	12.0	8.7
Natural resources and environment	13.1	12.7	10.4	13.6	7.9	13.8	14.1	13.7	14.0	11.9
Agriculture	4.9	5.6	5.6	5.6	5.5	4.8	1.1	1.2	4.8	4.4
Commerce and housing credit	10.5	7.0	6.4	10.7	8.2	7.8	3.5	3.2	8.1	3.1
Transportation	20.2	26.3	25.5	25.5	20.5	21.1	24.1	24.0	21.6	19.9
Community and regional development	10.1	10.2	8.2	9.2	7.3	10.0	11.1	10.3	9.1	8.1
Education, training, employment, and social services	30.6	31.9	29.4	36.3	24.6	30.8	31.8	30.6	34.5	25.8
Health	59.8	71.9	71.3	86.1	83.5	58.2	66.0	66.7	74.6	73.4
Income security	224.2	255.2	249.9	279.6	261.8	193.1	231.7	229.7	255.0	241.4
Veterans' benefits and services	21.2	23.2	22.9	25.0	24.2	21.2	22.6	2.4	24.5	23.6
Administration of justice	4.4	4.5	4.4	4.8	4.2	4.6	4.8	4.7	4.9	4.4
General government	4.6	5.4	5.4	5.4	5.1	4.5	5.2	5.1	5.2	5.0
General-purpose fiscal assistance	8.7	6.2	6.2	6.9	6.5	8.6	6.9	6.8	6.9	6.4
Interest	64.5	80.4	77.2	89.9	82.5	64.5	80.4	77.2	89.9	82.5
Allowances	—	—	—	3.0	2.3	—	—	—	1.9	1.8
Undistributed offsetting receipts	-21.9	-27.8	-29.3	-31.9	-32.0	-21.9	-27.8	-29.3	-31.9	-32.0
Total[a]	$658.8	$726.5	$710.1	$809.8	$772.4	$579.6	$662.7	$655.2	$739.3	$695.3

Budget by agency

Legislative branch	$ 1.3	$ 1.3	$ 1.3	$ 1.5	$ 1.5	$ 1.2	$ 1.4	$ 1.5	$ 1.4	$ 1.4
The Judiciary	0.6	0.7	0.7	0.7	0.7	0.6	0.7	0.7	0.7	0.7
Executive Office of the President	0.1	0.1	0.1	0.1	0.1	0.1	0.1	0.1	0.1	0.1
Funds appropriated to the President	12.5	14.7	14.0	10.9	9.8	7.5	6.2	6.1	6.3	6.1
Agriculture	24.9	26.7	26.3	30.1	25.9	24.6	20.9	20.7	28.0	23.7
Commerce	3.1	2.9	2.4	3.1	2.1	3.8	3.0	2.9	3.2	2.5
Defense: military	142.6	170.3	177.1	195.7	221.8	132.8	157.6	158.6	180.0	184.8
Defense: civil	3.3	3.0	3.1	3.4	3.1	3.2	3.4	3.3	3.4	3.2
Education	13.8	15.6	13.5	17.0	12.3	13.1	14.8	14.3	15.7	12.4
Energy	10.0	11.7	10.5	14.6	11.9	6.5	9.7	10.5	14.1	11.1
Health and Human Services	195.9	225.5	226.2	258.4	255.3	194.7	227.3	227.6	258.2	250.7
Housing and Urban Development	35.7	38.4	32.8	38.2	29.0	12.6	13.3	13.5	15.5	14.3
Interior	4.6	4.5	3.9	4.5	3.4	4.4	4.7	4.4	4.1	3.3
Justice	2.5	2.4	2.3	2.6	2.3	2.6	2.7	2.6	2.7	2.5
Labor	28.8	33.6	32.2	37.0	27.9	29.7	37.6	35.5	34.5	26.7
State	2.1	2.4	2.3	3.0	2.8	1.9	2.1	2.2	2.6	2.4
Transportation	18.2	24.1	23.4	24.0	19.2	19.0	21.8	22.0	20.0	18.3
Treasury	90.6	90.9	86.2	104.7	92.9	76.7	91.2	87.7	104.3	92.6
Environmental Protection Agency	4.7	4.8	3.0	5.3	1.4	5.6	5.5	5.5	5.8	5.2
National Aeronautics and Space Administration	5.2	5.5	5.5	6.7	6.1	4.8	5.3	5.3	6.4	5.9
Veterans Administration	21.2	23.2	22.9	24.9	24.2	21.1	22.5	22.3	24.4	23.6
Office of Personnel Management	24.9	28.5	28.5	30.5	30.4	15.1	18.0	17.9	20.2	19.9
Other agencies	34.3	23.7	21.1	21.7	17.9	20.0	20.7	19.4	17.5	14.1
Allowances	—	—	—	3.0	2.3	—	—	—	1.9	1.8
Undistributed offsetting receipts	-21.9	-27.8	-29.3	-31.9	-32.0	-21.9	-27.8	-29.3	-31.9	-32.0
Total[a]	$658.8	$726.5	$710.1	$809.8	$772.4	$579.6	$662.7	$655.2	$739.3	$695.3

[a]Figures may not add due to rounding

SOURCE: *Congressional Quarterly*, March 14, 1981.

and Impoundment Control Act of 1974. This enactment severely restricted the President's freedom in holding back appropriated funds. Now the President can order a temporary deferral, with ninety days to make his case to the public, but must send Congress a report of his action. *Either* the House or the Senate can disapprove the deferral, and thereby make the funds available. The President can order a permanent rescission of appropriated funds. However, this must be approved by *both* the House and the Senate to have effect.[3]

The Congressional Phase

Macropolicy

The congressional phase of the budget process has two distinct components. One component, orchestrated by House and Senate budget committees and the staff of the Congressional Budget Office, deals with macropolicy. By means of a *first resolution*, which must be passed by May 15, Congress sets targets for total spending and deficits allowable for each functional category in the federal budget. These targets are supposed to guide the House and Senate appropriations committees as they work on the details of agency proposals. A *second resolution*, which must be passed by September 15, comes after making detailed decisions on agency budgets. The second resolution establishes the final budget totals and the permissible deficit. These macrototals are targets only. They do not have the force of law that limits the spending of government agencies. After the second resolution is passed, however, any spending proposal that goes beyond its limits can be ruled out of order by a simple action in either the House or the Senate.

This macropolicy stage of the congressional budget process represents a major reform that was undertaken as part of the Congressional Budget and Impoundment Control Act of 1974. The act established new budget committees in the House and Senate, a Congressional Budget Office (CBO) with impressive expertise in economic and policy analyses, elaborate procedures for congressional review of the overall budget, plus a restructuring of the fiscal year to allow for the meshing of these new procedures with the review of each budget category by appropriations subcommittees.

Before the 1974 act, Congress depended on the executive branch for overall policy guidance. There were no Congressional Budget Office and no budget committees. The House and Senate appropriations committees could do little more than review the President's budget piecemeal, without taking an overview of the budget's implications on the economy. Although

---

[3]D. S. Ippolito, *The Budget and National Politics* (San Francisco: W. H. Freeman and Company, 1978).

Table 7-3 Congressional Budget Calendar

Date	Event
Oct.–Dec.	Congressional Budget Office submits five-year projection of current spending as soon as possible after Oct. 1.
Nov. 10	President submits current services budget, showing projected spending for existing programs.
Dec. 31	Joint Economic Committee reports analysis of current services budget to budget committees.
Late Jan.	President submits budget (15 days after Congress convenes), including current services and new and enlarged activities.
Late Jan.–Mar.	Budget committees hold hearings and begin work on first budget resolution.
Mar. 15	All legislative committees submit estimates and views to budget committees.
Apr. 15	Budget committees report first resolution.
May 15	Congress completes action on first resolution. Before adoption of first resolution, neither house may consider new budget-authority or spending-authority bills, revenue changes, or debt-limit changes.
May 15 through 7th day after Labor Day	Appropriation subcommittees and Congress complete action on all budget-authority and spending-authority bills. Before reporting first regular appropriations bill, House Appropriations Committee, "to extent practicable," marks up all regular appropriations bills and submits summary report to House, comparing proposed outlays and budget-authority levels with first-resolution targets. CBO issues periodic scorekeeping reports, comparing congressional action with first resolution. Reports on new budget-authority and tax-expenditure bills must contain comparisons with first resolution and five-year projections. "As possible," a CBO cost analysis and five-year projection accompanies all reported public bills, except appropriation bills.
Aug.	Budget committees prepare second budget resolution and report.
Sept. 15	Congress complete action on second resolution. Thereafter, neither house may consider any bill, amendment, or conference report that results in an increase over outlay or budget-authority figures or a reduction in revenues beyond amounts in second resolution.
Sept. 25	Congress completes action on reconciliation bill or another resolution. Congress may not adjourn until it completes action on second resolution and reconciliation measure, if any.
Oct. 1	Fiscal year begins.

SOURCE: Adapted from *Congressional Quarterly Almanac, 1975* (Washington, D.C.: Congressional Quarterly Service, 1976).

members of the appropriations committees had staff aides to help them study executive requests, Congress as a whole felt outstripped by the President. The executive's potential analytical capabilities, including planning-programming-budgeting, left the legislature increasingly dependent on the recommendations of the Office of Management and Budget, without comprehending the elaborate procedures and arguments used to justify those recommendations.

One attraction of the new procedures is that they are not so rigid as to break down in the face of changing realities. Exempt from the limits of the second budget resolution are "uncontrollable" items like social security and unemployment insurance, which can rise as high as demand requires. Also, the budget resolutions are entirely a matter of congressional action. They do not require the President's signature, and can be revised whenever Congress feels the situation warrants it.

Another attraction is the staff assistance that Congress has provided itself to operate the new procedures. Various staff units in the Congressional Budget Office concentrate on economic forecasting and policy analysis in various fields. The existence of the CBO lessens the dependence of elected legislators on program analyses provided by the agencies and the Office of Management and Budget. The CBO is one result of a long series of steps taken by recent Congresses to increase the staff assistance that is accountable directly to congressional members or committees.

Micropolicy

The most detailed examination of agency budgets by Congress takes place between the first and second resolutions, in the specialized subcommittees of the House of Representatives and Senate appropriations committees. The House examines budgets before the Senate does, owing to custom and to an interpretation of a constitutional provision that gives the House precedence in money bills. Further subcommittee deliberations on requests for supplemental appropriations occur after the passage of the second congressional budget resolution.

Recommendations of the subcommittees guide the full House and Senate in enacting the laws that define the sums that agencies may spend on each program. Subcommittees of the House and Senate appropriations committees consider the requests for each department and agency, keeping in mind the overall targets for budget totals set by the first resolution. These subcommittees show some of the benefits of the seniority system in Congress. Members have a continuing right to remain on the appropriations committee and particular subcommittees as long as they win reelection to Congress. After some years of looking at the budgets of the same agencies, subcommittee members acquire an expertise in the needs and problems of agency programs.

When the appropriations subcommittees examine agency budgets, they tend to be thorough in their investigation of the agencies that have been assertive in their requests for budget increases. In dealing with these agencies, subcommittee members do some or all of the following:

1. Ask more questions during the budget hearing.
2. Demand that the agencies justify certain portions of their request.
3. Ask the department secretary and budget officer about the agency's budget.
4. Reduce the agency's request and add special restrictions to the agency's use of its funds in the committee report or in the appropriations act.

While assertive agencies get some rough treatment from Congress, in the long run they usually increase their budgets more than timid agencies do. Harsh treatment does not usually cancel the impact of their more aggressive requests.[4]

Uncontrollable Spending

A problem for all participants in the budgeting process is the proportion of government funds that is "uncontrollable." These represent programs that are legally bound to meet the demands of citizens entitled to them, or are considered binding political commitments. Examples are social security, which spends enough to meet the legitimate applications that are made; ongoing contractual arrangements; pensions to retired federal employees; veterans' benefits; salaries to permanent staff; and interest payments on government debts. The OMB reported that 77 percent of the 1981 federal budget was uncontrollable, a proportion up from the 59 percent in 1967. Because of these continuing commitments of available revenues, budget-makers have proportionately less opportunity to create new programs or to add new features to existing programs that have proved attractive. Much of the activity of administrative, executive, and legislative participants in the budgetary process consists of formal actions to continue ongoing programs.

Tax Expenditures

An untappable budgetary resource is the monies left in private hands by virtue of being excused from tax collection. These resources—called *tax expenditures*—are enormous. They amounted to $136 billion in 1979,[5] or

---

[4]I. Sharkansky, "An Appropriations Subcommittee and Its Client Agencies: A Comparative Study of Supervision and Control," *American Political Science Review*, 59 (September 1965): 622–629.

[5]"Gimme Shelters" (Washington, D.C.: Common Cause, 1979), mimeo.

An important component in the uncontrollable budget is the benefits to which various classes of persons are entitled. These are written into laws and regulations, and have become commitments that defy White House or congressional wishes to cut the budget.

Table 7-4 Major Entitlement Programs (in thousands of dollars), 1980

Program	Budget authority
Defense	
Retired military personnel pay[a]	$11,652,500
Operations and maintenance, claims[a]	113,200
Agriculture: Farm price supports	248,530
Transportation: Coast Guard retirement pay[a]	202,500
Education, training, employment, and social services	
Social services grants[a]	2,774,777
Human development services[a]	817,484
Health	
Medicaid[a]	14,080,924
Medicare hospital insurance	25,370,000
Medicare supplementary insurance	10,248,000
Income security	
Supplemental feeding for women and children[a]	800,000
Child nutrition[a]	3,224,901
Supplemental Security Income[a]	6,323,436
Benefits for disabled coal miners[a]	1,005,202
Aid to Families with Dependent Children[a]	7,298,000
Federal unemployment benefits[a]	950,000
Black lung disability[a]	930,000
Food stamps[a]	6,188,600[b]
Old age and survivors' insurance	99,427,000
Disability insurance	17,381,000
Unemployment insurance	15,781,637
Foreign Service retirement	247,445
Earned income tax credit	1,874,300
Civil Service retirement	22,981,500
Civil Service retirement (special benefits)[a]	304,017
Railroad retirement	4,161,000
Veterans	
Compensation and benefits[a]	11,201,800
Readjustment benefits[a]	2,144,565
National service life insurance	968,423
General government: Claims against the government	152,000
Fiscal assistance	
Revenue sharing[a]	6,854,924
Forest Service	283,458
Bureau of Land Management	356,048
Payments to territories	220,000
Internal Revenue collections for Puerto Rico	220,000
Interest	
Interest on public debt	67,500,000
Interest on refunded Internal Revenue collections	326,000

[a]Spending that requires annual appropriations action by Congress; all other programs have permanent appropriations.
[b]Fiscal 1980 statutory spending ceiling. Entitlement status of program in doubt.

BOX 7-1   Legal Status of Entitlement Programs

Being eligible for federal entitlement programs is almost like having money in the bank.

A series of court rulings in recent years has elevated an eligible individual's right to receive benefits from entitlement programs to the status of a property right, albeit not in the traditional sense.

The property status of entitlement programs supplies the ultimate legal protection against congressional cuts in entitlement spending. Because of it, the courts presumably would force full spending for any entitlement program Congress sought to cut.

Traditionally, government benefits were held to be gratuities—gifts which could be conferred or denied at will. The privilege of receiving benefits was clearly distinct from the right to property.

However, beginning in the 1960s the traditional distinction between rights and privileges began to be questioned by the courts. The erosion of this distinction led to the concept of entitlements as property.

The important thing about that was that it gave entitlement benefits the protections given to property under the Constitution. This meant access to government benefits could not be denied without due process of law.

The Supreme Court solidified this doctrine in 1970, when it ruled on a case, *Goldberg* v. *Kelly*, involving New York State's Aid to Families with Dependent Children (AFDC) program. Some welfare clients had brought suit against the state, arguing that they had been denied their benefits without prior notice and a chance for a hearing.

The court ruled that, under the due process clause, the state could not withhold benefits without providing a hearing and a chance for a recipient to be represented by counsel. In support of its argument, the court noted, "It may be realistic today to regard welfare entitlements as more like 'property' than a 'gratuity.' "

This and other opinions that followed did not speak directly to the question of appropriations for entitlements, and what would happen if there was not enough money to provide benefits to all eligible applicants for entitlement programs. The courts have never ruled on that issue, because Congress has never failed to provide full funding for the programs.

However, the effect of the judicial rulings on entitlement status is clear—that the federal government is legally obliged to pay all the benefits promised by entitlement programs.

SOURCE: *Congressional Quarterly*, January 19, 1980.

BOX 7-2   Other Forms of "Backdoor" Spending

Entitlements are not the only form of government spending that is relatively uncontrollable by Congress.

While entitlements constitute by far the largest portion of uncontrollable outlays, other forms of "backdoor spending" still take up about one-sixth of the total budget.

Although the 1974 Congressional Budget Act limited some of the types of backdoor spending, there is still a great quantity of existing or potential federal obligations that Congress at some point may have to pay off. As a House Appropriations Committee staff report put it, "It is evident that Congress will have to appropriate large sums of liquidating cash in the years ahead to pay off the obligations that will be incurred. . . ."

The main kinds of uncontrollable spending, other than entitlements, are:

CONTRACT AUTHORITY

Before passage of the Budget Act, a favorite form of backdoor spending was the use of contract authority, which allows agencies to enter into contracts without immediately providing money to pay off the debts thereby incurred. When the bills do come due, the appropriations committees have no choice but to provide the money.

The Budget Act required that new contract authority be subject to the appropriations process. But it did not affect existing authority, which agencies can continue to use to enter into contracts. According to a 1976 study, there was more than $200 billion in existing contract authority that could be used in the future.

Moreover, the Budget Act exempted some new contract authorities from appropriations. Contracts taken out by the highway and airport trust funds, for example, do not have to be included in annual appropriations.

BORROWING AUTHORITY

A similar type of backdoor spending comes in the form of borrowing authority granted by Congress to federal agencies. Agencies can either borrow from the Treasury or the public; spending is required to pay off the debts incurred.

Like contract authority, new borrowing authority was controlled by the Budget Act. But there continues to be a large volume of past authorities that can still be used in the future. Federal agencies have about $90 billion in specific unused borrowing authority, which can be used without congressional action. In addition, agencies such as the Farmers Home Administration and Federal Housing Administration can borrow unlimited amounts from the Treasury.

"All told, federal agencies potentially possess several hundred billion dollars of borrowing authority beyond the reach of the budget or the appropriations process," according to a study by Allen Schick of the Congressional Research Service.

GUARANTEED LOANS

Another type of uncontrollable spending, which has gained in popularity in recent years, is the use of federal guarantees for private loans. Under these arrangements the federal government does not put up any money to begin with, but only promises to repay a loan if the borrower is unable to do so.

Most federal guaranteed loans go to encourage home ownership. Federal Housing Administration and Veterans Administration loan programs account for two-thirds of federal loan guarantees.

Guaranteed loans have appeal because they allow Congress to encourage the flow of capital to a desirable enterprise without any initial cost. Not controlled by the Budget Act, loan guarantees have become increasingly attractive as a way of getting around spending limits.

However, loan guarantees are particularly uncontrollable, since spending is dependent on the financial health of millions of borrowers, large and small. Each homeowner or business that defaults on a loan creates an unavoidable obligation on the government.

OFF-BUDGET AGENCIES

A different kind of uncontrollable spending involves the off-budget agencies. The budgets for these agencies, which include the Postal Service and the Federal Financing Bank, are not included in the total spending limits of the Budget Act.

No clear rule explains why some agencies are on the budget and some are not. In many cases, activities that are carried out off the budget are similar to activities that are included in the budget. Historically, a number of agencies were converted to off-budget status in order to avoid presidential impoundments.

While they are not included in the budget, and thus are not part of the three-quarters of the budget that is uncontrollable, off-budget agency spending nevertheless affects the economy. "In terms of their impact on the economy, the financial activities of off-budget agencies have the same effects as those of the agencies included in the budget," Schick wrote.

SOURCE: *Congressional Quarterly,* January 19, 1980.

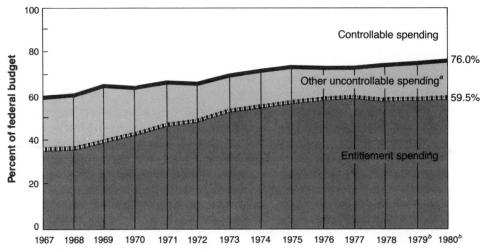

Figure 7-1 Controllable and Uncontrollable Spending. The growth of uncontrollable spending means less money for executive and legislative branches to use for new policy initiatives. [SOURCE: *Congressional Quarterly,* January 19, 1980.]

some 20 percent of the total expenditures budget. The U.S. government allows many separate reasons for excluding items from taxable income. Excluded items include taxes paid to state and local governments; interest paid on loans; interest received from lending to state and local governments; payments made for certain devices for pollution control or energy saving; certain investments in mining, timber, agriculture, real estate, and energy production, or made outside of the country; and contributions to one's own pension and approved charitable contributions. Each of these "tax shelters" has its justification in terms of the economic or social consequences that are envisioned. Unlike overt budgeting, however, these grants of resources are not reviewed in a regular fashion. We can only speculate why some groups benefit instead of or more than others. Incrementalism seems to prevail in tax expenditures as well as in budget expenditures. Once a tax benefit is written into the law, it seems rare indeed that the matter receives a serious reexamination.

INCREMENTALISM

Incrementalism is a primary feature of making budget decisions. Incrementalists view previous decisions as legitimate; they begin with the base of current expenditures and concentrate their inquiries on the increments of

Only part of what the government "spends" is listed in each year's budget and reviewed by the executive and legislative branches. Also to be counted are "tax expenditures," or taxes that do not have to be paid for various reasons. Here they are projected according to the field related to each exemption.

Table 7-5 Tax Expenditures on the Rise (in millions of dollars), 1979 and 1984

	Corporations		Individuals	
Function	1979	1984	1979	1984
National defense	—	—	$ 1,490	$ 2,160
International affairs	$ 1,715	$ 2,245	530	755
General science, space, and technology	1,550	2,780	30	55
Energy	2,480	3,405	1,645	2,300
Natural resources and environment	540	1,070	320	520
Agriculture	590	820	810	1,125
Commerce and housing credit	25,155	40,570	38,625	72,720
Transportation	75	90	350	—
Community and regional development	5	5	10	10
Education, training, employment, and social services	2,315	1,790	10,505	19,240
Health	205	300	12,210	24,740
Income security	—	—	30,071	55,855
Veterans' benefits and services	—	—	1,145	1,510
General government	—	—	80	100
General-purpose fiscal assistance	3,930	6,430	13,055	27,735
Interest	—	—	615	505
Total	$38,560	$59,505	$111,491	$209,505

Note: Tax expenditures—selective tax relief for particular groups of taxpayers—will rise by almost 80 percent over the next five years, or faster than direct spending, according to a new report by the Congressional Budget Office. In the current fiscal year, tax expenditures will produce an estimated revenue loss of $150.1 billion; assuming no change in the tax laws, the revenue loss in fiscal 1984 will be $269 billion, the CBO reports. This table gives the CBO breakdown of current and projected tax expenditures by type of taxpayer and by standard budgetary function.

SOURCE: *National Journal,* July 14, 1979. Reprinted with permission.

growth that are requested.[6] Agency personnel are concerned with the percentage of increase over their existing budget that they should request for the coming year. Reviewers in the department budget offices and the OMB think in terms of percentage cuts to be imposed on the agencies' requests. Members of the House of Representatives discuss the percentage changes they want to make in the President's budget. Senators talk about the percentage changes they want to make in House decisions.

Agency spenders typically request larger increments than budget reviewers grant. A study of federal agencies provides some information about the increments that get voted.[7] Annual requests made by 24 agencies averaged at least 10 percent above previous appropriations; 11 made annual requests that averaged at least 20 percent above their previous appropriations; and the annual requests of two agencies averaged at least 75 percent above earlier funds. The House of Representatives Appropriations Committee permitted annual growth rates in excess of 10 percent for only 12 of the agencies and an annual growth rate in excess of 20 percent for only one of them. The Senate Appropriations Committee serves as a court of appeals for House decisions. The Senate concentrates on the grievances that agencies hold after their House experience, and the process typically adds to the House grant. A House appropriation is the base from which the Senate works, and the increment between the House and Senate figure is usually small. For only 10 of the 36 agencies in the study did the Senate provide 5 percent more of the request than did the House, and for only two of the agencies was the Senate's generosity as much as 10 percent above the House grant.

State governments provide useful laboratories for the observation of incremental budgeting. Their many agencies and diverse economic, social, and political environments provide opportunities for several varieties of incremental budgeting to show themselves. As in federal budgeting, the common ingredient of incrementalism in state governments is a fixation on the increment over the previous budget. When administrators in state agencies plan requests, the paperwork requires them to list current and previous expenditures and to compare these figures with the requests for the coming year. Budget examiners in executive and legislative branches are most likely to question the funds that would increase appropriations and to cut from these requests in order to minimize budget growth.

If anything can be said about the differences in incremental budgeting at state and federal levels, it is that state personnel seem to be even more fascinated with the dollar increment of change in an agency's budget proposal. Studies of federal budgeting indicate that budget reviewers often

[6]Wildavsky, op. cit.; and I. Sharkansky, *The Routines of Politics* (New York: Van Nostrand, 1970).

[7]R. F. Fenno, Jr., *The Power of the Purse: Appropriation Politics in Congress* (Boston: Little, Brown, 1966).

question the substance of programs that are to be purchased with a budget increment. One study of state decision-makers, however, indicates a narrow fixation on the dollar amount of the increment, with virtually no attention paid to the substance of the program at issue.[8] There are several explanations for the narrower inquiry of state budget-makers. The budget offices of state governments have smaller staffs than the U.S. Office of Management and Budget, so their inquiries are more cursory. State legislators have less staff assistance than do members of Congress. Also, many state legislatures have high rates of turnover and are without a well-developed seniority system. Thus, the members of state appropriations committees are likely to be inexperienced at their work.

By looking at the nature of the relationships between agency requests, a governor's recommendations to the legislature, and the subsequent actions of the legislature, we can see how the governor and the legislature actually make their budget decisions in an incremental fashion.[9] In 19 states included in one study, the agencies requested an average increase of 24 percent over their current budgets, and the governors' recommendations trimmed an average of 14 percent from their requests. The legislatures' final appropriations typically remained close to the governors' recommendations, but appropriations varied from a cut of 8 percent below a recommendation to an increase of 19 percent above a recommendation. Six of the legislatures cut agencies' budgets below the governors' figures, and 11 appropriated more than the governors asked. In only one case, however, did a legislature give more money to the agencies than they had requested themselves. The overall average legislative grant for the coming period was 13 percent below the agencies' requests.

The responses of governors and legislatures to the budgets of individual agencies show that the acquisitiveness of agency requests plays a crucial role in budgetary decisions. In most of the states examined, the governor and legislature directed the greatest percentage of cuts at the agencies that requested the greatest percentage of increases. However, these acquisitive agencies still came out of the legislature with the greatest increases over their previous budgets. Both governors and legislatures used similar incremental decision-making rules:

1. Cut the agencies that ask for a large increase.
2. Do not recommend a budget expansion for those agencies that ask for no increase.

The size of agency budget requests does not appear to influence state budgetary decisions. Like federal budget reviewers, governors' offices and state

---

[8]T. J. Anton, *The Politics of State Expenditures in Illinois* (Urbana: University of Illinois Press, 1966).

[9]I. Sharkansky, "Agency Requests, Gubernatorial Support, and Budget Success in State Legislatures," *American Political Science Review*, 62 (December 1968): 1220–1232.

legislatures are likely to pay attention to the percentage increment of change requested. The failure of either governors or legislatures to impose additional funds on those agencies that do not ask for them illustrates how much the executive and legislative branches let program initiation pass over to administrators.

Explanations

Budget-makers have several reasons for making decisions incrementally. One reason lies in the appeal of routine compared with the rational assessment of an entire budget document. Rather than attempting the impossible task of considering all the issues that are relevant to a budget, officials in administrative units, as well as in executive and legislative branches, concede the propriety of allowing for program expenditures that already exist. They focus on the increment that represents a growth in expenditure, and presumably a change in the agency's program. To do otherwise would continually reopen the question of validity for each item of an agency's program. If each program item were always controversial, administrators or clients would be precluded from counting on the continuation of any current program. Also, an extraordinary magnitude of investigatory resources would be required just to supervise each part of every agency's program and to prepare the information necessary for an annual decision.[10]

A second reason for incremental decision-making lies in the commitments built into each budget. In some cases, relatively little in an agency's expenditure can be changed from one budget period to the next. As noted above, the Office of Management and Budget considered uncontrollable some 77 percent of the federal budget for 1981. Some parts of an agency's budget may represent "earmarked funds." These monies can legally be spent only for certain purposes, and thus are not likely to be challenged by either the executive or the legislative branch. Commitments to government employees and clients of public services also limit a serious inquiry into an agency's established level of expenditure. Large numbers of employees cannot be threatened with dismissal or transfer during each year's budget review, and large numbers of citizens cannot be threatened with curtailments or shifts in major components of their public services. These inflexibilities, reflecting common agreements about what is practical, impose real limits on the thorough review of an agency's budget. Think of your response if, during each year of your education, there was the prospect that your elementary and secondary schools and college were in danger of being eliminated from the local or state government budget.

---

[10] A. Schick, "Control Patterns in State Budget Execution," *Public Administration Review*, 24 (June 1964): 97–106.

3 Another reason for incremental budgeting lies in the lack of innovation that characterizes many governmental arenas. Budget growth tends to be slow, because few major proposals can survive all the veto power in administrative agencies and in legislative and executive branches. The constitutional framers set out to design a conservative government, and they were successful. Periods of dramatic growth tend to be short and to be followed by stability. After a surge of innovation in several programs, both the legislature and the chief executive tire of the political costs involved in getting lots of people to agree to major program changes. Administrators themselves tire of the expansion necessary to accommodate new programs. Often this means severe competition for new personnel and the need to integrate the new personnel, or perhaps new units, into the existing fabric of management. Programs that grow rapidly may get out of touch with their top administrators. Duplications in activities and lack of central control may bring charges of inefficiency or waste. It is often difficult to define these charges with precision. In any case, inefficiency and waste are powerful accusations in American politics. They are sufficient to lead some legislators, chief executives, and administrators to slow or stop the occasional spurt of growth in new programs.

Variations

The tradition of incrementalism in government budgeting sets vague outside limits to the changes that are feasible, but does not define precisely the direction and magnitude of the changes that occur. As we have seen, incremental routines lead budget reviewers to reduce the estimates of growth-oriented agencies and to withhold increases from the agencies that have not sought more funds. Nevertheless, these decisions are not made uniformly.

Occasionally, a situation of public-sector recession will occur, and budget-makers will cut into the base of existing spending. Then *incremental* budgeting turns into *decremental* spending. During the first year of the Reagan Administration, a number of programs suffered from decremental decision-making. Calculations still begin from the base of established spending, but the direction is downward rather than upward. At times, what appears on the surface to be incremental is actually decremental. This happens when the rate of inflation is greater than the rate of budget increase. Dollar amounts in the budget may increase, but purchasing power declines. When this happens, agency personnel have to make cuts in maintenance, supplies, personnel, and services.

Some governors and legislatures are more or less likely than their counterparts in other states (or in their own states during other years) to grant or withhold increments. Deviations from incremental budget routines are often not governed by objective forces of economics or politics. Instead, they appear to develop individually in the context of each state.

Some administrators have not rested in the face of incremental budget routines. Aaron Wildavsky identifies a number of strategies that assertive officials have developed within the confines of incremental budgeting. The following strategies defend the agency's current budget against attack from legislative committees:[11]

1. *Cut the popular program.* By anticipating legislative insistence on a pruned budget, administrators can cut their requests for programs that they know are popular. When this happens, it is more than likely that the legislature will restore the cut and not make up for the restoration by taking a cut elsewhere.

2. *Claim that any cut in a program will require its sacrifice.* Administrators say that any cut will be too great to allow the program to be continued. The risk with this kind of claim is that the legislature might view such a program as existing on too tenuous a foundation and scrap the whole works.

3. *Separate programs in the budget presentation.* This makes it difficult for legislators to cut across the board in a way that takes funds from anonymous programs. By forcing the legislature to cut out specific activities, an administrator can mobilize the supporters of those activities in opposition to the cut.

Administrators use other strategies to increase their budgets within the constraints of incrementalism. Wildavsky calls these strategies "increasing the base—inching ahead with existing programs":[12]

1. *The backlog.* This is the claim that existing activities have not accomplished the assigned tasks. Therefore, additional expenditures are necessary to clean up the backlog of unfinished business.

2. *The crisis.* A proposed new program is identified with an event or a set of circumstances that is widely viewed as a crisis: war, drought, depression, plant disease, social unrest. This strategy is related to the next device.

3. *The defense motif.* National defense has wide appeal. It often enjoys bipartisan support and a willingness to spend money. It is not only the military that has received the benefit of the defense motif. Other activities have tied themselves to this symbol with lucrative payoffs. The largest single highway program—and the costliest—in the nation's history is the Interstate and *Defense* Highway System. One of the most generous and wide-ranging federal aids for education enacted during the 1950s was the National *Defense* Education Act. Such labels vary in their appeal. In the years of the second Nixon Administration with a hostile Congress that was especially tired of

---

[11] Wildavsky, op. cit., pp. 102ff.

[12] Ibid., pp. 108ff.

the war effort, the defense label was of questionable value in the budget game.

EFFORTS TO RATIONALIZE BUDGET-MAKING

Policy-makers have not been content to rely on incrementalism or the strategies of administrators and other participants in budgeting. Congress and the President, as well as reformers outside of government, have sought to rationalize budgeting. Prominent recent efforts in the executive branch include the budgeting systems of PPB, MBO, and ZBB. The legislature's own efforts via the Congressional Budget and Impoundments Control Act of 1974 were done largely to reach parity of budgetary control with the executive branch.

Planning-Programming-Budgeting (PPB)

Planning-Programming-Budgeting's heyday was during the Johnson Administration. It was formally adopted by the President for the entire federal bureaucracy, and was made the subject of extensive training sessions and working manuals. PPB is an interrelated series of devices whose description is clouded by the failure of advocates to agree on a common set of terms. Systems analysis, cost–benefit analysis, cost effectiveness, and program budgeting have been used to describe individual components and sometimes the entirety of PPB. PPB seeks greater rationality in budgeting by clarifying the choice of means used to attain agency goals. Its decision stages include:

1. Defining the major programs in each area of public service.
2. Defining the principal outputs (goals) of each program.
3. Identifying the inputs that generate outputs; inputs include various combinations of personnel, facilities, and techniques of rendering service.
4. Computing the costs of alternative combinations of inputs and the value of the outputs likely to be produced by each combination.
5. Calculating the cost–benefit ratio associated with each combination of inputs and outputs.

PPB guides those who wish to employ public resources in the most efficient manner. If its practitioners are thorough, they should be able to clarify alternatives among goals and policies and to identify the set of inputs that produces the lowest cost–benefit ratio of inputs to outputs.

When the proponents of PPB speak about "systems analysis," they refer to the relationships between components 1–5 and the hope of taking "everything into consideration" in making budget recommendations. By combining PPB's five decision stages, their goal is to obtain a "systemswide" view of a policy problem. In practice, however, some aspects of PPB are developed more fully than others. Analyses that claim to reflect a systemswide view of a policy problem may actually produce only a microscopic examination into one part of a complex picture. Some shortcomings of PPB point to the continuing problems that have cropped up in other attempts to make decisions rationally: an inability to assess the full range of political and economic issues associated with each major policy, and the failure of participants to subordinate their loyalties to the recommendations that evolve from a new system.

PPB leaves much room for dispute. Depending on the approach, the kinds of assumptions made, and the nature of the data collected, a skilled analyst can produce a favorable or unfavorable recommendation.

PPB threatens to perpetuate controversy (and discomfort for budget-makers) with its rationalistic analysis of alternative approaches to each major program. An advantage to incremental budget-making is that it sharply limits the issues that have to be calculated. When incrementalists accept the base of previous expenditures as legitimate, they excuse themselves from reviewing the whole range of tradition, habits, and prior commitments that are subsumed within existing programs.

Another common accusation directed at PPB is that it focuses on the ingredients of program inputs and outputs that are easy to investigate. Many systems analyses introduce their subject matter with an impressive list of potential service determinants and likely products of the service. But the analysis itself typically deals with a few of the inputs and outputs, seemingly selected on no more substantial basis than the analyst's convenience. The inputs and outputs that are measured and subject to analysis may not be representative of other unmeasured components of the program. Budget allocations can be led astray by information that appears sophisticated, but that deals with only a small portion of the relevant picture. Thus, practitioners of PPB may base their recommendations on a routine that is no more systematic and comprehensive in its rationality than is incremental budgeting.

PPB made its start in the military, where the major goals seem clear and widely accepted among the officials who make budget decisions: deterrence of war, defense of country, and victory in war. Elsewhere, the goals of programs are subject to intense controversy. In many cases, different legislators and interest groups agree to support specific activities, even though bitter conflict would result if they had to agree about the long-range goals of the programs. Even in the case of agencies with goals that are relatively clear, the value of PPB is limited by the extent to which goals can be defined with precision and costs and benefits of programs can be measured. Definitions of the "victory" being pursued in a military encounter may, as in Korea and

Vietnam, be so ambiguous and controversial as to defy any precise statement. The life of an unlettered peasant in a foreign country, the value of an American soldier's life, or the payoffs of a research and development project must be considered in many phases of military planning, but they hardly lend themselves to simple or indisputable pricing. Some factors are worth more than their market prices indicate.

One more problem is that PPB encourages centralized decision-making by executive branch officials who assess information relevant to goals, resources, and prospective performance. Yet a prominent characteristic of American government is decentralized decision-making, with representatives of different government units or interest groups bargaining with one another. A participant's definition of a policy's feasibility is "a seat-of-the-pants judgment." The relevant "cost" questions are:

Will it "go" on the hill?
Will the public buy it?
Does it have political "sex appeal"?[13]

The death of PPB in the national government came with an Office of Management and Budget memorandum of June 21, 1971. No longer were agencies "required to submit with their budget submissions the multiyear program and financing plans, program memoranda and special analytical studies."

According to one political scientist who followed its life from the beginning, "PPB failed because it did not penetrate the vital routines of putting together and justifying a budget."[14] And yet, features of sophisticated analysis did remain in certain federal units after the demise of PPB. The OMB allowed agencies to continue with PPB-type analysis on a voluntary basis. Administrators in a number of states, localities, and other countries that took up PPB as it was developed and propagated by the national government remain convinced of its usefulness.[15] Any judgment of PPB is made difficult by the diversity of its evolution in various settings and by the differences in what people mean by PPB. As a head-on effort to rationalize the budgetary process, PPB did not master the full range of difficulties. However, sophisticated procedures remain for costing certain inputs to programs and for weighing the values of competing goals. (As an effort at rationalizing policy-making, PPB is discussed again in Chapter 10.)

---

[13] R. Huitt, "Political Feasibility," in A. Ranney, ed., *Political Science and Public Policy* (Chicago: Markham, 1968).

[14] A. Schick, "A Death in the Bureaucracy: The Demise of Federal PPB," *Public Administration Review*, 33 (March–April 1973): 146–156.

[15] A. Schick, *Budget Innovation in the States* (Washington, D.C.: Brookings Institution, 1971); N. Caiden and A. Wildavsky, *Planning and Budgeting in Poor Countries* (New York: Wiley, 1974).

Management by Objectives (MBO)

The principles behind management by objectives are much simpler than
those of planning-programming-budgeting. MBO was introduced to the
federal administration with much less fanfare. It was a creature of the
Nixon Administration and was prominent for a brief period in 1973–1974.
Put in its simplest terms, MBO requires agency administrators to identify
what they are doing—their *objectives*—in terms that allow them and their
superiors to monitor progress. While the scheme is not necessarily tied to
budgeting, President Nixon instructed the Office of Management and Budget to implement it, and several agencies tried to relate their annual objectives to the amount of money needed to accomplish them.

MBO resembles PPB in its acceptance of rational doctrine (as is explained
in Chapter 10): that the work of government can be clearly stated in terms
to be monitored in measurable units. If an agency targets the accomplishment of x number of y program units for the next fiscal year, then it should
be possible to hold agency management accountable for that goal. If the
goal is not met, then management has something to explain, and may learn
how to improve its operations.

MBO was implemented in the national government, at least according to
superficial measures. The OMB created 30 personnel positions to introduce
and monitor MBO in a group of 21 agencies. Within five months of its
formal introduction by the President, OMB had received 237 formal objectives from the agencies.[16]

The problem with MBO was in the quality of the objectives identified.
Agencies tended to identify objectives drawn from routine procedures
rather than from sensitive issues of program substance. Agency administrators wanted the OMB to judge them by the number of reports filed or
the start of work on activities approved by Congress. By one calculation,
some 80 percent of the objectives identified by the agencies were noncontroversial.[17] The OMB got the message of agency disinterest or evasion, and
allowed MBO to wither away. OMB officials began to cancel meetings scheduled to discuss agency objectives. The President sent out his last circular
asking for objectives in 1974. Yet the scheme caught on in some agencies
that continue to use it for purposes of internal management. As late as 1976
the Civil Service Commission continued to receive applications for its training courses in MBO, even though the Executive Office of the President
considered MBO a dead issue.

What went wrong? Seemingly, a combination of inherent complexity in

---

[16]R. Rose, "Implementation and Evaporation: The Record of MBO," in F. A. Kramer, ed., *Contemporary Approaches to Public Budgeting* (Cambridge, Mass.: Winthrop, 1979).

[17]Ibid.

the objectives of government agencies, plus the unwillingness of personnel in the agencies or the OMB to force hard decisions. MBO developed originally in the private sector, where objectives of production and profit lend themselves to clear definition. Not so the objectives of many government agencies. Much of what the government does has been undertaken because it is too risky or too costly for private enterprise. Also, the political process that pervades government may hinder the clear statement of objectives. Politicians seek agreement among themselves by means of expressions that mean all things to all people. Clarity in intentions might upset a coalition that hangs together on the basis of ambiguous statement. Government agencies may claim to pursue activities that have economic, social, political, and moral objectives, but with the participants being skittish about identifying their goals in a clear fashion.

Take elementary and secondary education, for example. The objectives are various kinds of book learning (reading, writing, arithmetic, history), plus certain physical skills (driving an auto, playing football), social skills (through student government, clubs, and proms), and a long-term capacity to earn a living and participate in the cultural and political activities of adult communities. There may also be some political objectives, such as patriotism or support for free enterprise. Which of these objectives to measure? Obviously, the long-term goals do not lend themselves to analysis in the annual budget cycle. What do lend themselves to analysis are the simpler short-term goals. Some of them can be defined in ways that make program administrators (the superintendent, principals, teachers) look good. Test scores can be improved by drilling students on the kinds of questions to be asked. Extracurricular events can be increased in number. Maintenance objectives (for example, the number of school rooms to be painted) can be predicted with precision.[18] The results of such analysis may add up to great piles of paper, without being substantially helpful to administrators or policy-makers.

Zero-Based Budgeting (ZBB)

Zero-based budgeting attracts our attention, not only because it is the latest in a series of reforms claiming to rationalize budgeting, but also because it attracted the personal attention of President Carter. Like Johnson's PPB, ZBB provides an insight into the capacity of the Chief Executive to leave a mark on public administration.

As Carter explained zero-based budgeting when he was Governor of Georgia, and later President, it would lead government officials to examine

---

[18] F. P. Sherwood and W. J. Page, Jr., "MBO and Public Management," in Kramer, op. cit.

each of their programs from the ground up—to see what was worth continuing, and if it was, to what extent. Its name implies that budget calculations start, not at the incrementalist's base of current spending, but at the prospect of zero spending. To Carter, ZBB requires "total rejustification of everything from scratch—from zero." To the Georgia legislature, he insisted "that the entire range of State services be re-examined [to] cut back or eliminate established programs if they are judged to be ineffective or of low priority."[19]

ZBB requires agency administrators to divide activities into "decision packages" that indicate the amount of program activity to be conducted at various levels of funding. Typically, the agencies are asked to show three levels of activity and funding for each decision package: a minimum level, the current level (or perhaps an optimal level above current activities), and an intermediate level. Agency officials also describe what would occur if each package were not funded at least to its minimum level. They indicate consequences for the clients of each decision package, the staff currently assigned to the activities, and the impact on other government activities that depend on each decision package. Paperwork flows upward from the working agencies, with managers at each level ranking the decision packages within their jurisdiction, and explaining to their own superiors the consequences of doing away with the low-ranking packages.

Several problems have appeared in the operation of ZBB. First, it seldom begins at a base of zero. The lowest calculation sought by budget units from the working agencies is typically in the range of 80 percent to 95 percent of current funding. Thus, it should be called 80-percent budgeting, or 95-percent budgeting, but not zero-based budgeting! Second, it depends on administrators to offer up their own activities for sacrifice, and invites them to avoid this prospect by describing the horrible consequences of program termination. Neither in Georgia nor in the federal government did President Carter approach his proclaimed goal of looking to the foundations of governmental activities.

Budget-makers can accept the terminology of ZBB without changing their behavior in important ways. Of 28 agency budget officers interviewed in Georgia, none claimed to have made a systematic reconsideration of programs as a result of ZBB.[20] In another group surveyed, no one claimed that funds had shifted from one activity to another as a result of ZBB. A study of fiscal years 1973–1975 in Georgia found not a single instance where a function received less money than in the previous budget.[21] One observer

---

[19] T. P. Lauth, "Zero-Based Budgeting in Georgia State Government: Myth and Reality," in Kramer, op. cit.; and A. Schick, "The Road from ZBB," in Kramer, op. cit.

[20] Lauth, op. cit.

[21] Wildavsky, op. cit., pp. 211–212.

of Carter's efforts in Washington found that his fiscal 1979 budget "hardly terminates or curtails anything of significance, continues most spending at inflation-adjusted levels, and offers few program initiatives." He labeled the 1979 budget "the most incremental financial statement since Wildavsky canonized that form of budget-making more than a dozen years ago."[22]

While some see nothing beyond a new cascade of paperwork in ZBB, others find that it leads administrators to examine their programs more thoroughly than usual. According to one agency official, it "is a useful management control device. . . . Managers are better able, I think, to make decisions on the basis of an improved reporting system."[23]

Is ZBB worth its own costs in the time devoted to it? Does it produce substantially better understanding of program administration than simpler methods of budgeting that are overtly incremental? Unfortunately, these questions do not lend themselves to clear answers. There is so much going on in the orbit of government agencies at any one time that it is virtually impossible to isolate the effects of one factor, such as a new budget scheme. This is particularly true when personnel in the working agencies and the budget staff are skillful in adopting the terminology but not the substance of the scheme. Moreover, the political stakes involved (i.e., the President's own reputation) are sufficiently high to preclude admission of failure during the term of the originator. While President Carter may not have been able to abandon ZBB, President Reagan may not be inclined to tout its virtues.

SUMMARY

If money is the blood of government, the budget is the circulatory system. While budgeting charts the flow of financial resources, it also tends to distort the picture. Typically, a budget shows only the activities of the core departments of government, and not special authorities or organizations that do the work of government under contract. Also, the budget shows only resources allocated to spending. It does not show money that is allocated to tax incentives, resources that are forfeited in order to encourage or reward certain kinds of activity by individuals or business firms.

The question *Why budget?* is as simple to answer as *Why does blood flow?* There are as many perspectives on budgeting as there are interests that are involved with government: line agencies, the Chief Executive's budget office, the legislature, interest groups, and clients. Academic observers of budgeting also reflect different perspectives. Economists, political scientists,

---

[22]Schick, "The Road from ZBB."
[23]Lauth, op. cit.

and specialists in public administration each offer their own reasons for studying a budget.

Answers to *How to budget?* likewise reveal varied processes that support their cadres of specialists. Budgeting is a profession unto itself, with its own vocabulary, calendar, training programs, and associations of practitioners. Both practitioners and commentators seek budget reform to make budgeting a more effective tool of policy-making. PPB, MBO, and ZBB are the major reform efforts in recent years, attracting the support of Presidents Johnson, Nixon, and Carter. Perhaps nowhere else in government has the clash between formal controls and informal behavior been as prominent. Despite these reform efforts, deep-seated procedures of incrementalism go a long way to explain how budgeting really works.

8

Personnel

Government is people. The quality of its people affects the quality of government. This truism carries a double meaning. Quality can mean caliber. If the caliber of public administrators is not high, then it is difficult to see how government can be well run and offer attractive programs. Quality can also mean characteristic. The characteristics of public administrators—their racial, ethnic, social-class backgrounds, and the proportions of males to females—may influence the judgments that citizens make about the effectiveness of government.

Personnel are resources that government uses to implement its programs and personnel are ends in themselves. Legislators debate and enact laws about the kinds of people to be favored in government employment and about the procedures to be used in selecting them. Involved here are policy disputes of some intensity, which make themselves felt in government agencies and public discussion. Government personnel are both means and objectives of public policy.

When viewed as resources, public personnel are like money. For this reason, this chapter parallels in some respects Chapter 7 on budgeting. In other respects, however, personnel management differs greatly from budgeting. Government employees have feelings, and vote, and put policies into practice. Unlike dollar bills, public employees are not alike. They claim rights and privileges based on traits of color, race, sex, and their status as military veterans or handicapped persons.

The key questions of this chapter reflect the peculiarities of personnel management, as well as its parallels with budgeting. They are:

Who are public administrators?
How do their backgrounds, values, and behaviors affect policy-making?
What are the controversial issues in personnel administration?
How is personnel administration done?

The last question deals with major details of personnel administration in the national government of the United States.

WHO ARE PUBLIC ADMINISTRATORS?

In response to the question *Who are public administrators?* it is appropriate to ask, *Which ones do you mean?* The personal, social, and political characteristics of public employees differ greatly—from the mass of lower-level government employees to the elite levels involved in policy-relevant decisions. The mass shows traits that are fairly representative of the population in terms of racial, ethnic, and sex balance, and the levels of education attained. If the query is directed at high-level administrators, the picture changes.

Just who high-level administrators are can vary with the study. In the federal government, the rankings that apply to most employees range from GS–1 for menial employees to GS–18 for the most senior officials. Typical college graduates may expect to take their first jobs at about GS–7 as management trainees or junior analysts. A beginning-level professional employee with a graduate degree might start at GS–11. Many studies of federal administrators consider high-level posts to apply to people with ratings of GS–14 and above. A person of GS–14 rank is likely to be a program head, the chief of a sizable field office, or a professional with some seniority.

Background

Compared to the population as a whole, high-level administrators in the federal government come disproportionately from communities having a large population and from families in the middle and upper ranges of occupational status. Also, they are disproportionately white males. High-level administrators have enjoyed a number of childhood benefits. These benefits increase the likelihood of cosmopolitan rather than parochial perspectives, and make available attractive educational opportunities and career prospects in science, the professions, or management. The administrators' educational experiences complement their middle- and upper-class backgrounds. Almost all of them have graduated from college, and a sizable proportion have obtained advanced degrees. A high percentage have received their precollegiate education in private high schools and have taken their degrees at the most prestigious colleges and graduate schools.[1]

Within the federal government, career paths show the influence of parents' social and economic characteristics. Among persons who have reached high-level positions in the federal bureaucracy, the children of laborers and farmers are more likely to have reached only the lower echelons of the policy-making corps (GS–14 and GS–15), while the children of professionals and executives are more likely to reach positions of GS–16 to GS–18. The offspring of major executives who become high-level political appointees reach such positions five years *earlier* in their careers than do the children of laborers. The children of lower-class parents who become upper-level civil servants are less likely than children of more advantaged homes to reach as high in the bureaucracy, and they take longer to reach their positions.[2]

Federal administrators at policy-making levels differ from the general adult population in their social backgrounds and educational experiences. However, they do not differ markedly from individuals in positions of responsibility in other branches of government or in large business firms. Some studies indicate that, among government administrators, a higher proportion have advanced education and a lesser proportion come from upper-class families than do members of the legislative branch or executives of large private firms; the differences are not great, however. In these and other traits, the high-level personnel of public agencies are more like their counterparts elsewhere in government or business than like adults in the society as a whole. Generally speaking, responsible positions in many fields attract persons with more-than-average education and from upper-income families. There is no indication that the personal traits of government administrators are so different from those of other policy-makers that their presence is likely to distinguish the decisions of government agencies from those of other institutions.

An individual's career route is another background element of potential importance. The first job, and the length of time spent in earlier occupations, may shape the way an administrator views work. Family background influences the nature of one's early career. Thus, family background may affect the personnel of administrative agencies, because it influences the early career choices of persons who later become high-level administrators.

Of all career routes, those in the professions most consistently supply individuals for high-level positions in the federal administration. One study showed that 46 percent of those who were high-level administrators (GS–14

---

[1] H. Heclo, *Government of Strangers* (Washington, D.C.: Brookings Institution, 1977); W. L. Warner et al., *The American Federal Executive* (New Haven: Yale University Press, 1963).

[2] Warner, op. cit.

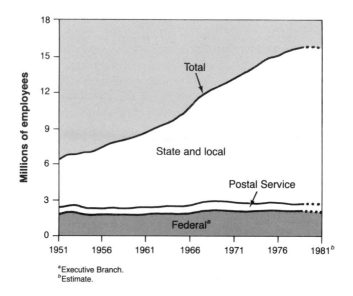

Figure 8-1 Government Civilian Employment. State and local employment has grown far more than federal employment in the last three decades. [SOURCE: *Congressional Quarterly*, February 2, 1980.]

and higher) started their careers in a profession. Many who worked first in the categories of laborer and white-collar worker moved into a professional category before reaching higher administrative positions. A breakdown of the professional routes shows that about one-third have been lawyers or scientists. Other professional groups that supply upper-level administrators are physicians, professors, accountants, and public school teachers.

It is interesting that the career route for business leaders is different from that of upper-level civil servants. Only 24 percent of the business leaders considered in one study began their careers as professionals, while 44 percent began in the white-collar sectors of clerical and sales. These findings have serious implications for the common stereotypes of government administrators as bureaucrats who glory in red tape and of business leaders who are more flexible individualists. It is business leaders who follow the route of white-collar worker to minor manager to major manager through the business bureaucracies. Government officials—especially political appointees—more often are educated in professional or graduate schools and then transfer into government at levels where they enjoy prestige, discretion, and responsibility for policy decisions. If any class of leaders shows the behavioral effects of a bureaucratic career, it is more likely to be the manager in business than the higher-level civil servant in government.

Values and Behavior

The family background, education, and career experiences of high-level administrators suggest the most likely routes to responsible positions in administrative agencies. From their background alone, however, we cannot infer that government administrators have any particular values or behavioral traits that set them apart from other individuals in society.

Some intensive research has been done on the personalities of government administrators. One group of scholars, headed by W. Lloyd Warner, conducted intensive interviews with a random sample of 257 civilian administrators in the federal government at the levels of GS–14 and above.[3] The interviews included Thematic Apperception Tests and lasted three to four hours each. More recently, Hugh Heclo had extensive interviews with some 200 present and former government executives.[4] The information from the two studies is consistent in some important ways.

The personal values, aspirations, and personalities of federal administrators suggest persons with large perspectives. They see themselves as functioning within a complex and demanding set of institutions and as being responsible for programs with great social value. They view their authority as coming from outside of themselves. Authority is a source of support as well as instruction; they generally accept authority as legitimate, although sometimes resent intrusions on their own activities. By and large, they accept the restrictions of large organizations, and they accept the need for coordination and cooperation. They show the traits of group workers rather than individualists.

High-level administrators tend to have lofty ideals. They aspire to community improvement more than to self-aggrandizement. Along with this idealism, government administrators have strong needs for achievement. This combination of traits may add up to public-minded realism. Their need for achievement, as well as their appreciation for organizational constraints, may temper their idealism so that goals come within the range of feasibility. Perhaps because of this, their goals are usually expressed in concrete terms that are relevant to their field of specialization. Instead of abstract principles that do not lend themselves to clear definition or attainment, they desire improved services in education, health, welfare, transportation, or resource development. These findings suggest that upper-level administrators seldom ponder the abstract ideals of justice, equality, freedom, and democracy discussed in Chapter 5. Perhaps they think of these values only when making difficult decisions, which they nevertheless resolve in pragmatic terms.

---

[3] Ibid.

[4] Heclo, op. cit.

incrementalism

Heclo found inclinations toward "gradualism" in his contacts. Administrators seek change by indirect means rather than by a frontal assault on the status quo and those who defend it. They are careful politically. Rather than identify themselves with the political appointees currently serving as heads of their departments, they identify themselves with their programs.

The values of senior administrators also reveal a great respect for the institutions of government and a strong motivation to serve the interests of the public. They appear more oriented to public service than to private gain.

The data on high-level government administrators are not without contradictions. They show values and attitudes that appear strange in combination with one another. Yet, this is to be expected. Administrators in policy-making roles must deal with the constraints of large organizations, active client groups, and legislators who may pressure agencies for certain decisions. Administrators also have powerful motivations and strong ideals of public service. It seems inevitable that many administrators experience internal conflicts. Intensive interviews reveal not only an expressed ease about their dependence on a large system, but also a drive for independence and an anxiety about the dependence that is necessary. Administrators both need and reject authority. Occasionally they show their rejection with expressions of resentment and with ineffectual behavior.

Another survey of 405 senior executives, reported by Bob Wynia, found that the large majority express liberal-democratic opinions with respect to such issues as upholding fair-play rules of the game; allowing freedom of speech; protecting due process; and the equality of various political, social, and economic groups. They also feel that politics offers meaningful opportunities for citizens to influence government. In these traits, senior administrators resemble other elite groups of high income and high educational and occupational status in the private sector. But the senior administrators are not homogeneous. Those with more formal education are the most likely to express liberal-democratic views, and those in social agencies are more likely to express these views than those in defense-related agencies. Of most concern, perhaps, is the finding that senior administrators with the longest service are less likely than their younger colleagues to express respect for democratic values or to believe that the political process offers a meaningful opportunity to change public policy.[5]

The multiple influences on agency policies provide some check against whatever influences may come from the personal traits of administrators. The personal attributes of administrators must compete for influence over policy with formal and informal communications from the legislative,

---

[5]B. L. Wynia, "Federal Bureaucrats' Attitudes Toward a Democratic Ideology," *Public Administration Review*, 34 (March–April 1974): 156–162.

executive, and judicial branches of government, from officials at other levels of the federal system, and from clients and other members of the public. Moreover, administrators may have to do battle with themselves, because of their own conflicting values. The values identified with family social status, for example, may conflict with professional standards acquired as part of formal training. Within one administrative unit, administrators may compete with one another for their personal interests, making it unlikely that anyone's sole interest can shape an agency's decision. Formal procedures help to guard against the overt influence of personal interests on official decisions. They include multiple decision-makers within one agency; the separation of powers, which provides an agency with several executive and legislative supervisors; and conflict-of-interest procedures used to screen out job applicants who would have a substantial personal financial stake in an agency's policies.

The information about the backgrounds and the personalities of high-ranking administrators does not point clearly to their distinctive impact on policy decisions. It appears that administrators' roles—their official duties—are more important than their personal traits in shaping official actions.

BACKGROUND AND TRAITS AS POLICY ISSUES

Even though there may be little discernible effect of administrators' background and traits on the policies of administrative organizations, they are important to know about for other reasons. The composition of the public service system has significance for employment opportunities within it. *To what extent do children of different social classes or ethnic groups have equal opportunities to enter public employment and reach policy-making levels?* For some groups that have been the target of discrimination in private industry, the government may be the most likely source of jobs commensurate with their skills and training. The opportunity for government employment is one of the policy benefits an administrative organization provides to such groups in the population. In addressing this issue, we turn from a concern with government personnel as a resource used to achieve policy goals to a concern with the character of personnel as a policy goal in itself.

In Chapter 6 we raised some of the issues concerned with administrative management. Managers have much to ponder as they operate their departments and agencies. They cannot focus on issues of program substance without also referring to issues of personnel selection and management. The person in charge of the Justice Department's Civil Rights Division, for example, may have to cope with lawyers who want to pursue a more aggressive policy with respect to civil rights enforcement than that chosen by the department. The head must also reach for a balance of employees with respect to traits of race and sex.

Representative Bureaucracy

One of the questions that is properly asked about administrative agencies is *To what extent do they include members of groups that are discriminated against in the private sector?* The answer to such a question has several implications. It indicates the commitment of administrative agencies to provide some opportunities to individuals who are socially disadvantaged. If this commitment is sizable, it can provide important policy benefits. The employment of the disadvantaged can provide members of these groups with positive feelings toward the established order. The employment policies may thereby lessen whatever tendencies toward nihilism and violence that may develop among disadvantaged groups. The employment of individuals from such groups also suggests the efforts of government recruiters to search all potential labor markets. When government employment is skewed against disadvantaged groups, large pools of labor will remain untapped. These pools may require cultivation with special educational and employment opportunities. If they remain unexploited, however, administrative agencies deprive themselves of important resources.

The efforts of blacks, women, and other underprivileged groups to increase their share of social benefits have led them to demand more and better jobs in government. Their claims bear some resemblance to the traditional demands for special privileges that have come from veterans and the supporters of victorious political parties. Each of these groups raises the issue of a *representative bureaucracy.*[6]

A representative bureaucracy is difficult to create. In one sense, completely equal representation is impossible to achieve; the bureaucracy of a modern government must include a disproportionate number of highly educated and well-paid lawyers, accountants, scientists, engineers, and managers, which, at least at present, are white-male-dominated professions. A more relevant conception of a representative bureaucracy is one that employs ample numbers of certain groups, especially in jobs that are considered important. The groups identified as "sensitive" earn this designation in the political process. The demands of blacks, women, Hispanics, Asians, native Americans, gays, and the physically handicapped reflect their heightened political consciousness and organizational clout.

The generally positive responses to demands for special consideration have been challenged by those who prize a *neutral* bureaucracy—that is, one selected purely on merit. Official policies require personnel officers to display "affirmative action" in recruiting women, the physically handicapped, and certain minorities according to established "goals." Programs to recruit

---

[6]S. Krislov, *Representative Bureaucracy* (Englewood Cliffs, N.J.: Prentice-Hall, 1974); and S. Krislov, *The Negro in Federal Employment: The Quest for Equal Opportunity* (Minneapolis: University of Minnesota Press, 1967).

the disadvantaged work best during program expansion. Expansion affords opportunities for affirmative action without constantly colliding with staff members seeking to protect their positions. The newer and expanding agencies, or those with low government status, now recruit the highest number of people from disadvantaged groups. Since the mid-1960s, the Office of Economic Opportunity, ACTION, and the departments of Health and Human Services, Education, and Housing and Urban Development have recruited the highest percentages of underprivileged people to high-ranking positions.

Blacks

In recent years, the incidence of nonwhites in government employment has resembled their proportion in the total population. By this measure alone, nonwhites have "equal" access to administrative systems. Yet, their skewed distribution among job categories testifies to continued disadvantages. Nonwhites are employed mostly in low-wage, low-status positions.

However, the distribution of blacks in the federal service is improving. Blacks fill an increasing number of middle- and upper-level positions. From 1972 to 1976, for example, blacks in grades GS–9 to GS–18 increased from 4.5 to 6.2 percent. In the same period, the percentage of all minorities in these ranks increased from 14.3 to 19.6. Blacks in middle- and upper-level positions face a new problem of feeling they were hired as symbols rather than as skilled professionals.[7]

Women

The status and problems of women in administrative agencies are similar to those of blacks. The exclusion of women from certain positions raises similar questions about discrimination and the failure of administrative agencies to exploit potential resources. The number of women in white-collar federal positions is about the same as the proportion (49 percent) of women in the population. As in the case of blacks, the problem is not so much in their numbers as in their distribution. As of 1975, only 5 percent of the federal employees above the level of GS–12 were women, a figure that increased by only 1.5 percent in the 1959–1975 period. As with blacks, women are employed disproportionately in certain kinds of jobs: they are concentrated in the fields of child welfare, public assistance, and vocational rehabilitation.[8]

---

[7] *Statistical Abstract of the United States, 1979* (Washington, D.C.: U.S. Government Printing Office, 1980).
[8] Ibid.

WHAT IS PERSONNEL ADMINISTRATION?

Administrative Tasks and Agencies

The tasks of personnel administration can be boiled down to hiring, assignments of personnel, determining proper salaries and other rewards, and disciplining wayward employees. In a large government with concerns for equity, efficiency, and effectiveness, personnel administration is a sophisticated profession, at the same time that it is influenced by politics. A model system of personnel management includes the following activities:

1. A classification of jobs, including the duties to be performed and the skills required of employees.
2. A schedule of compensation and other benefits, done with an eye to comparability of pay and benefits between different tasks in the government, and the need to compete effectively with the private sector for attractive candidates.
3. Procedures for recruiting appropriate applicants, and testing applicants to judge their suitability for employment in particular positions.
4. Procedures to train employees for their present positions, and to develop their potential for continued occupational growth.
5. Procedures for evaluating employees with respect to their suitability in their present positions and/or their prospects for promotion.
6. Procedures for monitoring the activities of personnel, rewarding good performance and selecting out those who do not perform at minimum levels.

The principal agencies charged with overseeing personnel administration in the U.S. government are the Office of Personnel Management (OPM), the Merit System Protection Board (MSPB), and the Federal Labor Relations Authority (FLRA). They emerged from the venerable Civil Service Commission as a result of the Civil Service Reform Act of 1978. The OPM is responsible for proclaiming and enforcing personnel policies, as defined by appropriate laws and executive orders. The MSPB has quasi-judicial powers—it hears and decides appeals by individuals with respect to personnel practices, and it imposes disciplinary actions. The MSPB also has oversight functions—it assesses and makes recommendations about personnel policies. The FLRA is the equivalent in the government sector of the private sector's National Labor Relations Board (NLRB). The FLRA establishes and oversees procedures for the organization of federal employees, and negotiates within the context of rules and regulations that apply to government employees.

The principles of the federal merit system are established in law. They can be summarized as:[9]

1. Recruitment to achieve a work force from all segments of society, with selection and advancement solely on the basis of merit, after fair and open competition that assures equal opportunity.

2. Fair treatment for all applicants and employees, with no illegal discrimination and with proper regard for their privacy and constitutional rights.

3. Equal pay for work of equal value, with consideration of local and national private-sector pay rates and with incentives and recognition for excellence in performance.

4. Employees that maintain high standards of integrity, conduct, and concern for the public interest.

5. Efficient and effective use of the federal work force.

6. Retention based on performance and training to improve performance.

7. Protection of employees against arbitrary action, personal favoritism, or coercion for partisan political purposes, and prohibition from employees using the workplace for partisan purposes.

8. Protection of employees against reprisal for lawful disclosures of information.

To deliver on these principles requires an annual expenditure of some $3.2 billion by OPM, MSPB, and FLRA. The details of salary surveys, position classification, testing, recruiting, training, and evaluating are the subjects of specialized courses and texts.[10] Especially in regard to the large numbers of lower- and middle-grade positions, activities are subject to precise regulation, written tests for recruitment and promotions, plus explicit standards of assessment. By one measurement, the Federal Personnel Manual occupies five linear feet of shelf space![11]

Employee Selection

The field of personnel administration is beset with controversy. We have already seen such controversy in discussing the issues of representative bureaucracy and affirmative action. Groups that feel disadvantaged want

---

[9]"Civil Service Reform Act of 1978: Detailed Summary" (Washington, D.C.: U.S. Office of Personnel Management, 1979), mimeo.

[10]F. A. Nigro and L. G. Nigro, *The New Public Personnel Administration* (Itasca, Ill.: Peacock, 1976); and O. G. Stahl, *Public Personnel Administration* (New York: Harper, 1976).

[11]Heclo, op. cit., Chapter 4.

greater access, while others oppose it as a new form of discrimination. Chapter 6 dealt with techniques of managing personnel. It touched on the problems of how to control administrators most effectively and the mirror-image problem of administrators who feel that their rights are trampled on by managers who are overly assertive. Many public employees want to speak freely in behalf of political candidates and policy goals, and to organize collectively in a trade-union framework.

Squabbles about selecting personnel are not new on the American scene. President Andrew Jackson came to office in 1829 with strong feelings about the bureaucracy. The federal bureaucracy had grown to over 11,000 civilian employees and was populated largely by members of upper-class families appointed during the administrations of John Quincy Adams and James Monroe. To Jackson, the incumbents were aliens in both social class and partisan loyalties. He saw them as a hindrance to reform. Unless he removed large numbers of incumbents and replaced them with his own supporters, he felt he could not count on the departments to carry out his programs. President Jackson believed that the responsibilities of public officials were "so plain and simple that men of intelligence may readily qualify themselves for their performance."[12] He had a dual justification for removing the appointees of his predecessor and replacing them with his own people:

1. The Administration's policies should conform to those of elected officials.
2. Government jobs are simple enough to permit frequent turnover without significant loss in expertise.

The Jacksonian personnel administration appointed and dismissed employees on the basis of political rather than technical qualifications. This practice continues to varying degrees today. It is identified with Jackson, not because he was the first to sweep out existing employees when he came to office, but because he provided the rationale and practiced it in an overt manner. Actually, he removed no larger a percentage of federal employees than did President Jefferson 20 years earlier.[13] The public service may have reached its most political level at the time of the Civil War. President Lincoln used his powers of appointment and removal to select pro-Union administrators to assure that government officers would use their powers in support of the Union. The civil service was not freed from political control after the Civil War. It experienced the clash of noble and ignoble values that

---

[12]From Jackson's First Annual Message to Congress, December 8, 1829.

[13]L. D. White, *The Federalists* (New York: Macmillan, 1948); and P. D. Van Riper, *History of the United States Civil Service* (Evanston, Ill.: Row, Peterson, 1958).

typified Reconstruction. It included persons who were consciously "hard" in dealing with the South, as well as those who were simply corrupt.

Throughout the period from President Jackson to President Arthur, several efforts were made to isolate government employment from excesses of venality and partisanship. Reform at the national level took a major step forward with the Pendleton Act of 1883. Its major features were:

1. A Civil Service Commission to administer personnel policies with some independence of the President.
2. The explicit use of merit as a primary criterion for government employment.
3. The use of competitive examinations for the selection of employees.
4. The protection of employees from being coerced to support the campaigns of political parties.
5. The immediate coverage of about 10 percent of federal employees under provisions of the act.
6. Authority given to the President to expand coverage to other employees by means of executive order.

There are still sharp disputes about personnel selection and administration. By now, however, administrators are sufficiently "professional" for most disputes to avoid extreme charges of patronage and venality. Any discussion of personnel procedures is complicated by differences between career and political appointees. Both categories include people who are at the highest levels in administrative units and who are involved in policy-making. However, the two groups differ in their overt alignment with political parties and involvement in election campaigns, as well as in the kinds of job protection they enjoy. Control over political appointees is generally given to popularly elected executives, while control over the career service is given to institutions protected from partisanship. However, administrators at the very top of the civil service must be accountable to some degree to the prevailing political leadership. For this reason, differences between politics and career become blurred.

In the middle and upper ranges (GS–9 to GS–18), the career service deals with professional and managerial personnel. Procedures of selection are less mechanistic than for clerical and technical tasks, leaving more room for subjective choice. Instead of written exams administered in post offices and other local testing centers, selection depends heavily on the assessment of educational and training qualifications, prior work experience, and personal interviews. The OPM relies less on mass publicity of job openings at these levels than on notices selectively sent to various government offices, universities, and other professional networks. Hiring agencies may refer specific names, and ask the OPM to certify them as eligible for the positon.

In this way, actual recruitment may depend on the searches done by the hiring agency, who canvasses the networks thought likely to produce attractive candidates. Such referrals to the OPM also are an opportunity for members of the President's team in each agency to affect the recruitment of personnel considered compatible with the President's goals.

The Civil Service Reform Act of 1978

President Carter made civil service reform a major goal of his Administration. He set the tone in a message in March 1978, when he told Congress that existing procedures had created a

> bureaucratic maze which neglects merit, tolerates poor performance, permits abuse of legitimate employee rights and mires every personnel action in red tape, delay and confusion.

The President sent his proposals to Congress in March 1978, and thus began a process of hearings—testimony by inside and outside experts on the civil service, representatives of veterans' groups, women, minorities, the handicapped, and unions of government employees.

The hearings provided an occasion for groups to press for the implementation of reforms that had been talked about for years:

1. To adopt an idea from Britain and Europe that high-ranking members of the civil service could be moved from one key assignment to another that required managerial expertise and prestige.

2. To sharpen the concern for merit in the middle ranges of the services, with substantial financial rewards for those truly deserving them by virtue of hard work or creativity.

3. To protect outspoken but responsible civil servants who criticize government programs (all too often these "whistle blowers" had been "rewarded" with blocked advancement or outright dismissal).

4. To ease the plight of managers who are frustrated by complex and long procedures in their efforts to dismiss incompetent or uncooperative employees.

5. To provide orderly procedures for dealing with recently expanded unions of government employees.

The list of desired reforms looked more like a smorgasbord than a well-planned meal. It included proposals to protect employees more completely from arbitrary dismissal, as well as proposals to ease the tasks of managers in dismissing those they considered to be unfit. The bills that moved through the House and Senate tried to provide something for many perspectives, and made an effort to balance conflicting interests.

The House of Representatives and the Senate passed separate versions of a bill, but a compromise acceptable to the President was approved and signed into law in October. Its provisions include:

1. Dividing the work of the old Civil Service Commission among the new bodies (OPM, MSPB, FLRA), as previously noted.
2. Spelling out in greater detail prohibited personnel practices, including more protection for employees who report government wrongdoing and then charge reprisals against their careers.
3. Providing somewhat more flexibility for managers in firing incompetent workers.
4. A new system of merit pay for employees in the GS–13 to GS–15 range, which, along with a system of bonuses, is designed to encourage greater effort from this cadre of managers.
5. Clarifying the rights of federal employees to join labor unions and bargain collectively on certain issues.
6. Establishing a Senior Executive Service, as detailed below.

The Civil Service Reform Act of 1978 will become a landmark in the development of the American public service. That status is assured by its many features that seek to alter adverse conditions that had developed under earlier civil service legislation. Supporters of the 1978 enactment see it as setting the tone of public administration, as did the Pendleton Act 90 years earlier. At this time, however, an observer should withhold judgment. In Chapter 11, the discussion of implementation details the many delays, detours, and distortions that may intrude between a policy's enactment and the actual delivery of its promises. There are special dangers when a policy is innovative or when it attempts to balance contrary themes, like greater protection for employees and greater discretion for managers.

The Senior Executive Service

A prominent feature of the Civil Service Reform Act of 1978 was the creation of the Senior Executive Service (SES). Long sought by commentators on the civil service, the SES is to be an elite group of managers and professionals, with special designations and perquisites. Pay within the SES is to depend on judgments about the merit of the executives, with provisions for substantial cash awards in cases of unusual accomplishment. The goal is to establish a service whose members will give up the comfort and automatic pay increases of routine career protections for the challenging opportunities of jobs designated by the OPM and the agencies as suitable for SES personnel. SES members will not have fixed attachment to particular agen-

The Office of Personnel Management counts the initiatives it has taken with respect to the Civil Service Reform Act of 1978.

Table 8-1 OPM Implementation Initiatives

Subject	Audiovisual presentations	Publications	New training courses	Meetings and conferences	Regulations published	Consultation projects	Evaluations	Delegated authorities	Delegations negotiated	Delegations studied	Research grant awards	LAIRS requests	Interventions in MSPB cases
Civil service reform (overall)	3	5											
Performance appraisal	1	7	5	15		17	178						
Work-force discipline	1	3		12	3		3,500						
Delegation of authority		2			3			55	28	33			
Research and demonstration		2									2		
Staffing		13		1	11			1					
Intergovernmental personnel program		6		1	1						4		
Labor–management relations	1	15	4	52		108						500	
Productivity		3		75									
Senior Executive Service	2	32		21	5								
Executive management and development		5		6									
Legal action and support		4		3			Numerous opinions						50
Merit pay	2	15	2	7									

Note: The Civil Service Reform Act directly affects all aspects of federal personnel management. OPM has extensively revised all its training programs, publications, and public presentations to reflect these changes. In addition, as this chart reflects, many completely new initiatives have been undertaken as part of OPM's campaign to inform the 2.1 million federal employees and the public about the reforms.

SOURCE: U.S. Office of Personnel Management, *Civil Service Reform: A Report on the First Year* (Washington, D.C.: U.S. Government Printing Office, 1980).

cies, but may shift from one important job to another, while retaining their rank in the SES.

The future of the SES will depend on the willingness of qualified managers to take the risks associated with its opportunities, and on the support given the SES by the OPM, the White House, and Congress. Early signs have been mixed. Congress and the White House were reluctant to relax a federal pay freeze to allow the salaries for the SES to reach levels set in the 1978 Civil Service Reform Act. Despite this, a promising sign is that some 95 percent of eligible senior personnel already in the federal service have sought transfer to the SES. This figure matches or exceeds the arguments of SES advocates that senior staff members have been chafing under conventional career opportunities, and would welcome the risks and the opportunities of the new service.

Political Appointees

The Office of Personnel Management is responsible for the majority of personnel appointments in the federal government. However, some appointments are left in the President's hands. He operates a separate unit, staffed by White House aides, to help recruit, screen, and select these persons.

Civil reformers of the nineteenth century portrayed hordes of office-seekers descending on a newly elected President. In their cartoons, the Chief Executive was unable to attend to important business because of the job applicants. Today this is a false image. Some people, including a fair number of professors, do hint at their availability during those times when administrations change in Washington. However, the President must search for talent and may have to persuade the people chosen to leave well-established situations in business or in their professions. To the prospects, the President offers the opportunity to serve the Administration, perhaps at a substantial reduction in salary and at an increase in personal expenses.

Recent presidential candidates have postponed decisions on political appointments until after the election. Although this delay has disturbed some observers of the presidential transition, the campaign itself has consumed the most important resources of the candidates and their assistants. One of John Kennedy's aides said that "Kennedy wouldn't have won" if his staff had devoted any more attention to postelection matters."[14] Eisenhower, Kennedy, Nixon, Carter, and Reagan detailed a group of advisers to concentrate on high-level personnel immediately after their elections. The cen-

---

[14]D. E. Mann, *The Assistant Secretaries: Problems and Processes of Appointment* (Washington, D.C.: Brookings Institution, 1965).

tral figures in Eisenhower's group were Herbert Brownell and Lucius Clay. Brownell was experienced in Republican party politics as a former national party chairman and campaign manager for Thomas Dewey. Clay was a military associate of the President-elect, had been active in the 1952 political campaign, and was chairman of the board at Continental Can Company. The key people in Kennedy's personnel team (the "Talent Hunt") were his brother and campaign manager Robert Kennedy and his brother-in-law R. Sargent Shriver. Nixon's team had Californians and New Yorkers drawn from his former close associates. The Carter group had a heavy representation of Georgians. President Reagan relied heavily on Californians. The practice has been to solicit names of prospective appointees from contacts in politics, business, the professions, and universities; screen the qualifications of various prospects; clear them with political leaders and professional or business associates; and make recommendations for each cabinet position.

There is no question about the direct involvement of the President-elect in the selection of cabinet secretaries and the heads of major independent offices. There have been differences, however, in their involvement in making appointments just below those levels. President Eisenhower left the selection of subordinate appointees to the new cabinet secretaries and agency heads. This course was consistent with his policy of delegating decisions and permitting administrators to operate their own organizations. And it left disappointed some Republican members of Congress who could not get presidential intervention for the sake of a "deserving" constituent. On some occasions, Eisenhower's staff urged a department to take "political considerations" into account; but the President-elect did not involve himself directly. Generally speaking, Kennedy exercised more control over subordinate appointments than did Eisenhower. Indeed, Kennedy's first announced appointment—made even before the announcement of a secretary of state—was G. Mennan Williams as assistant secretary of state for African affairs. This presidential concern may have won some credits among elites in the new African states, but it also signaled to the State Department that Kennedy would make decisions formerly delegated to the secretary. President-elect Kennedy appointed Chester Bowles as undersecretary of state and Adlai Stevenson as ambassador to the United Nations. Also, each of Kennedy's cabinet secretaries was assigned a member of the personnel team to review candidates available for subordinate appointments.

Presidents have used a combination of occupational competence and political acceptability as personnel criteria. The Kennedy team asked about a prospect's judgment, toughness, integrity, ability to work with others, industry, and devotion to the principles of the President-elect. The team also asked whether their appointments would enhance the Administration's prestige nationally, in their states, in their communities, or in their professional groups. With the press of time and many prospects to be reviewed, however, evaluations were simplified to highly qualified, qualified, or some qualifications with respect to competence; and good Democrat, political neutral, Republican, or politically disqualified with respect to partisanship.

As Presidents pass the period of inauguration, they change procedures for political appointments. Without the crush of numbers, they no longer require a special task force. Eisenhower, Kennedy, and Nixon assigned the review of later political appointees to the White House Office. As the Presidents themselves concentrate increasingly on substantive problems, their cabinet secretaries take a prominent role in personnel decisions, most of which involve the selection of replacements for subordinates who resign.

Congress also has a role in political appointments. All department secretaries, undersecretaries, and assistant secretaries, as well as ambassadors, the heads of many independent offices, and federal judges, are subject to senatorial confirmation. Within some cabinet departments and independent offices, administrative assistant secretaries do not require senatorial confirmation. Often they are named by immediate superiors to serve as personal assistants. Sometimes they represent the White House in an agency, with the job of riding herd on personnel actions and other matters that are politically sensitive.

Many senators would grant the Chief Executive considerable discretion over the selection of key personnel, especially in the "honeymoon" following a presidential election. The Senate undertakes only a casual examination of some candidates. The individual is introduced to the Senate committee that has charge of legislation for the nominee's department; there may be no searching probe and no formal record of the committee meeting. Such a nominee's name would go before the Senate with no debate and be approved by unanimous consent.

When opposition to an appointment does come from the Senate, it can take several forms. It can be a serious effort to block an appointment or merely the attempt of one senator to make a record of opposition. Alexander Haig's nomination as secretary of state drew fire from Democrats, who recalled his close association with Richard Nixon. Some opposition may be designed to elicit policy commitments from the nominee. Few candidates for administrative posts actually are rejected by the Senate. Yet formal rejections are not the full story. Some nominations are withdrawn by the President because he fears the embarrassment of a formal rejection. Some nominees withdraw themselves—like Theodore Sorensen, slated by President Carter to be head of the Central Intelligence Agency—when intensive opposition appears in the Senate. Some nominees are never formally submitted, because key senators express intense opposition during a preliminary clearance.

POLITICAL CONTROVERSIES

The personnel practices of government are contentious policies in their own right.

How many employees?

To pursue affirmative recruiting campaigns in behalf of women and certain racial and ethnic minorities?

To extend veterans' preferences in hiring criteria?

What levels of salary and fringe benefits?

What techniques of management?

To permit unionization?

What controls to impose on employees' rights to criticize government policy, to engage in electoral politics, or to lead the private lives that they desire?

Each of these questions can produce disputes between managers and employees of government departments, and can spill over to the private sector. Private employers see too-generous government salary scales and fringe benefits as providing models for their own workers to emulate. Organizations of ethnic groups, women, the handicapped, veterans, and the unions of government employees seek to maintain or expand the programs that benefit their members. Claims of government employees for equal rights to unionize or to engage freely in political or personal activities can rouse both support and opposition from citizens who take an ideological interest in these matters. The American Civil Liberties Union has been a prominent advocate for expanded conceptions of employees' rights.

Collective Bargaining

Government employees are not content to be controlled as inert resources in the policy process. Their organizations, whether they are called unions, associations, or councils, seek improved compensation, greater rights of political expression, and influence over the details of agency programs.

Unionization can be a tough problem for personnel managers. The issues include employee challenges of established antiunion or antistrike statutes and political squeezes between civil servants and citizens who are outraged at their own lack of desirable salaries or working conditions, or at the prospect of higher taxes. There are moral confrontations. On the one side are those who argue that government employees should have the same rights to organize and bargain collectively as do employees in the private sector. On the other side are those who argue that the state's sovereignty cannot be compromised by granting public employees the right to thwart the policies of constitutional offices.[15]

A source of difficulties both for the employees who organize and for the administrators who must deal with them reflects the insensitivity of earlier civil service reformers to the collective demands of employees. The merit system and related mechanisms are on the side of individuals rather than groups. Features of the merit system include open competitive examinations, criteria that reward individual excellence, and employee classifications on the basis of objective analyses of performance. Against these principles, union demands are in the tradition of a closed shop—recruitment on the basis of union membership or occupational license, promotion on the basis of seniority, and collective negotiations of employee classifications and working conditions.

Some politicians who are otherwise prolabor oppose collective bargaining with public employees. President Franklin Roosevelt, for example, said:

> [Collective bargaining] has its distinct and insurmountable limitations when applied to public personnel management. The very nature and purposes of government make it impossible for administrative officials to represent fully or to bind the employer in mutual discussions with government employee organizations.[16]

The unions of government workers have not been confined by these principles or by the antistrike laws that exist in many jurisdictions. Government unions, especially at state and local levels, are the fastest-growing sector of the union movement. Prominent unions or unionlike organizations include the American Federation of Government Employees, American Postal Workers Union, American Federation of State, County, and Municipal Employees, American Federation of Teachers, and the National Education Association. Numerous private-sector unions have representation in the public sector: the Teamsters Union, for example, enrolls members from police, fire, sanitation, and other public service units.

Among the mechanisms established by the Civil Service Reform Act of 1978 was the Federal Labor Relations Authority (FLRA). The FLRA defines bargaining units, supervises elections, and decides other issues in the framework of federal employee organizations.

Some 88 percent of postal employees and 58 percent of all other federal employees were represented by unions in 1977. Among state and local government employees, 48 percent were represented in 1978. Firefighters and school teachers were the most heavily represented of these employees, with respectively 72 and 69 percent of them enrolled.

---

[15] F. C. Mosher, *Democracy and the Public Service* (New York: Oxford University Press, 1968).
[16] Ibid., p. 177.

Along with growing size, there is a growing militancy among public employee unions. Although many of them exist in jurisdictions that formally outlaw the strike for government employees, 36 strikes were recorded in 1960, 42 in 1965, and over 350 in 5 of the 6 years between 1969 and 1975. In 1955, 7,000 worker days were lost to strikes in government, over 1 million worker days in 6 of the 8 years between 1967 and 1975, and substantially over 2 million worker days per year at the end of that period. School teachers are more likely to strike than other government employees. During 1978, they accounted for 54 percent of the state and local government employee days lost to strikes. In many actions, the leaders take care to avoid the term strike. However, slowdowns or sick leaves that occur in a cohesive manner during crucial periods of collective bargaining leave no doubt about their purpose. Some "strikes" take the form of strict enforcement of regulations that are otherwise slighted for the sake of convenience. Local police officers have enforced parking regulations with unusual thoroughness, sometimes against the vehicles of prominent citizens or policy-makers. The air traffic controllers of the Federal Aviation Agency have expressed their displeasure by refusing any of the customary deviations from strict safety requirements. The resulting delays at the major airports have led Congress and the OMB to release additional funds for recruiting and training additional traffic controllers.

Most employees that confront public agencies seek improved wages or fringe benefits. However, some focus on the ways services are administered. The air traffic controllers defended their demands for additional personnel in the name of improved air safety. Likewise, welfare workers and nurses have gone on strike, or taken equivalent actions, to obtain reduced caseloads, ostensibly to provide better services for their clients. Teachers have gone on strike to reduce the number of pupils in a classroom. During the fall of 1968, New York City teachers stayed out for 11 weeks over the decentralization of policy-making and over the school board's use of "nonprofessional" standards for assigning teachers. When government workers are numerically strong and are unified behind certain proposals, they can mount an awesome force in election campaigns. Organized public employees find a receptive hearing from elected executives and legislators. A strike of air traffic controllers in 1981 led to mass dismissals, an action that signaled the effort of the Reagan Administration to act tough with government unions.

Employees' Rights

Government employees are restive in the face of constraints imposed on their personal and political lives. The sources of these restrictions are laws passed by the U.S. Congress, as well as regulations and decisions on individual cases formerly made by the Civil Service Commission and now by the Office of Personnel Management, the Merit System Protection Board, and the Federal Labor Relations Authority. Especially important are the Hatch Acts of 1939 and 1940, which have restricted the rights of government employees in political campaigns. State and local employees are constrained by laws, ordinances, and rules enacted by their employers. Among the issues that cause difficulties for individual employees are:[17]

1. Restrictions against public criticism of the government, its policies, or the activities of one's own department.
2. Involvement in political campaigns as candidate, campaign manager, aide, or speaker including wearing a campaign button or posting a campaign advertisement on one's own car bumper, on one's home, or in one's front yard.
3. Pursuit of certain personal practices, such as those involving hairstyle, dress, the character of one's associates, or sexual preferences.
4. Affiliation with "radical" political organizations.
5. Required lie detector tests or other inquiries, with respect to behavior on the job or personal activities that may be considered suspect.

The courts are the final arbiters of employees' rights in these matters. On the one side are government claims of its rights, as employer, to carry out personnel policies that are consistent with the enactments of the legislature. On the other side are employee assertions of their own inalienable rights, especially those guaranteed in the First Amendment to the U.S. Constitution. That amendment speaks explicitly about freedom of speech and press, of peaceful assembly, and of the right to petition government for a redress of grievances.

No rights are absolute. Courts have granted some rights to governments to limit the behavior of employees in greater ways than are imposed on citizens generally. However, the courts have also upheld employees' claims against certain infringements. Among the tests that have been used by the courts are the following:

1. *How serious is the employees' role in a political campaign?* In general, federal employees are barred from running as candidates or taking a prominent role in a *partisan* campaign. They generally are allowed to wear campaign buttons, although perhaps not in a work setting where they meet the public, and they are allowed to put bumper stickers on their cars. Also, they can run for and take part in local, nonpartisan contests, such as for a school board.

---

[17]R. O'Neil, *The Rights of Government Employees: The Basic ACLU Guide to a Government Employee's Rights* (New York: Avon, 1978).

2. *How important is the person's job in the government?* In general, more restrictions will be allowed for an employee in a prominent position, who is well-known to the public and/or who takes part in policy-making duties.

3. *Is there a connection between the character of the restriction and the character of a person's job?* Officials wanting to restrict the private life of a government employee must show how the restriction adds to the capacity of the employee to perform the job.

4. *What is the character, tone, or style of the infringement?* Courts seem more inclined to accept disciplinary action against an errant employee if the action was blatant and prominent. For example, harsh, sarcastic, and repeated public criticism of one's department's policy might be accepted as cause for dismissal, whereas temperate comments would be accepted as within an employee's rights of free expression. Or an unpopular sexual lifestyle pursued in private might be protected, while the same lifestyle publicized in a provocative manner would be held as proper grounds for dismissal.

In general, the direction is toward more permissive behavior for government employees. This direction reflects the increased clout of employees' unions and the willingness of the legislative and executive branches to loosen prior controls. Undoubtedly, it is due in part to larger cultural movements in behalf of greater privacy for everyone and in behalf of more due process guarantees for those accused of wrongdoing.

In 1972, the U.S. District Court in the District of Columbia struck down key provisions of the Hatch Acts restrictions of political activities, because they were vague or overbroad when measured against guarantees of the First Amendment to the Constitution. In 1973, however, the Supreme Court reversed that decision. The Federal Campaign Act of 1974 loosened some of the controls on federal employees, but they still may not seek a partisan office. The employees of many state and local governments continue to face strict controls patterned after the original Hatch Acts.

SUMMARY

Government personnel are both an important resource for policy-makers and an object of policy in their own right. Prominent among the issues of political controversy that involve personnel are representative bureaucracy, affirmative action, and the rights of government employees to engage in collective bargaining and partisan political activity. *Who are government employees?* and *How to select and manage government personnel?* are questions that attract ideologies as well as concerned citizens and social scientists.

Government employees resemble the entire population or other groups of elites, depending on whether the focus is on the whole government work force or just those in managerial and professional positions. Prospects for change in the character of government employees seem best in times of growth, or in those sectors that experience growth amid a general picture of stability. When many positions need to be filled, an affirmative action program can operate with the least opposition from employees that feel threatened.

Administrators must be aware of the many tasks necessary in the personnel field: techniques of recruitment, job placement, promotion, discipline, salaries, and rewards. Public employees have also begun to take more responsibility for personnel matters. Recent changes in national, state, and local governments have moved in the direction of more explicit recognition of collective bargaining. At the same time, a new federal Senior Executive Service should provide an outlet for ambitious and talented individuals, who will give up some of the protections of the regular civil service for exciting opportunities to have a distinctive impact on government policymaking.

9

Program Evaluation

You evaluate government programs several times each day. You wake up to a radio commentator who praises or criticizes U.S. foreign policy toward the Soviet Union, Israel, or Japan. The morning newspaper offers more of the same. On the way to school you comment on the tardiness or the dirtiness of the municipal bus company. You have good or bad things to say about your courses at the public university. Some of your courses have lectures or discussions concerning government programs—about their benefits and costs and how both affect various people. And so it goes; in both casual and serious ways, government programs are never far from your thoughts and comments. Often you complain. Your taxes and the bureaucrats you deal with seem a bit more onerous than other people's. Sometimes you boast about the quality of government services. At other times you neither complain nor boast explicitly, but try only to describe public services. Here, your choices of adjectives require evaluation; if judgment is not explicit, it is likely to be implicit.

Several chapters of this book deal with the stuff of program evaluation. Chapter 3 reported the lack of congruity between the policies desired by the public and those in existence. Chapters 7 and 8, on budgeting and personnel, dealt with the mechanisms used to judge government programs and the amount of financial and human resources that should be allocated to them. Chapter 4 discussed the functions of the Office of Management and Budget, the Congressional Budget Office, and the General Accounting Office. Each of these offices is a program evaluator.

This chapter focuses on evaluation. While you may recognize themes repeated from earlier chapters, here they are treated integrally in order for you to understand how evaluation fits into the larger scheme of administration and to describe briefly the activities of professional evaluators. The key question is:

How to evaluate government programs?

However, such a formulation hides more than it reveals. Before dealing with the question of *How?* it is necessary to consider the questions

What to evaluate?
Why evaluate?

Evaluation is a vague term. Its meanings include measurement and judgment, according to quantitative and qualitative standards. The standards that may be employed range from the simple (such as height, weight, and market worth in dollar terms) to the profound (such as the moral values of justice and equity, and the aesthetic values of beautiful, provocative, sweet-smelling, and musical). The kinds of judgments that are appropriate depend on the kinds of programs at issue, on the purposes of evaluation, and on the natures of the evaluators. In other words, evaluation comes in many varieties.[1]

WHO EVALUATES?

There are many different kinds of evaluators. Some have no connection with government. They operate as concerned citizens, academicians, reformers, and journalists. They may wish to expose the wrongdoing they see in government. They may promote a particular point of view. Or they may seek spectacular revelations that will sell their books or earn a newspaper award. Some evaluators do basic research in political science and public administration while teaching or studying in professional schools of education, social work, and planning. Chapter 14 credits Ralph Nader and his associates for contributing to our understanding of administrative laws and rules and for alerting the public to problems of implementation.

---

[1]C. H. Weiss, *Evaluation Research: Methods for Assessing Program Effectiveness* (Englewood Cliffs, N.J.: Prentice-Hall, 1972); R. Dorfman, ed., *Measuring Benefits of Government Investments* (Washington, D.C.: Brookings Institution, 1965); E. A. Suchman, *Evaluative Research: Principles and Practice in Public Service and Social Action Programs* (New York: Russell Sage Foundation, 1967); J. S. Wholey et al., *Federal Evaluation Policy* (Washington, D.C.: Urban Institute, 1970).

A great deal of evaluation is done by government officials. Agency personnel evaluate their own programs under the requirements of Congress or the Office of Management and Budget. The OMB does its own evaluations as part of the annual budget review. The General Accounting Office evaluates the efficiency and effectiveness of agency programs alongside its more traditional concern with the integrity of financial records. A number of federal aid programs require state and local agencies to evaluate their activities.

With such diversity in official and unofficial evaluators, it is risky to generalize about their work. Some groups of unofficial evaluators tend toward sensationalism. Yet that trait is also prevalent in some of the work done by official evaluators. Some critics charge the General Accounting Office with puffing up discovered instances of inefficient or ineffective programs in order to look good in the eyes of its congressional patrons. Agency evaluations of its own programs are often temperate in tone, and may even purposefully be aimed at seeming routine, dull, and therefore undeserving of scrutiny. However, this style may be true only of the evaluations that turn up little in favorable information. Agencies are not innocent of exaggerating good news about themselves to try to look good to the public and to Congress.

Some evaluators are quasi-official. State and local governments contract with private firms to evaluate federally aided activities, and add the cost of the evaluation into the budget that is supported by Washington. The General Accounting Office also finds that its staff cannot handle the workload. The GAO contracts out work when it lacks the expertise to handle a sophisticated task or when its own staff is not able to handle a rush job.

The field of evaluation lends itself to many approaches. It is possible to find insightful and careful work among the evaluations that are contracted out to private firms. However, contracted work is also the source of much that is uninspired and uninformative. Contractors' independence can be a source of good research, since they are neither beholden to administrative superiors nor dependent on the nature of their findings. However, this independence can also produce shoddy and uninformed results. Federal grants requiring evaluations typically do not specify the quality of the evaluation or provide incentives for contractors to be creative or responsible.

KINDS OF PROGRAMS

Government programs range from the simple and routine (such as fixing the streets) to the complex and controversial (such as research and development on the frontiers of science and trying to regulate the trillion-dollars-plus American economy). The techniques suitable for evaluating one kind of program are not suitable for evaluating another. Indeed, some programs are so mundane that the value of a formal evaluation is questionable. The road maintenance program in a small town is known firsthand to each resident. Other programs are so experimental and so incomprehensible except to a small number of experts that the merits of a formal evaluation beyond that made by the experimenters are questionable.

In between the simple programs of a small community and the specialized experiments on the frontiers of science, a wide range of programs exists that invites formal evaluation. Three types of programs warrant our attention, because they imply different styles of evaluation.

Programs with Clearly Defined Results

Clearly defined programs are the simplest programs to evaluate. A minimum of quarreling arises about what these programs should be doing and about how their accomplishments should be measured. The work completed can be compared with the work projected during a certain period of time, as well as compared with the budget allocation. Figures for work done in relation to expenditures can be compared for different settings and for different periods of time. In this way, the activities of one community can be rated in relation to other communities with similar characteristics that are likely to affect a program (such as population size). A community can also measure its activities against its own past records.

The "dirty" jobs of local government give examples of simple kinds of evaluation. Programs of solid-waste collection can be measured by the tonnage collected and by the incidence of citizen complaints. A community's sewage plan can be measured by the gallons treated and by the quality of the water after treatment. The treatment of drinking water can be measured by the gallons processed and by several indices of water purity. A city's firefighting program can be measured by dollar figures of fire damage, by information about fire-related injuries or lives lost, and by the ratings used by fire insurance companies for local households and business firms.[2]

Some programs border on having clearly defined results. Often, there is some dispute about the nature of the results or the ways in which to measure them. If the local water board claims that its program includes conservation and aesthetics as well as water collection, delivery, and public recreation, then its managers may find program evaluation more difficult. A recreation program can be easily evaluated by referring to attendance figures and surveys of citizen views about facilities. But its managers may insist on the importance of wild reserves as part of the program's recreational output, clouding the evaluation, since the sites are closed to visitors.

---

[2]H. P. Hatry and D. M. Fisk, *Improving Productivity and Productivity Measurement in Local Government* (Washington, D.C.: National Commission on Productivity, 1971).

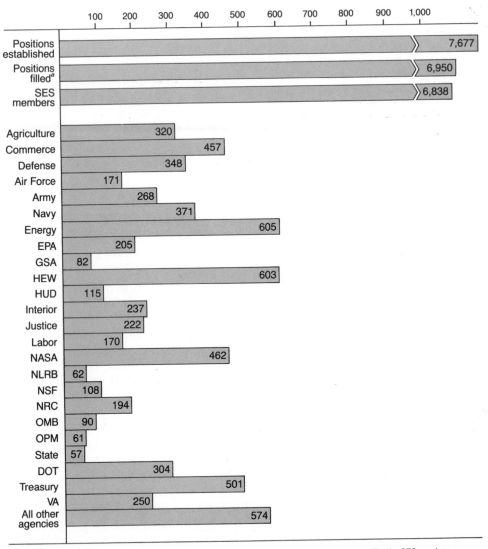

	100	200	300	400	500	600	700	800	900	1,000

Positions established — 7,677

Positions filled[a] — 6,950

SES members — 6,838

Agriculture — 320
Commerce — 457
Defense — 348
Air Force — 171
Army — 268
Navy — 371
Energy — 605
EPA — 205
GSA — 82
HEW — 603
HUD — 115
Interior — 237
Justice — 222
Labor — 170
NASA — 462
NLRB — 62
NSF — 108
NRC — 194
OMB — 90
OPM — 61
State — 57
DOT — 304
Treasury — 501
VA — 250
All other agencies — 574

[a]Due to pending conversions, temporary assignments, and nonconversions, not all of these positions are filled by SES members.

Figure 9-1 Senior Executive Service, Membership by Agency, July 1979. One way of evaluating the new Senior Executive Service is to count the number of eligible candidates who have enrolled. [SOURCE: U.S. Office of Personnel Management, *Civil Service Reform: A Report on the First Year* (Washington, D.C.: U.S. Government Printing Office, 1980).]

② Programs with Long-Term Goals

The manager of a closed recreation facility that is being saved for future generations raises the issue of nonevaluability. Such a claim is often heard in the social services. Programs such as education, counseling, mental health, services for the aged, income assistance, and support of the arts raise more issues than evaluators are prepared to assess in one sitting. While the superficial or short-term features of these programs can be assessed with routine measures (such as attendance figures for schools, clinics, and museums), their long-range benefits are crucial program features. It is a rare program manager or legislative audit bureau that can wait the many years required for such programs to produce their most important benefits.

The ways of coping with long-term problems of evaluation are not as definitive as those for dealing with sewage treatment or solid-waste collection. Professionals in the social services can render qualitative evaluations of professional activities after appropriate periods of observing the program, talking with clients, and examining program files. Certain aspects of "soft" programs are particularly subject to detailed scrutiny. Elementary and secondary education programs are judged according to annual achievement tests and dropout rates on the assumption that these features have something to do with long-term program effects. Mental health programs are evaluated by the incidence of clients who leave a program judged capable of independent living, perhaps measured by their lack of returning (recidivism) within a certain period of time.

③ Controversial Programs

Controversial cases are the toughest to evaluate. Skilled politicians and bureaucratic infighters can so harass evaluators or attack their findings as to render their evaluations nothing but the lettuce in a political sandwich. It is no easier to evaluate a program of school busing than it is to evaluate the United States' role in the Vietnam war. Such projects are imbued with ideology. Advocates are skilled at countering each attempt at evaluation with a contrary set of measurements and conclusions. The argument over busing raises the questions of whether to measure the impact on blacks *or* whites, to measure changes in student achievement *or* in student attitudes. Lurking in the wings are such "principles" as neighborhood schools and freedom of choice, which do not accommodate measurement. Few people can evaluate busing programs without being influenced by preconceived attitudes about racial integration or local control of education.

Seemingly mundane programs also raise hot issues that deter evaluation. As noted in a previous chapter, local hospitals compete furiously over whether they are evaluated as fit to purchase new equipment or establish

It is possible to evaluate complex activities, such as the quality of college teaching. If the activity to be evaluated is composed of several dimensions, each of them can be surveyed. There can also be an overall survey of general performance.

BOX 9-1   Evaluating a College Course

Each of the following questions is meant to be answered with a five-point scale, ranging from a very positive to a very negative score.

1. About what proportion of this professor's lectures were clear and well prepared?
2. What proportion of this professor's lectures were relevant to learning the subject matter?
3. What proportion of this professor's lectures have you attended this semester?
4. All in all, in comparison with other professors you have had, how do you rate this professor's lecturing ability?
5. How useful were the assigned readings?
6. How well did the readings prepare you for examinations taken thus far?
7. Were the objectives of this course clearly laid out and explained early in the course?
8. Taking into consideration the previous question, how well did the lectures and readings meet the objectives defined for the course?
9. Taking into account the size of this class, how willing was your professor to consult with you on an individual basis?
10. How do you rank the effectiveness of these contacts?
11. What was the work load for this course in relation to other courses of equal credit (much heavier to much lighter)?
12. For preparation and ability, the level of difficulty of this course was (very difficult to very elementary)?
13. How do you rate the grading in this course in comparison to other similar courses?
14. Do you feel the grading was fair in the sense of careful and thoughtful, neither arbitrary nor capricious?
15. Did this course make you think? Did it cause you to challenge and think through your beliefs and assumptions? Were you sometimes provoked and challenged to the point where you had to reformulate your ideas or wanted to present a counterargument to the lectures or readings? In short, was this a learning experience?
16. Would you recommend this course to a friend?
17. Would you recommend this professor to a friend?
18. Taking into consideration your own responses and the opportunity it has given you to review and evaluate the various elements of this course and your reactions to them, how do you rank the overall performance of the professor?

SOURCE: From a survey used routinely by students at the University of Wisconsin, Madison.

new services. Because of cost-containment programs designed to minimize excess capacity, local hospitals may arrange deals among themselves: one may develop the capacity for open-heart surgery, while the other pursues intensive care for premature babies. Formal evaluations may have to justify these outcomes. However, the details of formal evaluations may bend to the agreements already worked out between the hospitals.

WHY EVALUATE?

Motivation plays an important role in evaluation. For programs affected by "soft" goals or by controversy, evaluation is at least as much an art as it is a science. Even the evaluations that seem heavily loaded with objectivity require judgments about appropriate measurements. However, scientists as well as artists have their price, with the results of evaluation being tilted accordingly.

The motives behind an evaluation can be benign or perverse. They can be supportive or destructive with respect to a program or its agency. Most evaluations are routine procedures undertaken with no reason more complicated than a requirement handed down by a federal granting agency or the Office of Management and Budget. However, the controversies in public administration are many. Evaluations are one of many tools that politicians and bureaucrats use to help their friends and hurt their enemies.

Traditionally, members of congressional committees enjoy lobbing "soft balls" to administrators of favored programs that are being evaluated. Soft balls are easy questions designed to elicit responses that put a program in a good light. Such questions may even be supplied in advance by administrators who enjoy a good relationship with the committee member who asks them. Program antagonists get their ammunition from other sources: interest groups, constituents, or disaffected agency administrators who have a bone to pick with a program as it is currently operated. Private firms that do evaluations under contract acquire reputations for the character of their work. In selecting a contractor, officers can often predict the kind of evaluation that will be received.

At times, the process of evaluation becomes a game of competing efforts guaranteed to produce a mélange of findings sufficient both to please and to confound program administrators, executive and legislative branch officers, and the general public. Such is the case with the investigations into the spring 1979 accident and shutdown of the nuclear plant at Three-Mile Island, Pennsylvania. At one time, 14 separate inquiries were under way, arranged by separate committees of Congress, the U.S. Nuclear Regulatory Commission, and Pennsylvania agencies. Each had its professional staff or its contracted evaluators. There will be a grand war of evaluation among the experts, with the result that few of the rest of us will be better able to judge the event than we did by simply referring to our own predilections.

HOW TO EVALUATE?

The obvious answer to the question of *How to evaluate?* is *It depends on who you are, what you are evaluating, and why you are evaluating it.* Each important field of service has its own traditions, details, and pitfalls that must be addressed in specialized courses, literature, and practical experience. This discussion offers only general guidelines and a sampling of tricky issues.

Determining Program Goals

The simple model of evaluation derives from the model of rational policy-making (which guides us again in Chapter 10). The rational model offers a recipe for evaluation in an ideal world.[3]

1. Find out the program's goals.
2. Translate the goals into measurable indicators of goal achievement.
3. Collect data on the indicators for those who participated in the program and for an equivalent control group who did not.
4. Compare the data on participants and controls with the goal criteria.

Chapter 10 describes the problems of conceptualization, information, and political wrangling that make rational policy-making difficult to attain in the real world. At this point, you can probably already see the problems that get in the way of an ideal evaluation: There are too many goals that *may* be evaluated, and our capacity to define and measure any, much less all, of them is severely limited. Political feasibility imposes great constraints on the techniques of evaluation and the use of results.

The first task of evaluators is to select goals that can—more or less—be subject to evaluation. Here the art of evaluation and political common sense both come into play. Evaluators must discern which goals are appropriate to evaluate. Some goals they can select from are:

1. Goals that are important, as determined by the money or program personnel devoted to certain aspects of a program, the number of clients affected, the expressed interest of the media or key politicians, and the impact of certain goals on other important program components.
2. Goals that are malleable, that is, subject to some control in the event that evaluation shows them in need of change. For example, it is better to evaluate a program component that is wholly within the

---

[3]Weiss, op. cit., Chapter 3.

jurisdiction of one government, than divided between various government authorities, such as states or localities.

3. Goals that fit the existing background of the evaluator. It is better to examine something you know at least a little about than to examine areas where you have to begin learning from scratch.

4. Goals that are relatively free from sharp controversy. Evaluators can save a lot of energy by not devoting themselves to activities that prove unfeasible politically—unless evaluators *want* to engage in polemic as well as analysis.

5. Goals that are not so well known as to make another evaluation redundant.

6. Goals that can be achieved in the short or medium term, as opposed to long-term goals that preclude evaluation within a reasonable time frame.[4]

7. Goals for which achievement is measurable.

Making Program Models

A model of program activities can aid an evaluator in deciding which features are worth examining and how they fit into the larger picture of program components. Two kinds of models can prove helpful. One is a *descriptive model* or *flow chart* of the various program components, showing how each part feeds into the other parts. An example appears in Figure 9-2. With such a device, an evaluator can choose subordinate goals that are important by virtue of their strategic character—their importance as contributors to other goals. In Figure 9-2, an evaluator might focus on the financial aspect of a program in the belief that financial success or failure will have an impact on such other activities as staff salaries, the quality of teachers, plant value, teacher–pupil ratio, and, ultimately, the quality of education.

A second kind of model is more sophisticated in that it shows the *weights* of various program features according to how they contribute to goal accomplishment. Such a model requires extensive prior analysis, so that statistical relationships can be determined between measurements of each component in the model. Such a model can have great value, but it depends on the quality of the prior analysis. The model is only as good as the theory that posits likely relationships and the measurements employed for each component of the model. An example appears in Figure 9-3, which shows that favorable teacher–pupil ratios (small classes) are more strongly related

---

[4]A. Meltsner, *Policy Analysis in the Bureaucracy* (Berkeley: University of California Press, 1976).

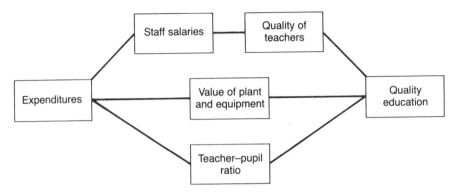

Figure 9-2 Policy Components of Quality Education.

to measures of program success than are other likely influences (quality of teachers, salaries, or total expenditures). Logic would lead us to measure teacher–pupil ratios in various schools, and to encourage programs that have smaller class sizes.

Measuring Accomplishment

The measurement of accomplishment can be as tricky as deciding which program items to assess. Even assuming that the most ephemeral goals are avoided as being outside the scope of evaluation, serious problems may remain. Making ideal evaluations—such as measuring changes in the traits of clients or communities as a result of program experiences—may be too costly. It may be necessary to measure perceived changes in place of objective changes. Then the question is *Whose perception?* For some programs that are targeted at the public, it may be easy and inexpensive to survey program clients. However, a survey of clients leaves out those citizens who do not participate. Surveying library patrons does not help to explain why many people do *not* use the library. A survey of welfare recipients could turn up much useful information about existing counseling activities, but less about outreach efforts that fail to inform prospective clients about the program. Programs generate a great deal of data as part of their operations. Schools produce endless reports about pupil attendance and test scores. Clinics gush forth information about patient visits, medications, and other therapies. Police departments record the mileage traveled by each official vehicle and the number of calls phoned in by the public. The questions to be asked about such data are:

Can they be assembled from the agency files at reasonable cost?
Are they worth it?

An evaluator requires a good reservoir of common sense, as well as some willingness to dive into agency files, to see which of its existing records can be used to judge the value of its programs.

In selecting appropriate measurements, an evaluator should remember the value of comparison. Summarizing an agency's activities during a single period will not be very informative. The data selected should enable comparison of the target agency with others having similar functions or with the agency's own past. The data might also suggest how the agency could improve its programs. One approach is to focus on groups of clients likely to be receiving different benefits. Comparing clients according to age, sex, occupation, and place of residence might reflect the relative successes of various program aspects. Likewise, dividing the agency's records according to field offices or according to staff members might reveal where the evaluator can take a closer look at operations. A well-known study of educational achievement analyzed the achievements experienced by teachers with different levels of professional training, and found that this trait bore no significant statistical relationship with student achievement. However, the same study did find a relationship between class size and level of student achievement.[5] See Figure 9-3.

The Hawthorne Effect

Evaluations of social services have to be aware of the "Hawthorne effect." Research done years ago in the Hawthorne plant of the Western Electric Company showed that workers being observed were induced by the observation to behave in special ways. Sometimes employees tended to work a bit harder than usual while under observation. Likewise, clients of social services may be more likely to express satisfaction with a program when they know they are being observed.

An evaluator can cope with the Hawthorne effect by comparing a sample group of program clients with a control group that is assessed in a similar way, but that is not subject to the program's treatment. Ideally, the control group resembles the sample group in every way except experience with the program that is the subject of evaluation. A pure experiment would randomly assign equivalent subjects to the project being evaluated or to the control group, and then compare the results of the project being tested. Subjects in the control group might be given a placebo, or an indication of being the subjects of research without actually being given the experiences of the program's group. Under these conditions, it should be possible to

---

[5] J. S. Coleman, *Equality of Educational Opportunity* (Washington, D.C.: U.S. Government Printing Office, 1966).

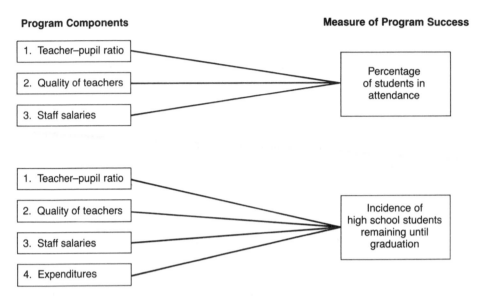

Program Components   **Measure of Program Success**

Figure 9-3 Policy Components of Quality Education, Ranked According to Scores in Statistical Analysis. [SOURCE: Ira Sharkansky, "Environment, Policy, Output and Impact: Problems of Theory and Method in the Analysis of Public Policy," in Ira Sharkansky, ed., *Policy Analysis in Political Science* (Chicago: Markham, 1970), pp. 68–75, with some rewording of concepts.]

determine what difference it made for the sample group to experience the program. In practice, however, ideal control conditions seldom appear. By means of "quasi-experimental" techniques, the evaluator can work with the populations that are really available. The evaluator employs statistical tests to measure the likelihood that a person's experience of a program is associated with traits that the program is supposed to produce. To the extent that variable x (the program goal being measured) shows high or low values along with variable y (the experience of the program being evaluated), an evaluator can conclude that the program has—or fails to have—its expected results.

Sometimes a simple graphic presentation can demonstrate that an apparent effect is not, in fact, attributable to a program. Figure 9-4 shows a hypothetical increase in a value that was thought to be associated with a program, which, when plotted over time, appears to be only a continuation of ongoing development likely to be associated with causes other than the program. In more complex cases, it may be possible to employ sophisticated statistical procedures that can test whether subjects' traits are related independently to a program's experience or are more directly related to such considerations as economic background or social conditions.

The moral and legal problems of dealing with human subjects make themselves felt in evaluating social services. It may not be desirable or fea-

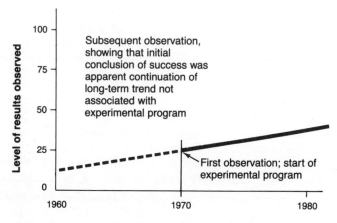

Figure 9-4   The Value of Long-Term Analysis.

sible to deprive certain subjects of a recognized treatment in order to assess their response to certain stimuli. The U.S. Department of Health and Human Services monitors research in the social and biological sciences to make sure that procedures would not subject persons to undue physical or emotional stresses.

Evaluating a Shifting Target

As if there were not enough problems for evaluators amid ambiguous program goals and elusive measurements, frequently there is the additional problem of program drift.[6] Public agencies are not laboratory settings under the evaluator's control. Individuals move in and out of sample and control groups. Staff persons change. Agency heads or members of the executive and legislative branches want instant evaluation conclusions in order to meet their own timetables. They may settle for "preliminary" findings. Insofar as these findings are the ones that figure in their determinations, however, they can be far more important than later conclusions that languish in the files. When data collection and analysis are not complete, evaluators may be even more vulnerable to requests that an interim report be shaded to please agency management or an executive or legislative control body.

FOLLOWING UP ON AN EVALUATION

Evaluators can take a lesson from Chapter 11 on program implementation. Policy-makers are urged to anticipate problems of implementation and to build a staff with the continuing responsibility of monitoring progress and

---

[6]Weiss, op. cit., Chapter 5.

problems. Evaluators who want to have an impact on program development should be sensitive to the followthrough phase of analysis. To enhance their usefulness, they might consider the following possibilities. Like other checkpoints, they offer general advice and are unlikely to be useful in their simplest terms.

1. Formulate the evaluation and its reports with an eye toward having an impact on policy. If possible, use comparisons between the current program of the target agency and programs within officials' reference groups: similar agencies of other jurisdictions or past activities of the target agency; or divide the data into subgroups that fit officials' frames of reference (by different field offices or according to clients' age, sex, or occupation).

2. Be sensitive to the constraints of political feasibility. This need not be a code word for kowtowing to agency managers or key members of the executive and legislative branches. The range of political feasibility can be wide. The tests of *un*feasible options are not those that provoke *some* opposition. Such timidity has no place in an evaluator. An evaluator with a sense of what is unfeasible might avoid testing program goals that are known to arouse intense feelings—pro or con—among individuals or groups with recognized power. Findings that might be unpopular can be brought within the feasible range. The timing of a report can put the stress on gradual change as opposed to a frontal assault on an entrenched interest. Language that is circumspect could begin the spread of a message that would not survive a flamboyant press release.

3. Time the release of findings with an eye toward the policy-making calendar. Schedules in the budget process are fixed far in advance and provide opportunities for evaluations to be useful. Major program reauthorizations occur less frequently, but can be anticipated if a program is limited by a fixed date of expiration or if pressure is building for legislative amendments. Budget staffs, the department head, the Office of Management and Budget, and congressional staffs can offer a warm reception to a program evaluation, but only if it comes at a time to affect staff thinking about an upcoming decision. Material that is too early or too late can get lost in the files or amid the noise just before a key decision is made. We know little about why certain information affects decisions, while other information has little influence. One of the explanations that is most persuasive, however, is good timing.

4. Offer suggestions. Explain the implications for reform that lie in the findings about current programs. The evaluator may be more aware of existing problems and the potential for change than anyone else in the program's orbit. Again, there is a need for sensitivity. Suggestions for incremental change will more often be acceptable than a proposal for a radical overhaul. As we have seen in other chapters, however, significant change can occur in the clothing of incrementalism. If a major budget shift is not

in the cards, it may be time for a change in key personnel. Or a change in the language of program statutes or administrative rules may offer some prospects where other resource lines seem fixed. It is to be hoped that the skills of judgment that help evaluators to get their project to the stage of making a report will not be abandoned at the point of offering suggestions.

SUMMARY

Doing program evaluation is like speaking prose. We do it all the time, but seldom realize it. This chapter deals with formal evaluations, mostly done by the professionals who work for government.

To understand the problems in evaluation, it is helpful to reflect on all the previous chapters of this book. The many perspectives and policy preferences mean that programs seek to serve diverse interests and have many components. Especially resistant to evaluation are "soft" social services with goals that are not clearly specified and programs that are permeated with controversy.

The motives of evaluators also range across a broad scale: from mechanistic (it's a job) to benign (to help judge programs fairly), to perverse (to make programs appear good or bad, depending on predispositions). This range of motives makes all evaluations suspect. Yet, an evaluator can improve a program's product. Care can be taken when choosing which aspects of a program should be evaluated. Goals should be important, somewhat malleable, fairly noncontroversial, testable, and familiar to the evaluator. Comparative testing can be done, showing differences between a sample and a control group, between the program being evaluated and those of other jurisdictions, or between the same program at different points of time. Administrators can thereby be shown how well an agency is performing compared to similar agencies or compared to their agency's earlier performance.

Evaluators can maximize their usefulness by recognizing the problems they are likely to encounter. They can plan their evaluations with an eye to having an impact on policy-makers. They can be sensitive to appropriate standards of political feasibility. They can make their reports timely according to the schedules of policy-makers. And they can offer concrete suggestions for program improvements.

PART IV

Making and Implementing Policies

As noted in Chapter 1, policies are the important things that government makes. Because they are important, the making of policies attracts the attention of many people. Besides elected officials and high-ranking administrators with formal roles in policy-making, there are likely to be observers and participants from various interested parties. How should policies be made? is a question that has long concerned philosophers and reformers. How are policies made? is a question for academics in the fields of political science and public administration, and it is the principal question of Chapter 10.

Policies made are not necessarily policies delivered. Chapter 11 takes on the issue of implementation or policy execution. It describes some of the conditions that frustrate policy-makers' aspirations, and suggests a number of checkpoints to help policy-makers improve the quality of program implementation.

10

Policy-Making

Policy-makers cannot make whatever decisions suit their fancies. To understand their decisions is not simply to understand their personal predilections. Previous chapters have described influences that come to them from citizens, elected officials, and employees of government agencies. Chapter 13 details the intergovernmental character of domestic policy-making in the United States. For example, a person who designs a program of U.S. aid to elementary and secondary education must ponder the likely responses of 50 state departments of education and more than 15,000 school districts.

A *policy-maker* in the national arena may be the President or one of the presidential staff aides; an elected member of the House of Representatives or the Senate, or one of the staff aides; a manager or an employee of a government agency; a judge; or a private citizen who works as a government consultant or who submits a proposal to those in official positions. Recalling the definition of public policy from Chapter 1, policy-makers are those people who shape "the important things that government makes." People make policies by writing laws (that may be enacted by the legislature) and regulations (that may be proclaimed by the Chief Executive) that affect the use of substantial resources or the interests of many people. Courts make policies by deciding unusual cases that serve as precedents for similar cases in the future. Private citizens also contribute to policy-making by enunciating positions that are followed by administrators in implementing laws and regulations.

Policy-makers are subject to numerous influences, which include:

1. Demands, resources, and political support from individual citizens, political parties, and interest groups.

2. Demands, resources, and political support from the legislative, executive, and judicial branches of government.

3. Demands, resources, and political support from the administrative units involved in an activity.

4. Demands, resources, and political support from individuals and institutions in other governments, through intergovernmental relations.

5. The social backgrounds, skills, and values of policy-makers themselves.

6. The structures, procedures, and precedents of policy-making bodies.

The sheer number and variety of influences complicate the task of policy-makers. No simple procedure for making decisions can accommodate the factors that must be taken into consideration. In an effort to clarify how policy is actually made amid this complexity, we first describe a purely rational model of policy-making that urges policy-makers to take everything into consideration. Then we consider several features that frustrate this kind of rationalism. Finally, we discuss some procedures that have evolved to ease making policy decisions. The actual methods of policy-making do not meet the standards of the purely rational model. Indeed, actual methods of making policy are attractive partly because they permit policy-makers to ignore all but certain limited sets of factors, which thus make their task simpler than if they followed the procedures of the rational model.

The participants in policy-making are many and their perspectives are broad. While most of the examples in this chapter come from the activities of administrators, our primary concern is not with the *who* of policy-making. The key question is:

How is policy made?

The focus is on the general problems of defining policy goals and the planning of program details amid conflicting influences.

A MODEL OF RATIONAL POLICY-MAKING

Rationality is a value that has wide respect in our culture. Public administrators and policy-makers like to be as rational as the rest of us. Certainly, they do not admit to making decisions irrationally or without taking into consideration all the important issues. However, the likelihood of making a completely rational decision is remote. It is unfair, however, to accuse policy-makers of making irrational decisions. This term implies that choices are made in an undisciplined fashion, without paying heed to many important considerations. Policy-making is neither completely rational nor completely irrational. While complete rationality is an unattainable goal in all but the most simple kinds of problems, policy decisions are usually made with discipline, after assessing the issues at hand.[1]

What is this purely rational and idealistic model? According to one common formulation, a rational policy-maker would:

1. Identify the problem.
2. Clarify goals, and then rank them according to their importance.
3. List all the possible means or policies for achieving each goal.
4. Assess all the costs and benefits that would seem to accrue from each alternative policy.
5. Select the package of goals and associated policies that would bring the greatest relative benefits and the least relative disadvantages.[2]

Rational policy-makers would take into consideration all information pertaining to a problem and would make a decision on the facts alone. First they would decide what was wrong, then what the best course of action would be to right the situation. Rationality assumes that vast resources can be used to gather intelligence about the problem and about the programs that are proposed. It also assumes that personnel will make decisions on the basis of information that is systematically collected; in other words, that they are not already committed to a particular set of goals or policies. Rationality conflicts with politics. Political demands require that certain goals and policies be favored in policy deliberations and that other goals and policies be avoided.

PROBLEMS WITH THE RATIONAL MODEL

Five major features of public policy-making block the fulfillment of the rational model. They are:

1. Defining the problems, then formulating goals and policies based on a multitude of considerations, including symptoms of problems, political expediency, and the demands of interested parties.
2. Barriers to collecting adequate information about the variety of politically acceptable goals and policies.

---

[1] H. Simon, *Administrative Behavior: A Study of Decision-Making Processes in Administrative Organizations*, 3d ed. (New York: Free Press, 1976).

[2] C. E. Lindblom, *The Policy-Making Process* (Englewood Cliffs, N.J.: Prentice-Hall, 1968), p. 13.

3. Structural difficulties within administrative units, involving their relations with legislative and executive branches of government.

4. The personal needs, commitments, inhibitions, and inadequacies of policy-makers, which interfere in their assessment of goals and policies that are acceptable.

5. The deviant behavior of individual administrators and other policy-makers.

These five items are not entirely separable; each includes some features that are also apparent in the others. However, each has been the subject of separate inquiries and imposes its own set of limitations on decision-makers.

Defining Problems, Goals, and Policies

A variety of problems can be selected as the target of policy-making, but commitments among policy-makers preclude a thorough assessment of each possible problem. Frequently, the full range of possibilities is so great that even the task of defining the problem—Step 1 in the sequence of rational policy-making—is obscured. Presumably, a problem is signaled by difficulties that are perceived. However, these difficulties may not translate themselves directly into a definable problem. One stumbling block can occur when officials try to conceptualize a problem based solely on the symptoms they see.

Why do many taxpayers fail to report the income they receive from savings interest and stock dividends?

Should this failure be viewed as willful evasion or blamed on tax forms that are too complicated?

What accounts for increased unemployment?

How does one account for survey results showing increased levels of political alienation?

Will specific goals and policies solve these problems? Or are they merely symptoms of deeper issues that are themselves the problems to be treated?

If underlying problems exist, what are they?

Does one common problem generate each of these symptoms?

If a common problem can be pointed to, the way in which it is defined can have important implications: Which agencies will deal with the problem? How will they define the goals and policies that treat the problem?

Without agreement on problems that lie beneath perceived difficulties, it is simply not feasible to select adequate goals and policies with which to attack them. Defining a problem is at best a difficult and ambiguous process. The definition of a problem is arrived at through a process of observation, assessment, and abstraction from reality. Only in theory is it possible to disengage from prior experiences and current commitments. Thus, even the process of determining the problem is less than rational.

A problem may exist for a long time in a dormant state without becoming an issue of public policy. Environmental pollution is often objectively worse in localities where it has failed to become an issue. Cynthia Enloe has described some of the elements that are needed to make a problem like pollution into an issue that policy-makers must face:[3]

1. Officeholders must be sensitive to an issue and also possess the legal authority and political clout to make their views count.
2. The mass media, business groups, labor unions, or other extragovernmental parties must be capable of developing public interest in the topic.
3. Economic and social settings must make it feasible to pursue the problem at a certain time. Environmental pollution is not likely to appear as a problem, for example, where factory smoke is considered a welcome sign of economic progress.

Once a problem is recognized and defined as such, additional difficulties involve defining appropriate goals and policies. They do not flow naturally from a sense of the problem. For example, a problem such as inadequate higher education might be met with a package of goals and policies that envisions changes in teaching techniques, the development of new curricula (such as courses on environmental quality), more financial aid for students, greater student freedom from university controls, a renewed emphasis on the merits of a liberal education, and the further refinement of specialization among institutions of higher education. When goals are formulated, agency personnel and other policy-makers—legislators, chief executives, and interest groups—receive signals about the likely course of agency activity. Because of the variety of people who have something at stake in an agency's activities, the choice of goals is not likely to produce a uniform reception. Disagreements will arise between agency members and outsiders who are affected by agency decisions. In fact, long before an agency chooses a course of action, it is likely to be beset with demands by parties interested in policy result.

Limits on Information

Information is essential for good policy-making. To identify problems and ponder options, policy-makers consult many sources:

---

[3]C. H. Enloe, *The Politics of Pollution in a Comparative Perspective: Ecology and Power in Four Nations* (New York: Longman, 1975), especially Chapters 1 and 2.

1. Statistics about economic and social traits.
2. Surveys of public opinion.
3. Complaints by agency clients.
4. Reports from administrators who work with clients and notice difficulties in current policies.
5. Stories or commentaries in the media.
6. Reports on programs adopted in other countries that detail new procedures and their results.

The more limited the information, the less rational it is possible for a policy to be. Avoiding certain information is sometimes intentional, such as when an agency restricts its discussion to topics that are politically acceptable. A second limitation is the sheer working time that can be devoted to analyzing a situation and assessing the advantages and disadvantages associated with alternative sets of goals and policies. Politicians and citizen activists demand fast action, and have a limited tolerance for lengthy deliberations. A third limitation is the ineradicable ignorance that may remain about a problem, even after an organization has invested a great deal of its members' time and has risked offending individuals by looking into areas that are politically sensitive. This ignorance often stems from inadequate techniques for gathering or evaluating information. Consequently, officials extrapolate a narrower range of information in order to make inferences about the future.

These inferences are called predictions, anticipations, or guesses, and require a leap beyond the edge of one's information. Some inferences are based on the assumption that past trends will continue. Inferences of this kind are not too risky if the trends being considered are simple ones that have shown past consistency in repeating themselves from one period of time to the next. On other occasions, however, extrapolations are complicated by the nature of the assumptions that must be made. Some of the most complicated inferences about the future are those that depend on assessments of both the intentions of individuals or organizations and the likelihood of changes in these intentions.[4]

When does a policy-maker stop gathering information? Perhaps never! Some units continue to gather and assess information, but they do not delay action indefinitely in the hope of obtaining complete information or a finished assessment. They proceed with activity, but try to hold open the possibility of altering their actions if new information warrants it.[5]

Information gathering and assessment may go into abeyance when a program actually reaches the operational stage. At this point, an agency

---

[4] Simon, op. cit., Chapter 5.

[5] A. Downs, *Inside Bureaucracy* (Boston: Little, Brown, 1967), p. 3.

Policy-makers feel political pressures to purchase food in the United States for use by American troops in Japan. American farm groups support such "buy American" programs. Japan, for its part, wants American troops to buy the produce of Japanese farmers. In considering the costs and benefits of these postures, let's hope that policy-makers also take into account the cost of moving the fruit from the United States to Japan.

BOX 10-1   Comparing Apples and Apples

The Pentagon has been paying $2 million to $3 million annually to comply with a Japanese ban on the import of 22 fruits and vegetables consumed by U.S. troops and their dependents stationed in Japan, according to the House Appropriations Committee in its report on the Defense Department appropriations bill.

According to the committee, the Japanese price per pound of several of these items was several times the U.S. price in fiscal 1978:

	Price in Japan	Price in U.S.
Apples	74¢	28¢
Pears	79¢	22¢
Carrots	41¢	15¢
Potatoes	29¢	6¢
Tomatoes	$1.00	42¢
Cabbage	74¢	11¢

"The committee believes that the presence of a large number of U.S. troops in Japan and its possessions is for the purpose of mutual defense of the United States and our Japanese ally and is not for the purpose of providing increased profits to the Japanese fresh fruits and vegetable industry," the committee complained.

So the panel reduced the appropriation by $2 million and added a ban on the purchase for U.S. military personnel of any Japanese produce that could be imported more cheaply from the United States.

SOURCE: *Congressional Quarterly,* September 29, 1979.

commits itself to a course of action. The commitments may become increasingly strong as persons inside and outside the organization get used to the established practice. Although new information can alter procedures, established procedures may acquire a life force of their own as they become ingrained in the expectations of officials and clients. Different agencies cut off their active research procedures at different times. Some have greater staff resources that can be devoted to information gathering; some may have greater tolerance for ambiguous or unresolved questions of policy; and some may experience greater conflicts, stimulating a prolonged search for policies that will appear bland to all protagonists.[6]

Government Structure

Several features in the structure of government hinder rational policy-making. Policy-makers may receive different messages from the legislative and executive branches, whose competition with each other reflects the separation of powers. And procedures within administrative units may hinder innovation.

Administrators may avoid making decisions about problems, goals, or policies, because they know powerful legislators or chief executives would oppose their action. Sometimes decisions appear vague or ambiguous to avoid opposition. Elected officials may support an administrator's program, even though they would reject certain results the program might produce. If the anticipated results are phrased unclearly, a program may receive support from elected officials whose own long-run goals *are likely* to be achieved, as well as from those who *can only hope* that their own goals will be achieved.

Several procedures endemic to administrative agencies also complicate policy-making. Some subordinates choose to follow their own policy inclinations. The heads of many public agencies cannot readily discipline a subordinate who does not accept the instructions necessitated by a rational choice among alternatives. Civil service sanction procedures are lengthy, and threaten to disrupt morale within an agency when invoked against an employee. New civil service procedures offer some protection to "whistle blowers" (employees who report wrongdoing within their agencies). Many administrators feel that it costs more in heartache to attempt dismissal proceedings than it would be worth to maintain greater efficiency. Administrators who wish to deviate from policy can shop around for legislators who

---

[6]A. L. Schiff, "Innovation and Administrative Decision-Making: A Study of the Conservation of Land Resources," *Administrative Science Quarterly*, 11 (June 1966): 1–32.

will support their positions or can seek public support through the media or interest groups. Legislators may decide to support independent-minded administrators with the intention of embarrassing an agency head or a chief executive who is a member of the opposite party or has an opposing viewpoint.[7]

Within administrative units, some procedures have a life force of their own and can resist changes in policy that might otherwise be dictated by a rational assessment of problems, goals, and policies. These procedures may be designed to inhibit hasty decisions or to keep individuals from making off with public resources. While such procedures are generally considered to be essential, they often limit policy-making flexibility. When this flexibility is lost, the procedures lose their quality of being safeguards, and become simply red tape.[8]

Personal Interests

An organization is more than the simple sum of its parts. A well-ordered group can accomplish more than if each of its members pursues his or her efforts alone. When it comes to the selection of goals and the development of policies, however, the organization must face the individuality of its members. Each person has different values and attitudes, which are the basis for different perceptions of the organization and its environment. Personal proclivities can create preferences about an organization's goals and policies.[9] The perceptions and preferences of individuals may gather strength through informal alliances among like-minded persons.

The goals of individuals and their alliances may reflect professional training or personal predilections. Professional training provides norms as well as skills; these norms affect the professional's view of problems as well as the goals adopted to confront them. Government administrators represent a wide range of professions—law, medicine, engineering, and various social and natural sciences. Different schools of thought have developed within each profession. Disputes occur between members of the same profession just as much as they do between the members of different professions. Some disputes reflect personality conflicts. Antagonisms developed in one

---

[7]L. C. Gawthrop, *Bureaucratic Behavior in the Executive Branch: An Analysis of Organizational Change* (New York: Free Press, 1969).

[8]V. A. Thompson, *Modern Organization: A General Theory* (New York: Knopf, 1964), especially Chapter 5. See also H. Kaufman, *Red Tape: Its Origins, Uses, and Abuses* (Washington, D.C.: Brookings Institution, 1977).

[9]This discussion relies on R. M. Cyert and J. G. March, *A Behavioral Theory of the Firm* (Englewood Cliffs, N.J.: Prentice-Hall, 1963), Chapter 3.

context may carry over to other encounters and may generate severe arguments about goals or policies.

Because of diverse personal and professional interests, the process of goal and policy formulation involves continuing learning and bargaining. There is no once-and-for-all decision that reflects a rational assessment of problems, goals, policies, and what benefits and costs are associated with each possible option. As changes occur, it is necessary for participants to learn about the implications of these changes for the current set of goals or policies, and perhaps to renegotiate. Coalitions in an organization form between members of similar professional and personal orientation. Coalitions are not always homogeneous or continuous. Certain coalitions may be viable only for a segment of the agency's activities. Changes in demands and resources may change conditions inside an organization. Also, personnel changes occur, due to retirement, resignation, and new recruitment. Certain coalitions may grow; others may disintegrate, their members redistributing themselves to a new set of coalitions.

The bargaining necessary in policy-making puts a premium on some skills not considered in the rational model. These skills include the capacity to express oneself clearly and the ability to resist the blandishments of antagonists. Points of view do not usually carry their own weight, but require a combination of tact, assertiveness, humor, and wisdom to move ideas into action.

Deviant Behavior

Certain individuals cannot relate to others in ways that are required to make rational decisions. Each of the preceding sections deals with behavior that is nonrational according to the severe standards of the rational model. The focus here is on individuals whose behavior is unreasonable in that it precludes cooperative communications. This kind of behavior prevents organizations from making decisions in ways that approach the standards of the rational model.

The deviant behavior mentioned here is not found equally in all settings. Undoubtedly, some organizations are free of most deviant behavior, while others have more than their share. Deviant actions may themselves reflect organizational stress, and the stress generated by certain deviancies may produce even more stress. Two stresses that are typically found in an organizational setting are insecurity and an inability to accept, either as superiors or subordinates, the status and power that adhere to hierarchical positions. Some deviant behavior reflects individual weaknesses for the temptations of alcohol, drugs, sex, or easy profit.

Chapter 2 described a deviance that derives from normal organizational behavior. The "bureaupath" is a bureaucrat who is pushed to pathological extremes.[10] The normal behavior of superiors toward subordinates may be formal, with a concern for separating professional judgments from personal feelings. Bureaupathic behavior, in contrast, involves an excessive and rigid attachment to formal procedures. Such behavior creates distrust among members of the organization and threatens the kind of rapport necessary for engaging in reasonable discussion. Bureaupathic attitudes hinder the process of redefining goals and reassessing policies, a process that is demanded by the rational model.[11]

COMPROMISES WITH THE RATIONAL MODEL

The failure of policy-makers to follow the rigorous prescriptions of the rational model does not mean that their decisions are frenetic, unpatterned, or made without benefit of human reason. Policy-makers have found several reasonable ways of coping with policy-making constraints, although none of them can claim to be rational according to the standards of the purely rational model of policy-making. The rational model can be labeled an *optimal* procedure—one that would work in the most ideal circumstances. In light of the various problems described, however, policy-makers must usually be content with *satisfactory* decisions. Decisions of this sort are not liked by everyone, but do meet the needs of participants in a policy-making situation, after taking into account the information feasible to assemble about goals, resources, and alternative courses of action.[12] Furthermore, for each of the features that hinder optimal policy-making, there are appropriate techniques for arriving at satisfactory policies.

Overcoming Other People's Priorities

One of the practices used by policy-makers who must be content with only satisfactory decisions is to define the problems, goals, and policies that permit the use of existing agency resources and that are consistent with the existing expectations of legislators, the chief executive, and interest groups.

Many policy-makers are skilled bargainers. They often settle disputes over goals and policies by accommodating diverse interests. Bargains are made between persons with different interests within administrative agencies, between agencies and officials in other branches of government, and

---

[10]Thompson, op. cit., Chapter 8. See also R. Presthus, *Organizational Society* (New York: Knopf, 1962), Chapter 9.

[11]D. Wise, *The Politics of Lying: Government Deception, Secrecy, and Power* (New York: Vintage, 1973).

[12]J. G. March and H. A. Simon, *Organizations* (New York: Wiley, 1958), pp. 140–141; and Simon, op. cit.

between agencies and interest groups or prominent citizens. The test of a good bargain is its acceptance by individuals and groups that have control over resources important to an agency. Such a test is not featured in the model of rational policy-making, but it is prominent in democratic political practice.

Bargainers often avoid *explicitly* defining problems or goals, which avoids severe conflicts and allows for the pursuit of concrete programs. People who might disagree about long-range goals might agree to work in behalf of specific programs. Several participants might support a particular policy without arguing about the long-range goals the policy *might* realize. Work on a policy can go forth in spite of the potential dissent that may lie dormant throughout the life of the policy. Administrators with different perspectives on the great problems of continued growth versus conservation, for example, might avoid their basic disagreements and still cooperate on certifying nuclear power plants. They could face each plant's certification on a case-by-case basis and let the local needs for electric power, the particular circumstances with respect to pollutants, and the local political weight of interested parties shape their decisions.

Getting Around Limits on Information

Policy-makers often cut off their search for information about problems, goals, or policies when they discover a mode of operation that will involve the least profound change in their established programs.[13] They do not search out all possible alternatives until they find "the one best way." Instead, they search until they find something that provides satisfactory relief from the perceived difficulties without threatening undesirable unrest within the agency and among the legislators, executives, and interest groups who involve themselves in its affairs.

Avoiding Structural Problems

Not making clear statements about long-range goals also skirts around conflicts between agencies, legislators, and the chief executive. Policies can proceed without the centralized deliberation and definitive choices prescribed by the rational model. The difficulties of coordinating different specialized units can be met by keeping coordination to a minimum. The news that specialized administrative units pursue duplicate, or even contradictory, programs reflects this lack of coordination.

---

[13]Downs, op. cit., p. 173.

The analysis of policy alternatives includes calculating "spillovers," or secondary effects. Here are some of the spillover costs calculated for one policy action, the embargo of agricultural exports to the U.S.S.R. as a result of the Soviet invasion of Afghanistan.

BOX 10-2 Budgetary Impact of the Embargo

When President Carter announced his decision on Jan. 4 to limit agricultural imports to the Soviet Union drastically, he stressed that he was "determined to minimize any adverse impact on the American farmer from this action."

As far as the federal budget is concerned, the Administration has estimated that its actions to protect farmers would cost $2 billion in the current fiscal year and another $800 million in fiscal 1981. More recently, however, Office of Management and Budget (OMB) officials have said that while total costs may turn out to be somewhat lower than that, the expenditures falling due this year will exceed the $2 billion estimate.

OMB's numbers change almost daily as new developments are reported and analyzed. One recent set of calculations made available to *National Journal* contain the following cost estimates (in millions of dollars):

	Estimates
Assumption of contractual obligations for corn, soybeans, and wheat that were to be delivered to the Soviet Union	+$2,165
Actions to isolate producer-owned grains from the market through increased loan rates for corn and wheat and an increase in storage payments for farmer-held reserves	+300
Forgiveness of first-year interest payments for first 13 million tons of corn placed in reserve after Oct. 22, 1979	+110
Receipts from expected sales of government-assumed soybeans and oil	−155
Offset of funds previously requested in a supplemental appropriation for the foreign aid program	−75
Expected receipts from sales of government-assumed corn	−1,115
Cost of placing additional corn in farmer-held reserve at $2.10 per bushel loan price	+890
Total fiscal 1980	$2,120
Estimated storage and loan costs, fiscal 1981	+600
Two-year total	$2,720

SOURCE: *National Journal*, March 8, 1980. Reprinted with permission.

Dealing with Personal Conflicts

The presence of personal conflict among personnel does not mean an agency will be rent apart. Practices that protect organizations from the worst consequences of internal conflict include:

1. The selection of highly ambiguous, nonoperational goals.
2. The use of slack resources to "buy off" members who are unhappy with the goals or policies selected.
3. The acceptance of precedent—goal and policy selections made in the past—to narrow the conflicts to be faced in the present.

Stating goals ambiguously defuses conflict, because participants can agree on them without feeling that they threaten their own goals. Conflict may come later when subgoals—the actual policies—are selected. At that time, however, new conditions may make the subgoals acceptable, or the choice of subgoals and their implementation may be shunted to another organization. A federal agency may announce general goals, for example, and leave the details to state or local administrators.

Organizational slack consists of resources that are not yet allocated, but that can be used to provide some rewards to officials who are dissatisfied with goal or policy selections. The resources include money, status and other symbolic rewards, and other policy commitments. When they are used to placate individuals who are miffed by major goal selections, they can be thought of as "side payments" that the organization makes to buy the acceptance of its decisions by unhappy personnel. A side payment can be an increase in salary or rank, a larger or more comfortable office or other amenities that make work easier or more pleasant, or a commitment to undertake a program tangential to the main effort of the agency. Such a program can be experimental or can be the continuation on a small scale of a project that had once been larger. A side payment of an experimental program might be given to an officer who failed in the attempt to convince the organization to adopt a massive effort in this new direction. A diminished continuation of a previously large activity might also be granted to an individual who fought unsuccessfully to retain the program at its previous size.[14]

The use of precedent may simplify decisions about goals and policies. If a new problem can be defined in a way that makes an existing goal relevant, then such a definition will spare the organization from the turmoil of a new goal conflict. Decisions can become "routinized," so that there is no longer any conflict when the agency makes similar decisions in the future.

---

[14]Cyert and March, op. cit., pp. 36–38.

Sidestepping Deviant Behavior

Participants in government agencies invent ways to minimize the problems of bureaupathic colleagues. Officials may present issues to the troublesome figure in ways to lessen the chance of a caustic incident. There may be a superficial show of courtesy that hides true feelings of fear, disdain, or embarrassment. Sidestepping may occur as officials refer all possible issues to other personnel in the organization. Sometimes bureaupathic figures are "kicked upstairs." They receive a new title and perhaps an increase in salary, but find themselves without significant duties.

MAKING CHOICES ABOUT CONTROVERSIAL ISSUES

The issue of economic growth versus the concept that "smaller is better" illustrates a few of the problems of making policy. By examining some of the conflicts inherent in this issue, you may begin to sympathize with officials who would prefer to decide issues rationally, but who bypass the rational model.

Growth Versus Limitation of Growth

On one side of the issue are those who find economic growth a necessity. Some regional and social groups do not share in the mainstream of economic benefits. Blacks and other ethnic minorities express strident demands for change from their economic and social deprivation. These calls from low-income regions and groups in the United States are in chorus with the statements from officials in less-developed countries that seek an increase in economic growth. (See Chapter 12.)

On the other side are those who point to the physical threats inherent in further economic growth. According to this view, there are too many people, too much industrial production, and too much consumption of nonrenewable resources. One predicted result of too much growth is that impending pollution will stifle the environment. In 1969, Paul Ehrlich, professor of biology, looked ahead only 10 years and saw an "eco-catastrophe," with "the end of the ocean [coming] late in 1979."[15]

In a more temperate piece, a group of researchers from the Massachusetts Institute of Technology projected growth rates for population, industrial and food production, resource consumption, and pollution. Their

---

[15]P. Ehrlich, "Eco-Catastrophe," *Ramparts* (September 1969), as reprinted in F. Tugwell, *Search for Alternatives: Public Policy and the Study of the Future* (Cambridge, Mass.: Winthrop, 1973), especially p. 186.

book, *The Limits to Growth,* reports that computer printouts show "the basic behavior mode of the world system is exponential growth of population and capital, followed by collapse."[16]

The view that growth produces doom makes serious demands on our attention. It is impossible to recommend continued economic growth without regard for avoidable consequences to the environment. However, the simple assertion that growth produces doom is not a sufficient reason to limit growth.

One group of demographers has challenged any projections that see population as continuously going upward. Their amount has two basic points. First, population forecasting should not be accepted without strong reservations:

> No demographer has ever succeeded in forecasting the future of any population. However, demographers today are much better informed about the reasons for their failure, and their product is much more likely to be regarded with justifiable doubt. We call that progress.[17]

Second, existing figures about recent trends severely question any expectation of continued population growth. Indeed, the long trend in countries with advanced levels of economic development is population decline. This trend is true in the United States, with the magnitude and duration of the post-World War II baby boom explained away as an aberrant phenomenon. The U.S. population stopped increasing by about the mid-1960s; the mean birth ratio declined by about 20–24 percent between the periods 1961–1965 and 1966–1970. Birth declines have come partly with changes in technology (more widespread use of better contraception) and values (later marriages and fewer children wanted). The implication is that economic growth brings about a modernization of attitudes and lifestyles—and fewer children. While occasional upward spurts in population occur, little in recent history seems to support the notion of continued exponential growth.

A group of researchers from Sussex University in England took direct aim at the MIT group. Their book, *Models of Doom: A Critique of the Limits to Growth,*[18] offers a systematic attack on the assumptions, methods, conclusions, and recommendations offered in *The Limits to Growth.* The Sussex group finds the MIT people to be "unreconstructed Malthusians." Thomas Malthus was a preacher of the early nineteenth century who forecast that population would grow so much faster than agriculture that mass starvation was inevitable. The Sussex group accuses its MIT colleagues of a failure to

---

[16] D. H. Meadows et al., *The Limits to Growth* (New York: Universe Books, 1972), p. 142. This discussion relies on I. Sharkansky, *The United States: A Study of a Developing Country* (New York: Longman, 1975).

[17] N. B. Ryder, "The Future Growth of the American Population," in C. F. Westoff et al., *Toward the End of Growth: Population in America* (Englewood Cliffs, N.J.: Prentice-Hall, 1973), pp. 85–86.

[18] H. S. D. Cole et al., *Models of Doom: A Critique of the Limits to Growth* (New York: Universe Books, 1973).

The social security trust fund invites reconsideration in the light of changing family patterns since the mid-1960s. Popular movements toward "zero population growth" may mean that people born in the present low-birth years will have to make heavy contributions when the large number of people of the baby boom years (1945–1965) reach retirement age.

Table 10-1   When the "Baby Boomers" Hit 65, 1970–2040

Age	1970	1978	2000	2015	2040
65+	9.8%	11.0%	12.2%	13.9%	17.9%
65–74	6.1	6.8	6.7	8.5	8.8
75–84	3.0	3.2	4.1	3.7	6.5
85+	0.7	1.0	1.4	1.7	2.6
Total population (in millions)	204.9	218.5	260.4	283.2	308.4

Note: In 2015, the peak of the "baby boom" generation will turn 65. That fact, combined with increasing longevity, will mean that the 65 and over age group will nearly double as a share of the total population between 1970 and 2040, as the table illustrates.

SOURCE: U.S. Bureau of the Census.

Table 10-2   The Trust Fund Picture (in billions of dollars, fiscal years), 1979–1984

	Old age and survivors' insurance trust fund					
	1979	1980	1981	1982	1983	1984
Outlays Revenue	$ 90.5	$104.0	$119.8	$135.7	$150.4	$165.3
Balance	86.7	99.4	113.1	131.7	147.3	163.8
Balance on Oct. 1	31.0	27.2	22.7	16.0	12.0	8.9
Balance as percent of outlays	34.3%	26.2%	18.9%	11.8%	8.0%	5.4%
	Above plus disability insurance trust fund					
	1979	1980	1981	1982	1983	1984
Outlays	$104.5	$120.1	$138.3	$157.6	$174.4	$192.0
Revenue	102.0	116.8	133.8	156.0	174.7	194.5
Balance on Oct. 1	35.4	32.9	29.7	25.1	23.5	23.8
Balance as percent of outlays	33.9%	27.4%	21.5%	15.9%	13.5%	12.4%

Note: The first section of the table shows the projected decline in reserves in the social security program's old age and survivors' insurance trust fund. The second shows that when that trust fund is combined with the disability insurance trust fund, the decline is not so steep.

SOURCE: *National Journal*, August 25, 1979. Reprinted with permission.

build technological changes into their projections, and reminds us that Malthus was proved wrong on the basis of higher agricultural yields, as well as on the uneven nature of population growth. Technological innovation has been a continuing feature of recent history. Just as any forecasting of energy supplies done in the mid-nineteenth century could not have taken into consideration the as yet undeveloped use of petroleum, so any energy projections to the year 2100 must concede unexpected new discoveries and innovation. Sussex also indicts MIT for working with a whole-world model, thereby masking the numerous opportunities for continued resource exploitation, industrialization, and population growth in as yet undeveloped regions.

The Sussex group concedes that there are theoretical limits to growth, but is more impressed with political than physical constraints. The 1973–1974 oil embargo on the United States and the 1979 shortages after the Iranian revolution lend weight to this argument. For them, the issue is not growth versus no growth, but the nature of growth, its location, and the use of its outputs. These issues lead to political analysis, which focuses on the most variable of elements and does not lend itself to computer projection.

Growth Versus Other Issues

Many decisions of administrators touch on the growing debate about growth and conservation. Since the 1973 Arab oil embargo and price increases in petroleum, energy issues have been linked with prospects for economic growth. Often, groups that are concerned for the environment express the skeptical view about growth and its long-term costs. Disputes about growth erupt over decisions concerning new power plants, oil storage and refining facilities, pipelines, licenses for companies to explore for oil and gas or to mine coal. Periodic fuel shortages produce disputes about gasoline rationing, an end to fuel price regulation as an incentive for greater exploration for new sources, and "windfall" taxes to soak up some of the oil companies' profits (thereby lessening their incentives to explore for new energy sources). Pollution contributes to the picture. Proposals to facilitate fuel exploration and transportation threaten spills. Dirty air and water are inevitable, to an extent, but technologies exist to minimize the damage. All this is costly. Disputes focus on which control technologies should be employed, who should pay for them, and whether the government should pursue its goals by mandatory requirements or by persuasion and inducements.

Despite the problems of analysis and the political conflicts that swirl through issues of growth, conservation, energy, and the environment, policies are made. A combination of legislative enactments and administrative rules indicate standards for the level of pollution to be allowed for factories or automobiles. Field officers from the Environmental Protection Agency monitor emissions from industrial smokestacks and water outlets, and evaluate a sample of each new car model. These policies result in added costs for manufacturers and consumers, and thereby may lessen the aggregate level of economic growth. At the same time, however, they help to conserve the quality of air and water. Just what standards are set and by how much each case is allowed to vary from these standards are determined partly by bargaining and compromise among interested parties. Imperfect knowledge and estimates about political feasibility can, and do, enter into such large questions as *Do we emphasize growth or conservation?* as well as such smaller questions as *Do we tighten or loosen pollution standards? How strictly do we enforce those standards?* (Does the enforcement agency allow an exemption for a large factory in a small town that might otherwise go out of business?) *Do we build a new road? If so, where do we build it?* When policy-making involves issues that are in conflict, the rationality of choices is always subject to debate.

DECISION RULES AS ALTERNATIVES TO THE RATIONAL MODEL

Contrary to the rational model, policy-makers do not take everything into consideration. They use decision rules to simplify their tasks. Three of these rules merit separate attention:

1. Rely on tension between established patterns and unmet needs to signal the need for a change in policy.
2. Make adjustments to demands rather than initiate decision processes that seek a clear definition of goals or policies.
3. Use routine procedures to simplify the complex considerations potentially relevant to a decision.

Common to each of these rules is the reluctance of policy-makers to make great departures from customary activities. This attitude is not a reflection of laziness, but rather an appreciation of the numerous demands made on the organization.

Reliance on Tension

Policy-makers do not look for trouble. There is usually a scarcity of personnel for research. Officials want to avoid provoking new conflicts that might upset delicate agreements reached on other matters. There is almost

Some data relevant to policy disputes about growth or conservation.

Table 10-3 U.S. Energy Supply and Demand, 1960–1978

	1960	1970	1971	1972	1973	1974	1975	1976	1977	1978
Energy supply (quads)[a]	46.01	70.91	71.57	74.28	77.19	75.64	74.17	76.93	80.47	79.89
Oil[b]	20.39	30.38	31.11	32.94	35.53	34.17	33.05	35.26	38.54	38.04
Natural gas	12.82	22.52	23.24	23.26	23.25	22.20	20.62	20.47	20.61	20.24
Coal	11.12	15.05	13.59	14.49	14.39	14.47	15.19	15.85	15.90	15.11
Nuclear	0.01	0.24	0.41	0.58	0.91	1.27	1.90	2.11	2.70	2.98
Hydro, other	1.67	2.72	3.22	3.01	3.11	3.53	3.41	3.24	2.72	3.47
Energy consumption (quads)[c]	44.08	66.82	68.30	71.63	74.61	72.35	70.71	74.16	76.56	78.01
Transportation	11.23	16.76	17.38	18.34	18.93	18.40	18.52	19.39	20.07	20.59
Residential, commercial	14.37	23.77	24.69	25.84	25.75	25.57	25.98	27.18	28.39	29.30
Industrial, other	18.48	26.29	26.23	27.45	29.92	28.39	26.21	27.59	28.11	28.13
Oil consumption (millions of barrels a day)	9.80	14.70	15.21	16.37	17.31	16.65	16.32	17.46	18.43	18.73
Oil imports	1.62	3.16	3.71	4.52	6.03	5.89	5.85	7.09	8.57	7.86
Proved U.S. oil reserves (billions of barrels)	31.6	39.0	38.1	36.3	35.3	34.2	32.7	30.9	29.5	27.8
Gasoline consumption (millions of barrels a day)	4.13	5.78	6.01	6.38	6.67	6.54	6.68	6.98	7.18	7.41
Natural gas consumption (trillion cubic feet a year)	11.97	21.14	21.79	22.10	22.05	21.22	19.54	19.95	19.52	19.41
Residential	3.10	4.84	4.97	5.13	4.88	4.79	4.92	5.05	4.82	4.97
Industrial	5.77	9.25	9.59	9.63	10.19	9.77	8.37	8.60	8.47	8.14
Electric utilities	1.73	3.93	3.98	3.98	3.66	3.44	3.16	3.08	3.19	3.22
Proved U.S. gas reserves (trillion cubic feet)	262.3	290.7	278.8	266.1	250.0	237.1	228.2	216.0	208.9	200.3

Coal production (million short tons)	415.5	602.9	552.2	595.4	591.7	603.4	648.4	678.7	688.6	653.8
Underground mines	284.9	338.8	275.9	304.1	299.4	277.3	292.8	294.9	271.6	243.5
Surface mines	130.6	264.1	276.3	291.3	292.4	326.1	355.6	383.8	416.9	410.3
Coal use										
Electric utilities	173.8	318.3	325.7	350.2	387.3	390.3	404.5	447.0	475.7	480.1
Coke	81.0	96.0	82.8	87.3	93.6	89.7	83.3	84.3	77.4	71.1
Exports	36.5	70.9	56.6	56.0	52.9	59.9	65.7	55.4	53.7	39.8
Electricity production (quads)	8.40	16.51	17.44	18.74	19.74	19.94	20.28	21.51	22.64	23.76
From coal (percent)	53.5	47.3	44.2	44.1	45.5	44.5	44.5	46.4	46.4	44.3
From oil	6.1	12.2	15.6	15.6	16.8	16.0	15.0	15.7	16.9	16.5
From natural gas	21.0	25.0	21.5	21.5	18.3	17.1	15.6	14.5	14.4	13.8
From hydro	19.4	16.7	15.6	15.6	14.6	16.1	15.6	13.9	10.4	12.7
From nuclear	0.0	1.5	3.0	3.1	4.5	6.1	9.0	9.4	11.8	12.5
Population (millions)	180.0	203.8	206.2	208.2	209.9	211.4	213.0	214.7	216.3	218.1
Automobiles (millions)	61.7	89.2	92.7	97.1	102.0	104.9	106.7	110.4	114.1	117.1
Gross national product (billions of 1972 dollars)	736.8	1,075.3	1,107.5	1,171.1	1,235.0	1,217.8	1,202.3	1,271.0	1,332.7	1,385.7
Energy consumption/GNP (thousands of Btu per dollar)	59.8	62.1	61.7	61.2	60.4	59.4	58.8	58.3	57.4	56.3

[a]Includes U.S. imports, U.S. exports, and changes in inventories (1 quad = 1 quadrillion British thermal units).
[b]Includes natural gas liquids.
[c]Includes distribution loss from electrical generation.

SOURCE: *National Journal*, July 21, 1919. Reprinted with permission.

Here are some of the economic indicators used in deciding about the President's budget requests. Information like this concerns the Council of Economic Advisers, whose macroeconomic projections are fed into the calculations of generosity or constraint toward particular programs made by the Office of Management and Budget.

Table 10-4 Economic Indicators (in billions of dollars, calendar years), 1978–1985

Item	Actual 1978	Forecast			Assumptions			
		1979ᵃ	1980	1981	1982	1983	1984	1985
Major economic indicators								
Gross national product (percent change, fourth quarter over fourth quarter)								
Current dollars	13.4	10.0	7.9	11.7	13.3	12.6	11.6	10.7
Constant (1972) dollars	4.8	0.8	-1.0	2.8	5.0	5.0	4.8	4.6
GNP deflator (percent change, fourth quarter over fourth quarter)	8.2	9.1	9.0	8.6	7.9	7.2	6.5	5.8
Consumer Price Index (percent change, December over December)ᵇ	9.0	13.2	10.4	8.6	7.8	7.2	6.4	5.7
Unemployment rate (percent fourth quarter)	5.8	5.9	7.5	7.3	6.5	5.6	4.8	4.0
Annual economic assumptions								
Gross national product								
Current dollars								
Amount	2,128	2,369	2,567	2,842	3,206	3,619	4,052	4,498
Percent change, year over year	12.0	11.4	8.3	10.7	12.8	12.9	12.0	11.0
Constant (1972) dollars								
Amount	1,399	1,431	1,423	1,448	1,510	1,586	1,664	1,742
Percent change, year over year	4.4	2.3	-0.6	1.7	4.3	5.0	4.9	4.7

Incomes							
Personal income	1,717	1,923	2,109	2,314	2,591	2,914	3,256	3,610
Wages and salaries	1,103	1,227	1,342	1,478	1,663	1,874	2,094	2,316
Corporate profits	206	238	228	242	277	324	369	415
Price level								
GNP deflator								
Level (1972 = 100), annual average	152.1	165.5	180.4	196.3	212.3	228.1	243.5	258.3
Percent change, year over year	7.3	8.9	8.9	8.8	8.2	7.4	6.8	6.1
Consumer Price Index[b]								
Level (1967 = 100), annual average	195.3	217.6	243.4	265.8	287.4	308.8	329.8	349.7
Percent change, year over year	7.6	11.4	11.8	9.2	8.2	7.4	6.8	6.1
Unemployment rates								
Total, annual average[b]	6.0	5.8	7.0	7.4	6.8	5.9	5.1	4.3
Insured, annual average[c]	3.3	3.1	3.9	4.0	3.6	3.0	2.4	2.0
Federal pay raise, October (percent)[d]	5.5	7.0	6.2[e]	8.0	8.0	7.5	7.0	6.5
Interest rate, 91-day Treasury bills (percent)[f]	7.2	10.0	10.5	9.0	8.4	7.7	7.0	6.3

[a] Actual data for the 1979 unemployment rate, federal pay raise, and 91-day Treasury bill rate.
[b] CPI for urban wage earners and clerical workers. Two versions of the CPI are now published. The index shown here is that currently used, as required by law, in calculating automatic cost-of-living increases for indexed federal programs.
[c] This indicator measures unemployment under state regular unemployment insurance as a percentage of covered employment under that program. It does not include recipients of extended benefits under that program.
[d] General schedule pay raises become effective in October of each year—the first month of the fiscal year. Thus, the October 1980 pay raise will set new pay scales that will be in effect during fiscal year 1981, and the October 1982 pay raise will set new pay scales that will be in effect during fiscal year 1983.
[e] This is the projected pay increase for white-collar workers and wage-board employees. The pay raise for military personnel is estimated to be 7.4%.
[f] Average rate on new issues within period. These projections assume, by convention, that interest rates decline with the rate of inflation. They do not represent a forecast of interest rates.

SOURCE: *Congressional Quarterly*, February 2, 1980.

always a scarcity of resources for new programs. Policy-makers rely on problems to present themselves. When problems become sufficiently severe to cause tension, administrators make some effort to respond. Tension can be thought of as a screening device between a policy unit and its environment; unit members use it to determine when unmet demands are severe enough to require a response. The quality of the tension may indicate the source of the stress, the participants involved, and the intensity of their problems.[19]

Mutual Adjustment

A policy unit that responds to tension does not initiate policy change according to any rationally defined set of priorities. Instead, it waits until a change is demanded. A set of procedures for accommodating demands has been labeled "mutual adjustment." Like the reliance on tension, the concept of mutual adjustment refers not to a rational assessment of priorities, but rather to a particular pattern of response and negotiation. One of the terms used to identify decision-making by mutual adjustment is "muddling through."[20] This term suggests a lethargic organism that detours around a problem rather than meeting it head-on.

The techniques of adjustment include discussions with representatives of various interests; a reluctance to view any part of a position as inflexible; a willingness to bargain with a protagonist; the expectation that protagonists will negotiate in good faith and relinquish part of their demands in exchange for concessions made to them; and the view that goal formation and policy-making are continuing processes, so that desires that are not satisfied in one period may be realized sometime in the future.[21]

Flexibility in the face of others' demands is a primary feature of mutual adjustment. It represents an admission that decision-makers lack clear evidence that any one set of goals or policies is "the one best way" to resolve their problems. Intellectual search and discovery is less to the point of mutual adjustment than is the accommodation of demands. The number of individuals who support a demand, the intensity of their support, their

---

[19]W. J. Gore, *Administrative Decision-Making: A Heuristic Model* (New York: Wiley, 1964).

[20]C. E. Lindblom, "The Science of 'Muddling Through,'" *Public Administration Review*, 19 (Spring 1959): 79–88.

[21]This discussion relies on the works of C. E. Lindblom, especially *The Policy-Making Process* and "The Science of 'Muddling Through,'" and also "Decision-making in Taxation and Expenditure," in National Bureau of Economic Research, *Public Finances: Needs, Sources and Utilization* (Princeton, N.J.: Princeton University Press, 1961), pp. 295–336.

alliances with key officials, and the possibility of modifying their position so that it appeals to an even wider population are useful criteria for mutual adjustment.

Routines

Routines are decision rules that specify which of numerous factors should be considered in making decisions. Some routines are more elaborate than others and indicate the weight to be given each factor; some even specify the response to be made under certain conditions.[22]

There are different types of routines. At the extreme of simplicity, an electronic computer uses a routine when it decides whether the arithmetic is accurate on a citizen's tax return. At another stage, the computer uses a slightly more elaborate routine to determine whether the citizen claims more for charitable contributions than is commensurate with total income. If the citizen does claim more, the computer identifies the tax return for human scrutiny. When the auditor examines the tax return and other documents the taxpayer is asked to produce, the auditor employs additional routines. These routines are more flexible than those programmed into the computer, but they likewise provide an important screening process for the material to be considered in making a decision. They identify the kinds of evidence that are acceptable—and unacceptable—for proving the citizen's contributions. Other routines help the tax agency determine whether the citizen will simply pay back taxes with interest, pay a fine in addition to the taxes and interest, or be prosecuted for tax evasion.

Many of the routines used by subordinates in administrative agencies reflect the working out of procedures explicitly designed by their superiors. However, some of the most interesting routines are used in making policy decisions. They affect enormous financial, material, and personal resources. Often they are not pursued in a conscious manner. Decision-makers accept them because they simplify complex situations. Like workaday routines, those used by policy-makers select a few *inputs* from the many that face them; sometimes they assign a weight to each of these inputs or determine in advance appropriate responses to certain kinds of inputs. At the same time that routines simplify the tasks of policy-makers, they also help stabilize the political system. They do this by screening out certain kinds of inputs, especially those that would produce marked departures from prevailing activities.

---

[22] I. Sharkansky, *The Routines of Politics* (New York: Van Nostrand, 1970).

Three policy-making routines are illustrated here: incremental budgeting, the tendency of state and local administrators to copy regional neighbors in formulating their own policies, and the tendency of policy-makers to seek an increase in spending when they perceive a need to improve their programs.

Incremental Budgeting

Incrementalism is a routine found in many types of government decision-making, but most clearly in the budgetary process. Budget-makers who follow an incremental approach fail to consider all of the alternatives that face them. They do not make their decisions on the basis of all relevant information. Incrementalists do not debate grand social goals. Their most salient concerns are immediate approprations for specific agencies, rather than long-run benefits for society. They generally accept the legitimacy of established programs and agree to continue the previous level of expenditure. Under incremental budgeting, budget-makers assume that their past decisions are good ones. They limit their task by considering only the increments of change proposed for the new budget and the narrow range of goals embodied in departures from established activities. Their expectations tend to be short-range and pragmatic.

John Crecine's findings about budgeting in Detroit, Cleveland, and Pittsburgh document how incremental budget-makers can parcel out annual increases in revenues with little concern for program value.[23] When budget-makers expect a revenue surplus, they distribute it on the basis of routine priorities, which are not rationally derived. Salaries are given first preference, equipment gets the second reward, and maintenance gets the remainder. Opposite priorities are used when the forecast indicates a need to reduce budgets. Cuts are made first in maintenance, then in equipment, and last in salaries. Those items that promise the greatest political appeal, regardless of program value, receive the best treatment. (More details on incremental budgeting appear in Chapter 7.)

Regional Consultation

The routine of regional consultation often gives decision cues to policy-makers of state and local government. When policy-makers look elsewhere for a problem-solving model for their own jurisdiction, they do not survey

---

[23]J. P. Crecine, *Governmental Problem-Solving: A Computer Simulation Model of Municipal Budgeting* (Chicago: Rand McNally, 1969).

all the possible models throughout the country, as the rational model suggests. Instead, they usually rely on their geographic region or, more typically, on a jurisdiction that borders directly on their own. Many policy-makers believe that neighboring jurisdictions have problems similar to their own.[24] Because neighboring governments serve similar populations, it is likely that the people have common needs for public services and present similar demands to government agencies. The economies of the neighboring governments are generally alike, and they present to government agencies a comparable set of resources and needs. The political environment is also likely to be similar in neighboring jurisdictions. Politicians will probably support comparable levels of service, and there may be similar relationships among administrators, the chief executive, and the legislature. State bureaus of research usually publish comparisons of their own state's demographic, economic, and public service characteristics with those of regional partners. For example, the *Georgia Statistical Abstract* (published by the University of Georgia's Bureau of Business and Economic Research) compares data for the state as a whole with a figure for the entire United States and with separate figures for Alabama, Florida, North Carolina, and Tennessee. Wisconsin officials commonly compare their state with Illinois, Indiana, Iowa, Michigan, Minnesota, and Ohio.

The professional activities of officials also lead them to regional neighbors for policy cues. Policy-makers of state and local governments belong to formal organizations according to their subject-matter specialties. They include the National Association of State Budget Officers, the National Association of State Conservation Officers, and the National Association of Housing and Redevelopment Officials. They have national and regional meetings that provide the opportunity for trading information about current problems and reinforcing friendships formed at earlier meetings. State and local officials indicate that they are more likely to attend the regional than the national meetings of these groups, and that they acquire many of their professional contacts at these meetings.

Because policy-makers have consulted in the past with their counterparts in nearby governments, they have learned who can be trusted for credible information, candor, and good judgment. Unless officials are committed to extensive research before making their own policy decisions, they will feel it necessary to make only a few calls to individuals with whom they have dealt amicably in the past.

Some elements favor the development of nationwide similarities in the public policies of state and local governments. They include federal aid, improvements in transportation and communication, and the mobility of professional and technical personnel from schools or previous government

---

[24]I. Sharkansky, *Regionalism in American Politics* (Indianapolis: Bobbs-Merrill, 1970).

jobs in one state to new jobs in other states. Yet regional patterns in policy have not succumbed to these influences. Distinct regional patterns remain in spending and service levels for the fields of education, highways, and welfare; in the nature of state and local revenue systems; and in the use of federal and state aids. The presence of these regional similarities in policy is a prominent indication of the deeply entrenched routine of regional consultation.

The Spending–Service Cliché

The spending–service cliché is a routine that leads policy-makers to equate levels of expenditure with levels of service output. Like other routines, the spending–service cliché gets its support from decision-makers' need for a device that simplifies reality. In the field of program development, five principal elements add to the appeal of the spending–service cliché:

1. The large number of factors, and complex interrelationships among these factors, that actually has an influence on the character of services an agency provides.
2. The lack of information among policy-makers about these service factors.
3. The belief that some factors that influence the level of outputs are not conveniently subject to manipulation by public officials.
4. The commonality of money as an element that may influence many potential service factors.
5. The widespread belief among analysts and observers outside the decision-making arena that money is crucial among the factors that influence the character of services.

Among the factors that can influence the nature of public services are the nature of staff and leadership, physical facilities, the clientele who is to be served, the organizational structure of the service agencies, the economy of the jurisdiction receiving the service, and the political environment in which policy decisions are made. The folklore abounds about the elements that will help to improve services, but little hard information exists about the results to be expected from certain combinations of ingredients under certain conditions. In a number of federal, state, and local agencies that have access to sophisticated staff assistance and electronic data-processing equipment, efforts are being made to identify salient features that have a bearing on the level of services produced. However, much of this work is still in the exploratory stage. So far, research into what makes programs tick is not sufficiently widespread among government agencies and the research techniques are not sufficiently well accepted for the results to have broad application.

Among the many elements that seem likely to influence service levels, a number of them appear unamenable to direct manipulation by government officials. Because of this, decision-makers may be dissuaded from making a thorough analysis of service determinants and led to rely on a simple routine that assumes a spending–service relationship. The preparation of clients, motivations for rendering services, market costs, the level of economic development in a community, and the attractiveness of a community as a residence for professional and technical personnel can have a bearing on the services that an agency can render. Each of these elements may be altered by long-range campaigns directed specifically at them. However, it is unlikely that such changes can be made the responsibility of service agencies that have other, more immediate goals.

In the face of the complexities that face policy-makers who undertake a thorough analysis, the routine of the spending–service cliché offers both simplicity and credibility. Although money, per se, does not affect levels of service, it seems reasonable to believe that money will purchase many of the commodities that do affect services. Money is also subject to manipulation by government officials. If the present level of service is not satisfactory, it is always possible—assuming sufficient resources or sufficient willingness to increase taxes—to spend more money. With additional dollars, officials can seek to recruit and/or train leaders and scientific–technical–professional personnel for their agencies; they can pay existing personnel enough money to make it difficult for them to accept employment elsewhere; they can offer financial inducements so that employees will accept changes in organizational structure or changes in agency norms; and they can buy the material and talents necessary to construct and maintain attractive physical facilities.

One of the factors that helps to make the spending–service cliché attractive to policy-makers is its popularity among those who observe and analyze public policy. Journalists frequently rank federal agencies and state and local governments on some readily available financial scale. Total spending, expenditures per client, and average salaries are favorite subjects for comparison.

Unfortunately, the willingness to spend more money may not solve the service problem. Not only is it true that some service determinants are not subject to alteration by current spending, but it may also be unclear which of the purchasable commodities, and how much of each, will produce the desired results.

Opportunities for Innovation

The use of rules in making routine decisions does not fix the decisions of policy-makers. As noted earlier, routines are only one of several devices used in making decisions. Others, such as mutual adjustment, are more hospitable to innovative stimuli. Moreover, some officials recognize the biases in policy-makers' routines, and they devise strategies that play on the weaknesses of routines. Events may weaken routines and permit innovative proposals to affect policy. Some officials are sufficiently won over to new ideas that they disregard their normal routines and make new kinds of decisions.

Even the spending–service cliché is not invincible. Despite its widespread appeal, some politicians are skeptical about big spending that produces few tangible improvements in social problems (Chapter 7 describes the efforts, and the problems, with such efforts to rationalize budgeting as PPB, MBO, and ZBB). The massive size of the policy machinery, as well as all the inputs policy-makers would prefer to consider, will challenge any new perspectives introduced at the top. Decision rules that simplify policy-makers' consid-erations, such as incrementalism, regional consultation, and the spend-ing–service cliché, may resist changes in routine, even with the most highly placed opposition.

SUMMARY

If policy-makers followed the standards of the rational model, they would list and assess all goals that appear relevant to the problems they perceive and would then do likewise for each of the policies that appeared capable of achieving each potential goal. On the basis of all relevant information about the probable advantages and disadvantages associated with each pack-age of goals and policies, a policy-maker would then select the one best goal-and-policy combination.

The rational model is widely respected by individuals and groups who comment about government activities. It presents a standard of "right think-ing," which asks that officials take every issue into consideration and make clear decisions that can then guide the actions of subordinates. The result promises to be integrated policies that complement rather than conflict with one another. However, policy-makers who would otherwise accept the pro-cedures of the rational model find their way blocked by a number of con-straints. These constraints, which are integral to American politics, reflect the heterogeneity and conflict that many consider to be components of the democratic process. The finding that these limitations hinder rational pol-icy-making is frustrating, however, and may account for part of the alien-ation that sets some citizens against their government.

The factors that stand in the way of rational policy-making include the numerous goals and policies that are potentially feasible; the high cost of information; the personal, ideological, and professional interests of policy-makers; structural disharmonies that generate conflict among policy-makers; and deviant (sometimes bureaupathic) behaviors that occur in administrative units.

In the face of these problems, policy-makers tend to avoid centralized decisions that are announced in an unambiguous fashion. They seek decisions that will be satisfactory rather than optimal. They make as few difficult choices as possible. Problems are avoided unless they appear with enough severity to generate tension in an organization or its environment. Once tension occurs, policy-makers may use the procedures of mutual adjustment, which include a combination of negotiation among interested parties, flexibility on the part of each protagonist in the face of others' demands, and an expectation that problem-solving will be a continuing process. Mutual adjusters do not seek final solutions to social or economic problems, but instead recognize that perceptions of problems, as well as goals and policies, are matters of dispute among reasonable individuals. These disputes provide opportunities for dissatisfied interests to express their demands. It frequently happens that a demand raised and rejected in one context may be raised later under other conditions and receive support from decision-makers.

A variety of possible problems can be perceived in one environment. Even when trying to apply the principles of the rational model, it is everyone's guess as to which decisions will turn out to make the most sense in the long run. Is it more important, in the long run, to give people jobs in a factory or to clean up the air by closing the factory? Will a growing industrial economy eventually destroy life? Or will the answers to potential eco-catastrophe be provided by technology as it evolves? If we must make a choice, do we favor human welfare or the planet's? To make good policies concerning such deeply controversial issues, policy-makers must rely on whatever projections of the future seem the most relevant and correct, based on what we know today.

Another device that compromises the rational model is of decision-making routine. Decision rules identify which of numerous inputs policy-makers should take into account and sometimes specify how they should respond to specific inputs. Routines appeal to policy-makers because they simplify choices. They limit the influences likely to have an impact on policies, thus helping to stabilize policy as well as complicating the task of those who demand major innovations. The routines considered in this chapter are incremental budgeting, regional consultations, and the spending–service cliché.

While routines bring considerable stability to policy-making, they do not choke off all innovation. As is evident in the strategies used in federal budgeting, participants can be innovative within the constraints of a routine. Stimuli associated with national crises (such as wars, postwar reconversions, and depressions) have occasioned major departures from routine policy-making. Occasionally, a powerful individual may upset the routines of entrenched officials. On the other hand, reformers have also not resisted the temptation to enhance the components of rationality in existing procedures. (Chapter 7 includes a discussion of a recent effort to rationalize policy-making—PPB—which recently disappeared from the manuals of the national government. Yet aspects of this reform survive.) If rationality, in the strict sense of the word, does not prevail in policy-making, there is nevertheless considerable hope of improving the information and decision-making employed in government.

Program Implementation

By now, you should be attuned to the complexities of government. Policy-making is not easy. Neither is implementation. Once a law is enacted, there is no assurance that a program will result. And once a program has begun, there is no assurance that it will produce the results expected. Perhaps there will be no significant results. Or perhaps the results obtained will be different from those predicted. "It does more harm than good" is a curse that is heard in the halls of government. A program designed to alleviate one problem may create others.

The authors of one prominent book about program implementation identified all the parties who must work together to implement a certain program. With some facetiousness, they figured that if there were a 95 percent probability that everyone cooperated, the overall probability of success was still only 0.000395.[1] Another leading author on implementation has concluded that government ought not to do many of the things that liberal reformers have sought.[2]

This discussion of implementation touches many of the issues considered in previous chapters. Implementation is affected by political constraints that come to administrative agencies from the populace and from branches of government. It also involves organizational structure, budgets, personnel, and law. Its key questions are:

Why don't programs work?

What can be done to improve their performance?

---

[1] J. L. Pressman and A. Wildavsky, *Implementation* (Berkeley: University of California Press, 1973).

[2] E. Bardach, *The Implementation Game: What Happens After a Bill Becomes a Law* (Cambridge, Mass.: MIT Press, 1977).

243

MEASURING IMPLEMENTATIONS

In general, *do government programs work or don't they?* Perhaps the principal source of confusion lies in the fact that almost all of the writing about implementation focuses on programs that do not work. Certain kinds of programs seem more likely to work than others; programs generally work well that are old and well-established, that are simple for administrators to operate and for clients to receive services, and that do not provoke significant political controversy. The programs that defy easy implementation are those that are new, that are complex for administrators to operate and for clients to receive services, and that provoke continuing political disputes.

Before getting into the problems of *Why don't programs work?* it is necessary to stress that most programs do work, most of the time. By all appearances, programs of traffic control succeed in leading most cars to drive on the right side of the road and to drive at or below the legal speed limit. The U.S. Social Security Administration sends checks for the proper amounts to most of the people entitled to old-age pensions. It is likely that most programs of federal aid to state and local government distribute most of their budget allocations. However, efficient functioning is only one measure of a program's workability. Programs are also judged according to whether they succeed in meeting each goal written into their laws, or each aspiration hoped for by program administrators, politicians, or clients.

Measuring the success of implementation can be difficult and contentious. Programs may accomplish some of their goals, but only at the price of unanticipated consequences (sometimes called "secondary effects"). Highway building and maintenance, flood control, and other large-scale construction projects are powerful programs that have multiple effects. Aside from their primary goals (to carry traffic and control flooding), they alter existing land uses suitable for housing and industry, and affect the habitat of wildlife. Welfare programs designed to benefit the children of women without husbands have encouraged illegitimate births and the breakdown of families. Often there are disagreements about the service levels that agencies should produce. There are other disagreements about the proper units to be used in measuring what the agencies actually produce. Those who are inclined to claim success for agency programs are likely to challenge the indicators used by those who claim failure.

Administrators and others concerned with the implementation of their programs make do with indicators that are, in a pure sense, inadequate. (The discussion of evaluation in Chapter 9 deals with similar issues.) Personnel officers concerned with affirmative action may be content to show the percentage increases of women, blacks, and other minorities in upper-grade civil service positions. The figures may show an increase, even though they may not allow observers to judge whether the increase was as great as it should have been, or if it was a product of the affirmative action program

Here is an example of what happens when laws are not enforced. The 160-acre limit of land ownership was written into laws authorizing certain federal land programs. When Congress wrote these laws, they reflected the interests of small farmers. In the interim, other influences have led federal administrators to overlook substantial numbers of violations.

Table 11-1   Excess Lands by State

State	Acreage	State	Acreage
Arizona	66,471	New Mexico	31,711
California	1,742,743	North Dakota	1,246
Colorado	1,056,293	Oklahoma	1,342
Hawaii	10,572	Oregon	32,238
Idaho	15,981	South Dakota	2,936
Kansas	446	Texas	30,863
Montana	22,794	Utah	3,433
Nebraska	22,729	Washington	24,180
Nevada	980	Wyoming	20,436
		Total	2,043,132

Note: This is a list of the lands in each state that are owned in excess of the 160-acre limit of the original reclamation law. The owners are required to sell the lands to family farmers under existing law. A bill passed by the Senate seeks to make some of this land available to small farmers, but exemptions and other provisions of the legislation would reduce the 2 million acres listed here to 355,000 to 400,000 acres.

SOURCE: *Congressional Quarterly*, September 29, 1979.

itself or some other factor, such as a general improvement in the economy and a lessening of unemployment.[3]

WHY SOME PROGRAMS DON'T WORK

Insufficient Resources

Earlier discussions about budgeting and personnel management should alert you to one of the reasons why programs do not work: They do not receive sufficient *monetary* resources. Most programs face two separate approvals in the executive and legislative branches. First, they must be approved in substance (authorized). Second, they must receive funding (appropriations). The funding must come annually for most national government programs. Even if the law has provided program administrators

---

[3]T. Sowell, *Race and Economics* (New York: Longman, 1975).

with all they need in program authority, their budgets might not allow them to hire sufficient staff or to purchase sufficient equipment and facilities. Budgets may not keep up with escalating costs or increases in the number of clients who seek services.

People are a resource that can affect program implementation. The staff must be of sufficient size and quality. Its skills must fit program characteristics and the needs of clients.

Another important resource is program support. The administrative staff must overcome the daily frustrations that are part of introducing new activities. Members of executive and legislative branches are in key positions to help a program along with public praise and encouragement or to kill it by dragging their feet at crucial times. The attitudes of the media and clients may reflect the comments of political leaders, and may boost staff morale enough to help a struggling program along.

Organizational Complexity

The problem of coordinating people in different organizations affects program implementation. Lack of coordination occurs between the different branches of government; between national, state, and local governments; and between different departments and agencies of the same government. Some agencies are sufficiently complex in themselves so that different officers cannot work together for smooth programming.

The United States may win the prize for having the most complex structure of government. The sheer number of authorities with some degree of autonomy from one another is in itself mind-boggling. (Chapter 13 details some of the problems in intergovernmental relations.)

Federal–Local Snafus

The story of "new towns in-town"—the federal effort to use government-owned land to help in the provision of low- and moderate-cost housing—illustrates several barriers to implementation.[4] Chief among them are the multilevel nature of American government, and the problems of national officials who can stimulate but cannot command local officials.

The idea of using federally owned surplus land in urban areas to house low- and moderate-income families was the invention of President Lyndon B. Johnson himself. As always, he wanted fast action. Aides devised a formal

---

[4]M. Derthick, *New Towns in-Town: Why a Federal Program Failed* (Washington, D.C.: Urban Institute, 1972).

plan within three days. Its appeal was partly because it seemed to require no congressional legislation and it could be put into operation by the Chief Executive acting alone and quickly.

But not quite. Early on, problems developed between the major departments of administration. Some departments wanted to save their vacant land for their own purposes. Some departments tried to add their own interests to the new-towns program. The Justice Department wanted clear language assuring the availability of housing without regard to the race of the applicants. Other departments wanted provisions for open spaces, environmental protection, and mass transportation.

The Department of Housing and Urban Development was dedicated to its own housing interests and resisted all moves to add provisions in the hope of preserving the program in its initial formulation. Yet HUD had its own problems with personnel in its regional offices. They considered themselves the experts in dealing with local government officials, and expressed the sentiment that a program that was directed too much from Washington—even from the White House—would run afoul of local sensitivities. Another snag developed when the Bureau of the Budget—a key component in the President's own Executive Office—pointed out that the government could not transfer federal land to local authorities or private firms for anything less than fair market value. The dream of a quick and inexpensive program without new law thereby evaporated.

Serious problems occurred at the local levels. Once sites were identified for housing developments, nearby residents organized in opposition. They did not want to spoil open land, to lose a view of the sea or fresh breezes, or to live near public housing with poor and black residents. In these settings it became difficult for local officials to usher the program through the stages of detailed planning, changes in zoning, and the pursuit of funds. There was a noticeable lack of support in most places that seemed eligible for the program. Some officials were annoyed at being upstaged by Washington. Others simply could not be bothered; too little federal aid was offered to justify the efforts needed to bring off the project.

Quasi-Governmental Bodies

The extensive development of quasi-governmental bodies adds greatly to organizational complexity. As Chapter 15 describes, private firms and non-profit organizations engage in social-service activities under contract with government agencies. They take part in the design, delivery, and monitoring of social programs from a position that is outside of government.[5]

---

[5] I. Sharkansky, *Wither the State? Politics and Public Enterprise in Three Countries* (Chatham, N.J.: Chatham, 1979).

The ambiguities of the contractual relationship often get in the way of smooth program implementation. In a contractual arrangement, the problems of government administrators include:

1. Lack of central records indicating the resources or personnel involved in contracting. Records may be dispersed among the agencies responsible for arranging contracts. Efforts by officials in executive offices or legislative committees to cull these records reveal the haphazard nature of recordkeeping, and the great costs needed to retrieve and assemble records in comprehensive formats.
2. Lack of program integration. Different pieces of related activities are in the hands of different agencies and contractors. Contractors' claims of autonomy retard efforts to standardize reporting or service delivery.
3. Lack of central control over service quality, cost overruns, or the prices charged to clients. This lack of control may be due to the lack of genuine competition between actual or potential contractors and/or the inability of government control officers to deal with the large number of separate service providers.
4. Irresponsibility of some government officers charged with arranging or monitoring contracts. Problems range from the avoidance of competitive bidding to the acceptance of bribes in order to favor certain contractors.
5. Control units that cannot function as intended because they are overloaded. Some government officers charged with reviewing requests to avoid competitive bidding, for example, must approve them routinely without thorough inquiry.

Some of these deficiencies are not due to contracting, per se, but to aspects of the larger system in which contracting operates. For example, the categorical structure of social services—as defined by federal aid programs, as well as state and local officials—results in a large number of particular activities. Contracting adds to this particularity of social service provision. Individual providers seek to make their activities distinctive by offering a slice of service that is not available elsewhere. They tend to take a proprietary view of their activities, and resist coordination by central authorities. Clients of social services are also likely to suffer from the confusing array of government agencies and contractors. There is no holistic promise of "welfare," nor an official mechanism to lead prospective clients from one service provider to another. (Chapter 16 explores clients' problems in detail.)

Inadequate Planning

Chapter 10, on policy-making, alerted you to connections between clear definitions of policy goals, careful planning, and program implementation. Policy-makers do not always know what to expect when a new activity gets under way. They estimate the number of people who will ask for a service or the cost of preparing an as yet untried piece of equipment. Some new programs represent one more stab at ancient and chronic problems, such as poverty, disease, ignorance, and crime. While hope and good will may be abundant, there is no certainty that new efforts will succeed.

When political dispute is sharp, policy-makers may be unable to make a clear statement of goals. Ambiguity is the politician's stock-in-trade. A program statement may list a number of goals, without clarifying which ones are the most important. Goals may have inherent conflicts, as in the case of the new-towns program that listed both new housing construction and the preservation of urban open spaces. How much of each? Which should prevail if both are impossible in a given site? Leaving such details to administrators may be a political way out of an impasse at the stage of program design, but it creates havoc at the stage of implementation. At the least, it may lead to delay as administrators worry and debate alternatives among themselves. At the worst, it kills a program by allowing unenthusiastic administrators to use the ambiguity as an excuse to do nothing.

If a politician insists on undue speed in planning, this in itself can hamper program preparation. Lyndon Johnson's political metabolism was hyperactive. His harassment of aides was legendary, as was his insistence on instant planning and implementation. He supervised the frenzied planning of his War on Poverty with an eye to shoving through Congress as much new legislation as possible before the inevitable cooling of the nation's ardor for social welfare. He recognized that planning had to suffer, and that much would prove unworkable in the agencies.[6]

The new-towns program also illustrates the problem of haste. President Johnson extracted a planned program some three days after his initial inspiration. When the plans were formalized, however, members of the President's own team objected to the initial simplicity of the program. The planning was too Washington-centered, and there seemed little awareness of the opposition that would emerge from local leaders whose cooperation was essential.

"Inadequate planning" is a simplistic explanation that is often given when a thorough inquiry is not made as to why a program has failed. If the

[6]T. R. Marmor, "The Congress: Medicare Politics and Policy," in A. P. Sindler, ed., *American Political Institutions and Public Policy* (Boston: Little, Brown, 1969); and D. P. Moynihan, *Maximum Feasible Misunderstanding: Community Action in the War on Poverty* (New York: Free Press, 1970).

A program that does not work as hoped.

BOX 11-1   Disclosure That Doesn't Disclose

The extensive disclosure requirements imposed on Congress in recent years have given voters more information than ever before about the financial dealings and personal wealth of elected representatives.

But, ironically, the methods of disclosure can distort the true picture of a member's wealth; moreover, the structure of the disclosure forms, in certain cases, presents an open invitation for members to obfuscate or to conceal information.

These problems make an exact calculation of a member's net worth impossible unless the individual voluntarily supplies additional information.

Several members have been doing this for years, most notably Rep. Paul Simon, D-Ill., who released his 24th annual public financial disclosure statement this year. It has been his practice since first taking public office in 1955 as a member of the Illinois state House. Rep. Philip M. Crane, R-Ill., a presidential hopeful, filed a statement over 100 pages in length. Sen. Claiborne Pell, D-R.I., released 67 pages of financial information, the most lengthy statement in the Senate.

CATEGORIES OF VALUE

The financial disclosure rules require a member to reveal the "category of value" owned by him or his spouse and dependents. Each category represents a "range" of wealth and not an actual amount. Examples are: "between $15,001–$50,000" and "between $100,001–$250,000." . . .

The misleading nature of the categories can be shown in the disclosure of Sen. Russell B. Long, D-La., who listed all his income and holdings, and voluntarily showed a net worth of $2,817,731. Using the categories, however, Long's net worth could be anywhere between $2,127,000 and $4,760,000.

Walter (Dee) Huddleston, D-Ky., gave the exact amount of his unearned income as $14,901. Using the categories, his income could be $12,301 to $38,000.

For most members, the most serious distortion is in the $15,001–$50,000 category.

If a member had three holdings of about $16,000 each, the actual total would be $48,000. But under the category system, those would total $45,000–$150,000.

Another distortion inherent in the category system is the largest category value. In the House it is over $250,000; in the Senate it is over $5 million.

Rep. Fred Richmond, D-N.Y., reported his holdings in Walco National Corp. as "over $250,000," which is all that is required by law for House members. Richmond held 750,000 shares of stock in Walco National in 1977, and sold 2,000 shares in June 1978, leaving him with 748,000 shares. At current stock market value, his financial interest in Walco National should be about $16.5 million—$16.25 million more than he had to disclose.

PROBLEMS WITH THE FORMS

The structure of the disclosure forms also permitted errors.

The House forms for 1978 were short on space for anything but the most miniscule of holdings for an individual member. The instructions were short on detail and briefly printed on the reverse side of each member's disclosure cover sheet. House Ethics Committee staffers were deluged with questions on procedures for filling out the forms.

On the other hand, the Senate Ethics Committee published a 43-page manual for senators and employees, and received far fewer procedural questions.

The different forms allowed the accuracy of information to vary, especially the value of financial interests.

The Ethics in Government Act requires members to disclose "the current value" of their real property holdings unless the current value "is not ascertainable without an appraisal." If the latter case is true, members could use different calculation methods to determine the value, providing the method used is explained.

Because of limited space on the House forms and the brevity of instructions, information about real property holdings was more likely to be reported at fair market value than through other methods.

The Senate forms provided a separate column for senators to list the method used to value their property. This appeared to invite senators not to report the current value. Hence, Sen. Long reporting an interest in "133 acres of timberland, Winn Parish, La." at a value of "not more than $5,000, purchase price in 1935."

The county assessor's office in Winn Parish, La., told a reporter that timberland there is valued between $500 and $750 per acre. This suggests that the current value of Long's timberland might be between $66,500 and $100,000. If the timber on the land is top-quality southern pine, the value could be as high as $1,500 per acre, which means Long's holding could be worth as much as $200,000.

Long also reported 800 acres of timberland in Livingston, La., at a 1935 purchase price of $36,246. Based on the U.S. Forest Service assessment that virtually no timberland in the United States today is worth less than $300 per acre, 800 acres would be worth at least $240,000 and could be worth over $1 million.

Although this avenue of disclosing as little as possible was open to all members, few took advantage of it. Only six senators listed most of their real estate holdings at acquisition cost.

FILLING OUT THE FORMS

Some members simply filled out the forms incorrectly or incompletely.

Several, such as Rep. Harold Runnels, D-N.M., reported income from dividends but listed no stockholdings. Rep. Charles Wilson, D-Texas, reported rental income without listing an interest in real property.

The winner of the "most illegible handwriting award" this year goes to freshman Rep. Ron Paul, R-Texas, who filled out his form himself in longhand. Paul is a doctor.

SOURCE: Andrea Yank, *Congressional Quarterly*, September 1, 1979.

problem is a shortage of resources—money, administrators, or details of law or rules that deprive administrators of essential authority—it may not be so much a case of inadequate planning as it is a lack of political support or too much competition from programs with higher priority. Planners may know which resources will make a program work, but may be unable to convince key people in the executive and legislative branches. Budgeting often works according to the criterion of what is available, rather than of what is needed. Personnel allocations come under the influence of government-wide ceilings or hiring freezes. Requests for new legal authority must compete with other matters for the attention of the Executive Office and key members of Congress, as well as run the gamut of opposing interests.

Inadequate planning is also the curse that is hurled unfairly at the people in charge of new or experimental activities. Research-and-development projects in the military are a favorite target of politicians and journalists, who use invective and ridicule against their cost overruns. Perhaps there is some waste in these programs. Also, their planners might be guilty of flim-flam in announcing cost estimates that are unrealistically low. However, it is the essence of research to deal with unknowns, and to come up short of some of the aspirations that motivated the research.

Inflated Aspirations

Some of what is labeled inadequate planning might really be inflated aspirations. What appears at first sight to be snafued implementation may be more a problem in the eye of the beholder than failure in the hands of administrators. The loftiest goals of President Johnson's War on Poverty were bound to failure. Sophisticates may have recognized them as the puffery necessary to gain support in the public and Congress. Likewise, President Carter's various targets for energy saving. Exaggeration is as much the tool of politicians as it is of commercial advertisers.

Care must be taken not to cite inflated aspirations as an excuse for poor implementation, thus providing administrators with a handy excuse: "We never believed we could attain much targets. It was the fault of politicians in describing their goals in too grand a style." The fault is not entirely in the hands of politicians. Program administrators provide many of the details that come out of the Executive Office and Congress. Administrators have a stake in their programs from the beginning, and they supply some of the propaganda that surrounds them—both to convince politicians to lend their support and to help politicians win public approval.

Perversity

Governments are not populated with angels. Perversity occurs both among the politicians who formulate and proclaim policies and among the administrators who implement them. Members of Congress can appeal to their constituents who support a program *and* to those who oppose it. They vote in behalf of provisions that define the principles of a bill, but against provisions that are essential to its implementation. The President or members of Congress can support a bill that authorizes a program, while they decide against appropriations or seek only a fraction of the money that is necessary. The reasons of "economic constraints" or "other pressing matters that require the funds available" are universal excuses that are difficult to rebut.

Administrators have their own reasons to be perverse, and their own tricks. They may oppose a program in principle, simply because they don't like it. They may want to hurt an enemy of long standing, and therefore drag their feet over a new program favored by the enemy. Administrators may see implications in the way a program is announced or in the funding formula that—if the program is successful—may become an unwanted precedent for future programs.

The common tactic of administrators who oppose a program is to do nothing. There are many ways to stall or to raise questions that send program advocates back to their drawing boards. A skillful player can make opposition look like support. "This sounds like a great program to add low-income housing in the inner city. Why don't you make it better by adding a provision in behalf of open spaces?"—knowing full well that open-space provisions cannot be resisted in an era that is concerned with the environment, but knowing too that such a provision will create delay, if not the death of the program.

Another device available to the perverse policy-maker is the use of program symbols in place of program substance.[7] This device is not new. Roman emperors recognized the value of a circus when bread was scarce. Demagogues have been quick to create the image of enemies to distract the public from difficult problems. Much of the writing that comes from Ralph Nader and his Center for the Study of Responsive Laws deals with regulatory programs that promise more than they deliver. Nader's central message—that programs legislated are not programs delivered—is a message both about problems of implementation and about perverse policy-makers. Nader's typical case is a regulatory program that is captured by the industries it is supposed to regulate, with the consumer getting little more than rhetoric. (See Chapter 14.)

Eugene Bardach's influential book, *The Implementation Game,* suggests by its title that officials may take programs less than seriously. Bardach lists several games that lessen the quality of program implementation.[8]

1. *Easy money.* Government agencies offer grants or contracts with less than a thorough review of proposals. Business firms, universities, and other nonprofit organizations can raid the public treasury with

---

[7]M. Edelman,*The Symbolic Uses of Politics* (Urbana: University of Illinois Press, 1964).
[8]Bardach, op. cit.

hyped-up proposals that stand little chance of being implemented as promised.

2. *The budget game.* One reason why the easy-money game works is that agencies have an incentive to spend their entire appropriation. Not to do so is to risk a cut in the next budget cycle. Toward the end of the year in particular, agencies that face an impending surplus may be an easy target for a grant proposal that is assembled rapidly.

3. *Pork barreling.* Program administrators have an incentive to please allies in Congress. One way to do this is to spread their program activities over many locales, even if some proposed projects seem unlikely to succeed. The need for broad appeal minimizes the prospect of good implementation.

4. *Piling on.* An attractive program can become the donkey to carry extraneous goals. Motives may be hard to discern. New goals may be designed to break the creature's back, or it may be hoped that a strong program will carry both itself and the new load.

5. *Up for grabs.* Designing a program with high-sounding, but ambiguous goals. Administrators might make something of it, or they might not.

6. *Tokenism.* Supporting a program verbally, but providing only enough resources to allow a small show of effort.

7. *Social entropy.* Waiting. Enough problems of incompetence, lack of coordination, or quarrels about a program may bring about further delay and eventual death.

8. *Not our problem.* An agency expected to cooperate with a program refuses to see that it fits into the agency's defined responsibilities.

Complex Environments

No program is implemented in a vacuum. A program's target is likely to be a situation that policy-makers consider a problem in need of repair. The problem may be more difficult than first envisioned. Or it may shift its character in response to the activities undertaken by government.

Some governmental problems are ages old—chronic and intractable. The poor, the diseased, the ignorant, and the criminal will probably always be with us. Programs that seek to alleviate such problems will, in all likelihood, fall somewhat short of their aspirations. The programs may improve conditions, but not cure them.

The economy provides the financial resources for government, and offers its own problems. An increase in unemployment will cut into the tax receipts available, and tilt priorities to favor certain programs instead of others. Inflation reduces the value of funds already budgeted, and may lead the President or Congress to lessen support for planned expansion of program activities. International crises may distract the White House and cut into the political support available to administrators in the domestic sector.

Some problems involve antagonists who seek to foil the implementation of programs. Such is most clearly the case in military and international relations. Our adversaries seek to outwit our efforts, and to set up new conditions to prevent whatever we might try.

Domestic programs also have their adversaries. Prime examples are policies designed to obtain wage and price stability. Unions seek to emphasize price stability, but want a boost in wages to catch up with the previous increases in prices. Business management, in contrast, seeks to emphasize wage stability, but wants to boost prices to catch up with recent increases in the costs of production. Efforts to control wages or prices in peacetime seem doomed to failure. These efforts have ranged from Richard Nixon's freeze of wages and prices during his second term to Gerald Ford's ridiculous and short-lived program to distribute WIN buttons (Whip Inflation Now) and urge business and labor to hold the line on prices and wages. Even Nixon's serious effort at economic stability succumbed to an onslaught of special circumstances. Claims in behalf of exemptions eroded the simple prohibition of wage and price increases until the program collapsed from complexity and lack of credibility.

Another frustrating feature of the political environment is its escalating appetite. Edward Banfield once used the image of the mechanical rabbit at the racetrack, always set just ahead of the fastest dog.[9] Insofar as aspirations for social programs increase faster than government's ability to deliver, we are bound to find that our newest programs have not been implemented fully. In recent years, groups have demanded not just minimum maintenance from welfare programs, but that they counsel and otherwise lead their clients to end their dependence. Parents have demanded that our educational programs expand their efforts for special students with physical and emotional handicaps, and that they integrate many of these students into the regular classrooms. Groups that were once submerged or invisible in the political process—ethnic minorities, women, and gay people—have asserted strong claims for staff positions. Such demands help to overload agencies that are already suffering from skimpy budgets. If resources do not increase along with demands, inadequate implementation is inevitable.

Some research looks at statistical associations between government expenditures and the benefits that clients expect to receive from administrative agencies. In order to make positive judgments of the implementation of policy intentions, the jurisdictions showing high (or low) levels of spending should show consistently high (or low) scores on most measures of ser-

---

[9]E. C. Banfield, *The Unheavenly City Revisited* (Boston: Little, Brown, 1974).

vice. Three studies in different contexts show that relationships between government expenditures and levels of public service are neither strong nor pervasive. A highly regarded study of education finds that school spending bears little relationship to the learning that occurs. More important are traits of the pupil's family and friends. Pupils who come from well-educated families and associate with friends who are academically motivated are likely to do better in school than if family and friends are not supportive.[10] A study of 163 Georgia school districts shows only weak relationships between measures of educational spending and service outputs.[11] Another study of state and local government spending and services across the country found that only 11 out of 27 service measures (41 percent) showed sizable and positive relationships with government spending.[12] Some relationships were negative, which means that high scores on spending corresponded with low scores on service. In the field of roads and highways, the mileage per capita of rural roads and a measure of traffic safety were negatively related with state and local government highway spending per capita. Apparently, the low-spending states have developed the most extensive systems of rural roads and also experience the most enviable record of highway safety.

Several social and economic features of the environment show stronger, and more consistent, relationships with services than does government spending. Road safety varies inversely with the incidence of motor vehicles. In the field of secondary education, service levels are highest where there is the greatest incidence of adults with at least a high school education. We can only speculate about explanations. Perhaps parental concern for education makes itself felt on children and school personnel. Children may be well prepared for school, and they may stimulate administrators to provide high-quality programs.

IMPROVING IMPLEMENTATION

Scholars who study implementation are more helpful in pointing to problems than to solutions. By noting some of the problems that are intractable, they imply that no solutions exist. Yet administrators may be able to alleviate some of the problems identified, and improve the general quality of program implementation without meeting all of the aspirations of program designers.

---

[10]J. S. Coleman, *Equality of Educational Opportunity* (Washington, D.C.: U.S. Government Printing Office, 1966).

[11]I. Sharkansky, "Environment, Policy, Output and Impact: Problems of Theory and Method in the Analysis of Public Policy" (paper presented at meeting of American Political Science Association, Washington, D.C., 1968).

[12]I. Sharkansky, *The Politics of Taxing and Spending* (Indianapolis: Bobbs-Merrill, 1969), Chapter 6.

Policy-makers can be alert to the pitfalls along the road to implementation. The following statements offer general advice. Sophisticated observers realize they cannot all be attained in the really tough cases. By attending to these points, however, policy-makers may improve implementation.

1. Be concerned with implementation. Have a staff member work on issues of implementation from the first conception of the program and through all its stages of definition, drafting, negotiation with executive and legislative branches, and into actual programming.
2. Define goals clearly, so that personnel in all relevant units of government understand and support a unified conception of the program.
3. Communicate essential details of the program to all who will be involved as administrators and clients.
4. Provide adequate funding, personnel, and program authority to permit the program to be administered as it was conceived.
5. Know what to expect from the environment. Be alert to continuing political opposition, adverse changes in the economy, the perspectives of relevant state and local authorities and key administrators.
6. Keep on top of program evolution. Be prepared to recognize and to respond to problems as they emerge. Keep lines of communication open to executive and legislative supporters who may help with additional money, personnel authorizations, new legislation or executive orders, and public support directed at the media.

So much for building a continuing concern with implementation into program planning and administration. The staff that concentrates on implementation will not always be able to comply with each of these points. When all is said and done, it is best to have modest expectations. Bardach's sobering thought sums up the problem:

> In the short run, it is essential to invest a great deal of energy in designing implementable policies and programs. For the longer run, however, it is equally essential to become more modest in our demands on, and expectations of, the institutions of representative government.[13]

SUMMARY

The study of implementation is, for the most part, the study of programs that do not work as planned. Actually, most programs seem to work most of the time. It may be that new and difficult cases attract our attention.

---

[13]Bardach, op. cit., p. 283.

Their problems deserve our concern, but they should not be exaggerated into a general condemnation of public administration.

It is not always easy to decide exactly what programs ought to be doing. The difficulties of policy-making are addressed in Chapter 10. Vague program goals haunt us in trying to assess the degree of actual implementation.

The question *Why don't programs work?* can receive several answers: insufficient resources; complex organizations that create snafus instead of coordination; inadequate planning; inflated aspirations; perversity among policy-makers and administrators; and complex environments that foil program planners.

What to do in the face of imperfect implementation? Two short answers are: plan better, with concern for the factors that are likely to frustrate implementation; and be modest, not seeking goals that are likely to be frustrated.

PART V

Special Topics

After reading Chapter 11 on implementation, you will have a bare-bones knowledge of public administration. Parts of the whole should attract greater attention; there is much that is fascinating in policy-making and public administration. Part V looks more deeply at five such areas that were described only briefly in earlier chapters.

Chapter 12 compares public administration in different settings: between different states of the United States, between different regions and countries of the world, and between some U.S. states and some nations. Chapter 13 looks at the intergovernmental links within the United States that are part of virtually all domestic programs. Chapter 14 explores the rule-making of administrative bodies, and focuses on the activities of regulatory agencies. Chapter 15 describes the growing issue of contracting, whereby much of domestic policy-making and program implementation is put into the hands of bodies that are not part of government. Chapter 16 takes an overview of public administration from the client's perspective. It traces several client problems to features of public administration described in earlier chapters, and offers some advice to clients who feel confused or short-changed by government departments.

12

Comparisons Between
States and Nations

The other chapters of this book focus on public administration within the United States. This chapter compares different administrative settings within the United States and throughout the world. The comparative method shows differences in form and process in varying contexts, identifies the range across which administrative phenomena vary, and demonstrates the patterns whereby certain features of administration tend to occur together. Comparative analysis reveals a great deal about the influence of economic conditions, for example, over the activities of administrative agencies. The key questions of this chapter are:

What variations exist between public administration in different settings?

What explains the variations?

VARIATIONS IN THE UNITED STATES

Economic Interpretations of Policy

Thomas Dye provides substantial evidence that the level of economic development within a jurisdiction affects the nature of government policies.[1] He has written mostly in the American context—comparing certain states and

---

[1] T. R. Dye, *Politics, Economics, and the Public: Policy Outcomes in the American States* (Chicago: Rand McNally, 1966).

localities to others. Much of what he finds, however, applies to international comparisons as well. Dye finds high levels of economic development generally associated with high levels of expenditure in the fields of education, welfare, and health; governments in the wealthiest settings spend the most and offer the most attractive programs. In the field of highways and natural resources, however, economic development is inversely associated with levels of spending and services. The poorest governments may offer the most attractive programs.

Dye suggests that the economy offers material resources that either provide the wherewithal or impose limits on administrators and other policy-makers:

> There is little doubt that the ability of states to raise revenues is a function of their level of economic development. Both tax revenues and total revenues per capita are closely related to wealth, as is the ability to carry larger per capita debt levels.[2]

This is a *resource* view of the economic–output link. In its simplest form, Dye's view implies that citizen demands are similar from one state to another. Governments in poor areas offer the most generous policies that their resources permit. Governments in wealthy areas generously provide whatever resources are necessary to meet a particular need. At the same time, because of the great resources available, policies in wealthy states may be supported with relatively low tax burdens.

It is not only through a resource–output connection that a level of economic development can affect administrators' programs. The economy may affect the needs felt by the population and perceived by policy-makers. This is a *need* view of the economic–output link. In low-income areas, policy-makers may tax their citizens with unusual severity to provide the demanded level of services. Dye uses a need explanation for his findings that low-income rural states score high on their road programs:

> Quite clearly, rural politics are much more highway-oriented than urban politics. Part of this phenomenon may be a product of the historical problems of rural isolation. "Let's Get Out of Mud" was a familiar battlecry in rural politics a few years ago.[3]

State Expenditures

The American states provide a natural laboratory for economic comparison. The expenditures of each state indicate which states give their administrators greater or lesser amounts of financial resources. Only a small fraction

---

[2]Ibid., p. 290.

[3]Ibid., p. 161.

of the total is used to support the governor, the legislature, and the judiciary. Figures compiled by the U.S. Bureau of the Census show that these three branches outside the administrative departments receive, on the average, less than 1 percent of total state government expenditures.[4]

In studying variations in states' expenditures, we must correct raw figures for state-to-state differences in population and other factors. The resulting figure—general expenditures per capita—is the measure that is used most frequently to judge the fiscal resources made available in each state to support its public services. Table 12-1 ranks the states according to this measure for 1978.

Table 12-1 State Government Expenditures per Capita, 1978

State	Amount	State	Amount
Alaska	$2,875	Idaho	$851
Hawaii	1,520	Pennsylvania	819
Delaware	1,125	Arizona	811
Wyoming	1,075	South Dakota	810
Minnesota	1,051	New Jersey	788
New Mexico	1,038	North Carolina	785
Vermont	1,037	Colorado	782
New York	1,005	Mississippi	781
North Dakota	987	Alabama	780
California	967	Illinois	779
Rhode Island	965	Connecticut	773
Montana	951	Virginia	764
Washington	947	South Carolina	752
Wisconsin	945	Oklahoma	734
West Virginia	935	Arkansas	718
Nevada	922	Georgia	712
Oregon	912	Nebraska	706
Michigan	910	Kansas	695
Massachusetts	908	Ohio	667
Utah	905	New Hampshire	662
Maryland	902	Tennessee	653
Louisiana	894	Indiana	647
Maine	865	Florida	621
Iowa	858	Texas	620
Kentucky	857	Missouri	565

SOURCE: U.S. Bureau of the Census, *State Government Finances in 1978* (Washington, D.C.: U.S. Government Printing Office, 1979).

---

[4]I. Sharkansky, "State Administrators in the Political Process," in H. Jacob and K. N. Vines, eds., *Politics in the American States*, 2d ed. (Boston: Little, Brown, 1971).

Alaska and Hawaii outspend the other states, which is partly due to the high cost of goods and services in these newest states. The lowest per capita spender is Missouri, which may come as a surprise to those who might have expected that a poorer southern state would hold this position. Other wealthy states scoring near the bottom of this list are Indiana and Ohio. Administrative agencies in these state governments have been lethargic in supporting programs that are popular elsewhere. When state and local spending is combined for each state, the lowest-ranking states are Arkansas, Missouri, and Indiana. State government expenditures are often highest where local governments are relatively weak and where private resources (as measured by personal income and industrialization) are meager. Where citizens and local governments are poor, state authorities tend to collect sizable revenues and provide them with a disproportionate share of the services received by the population.

Professionalism

States differ from one another in their efforts to professionalize administration. A professional cadre of administrators has several attributes: advanced training in their fields of specialization, an active concern to stay abreast of the latest developments, and a desire to implement the most advanced level of service that is available. Deil Wright made an opinion survey of 933 state administrators from across the country that shows one dimension of their professionalism. The large majority of his respondents (76 percent) want an expansion of their own agency's services and expenditures. The administrators had a choice of expansion at levels of 0–5 percent, 5–10 percent, 10–15 percent, and over 15 percent. Almost one-third of the respondents chose the uppermost range of expansion. If Wright's specific alternatives had gone beyond 15 percent, it might have been possible to gauge the upper limits of administrators' desires. As it is, many administrators seem to want a greater magnitude of expansion than Wright expected.[5]

Employees' salaries show part of the states' efforts to professionalize their administrative systems. One group of states scores consistently high in the salaries paid to employees in general and to the heads of major units, such as the chief budget officer and the heads of departments of education, welfare, and health. The highest-ranking states in this group are New York, California, Ohio, Michigan, Pennsylvania, and Illinois. The states with low scores on administrative salaries are Montana, Louisiana, Delaware, Idaho,

---

[5]D. S. Wright, "Executive Leadership in State Administration," *Midwest Journal of Political Science,* 11 (February 1967): 1–26.

Mississippi, and Wyoming. As this list suggests, salaries correspond with state economies. A high level of industrialization, in particular, may provide the resources necessary to support high levels of spending on the civil service, and it may provide models of salary levels in the private sector that are adopted by the state government.

The Influence of Economic Conditions on Policy

The influence of the economy on policy can change with conditions. The economy varies in its influence at different levels of government, at different periods of time, and among different kinds of public services. Economic development has greater influence on local governments than it does on state governments.[6] Most local governments must draw on a narrowly limited geographical area for resources. In addition, they are confined to only one major revenue source—the property tax—which generates a great deal of political controversy. State governments draw on their larger jurisdictions and can transfer resources from "have" to "have-not" communities. State officials also have wider revenue options that include taxes on income and retail sales. State officials can escape many of the constraints on policy that seem to originate in the economic sector of local government. Officials of the national government appear to be hindered even less by economic constraints, partly because of their power to tax the resources of the wealthy areas of the country and partly because of their ability to borrow in the face of current deficits in the taxing–spending balance. The national government operates numerous programs to influence levels of employment, interest, and wages. At times it may be as much the master as the subordinate of the economy.

The influence of economic conditions on state and local government policies appears to be diminishing.[7] Policy-makers now have more opportunities to spend at levels above the norm for their economic conditions. Some of this increased flexibility may reflect growth in the magnitude of federal aid. By transferring resources from have to have-not jurisdictions, the federal government makes up for some of the differentials among the states. Also, state and local governments now have more flexible tax structures. With state taxes on personal incomes or retail sales now used by over 40 of the states (no state used either tax at the beginning of the century), and with numerous local governments now also turning to these forms of

---

[6]Compare the findings reported in H. E. Brazer, *City Expenditures in the United States* (New York: National Bureau of Economic Research, 1959), with those in I. Sharkansky, *Spending in the American States* (Chicago: Rand McNally, 1968), Chapter 4.

[7]A. K. Campbell and S. Sachs, *Metropolitan America: Fiscal Patterns and Governmental Systems* (New York: Free Press, 1967), p. 57.

The states and regions of the United States differ greatly from one another. Information like this attracts the attention of political campaigners and policy-makers. Social and economic traits affect the kinds of campaign strategies that may be successful in each state and the kinds of programs that may be demanded by state residents.

Table 12-2 A Population Profile of the States (population 1978; other data 1970)

State	Population		Age		Median voting age	Racial composition		Employment	
	Total (in millions)	Urban	18–25	65+		White	Black	White-collar	Blue-collar
Alabama	3.7	58.4%	18.9%	14.7%	42.8	73.4%	26.4%	40.6%	42.7%
Alaska	0.4	48.7	26.0	3.8	33.9	78.8	0.3	64.8	35.2
Arizona	2.4	79.6	19.5	14.2	41.9	90.6	3.0	51.1	32.3
Arkansas	2.2	50.0	17.2	18.7	45.5	81.2	18.6	64.8	35.2
California	22.3	90.9	19.0	13.5	41.6	89.0	7.0	54.4	30.7
Colorado	2.7	78.5	21.1	13.0	40.2	95.7	2.9	53.8	28.3
Connecticut	3.1	77.4	16.8	14.3	43.7	93.5	6.0	52.4	36.2
Delaware	0.6	72.2	18.7	12.4	41.4	85.1	14.2	51.0	34.4
District of Columbia	0.7	100.0	21.3	13.2	40.2	27.7	71.1	73.6	26.4
Florida	8.6	80.5	16.0	21.1	46.5	84.1	15.5	49.8	32.0
Georgia	5.1	60.3	20.6	12.4	40.4	73.8	26.0	43.6	39.9
Hawaii	0.9	83.1	22.9	8.9	38.3	38.8	1.0	49.9	31.3
Idaho	0.9	54.1	12.5	9.5	43.2	98.0	0.3	46.7	33.2
Illinois	11.2	83.0	17.4	14.9	43.3	86.4	12.8	49.1	36.6
Indiana	5.4	64.9	18.7	14.7	42.5	92.8	6.9	42.0	42.7
Iowa	2.9	57.2	17.2	18.9	45.1	98.5	1.2	42.8	30.8
Kansas	2.3	66.1	18.9	17.7	44.0	94.5	4.8	47.8	30.6
Kentucky	3.5	52.3	19.3	16.0	43.0	92.3	7.5	40.1	41.2
Louisiana	4.0	66.1	20.4	13.5	41.5	69.7	29.9	45.2	36.1
Maine	1.1	50.8	17.7	17.6	44.5	99.3	0.3	40.6	44.1
Maryland	4.1	76.6	18.7	11.7	41.2	81.4	17.9	55.8	31.0

State									
Massachusetts	5.8	84.6	18.2	16.6	44.1	96.3	3.1	52.7	34.2
Michigan	9.2	73.8	19.0	13.3	42.2	88.3	11.2	44.8	40.7
Minnesota	4.0	66.4	18.5	16.8	43.2	98.2	1.0	48.5	30.9
Mississippi	2.4	44.5	19.8	16.1	43.2	62.8	36.8	38.6	41.0
Missouri	4.9	70.1	17.3	17.9	44.6	89.3	10.3	46.9	35.6
Montana	0.8	53.4	18.0	15.5	43.6	95.5	0.3	45.3	28.3
Nebraska	1.6	61.5	18.1	18.7	44.5	96.6	2.7	44.4	28.3
Nevada	0.7	80.9	17.3	9.7	40.5	91.8	5.7	47.1	26.2
New Hampshire	0.9	56.4	18.4	16.1	43.2	99.4	0.3	44.5	42.1
New Jersey	7.3	88.9	15.8	14.5	44.1	88.6	10.7	52.7	36.2
New Mexico	1.2	69.8	20.4	11.5	40.1	90.1	1.9	51.4	39.9
New York	17.7	81.7	16.5	15.8	44.1	86.8	11.9	55.1	30.8
North Carolina	5.6	45.0	21.1	12.4	40.8	76.6	22.4	38.5	45.8
North Dakota	0.7	44.3	19.3	16.9	43.9	97.0	0.4	42.4	21.0
Ohio	10.7	75.3	18.2	14.4	42.9	90.6	9.1	45.4	40.8
Oklahoma	2.9	68.0	18.1	17.3	44.2	88.9	7.0	47.8	33.2
Oregon	2.4	67.1	17.7	16.2	44.1	97.2	1.3	48.2	34.2
Pennsylvania	11.8	71.5	16.4	16.0	45.2	91.0	8.6	45.0	41.5
Rhode Island	0.9	87.1	19.8	16.0	44.1	96.6	2.7	45.1	42.3
South Carolina	3.0	47.6	22.1	11.6	40.1	69.3	30.5	37.3	46.8
South Dakota	0.7	44.6	18.3	18.9	45.2	94.7	0.2	41.0	22.3
Tennessee	4.4	58.8	18.7	14.7	42.6	83.7	16.1	41.4	42.2
Texas	13.0	79.7	19.8	13.7	41.4	86.6	12.7	48.4	34.2
Utah	1.3	80.4	23.3	12.1	39.2	97.4	0.6	51.8	32.2
Vermont	0.5	32.1	19.7	16.4	42.8	99.6	0.2	46.2	34.3
Virginia	5.1	63.1	20.8	11.9	40.5	80.8	18.6	48.9	36.2
Washington	3.7	72.6	19.5	14.2	42.3	95.4	2.1	50.7	32.9
West Virginia	1.9	39.0	17.3	16.6	45.2	95.6	4.2	40.4	45.2
Wisconsin	4.7	65.9	18.4	16.6	43.7	96.4	2.9	43.2	37.2
Wyoming	0.4	60.5	18.0	14.2	42.7	93.2	0.8	46.3	30.2

SOURCE: *National Journal*, October 20, 1979. Reprinted with permission.

[267]

taxation, policy-makers can tap an increasing proportion of the resources within their own jurisdictions. Even the poorest states (Mississippi, South Carolina, Arkansas, Vermont) have some pockets of wealth that can help support services in their poorest counties.

Economic conditions exercise fewer constraints on some kinds of policies than on others. The political saliency of a policy is one of the factors that can lessen the influence of economics. A program's popularity can provoke the use of substantially more resources than are normally associated with a jurisdiction's level of wealth. Officials "try harder" under the impetus of public demand. Under different conditions—when public sentiment runs counter to a program—there is less performance than would be expected on the basis of economic conditions.[8]

The findings about how economic conditions influence policy-makers and administrators may apply beyond the United States. It is possible that the administrative units of national governments in other countries are less constrained by economic conditions than are those of local or regional governments—owing to the greater jurisdiction of the national governments, their opportunity to redistribute resources from richer to poorer areas, and their opportunity to exercise greater controls over their own economic development. Perhaps the influence of economic conditions over policy has declined in recent years, along with increases in wealth and familiarity with taxation and government borrowing. Perhaps the politicization of issues makes policy decisions less dependent on economic resources.

INTERNATIONAL VARIATIONS

Development

In international comparisons, a characteristic that seems important for public administration is the level of a country's development.[9] Development is related to but not identical with the level of economic wealth, as used in the previous section on variation in the United States. The term refers to an aggregate of economic, social, and political variables, each of which exists on a continuum ranging from less developed to more developed. An individual country may simultaneously exhibit some traits that appear to be

---

[8]See C. F. Cnudde and D. J. McCrone, "Party Competition and Welfare Policies in the American States," *American Political Science Review*, 63 (September 1969): 858–866; and I. Sharkansky and R. I. Hofferbert, "Dimensions of State Politics, Economics and Public Policy," *American Political Science Review*, 63 (September 1969): 867–879.

[9]A number of labels have appeared for the "less-developed" countries. Some of the most common alternatives include "emergent," "transitional," "developing," and "expectant." "Underdeveloped" no longer seems to be popular, perhaps because it carries the onus of a connotation of permanence. Terms suggesting movement toward some more-developed stage seem to be the most acceptable.

developed and others that appear to be less developed. Some features of public administration may likewise appear developed, while others in the same country—indeed in the same capital city—may resemble the administrative features of a less-developed country. Differences in public administration at each pole of the development continuum do not reflect the stage of development so much as peculiar historical experiences or cultural traits. Great Britain, France, Germany, and the United States, for example, are currently at about the same stage of advanced development. However, each of these nations demonstrates peculiarities in public administration that reflect its own evolution.

Social scientists disagree among themselves about the characteristics of development. To some, it is equated with the capacity to produce large amounts of tangible resources in relation to size of population, which translates into industrial output, agricultural produce, raw materials, gross national product, and personal income. Others, who focus not so much on material production as on the forms of social and economic organization, argue that advanced development exists in societies that:

1. Have relatively equal distributions of benefits.
2. Utilize modern technology.
3. Assign rewards according to personal achievement and not according to family, caste, or tribal background.
4. Use specialists instead of generalists in economic and governmental roles, who provide leadership in a full range of activities.
5. Have government units that can adjust to social or economic change and acquire new capabilities to meet new demands.[10]

Each trait of development is a distinct variable. However, many countries that score as more developed in one variable also score as more developed in other variables. The dimensions of development seem to reinforce one another. For example, the use of sophisticated technologies seems to impel a society toward specialization and toward the distribution of rewards according to personal achievement. Where there are complicated programs of medicine, agriculture, or industry, it is typical to allocate many of the educational resources to the training of technicians and professionals. In such a context, it is incongruous to give prestige and political power to religious and tribal leaders and not to those who have mastered both the sophisticated technologies and the large-scale organizations that seem to accompany these technologies.

Despite the tendency toward a clustering of the development characteristics, each of the most well-developed nations also shows some features of

---

[10]The following discussion relies on materials in F. Heady, *Public Administration: A Comparative Perspective* (New York: Dekker, 1979).

less-developed societies. Each has experienced some civil strife that reflects an inability to resolve the intense demands of certain social groups. Moreover, each has some "backward" regions that have been bypassed by some of the organizational traits and material wealth of development. Indeed, certain regions in the United States offer economic and political traits sufficiently similar to those of Africa, Asia, and Latin America to question whether the United States should be designated a developed country.

Administration in More-Developed Countries

When writers describe well-developed nations, they generally focus on most of the countries of Europe and those countries elsewhere that have followed European models. Outside of Europe the list typically includes the United States, Canada, Australia, New Zealand, Japan, and Israel. The following features are generally shared by these countries:

1. The organization of government is patterned after the organization of the private sector. There is a high degree of task specialization, and roles are assigned according to the personal achievements of individuals rather than according to family status or social class.
2. Political decisions and legal judgments are made according to secular standards of rationality; traditional (religious or tribal) elites have lost any real power to affect major governmental decisions.
3. Government activity extends over a wide range of public and personal affairs, and it tends toward further expansion into all major spheres.
4. Popular interest and involvement in public affairs are widespread.
5. Those persons who occupy positions of political or governmental leadership are widely viewed as legitimate holders of those positions, and transfers of leadership tend to occur according to prescribed, orderly procedures.

Some of these characteristics have counterparts in public administration:

1. The administration is large and has numerous, distinct subunits. Many of these units require highly specialized employees, and together they represent the full range of occupational specializations that is found in the society. This reflects both task specialization and the wide range of government activities.
2. The administration tends to accept policy directions that come from other branches of government. This tendency reflects both task specialization and the legitimacy of elected officials.

3. The administration is considered to be professional, both by its own members and by other participants in the policy process. Professionalism is a sign of specialization among administrators.

Among the well-developed nations, considerable differences in bureaucratic forms and procedures reflect each country's historical background. One writer has compared public administration in France and Germany with that in Great Britain and the United States.[11] Officials in the upper levels of French and German administration have achieved a distinct status, separate from other occupational groups in their societies. They undergo a long period of training in elite institutions of higher education. This training helps to maintain both the historic upper-class backgrounds of public officials and the antidemocratic bias in their norms. The separateness of public administrators is enforced even further by elaborate procedures for administrative self-government. The recruiting of new officials is controlled by the administrators themselves. Upper-echelon administrators are promoted from within the career service. Each of these countries has a system of administrative courts that is distinct from the civil court system. Administrative courts hear complaints brought against administrative actions by private citizens and charges brought by administrators themselves concerning their ranks, salaries, or pensions.

In Great Britain and the United States, the tradition is to avoid any clear separation between public administrators and other occupational groups. In contrast to the continental model of distinctive training for high-level administrative positions, the British and American services recruit from persons with a generalized training. In some details of their selection procedures, however, the British and Americans diverge from one another. The British are more inclined to select recruits from among the graduates of elite universities than from schools that have curricula specifically designed for professional administrators. British graduates in literature or the classics have traditionally been favored by essay examinations in general knowledge.

Related to the Jacksonian tradition that any citizen is fit to perform the chores of a public employee is the American practice—still observed in numerous state and local governments and for some federal positions—of filling government jobs on the basis of political appointments, without regard to the details of a candidate's training. However, both Britain and the United States have moved toward selection procedures that emphasize specialized competence in the administrative tasks to be performed. Yet neither country provides elite training schools for professional administrators, as in France and Germany, thereby stressing the distinctiveness of a

---

[11] Ibid.

government career. In Britain and the United States, there is no pervasive concern among public officials to distinguish their rank and status from those of other citizens, and there are no separate administrative courts. One important difference between the United States and Britain, is that, by tradition, British civil servants have more typically come from the upper social class, while in America some effort has been made to ensure that civil servants are representative of the population. The British generally appoint high-level administrators from within the ranks of the civil service. At both federal and state levels in the United States, many high-level administrative positions are filled with noncivil servants. American executives in government and in the private sector believe that the "transient" business–government administrator can infuse the government bureaucracy with an innovative stimulus from the outside.

Administrative Incoherence

A problem that appears widely in more-developed countries is a lack of coherence and direction in the structures and procedures of public administration. The proliferation of nongovernmental bodies that do the work of government (see Chapters 2 and 15) appears in other countries besides the United States. The forms taken by nongovernmental bodies differ from one country to another, in keeping with underlying traits of culture, government, and the economy. The American setting has produced countless numbers of special authorities and private bodies that work for government under contract. Israel features limited-liability companies owned either wholly by the government or in partnership with the labor federation, international Jewish organizations, or private investors. Commonwealth and state governments in Australia have established several hundred statutory authorities. Such bodies involve themselves in a wide range of public activities: transportation, utilities, energy, banking, industrial production, commerce, and the provision of social services. By some estimates, these bodies on the margins of government are larger in the aggregate than the core departments of government. In fact, none of these countries has a clear record of how much the government does by means of these quasi-governmental bodies. The unclear lines of control between the government and quasi-governmental bodies result in problems of poor management and faulty accountability to the political branches of government.[12]

The lack of coherence may be most noticeable at local levels, where authorities design and implement their own programs, as well as implement

---

[12] I. Sharkansky, *Wither the State? Politics and Public Enterprise in Three Countries* (Chatham, N.J.: Chatham, 1979).

programs designed and funded in part by national authorities. *Who controls what?* is a topic of some concern when many units share policy design, funding, and implementation. A typical result is control by bureaucratic elites who operate within their specialized domains. Occasionally politicians dominate a particular matter in which they take an interest, but in general, elected officials lack control over the operation of programs.

Americans who wish to comprehend the true nature of their government must take into account the 78,000 local authorities, plus uncounted thousands of administrative entities within these authorities, as well as special authorities and contractors that operate in local settings. Some 22 percent of the resources that the federal government allocates to domestic activities are transferred to local, state, and regional governments, which adds a dimension that approaches international relations to activities that have shared financing, program design, and implementation.[13] Elected officials generally feel left out of decisions that are dominated by bureaucrats who speak for their different governments at the points at which program activities come together.[14] Much of the transfer of resources occurs in programs that are defined with a vagueness that defies control by elected officials or their immediate agents.[15] Intergovernmental mazes are thickest in metropolitan areas, where central city and suburban municipalities share territory with districts that provide schools and other services. Where this sharing of resources is complicated, there are often regional advisory bodies—like councils of governments—that try to systematize certain intergovernmental relations. In all of this, a fair amount of distrust and alienation is directed at officials.[16] (Chapter 13 returns to some of the special features of intergovernmental administration in the United States.)

The fragmented nature of British government in urban areas appears in the mixture of boroughs, urban and rural districts, parish councils and meetings, metropolitan counties and districts. Other bodies have responsibility for particular services, sometimes with their territories scattered in patchwork fashion. Within a single jurisdiction, the civil servants of different departments may follow their own procedures for recruitment, promotion, salary, and control. There is no unifying national civil service, as in several European countries, and no strong local chief executive along the

---

[13] I. Sharkansky, "Intergovernmental Relations," in P. C. Nystrom and W. H. Starbuck, eds., *Handbook of Organizational Design* (New York: Oxford University Press, 1981).

[14] See M. D. Reagan, *The New Federalism* (New York: Oxford University Press, 1972); and D. S. Wright, *Federal Grants-in-Aid: Perspectives and Alternatives* (Washington, D.C.: American Enterprise Institute, 1968).

[15] E. B. Staats, "New Problems of Accountability for Federal Programs," in B. L. R. Smith, ed., *The New Political Economy: The Public Use of the Private Sector* (London: Macmillan, 1975).

[16] M. K. Jennings and H. Zeigler, "The Salience of American State Politics," *American Political Science Review*, 64(June 1970): 523–535; and J. D. Aberbach and J. L. Walker, *Race in the City: Political Trust and Public Policy in the New Urban System* (Boston: Little, Brown, 1973).

lines of an American mayor or city manager, who might work to integrate the activities of different agencies or authorities.[17]

Sweden's localities also show a lack of coherence. Elected legislative councils exercise certain controls, while much administration is given over to executive boards. The boards deal with representatives of the national government and public corporations that also have a stake in common ventures. Protracted negotiation appears to be a dominant feature in their relation, with no single actor having clear authority to coordinate the bodies that must deal with each other.[18]

The incoherence of local authorities is no stranger to the socialist bloc. One Polish expert summarizes local decision-making in his country in words that fit many settings farther west:

> Everyone who has examined local power in Poland knows the difficulties encountered in obtaining information, or sometimes even the impossibility of getting answers to questions concerning roles in the decision process. In my opinion, the context . . . in which the majority of local decisions are made creates the situation in which the process seems unclear, even to the actors.[19]

Israel's cities depict a standoff between equally aggressive national ministers or senior civil servants on the one hand, and local officials on the other. Israel's public sector has its own maze of national and local authorities; universities, hospitals, and other public institutions; corporations associated with the state, local authorities, or the labor federation that deal with the urban-relevant areas of housing, industry, mass transit, and banking; plus other corporations that are subsidiaries of these corporations or joint ventures between them. Each unit may have its own source of funds in Israel, as well as a well-cultivated group of friends in the international Jewish community.

A certain degree of local incoherence may be inevitable in a state that provides many different services to the population. Incoherence may also be especially strong in any democratic context, but the Polish material suggests that democracy is not a requirement. Different aspects of social services develop at different times, with aggressive politicians and civil servants more concerned about their own activities than with the advantages of administrative integration. Local authorities provide the setting for the implementation of many activities designed and funded in part or wholly

---

[17]Lord Redcliffe-Maud and B. Wood, *English Local Government Reformed* (London: Oxford University Press, 1974.)

[18]H. Calmfors, F. F. Rabinowitz, and D. J. Alesch, *Urban Government for Greater Stockholm* (New York: Praeger, 1968).

[19]J. Tarkowski, "Decision-Making in the Polish Local Political System," in F. C. Bruhs, F. Cazzola, and J. Wiatr, eds., *Local Politics, Development and Participation: A Cross-National Study of Interrelationships* (Pittsburgh: University Center for International Studies, 1974).

by national ministries. There are incentives for people, involved both locally and nationally, to continue the lack of organizational coherence. Occasionally, a strong demand for reorganization may surface in order to simplify the structure for reasons of popular control, but such demands must compete with the incentives of senior bureaucrats and politicians to give priority to their own funding needs through existing arrangements.

Administration in Less-Developed Countries

Even more differences in public administration are observed among the many less-developed nations than among the relatively few societies that qualify as more developed. In part, this results from differences in numbers; it is also a result of the diverse cultures in which less- and more-developed groups are found. Almost all of the more-developed countries are European or are tied closely to the nations of Europe. They have shared many historical experiences with one another or were settled by immigrants who brought the governmental institutions of Europe with them. In contrast, the developing countries reflect a global range of political cultures. Some are in Europe (Portugal, Spain, and Albania), but most are in Latin America, Africa, and Asia. Most of these countries experienced a period of control by the colonial powers of Europe, but this period was too brief or too superficial to obliterate the centuries of pre-European experiences.

Despite the peculiarities in structures and processes in individual countries, the following traits have been observed throughout less-developed countries:

1. Among political elites, there is a widely shared commitment to development. The package of changes that is sought may vary from one country to another, but common goals include: an increase in agricultural or industrial production; an increase in personal living standards; improved programs for public health, education, and individual pensions; changes in the traditional roles of women or of the lower castes; and a change of loyalty from a tribe or region to the newly created nation.

2. The public sector is greatly relied on for leadership. Many developing countries have evolved structures that have a socialist or Marxist orientation. However, it is frequently a local variety of socialism, reflecting an evolution of Marxist doctrines outside of the European working-class context. Agriculture, rather than industry, is the economic base; and the people who feel oppressed have ethnic ties rather than an affinity for being an industrial working class. The proposals for specific reforms differ from one country to another. However, they typically seek rapid economic development, and identify government as the organized body most capable of generating this development and guiding it along socially desirable paths.

3. The society suffers from incipient or actual political instability. This instability may be a carryover of patterns that were developed within the native movements against a colonial power. In several countries, not only was there conflict between colonial and native forces, but also internal strife among the native leaders. In many cases, the "country" was an artificial creation of the colonial power, which combined into one administrative unit the lands of distinct tribal or ethnic groups. During the campaign for independence, or perhaps soon after independence was achieved, conflicts between traditional groups erupted into violent confrontations. Also contributing to violence are the frustrations associated with unmet goals for development. Many campaigns for independence are coupled with rash promises made by the new elites. However, their limited economic resources and scarce supply of skilled personnel make these promises unfulfillable. Military coups are a common experience in these settings.[20]

4. A gap exists between modern and traditional elites. Modern elites tend to be urban, western-oriented, young, well educated, and committed to economic, social, and political change. Traditional elites tend to be rural, oriented to local customs and to the indigenous religion, and opposed to change as a threat to these values. The new elites may control the technological skills that are vital to the nation's development, but the older elites may retain the intense loyalties of people in the countryside and the urban slums. The contrasting styles and orientations of the two types of leaders may generate severe conflict between them and their followers.

5. The development of various political features is imbalanced. Postcolonial countries tend to reproduce the legislative, executive, and administrative forms of the mother country. When these forms are imposed on the institutions originating in the colonial and precolonial periods, however, they can produce a wide gulf between formal procedures and actual practices. Legislative and executive branches often lack the ability to control civil or military agencies. The government administration generally receives the best-educated members of the new elite and thereby acquires the expertise to direct programs of social and economic development. The military sector may be even more well developed (at least in its office corps) than the civilian administration. The combination of a weak legislature and an ineffective chief executive, plus a professional military, often results in government takeovers that are either engineered behind the scenes by the military or led openly by military personnel. Less-developed nations throughout the world may share no one trait as much as they share the experience of having a uniformed and bemedaled chief executive, who either took over the gov-

---

[20] F. R. von der Mehden, *Politics of the Developing Nations* (Englewood Cliffs, N.J.: Prentice-Hall, 1964), pp. 1–2.

ernment in an overt putsch or used an election format—perhaps without tolerating real opposition—to obtain office.

6. Corruption tends to be pervasive. The corruption that exists in the bureaucracies of less-developed countries affects both small and large decisions and involves proportionately minor and major resources. It includes the small bribe that officials expect in exchange for "expediting" a decision in behalf of an individual; the willingness of officials to evade formal personnel procedures to hire their own relatives or fellow tribesmen; and the massive bribes from foreign investors that assure a favorable decision about mining rights, a utility monopoly, or a commercial concession. In some cases, this corruption is so taken for granted that it is defended as "part of the system," without which officials could not justify their decisions. Nepotism or tribal favoritism may be carryovers from traditional values. The truly massive corruption may, in contrast, be a product of colonial times when outside investors bought concessions from traditional elites.

7. There is a marked discrepancy between the forms and realities of administrative procedures. Governments establish procedures to resemble those observed by the former colonial power or those prescribed by visiting advisers from the United States or Europe. However, the forms do not operate in the poor country as they do in the rich. This trait has been labeled *formalism*.[21] It has many implications for the citizens and elites of less-developed countries. It means that announced procedures may provide no reliable guidelines about the activities to occur. Formalism rewards those who learn the informal procedures of administration and frustrates those who rest personal aspirations on the public promises of government.

Formalism also has important implications for students of comparative administration. It means that they cannot accept as similar (or comparable) those institutions that carry similar labels in different countries. An interior ministry may not only be—as in more-developed countries—the superstructure of the police service, but may also represent the single most powerful unit in the bureaucracy (perhaps excepting the army) and may actually select the chief executive. The leading political party may not simply be the organization that currently has control of major government offices, but may also be the only real vehicle that integrates the programs of leading figures in the army, the civilian bureaucracy, and other branches of the government. Elaborate programs for education, health benefits, or old-age pensions may be empty shells without operating administrators or budgets sufficient to meet the announced goals. The forms of federalism or local autonomy may belie the realities of strict central control through an authoritarian political party, a strong chief executive, or a centralized bureaucracy.

---

[21] F. W. Riggs, *Administration in Developing Countries: The Theory of Prismatic Society* (Boston: Houghton Mifflin, 1964), p. 12.

Some countries thought of as underdeveloped are not poor. Most of the oil-producing countries have substantial surpluses of foreign currency.

Table 12-3 Riding the OPEC Roller Coaster (in millions of dollars), 1973–1980

OPEC member	1973	1974	1975	1976	1977	1978	1979[a]	1980[b]
Algeria	-445	158	-1,662	-885	-2,325	-3,539	-2,740	-2,720
Ecuador	6	37	-219	-6	-341	-150	-50	-20
Gabon	-36	209	58	27	42	200	620	720
Indonesia	-475	597	-1,109	-908	-50	-1,249	1,025	1,300
Iran	155	12,267	4,708	4,713	5,082	1,900	4,500	3,400
Iraq	800	2,618	2,705	3,500	3,000	3,200	10,900	14,660
Kuwait	1,540	7,360	5,891	6,949	4,766	6,167	11,850	12,680
Libya	67	1,831	-68	2,437	2,906	1,025	3,980	5,510
Nigeria	26	4,945	63	-299	-1,357	3,782	4,440	4,690
Qatar	250	1,400	860	870	490	840	1,700	2,300
Saudi Arabia	2,204	23,007	13,931	13,791	12,791	-58	10,400	13,300
United Arab Emirates	300	3,140	2,270	2,670	990	925	2,550	4,540
Venezuela	861	5,810	2,306	967	-2,060	4,484	-1,610	-1,380
Total	5,253	63,379	29,734	33,834	23,944	995	48,135	58,980

Note: The table gives current account balances, including official transfers, of members of the Organization of Petroleum Exporting Countries, in millions of U.S. dollars.

[a]Estimate.

[b]Forecast at $26.55 a barrel; at $30 a barrel, surplus exceeds $90 billion.

SOURCE: *National Journal*, December 22, 1979. Reprinted with permission.

Administrative Structures

A variety of administrative structures—both formal and informal—can be found among less-developed countries. As in the more-developed countries, there is not a perfect correspondence between the level of development and public administration. Many factors peculiar to each country's history can shape its bureaucracy. Ferrel Heady suggests several kinds of administrations within the less-developed countries. Some of his categories suggest the differences to be found within them: traditional–autocratic, bureaucratic elite, polyarchal competitive, and dominant-party mobilization.[22] In describing each type and identifying some countries in each category, it is important to remember that instability is a prominent feature of less-developed countries. Instability is often close to the surface, and dramatic change can shift a government from one category to another in a short period of time.

The *traditional–autocratic* model is a traditional style of rule, with dominant political elites drawn from families with monarchic or aristocratic status. The political elite relies on military and civil bureaucracy to provide those changes in policy that are considered desirable and to inhibit those demands that are considered undesirable. With the exception of those countries that are blessed with huge oil deposits, little economic progress is demonstrated and little commitment toward such development is expressed by the political elite. Countries with traditional–autocratic governments include Saudi Arabia and Morocco. Ethiopia was in this category prior to its revolution of 1974, and Iran prior to the revolution of 1979.

In the system of the *bureaucratic elite,* traditional elites have been displaced from effective power, although they may retain some presence (perhaps as a figurehead monarch). Popular political participation is severely limited. Modernizing goals are proclaimed by leadership groups, but they are not embraced by the general public. Political power is largely in the hands of the civil and military bureaucracy. Military officials are usually in positions of the highest power, often as a result of having led a coup against the prior regime. However, the military depends on civil bureaucracy to carry out its nonmilitary developmental projects. Countries in this category include Brazil, Guatemala, Indonesia, Iraq, Pakistan, Paraguay, Peru, South Korea, Sudan, Syria, and Thailand. Nicaragua was run by a bureaucratic elite before Anastosia Somoza was ousted in 1979.

The political structures in a *polyarchal-competitive* system resemble the models of Western Europe and the United States with respect to popular participation, free elections, interest-oriented parties, and policy-making authority granted to representative government institutions. However, representative government is occasionally interrupted by military interventions

---

[22] Heady, op. cit., Chapters 8 and 9.

or other lapses. Typically, these interruptions are claimed to be only temporary. The polyarchal label denotes the existence of several political elites whose base of power may be spread among urban merchants, landlords, military officers, labor leaders, and professionals. Social mobility is greater than in more traditional societies. Due to competing parties' search for consensus, government programs emphasize pragmatic policies that are easy to understand and that offer short-range benefits in education, welfare, and health. Polyarchal-competitive countries include Greece, Jamaica, Malaysia, the Philippines, and Turkey.

In the type of government called *dominant-party mobilization,* there is little permissiveness in politics. The dominant party may be the only legal party, and it may assure its position by coercive techniques. A doctrinaire ideology usually backs up policy, and mass demonstrations of loyalty to the government are common. The elite group tends to be young, urban, well educated, and secular. Often a charismatic leader dominates the entire political movement, in which the programs stress nationalism and development. A well-trained civil service is essential to achieve the developmental goals; but frequent tension exists between the technical and professional people who work in the bureaucracy and the politicians who insist on the primacy of nationalism and loyalty to the current regime. Countries in this category include Algeria, Bolivia, Egypt, Guinea, Kenya, Mali, Tanzania, and Tunisia.

It is unclear what political, social, and economic features parallel the different types of administrative structures. As loosely conceived as these categories are, they may be more useful as illustrations of variety among less-developed administrative systems than as tools for rigorous comparative analysis.

COMPARISONS BETWEEN LESS-DEVELOPED U.S. STATES AND COUNTRIES

The traits of public policy and administration in certain less-developed American states have several parallels with developing countries. These similarities may be enough to challenge the validity of clear divisions between more- and less-developed countries.[23]

According to some measures of economic development, the United States is at or near the top of the world scale. Gross domestic product per capita (GDP/c) is the measure of economic development most widely used in international comparisons; it sums the market value of the total goods and ser-

---

[23]This section relies on I. Sharkansky, *The United States: A Study of a Developing Country* (New York: Longman, 1975).

vices in any economy. For 1970, the GDP/c of the United States was $4,734. The average for a group of 13 black African countries was $172; for 16 Asian countries, $253; and for 19 Latin American countries, $473. Despite these marked differences and all they mean in terms of economic security and living standards, there are major contrasts between the most- and least-affluent regions of the United States. The differences between the most comfortable sections of New York and California and the depressed regions of Mississippi, West Virginia, and New York City emphasize American problems of economic development. Depressed social classes in rural backwaters and urban slums have their counterparts in the Third World. Much can be learned about American policy and administration by looking at the American economy from a developmental perspective. Several policy-relevant parallels appear to link the less-developed states of the United States with the less-developed countries of Africa, Asia, and Latin America. The following traits tend to occur in the southern states, as well as in such other low-income states as Vermont, New Mexico, North Dakota, and Utah.

Parallels in Politics and Government

Developing states and countries receive significant inputs of financial grants, "soft" loans, and technical assistance from wealthier governments and outside private sources. The chief governments that supply aid to the developing countries are the former colonial powers, with other assistance coming from Canada, the Soviet Union, Sweden, the United States, and West Germany. In the United States, the federal government provides more in per capita aid to devloping states than to wealthier states.

Citizens in both the developing states and countries feel that they pay a price in the control of their economic resources by outsiders. Just as Chileans and Cubans have rallied against United States control of copper and sugar, so West Virginians, Kentuckians, and Georgians have declaimed Yankee control over their coalfields or railroads. One difference lies in the fewer options open to governments in less-developed countries. A developing country may try to expropriate the resources of foreigners at the risk of substantial changes in its international relations. In the developing states of the United States, the governments have some leverage through the weight of their own representatives in the national legislature.

In both less-developed countries and states, cultural traditions have a greater role in the political process. Political campaigns are less concerned with the hard details of policy alternatives than with the efforts of candidates to identify themselves with folk symbols. In Kenya, for example, the late President Jomo Kenyatta featured traditional dancing at many of his public appearances and often joined the dancers of different tribes to sway and kick through several routines. Likewise, an aspiring politician in the American South will mix with "the folks" and provide traditional food and music to attract them to his or her rallies. The importance of traditional symbols is not in the food or festivities of political rallies, but in their use in cementing political alliances. Developing countries and states both provide examples of where traditional loyalties slow the modernization that is feasible. Where traditional politics feature racial symbols in the United States (or tribalism in the Third World), the distribution of resources is likely to be unequal between the citizens in different racial groups.

Two policy-relevant political traits that appear in the less-developed states and countries are *centralization* and *concentration*. The centralization of government refers to the dominant role taken by central, as opposed to local, jurisdictions. In the less-developed American states, the central government is the state government. The patterns of centralization are evident in the state government's collection of revenue, its distribution of financial aid to local units, its establishment of program standards to be followed by local governments, and its direct provision of services throughout a jurisdiction by means of state government officers. For the less-developed American states, centralization appears most clearly in the ratios of state to local activities in revenue collection and spending.

Concentration pertains to the aggregation of political options in relatively few hands; it determines the political opportunities available to the mass of citizens. A hallmark of concentration is limited competition between political parties. The dominance of a single party lessens the opportunities for citizens to make decisions based on alternatives to present officeholders or public policies. In some developing countries, the major-party monopoly is written into the national laws or endorsed by the official police and the political elite. Concentration is not the same as centralization, which pertains to the aggregation of power to officials in the capital city. But concentration and centralization complement one another; both permit a narrow base of effective participation, with many citizens and officials left out of real decision-making.

Strong executive leadership frequently accompanies centralization and concentration. Powerful southern governors have been archetypes of strong executives in the context of less-developed American states. Men like George Wallace (Alabama), Orval Faubus (Arkansas), Huey Long (Louisiana), and Gene Talmadge (Georgia) dominated their legislatures and bureaucracies with a combination of patronage and demogogic appeals to the masses. Virtually all of the developing countries offer their own parallels, some of the most striking cases being those nationalist leaders who led their countries out of the colonial experience and became their first presidents or heads of government: Kwame Nkrumah in Ghana, Jomo Kenyatta in Kenya, Julius Nyere in Tanzania, Hastings Banda in Malawi, and Sukarno in Indonesia. In most of the least-developed countries, the bureaucracy—often the military sector of the bureaucracy—joins the chief executive in commanding the greatest leverage over public policy. The bureaucracy attracts members of the best families and the best graduates of the national universities; it commands a virtual monopoly over technical expertise; and its police and military segments may use their powers to control other branches of government.

Parallels in Public Policy

Developing states and countries resemble each other in certain efforts to induce economic growth. Both pursue industrialization with similar kinds of tax reductions for new industries, and both have problems with the marginal industries that are attracted by such schemes—firms that teeter on the brink of bankruptcy, require extensive nursing by the government offices charged with economic development, offer little in the way of transferable skills to their employees, or fail to pay back the jurisdiction's investment in the form of adding substantial taxes or resources to the economy.

Regressive tax and spending policies also appear in both developing states and countries. A regressive tax or expenditure is one that takes disproportionately from the lower-income population or provides its benefits disproportionately to upper-income classes. In the developing countries, typical regressive taxes are the excise taxes on fuel, cloth, processed food, beer, or manufactured goods; and the customs duty on goods that permeate the society, such as imported radios, printed cloth, and imported components that are assembled by local industries. In the United States the most prominent regressive taxes are those on retail sales and real property. State individual and corporate income taxes, in contract, are progressive. During 1971, the 10 states with the least-developed economies drew only 10.3 percent of their revenues from income taxes, while the 10 states with the most-developed economies took 20.6 percent of their revenues from such taxes.

The tendency to avoid progressive taxes has a further parallel in the tendency to give little support to those programs that have a progressive impact on the distribution of resources. Elementary and secondary education, welfare, and public health programs go disproportionately to citizens in the lower-income ranges. In the United States, these programs tend to receive smaller per capita allocations in the low-income states. Highway and natural resource programs, in contrast, represent investments in economic infrastructure and promise growth. They tend to receive greater per capita allocations in states that have little industry. Similar allocations appear in the development plans of many lower-income countries, which serve to complement their avoidance of progressive taxes. On the expenditure side, these plans feature transportation, electric power and communications facilities, plus investments in industry and commercial-scale agriculture.

How Traits Relate to Each Other

Elements of governmental centralization, political concentration, tradition-alism in politics, and such policies as industrial promotion, plus tax and spending regressivity fit together in a syndrome that both reflects conditions of relative deprivation and may affect the processes of further economic development. Traditional politics lessens the opportunities for new per-spectives to permeate policy-making. Centralization and concentration both serve to limit the claimants on public resources. With centralization, regional and local groups have minimum opportunities to make strong demands on public resources. Political concentration lessens the ability of citizens in regional or class groupings to claim resources for their own wel-fare. Centralization and concentration permit a small number of trained and experienced administrators to keep the management of scarce resources in their own hands. A regressive tax base means that allocatable resources remain scarce.

The view that prospects for economic development benefit from tradi-tionalism, centralization, concentration, and regressive policies is proble-matical and relies on one important assumption: that elites who benefit will use their economic and political leverage for public benefit rather than private gain. Traditional symbols may distract unsophisticated voters from their leaders' policies. Programs of industrialization, transportation, com-munications, improved agricultural techniques, public health and educa-tion, as well as general improvements in the standard of living can result when publicly minded elites invest rationally to stimulate economic devel-opment. On the other hand, some leaders can and often do use their lever-age to reinforce their political positions; keep taxes low for the social class they belong to or aspire to; and control the government for personal profit, either banking the proceeds overseas or consuming them in opulence at home. The developing states and countries provide examples of both extreme asceticism and extreme excess on the part of their elites.

FINANCIAL AID AND TECHNICAL ASSISTANCE

The economic and political traits of rich and poor areas are important not only for their impact on administration and on the domestic policies for economic growth. These traits also leave their mark on the financial aid and technical assistance that flow from richer to poorer areas. Although inter-national aid has declined in recent years, it is still considerable. U.S. aid to other nations was about $5 billion in 1977. Domestically, funds flow from wealthy to poor states through the mechanisms of the national government's taxes and aid programs. In 1975, the ten poorest states received some $5.3 billion from Washington, D.C., amounting to $235 per capita. Some American observers feel that the poorer states of the South have received more than their share of federal benefits and are growing economically at the expense of the more industrial northeastern region.

International Aid to Poor Countries

The diversity of poor regions is one of the factors that leaves its mark on the aid policies of outsiders. *What aid to offer?* is an issue that varies with the economic situation of the potential recipient as well as with the demands coming from the political leaders of the recipient. These economic and political realities combine with cultural traditions and traits of geography, climate, soil, and water to affect the workability of various proposals. The recipient's traits complicate an outsider's efforts to bring about changes in economic, social, or administrative patterns. Presumably, the problems of program design are easier when aid is given within a single country than when one country gives aid to another and both have sharp differences in cultures and politics. Yet, one observer of federal aid to American states and localities has written—it is hoped, with tongue in cheek—that 40 percent of both time and funds is spent in designing aid projects and another 40 percent is spent on evaluation.[24]

Not all of the problems associated with project choice and design reflect the complexities of recipient governments. Political inclinations and commitments also change in the donor governments. Such changes affect not only the size of aid budgets, but also the programs that are likely to have appeal. Some of the targets that have been stylish at various times are: economic growth, irrigation programs, and development of key industries; a more balanced distribution of economic opportunities through programs of education or job opportunities in rural areas; a concern for grass-roots political development resulting in greater participation, and assurances of democratic liberties; and a narrower concern with administrative reforms that would enhance an aid recipient's capacity to extract and manage the resources of its own economy.[25] The numerous motives for financial and technical assistance include the donor government's calculations of what will meet the current political demands coming out of its own society, as well as what efforts may win some support in international politics, plus some undefined measure of altruism. U.S. aid policies have changed considerably from the early 1960s, when the Alliance for Progress was pursuing political and economic reforms throughout Latin America. The Nixon–Ford Administrations were more inclined to military and economic aid for the

---

[24]D. T. Stanley, "How Safe the Streets, How Good the Grant?" *Public Administration Review*, 34 (July-August 1974): 380–389.

[25]See K. J. Rothwell, ed., *Administrative Issues in Developing Economies* (Lexington, Mass.: Heath, 1972).

purposes of strengthening selected allies or extracting concessions in international negotiations. The statements of the Carter Administration in behalf of human rights indicated a shift back toward reformist goals. The Reagan Administration began with a less explicit concern for human rights and moved closer to a "help our friends" approach to foreign aid.

Current definitions of *development administration* encompass diverse goals, with the participants in major projects having to face the conflicts that rage among the proponents of each. According to Milton Esman, development administration "refers to those activities of government that foster economic growth, strengthen human and organizational capabilities, and promote equality in the distribution of opportunities, income, and power.[26]

The problems of recipient governments often frustrate the goals of aid projects. The entrenched conservatism of traditional peasants hinders the reform of agriculture, while entrenched bureaucrats thwart campaigns against corruption. Shortages of trained personnel and the unwillingness of university graduates to live outside the capital city hinder projects that require effective administration in regional centers. A great number of bureaucratic procedures—typically inherited from colonial rulers concerned with controlling the work of suspect natives—hamper development programs that require personnel to move quickly in response to local problems or oportunities.[27] The elites of recipient governments may look to technical advisers only for the backing of projects already chosen. The elites may demand obeisance to local pride more than the candid use of the adviser's expertise.[28] The details of these problems vary from one country to another, and within a country, from region to region or project to project. Behind many of the problems lies the poverty of resources, personnel, and administrative capabilities that are both the targets and the frustrations of development programs.

The U.S. Internal Revenue Service has cooperated with the U.S. Agency for International Development (AID) in sending high-ranking experts in tax administration to poor countries on missions of technical assistance. Their "end-of-project" reports offer numerous examples of tax reforms that succeed in increasing government revenues. However, they also contain insights—sometimes veiled to protect the sensitivities of the recipient countries—into the problems faced by tax advisers: officials of the recipient

---

[26]M. J. Esman, "Administrative Doctrine and Developmental Needs," in E. P. Morgan, ed., *The Administration of Change in Africa* (New York: Dunellen, 1974), p. 3.

[27]See G. Myrdal, *An Approach to the Asian Drama* (New York: Vintage, 1970); and R. F. Taub, *Bureaucrats Under Stress: Administrators and Administration in an Indian State* (Berkeley: University of California Press, 1969).

[28]G. E. Caiden, "International Consultants and Development Administration," *International Review of Administrative Sciences*, 42 (1976): 1–7.

government who seem to accept an adviser's recommendation, but who then do not deliver the resources or reforms that they have promised; personnel resources that are too thin to make more than a symbolic effort at staffing field offices outside of the capital city; efforts at tax enforcement that run afoul of outright corruption or of political influence that protects errant taxpayers from an intensive audit or from prosecution; lack of elementary recordkeeping, which results in many eligible citizens not being placed on the tax rolls, or which hinders the revenue department from keeping track of tax returns and correspondence; and political instability, which hampers the implementation of any but the simplest of administrative reforms.[29]

Domestic Aid to Poor States

The United States has its own share of difficulties in the design and implementation of domestic strategies for development. The regional development program of the 1960s showed an undisciplined dissemination of resources over a wide variety of regions and for a diverse set of goals.[30] The early intention of the Kennedy Administration was the development of the Appalachian region, modeled after the Tennessee Valley Authority of the Roosevelt days. Under the pressure of representatives, senators, and governors from states on the periphery of the original target area, the concept of Appalachia moved outward from the coal-mining counties of West Virginia and eastern Kentucky to include parts of 13 states from New York to Mississippi. Later, the leaders of other poor regions demanded a piece of the action. Eventually, most sections of the country had their regional development schemes:

1. The Ozarks Regional Commission included parts of Arkansas, Oklahoma, Kansas, and Missouri.
2. The Four Corners Regional Commission included parts of Arizona, New Mexico, Colorado, and Utah.
3. The Coastal Plains Regional Commission included parts of Georgia, North Carolina, and South Carolina (other sections of these states were attached to the Appalachian region).
4. The Upper Great Lakes Regional Commission included parts of Michigan, Wisconsin, and Minnesota.

---

[29] An important study of tax administration in poor countries is A. Radian, *Resource Mobilization in Poor Countries: Implementing Tax Policies* (New Brunswick, N.J.: Transaction, 1980).

[30] See J. H. Cumberland, *Regional Development Experiences and Prospects in the United States of America* (Paris: Mouton, 1971); and M. Newman, *The Political Economy of Appalachia: A Case Study in Regional Intergration* (Lexington, Mass.: Heath, 1972).

5. The New England Regional Commission included all of Connecticut, Maine, Massachusetts, New Hampshire, Rhode Island, and Vermont.

A further diffusion of resources for regional development occurred in the choices of program goals. There were debates over whether the provision of aid should go to places or directly to individuals; over whether the focus should be on the most needy areas, on the areas most likely to develop, or in the dispersal of aid to many sites; and over which kinds of programs should be offered: humanitarian aid or inducements for economic growth. Just as the political process took the regional idea and applied it to many parts of the country at the same time, so there were tendencies to answer these issues in a multiplicity of ways and to divide resources among numerous kinds of projects.

SUMMARY

Comparisons of different administrative situations can find patterns in the occurrences of different kinds of agencies, controls, and policies, and can test hypotheses about the influence of certain traits—such as a well-developed economy—on administration. Characteristics of economic development seem important for public administration, both within the United States and around the world. There are complex disputes about the nature of development and about the level of development of individual countries according to several measures of development. This chapter illustrates the range of variations in public administration throughout the world, and suggests the importance of development on the variations.

Individual traits of a nation's culture and history also leave their mark. Public administration varies markedly between such countries with developed economies as the United States and Great Britain on the one hand and France and Germany on the other. Sharp differences also occur among the many countries grouped as "less developed." The United States shows wide variations within itself, from wealthy to poor states and regions.

Sharply varying levels of economic development prompt numerous programs of assistance from more-wealthy to less-wealthy areas. Such programs have their own problems of political constraints and administrative snafus— whether the aid flows between countries or within countries from the national capital to poor regions.

13

Intergovernmental Relations

The view from the top is awesome. Federal innovators in the field of education face 50 state departments of education and 15,000 local school districts, each of which may express a claim of independence. Whether the issue is one of great public controversy—like busing—or merely a professional squabble about the techniques of education—like something to do with audiovisual aids—great barriers lie in the way of national policy. To accomplish goals in this situation requires the patience of Job, the skills at bargaining shown by Lyndon Johnson in his prime, and many of the resources of the U.S. Treasury.

The view from the bottom is disturbing. Program requirements come to school administrators from Washington, D.C., and the state capitals, and from several sources in each. The Department of Agriculture administers food programs, the Department of Defense concerns itself with the education of military dependents, the Department of Education with techniques of instruction, and the Justice Department deals with racial integration. The money that comes from federal and state sources is attractive. Without the 51 percent of the school budget from those sources, local taxpayers would put even greater pressure on the school board, and parents would complain even more about the quality of their children's schooling. Actually, it costs a great deal to get the money. Not only is time spent studying the district's entitlements and pursuing funds through countless pages of applications and supplemental inquiries, but also the follow-up in reporting is equally burdensome. Along with federal aid come requirements for complying with numerous standards, many of them extraneous to the subject that is being aided—such as affirmative action in hiring staff and selecting students; the provision of ramps and other facilities for the handicapped; efforts to make contracts with small businesses and those owned by women or minorities; concerns about the nutritional content of food and the prices that can be charged in the cafeteria. Each of these requirements may be socially beneficial when individually considered, but collectively they also impose their burdens on the local educators.

This chapter deals with an issue that is distinctively American: the pervasive character of intergovernmental relations among so many governments that have a great deal of autonomy from one another. Program administration involves much negotiation and persuasion, and relatively little command. The key questions are:

How do officials and policies of one level of government impinge on others?

How do the target governments respond to the initiatives of others?

FEDERALISM AND ADMINISTRATION

The federal nature of American government means that administrators in most agencies at each level of government must reckon with demands from officials at other levels of government. These relationships are not simply rituals of public administration. Due to certain guarantees that are integral to the meaning of federalism and due to political customs that bolster these guarantees, the representatives of other governments have special status.

Every major government in the world has a central unit and local units of government. However, a federal arrangement is peculiar in that it provides certain assurances to both central and local levels of government. It is common to speak of the American national and state governments as "superior" and "subordinate" to one another, but this terminology is inaccurate. On some dimensions, the national government (often called the federal government) has prerogatives that are reserved to it alone. The states, however, are not the creatures of the national government. They have a prominent independent role in any amendments to the Constitution, important guarantees of equal representation in the Senate and proportional representation in the House, and a role in selecting the President.[1]

The constitutional structure of federalism helps to protect the interests of the state governments, but it does not protect local government institu-

---

[1] D. Elazar, *American Federalism: View from the States* (New York: Crowell, 1976).

tions from either the national or the state government. The cities are creatures of their state governments and are subject to whatever constraints are found in state constitutions or statutes. However, local governments (as well as states) benefit from the political customs that respect "localism" and "home rule." The respect for localism exists among officials at all levels of government and has been observed in the United States since the early nineteenth century.[2] These values overlay the structure of federalism and make local governments, as well as state and national governments, important participants in policy-making.

A feature that heightens the importance of federalism for administrators is the mixture of governmental responsibilities. No important domestic activity is staffed or financed solely by federal, state, or local government.[3] The fields that consume most domestic expenditures—education, highways, welfare, health, natural resources, and public safety—are funded with a combination of federal grants or loans, plus state and local taxes or service charges. Even when programs involve local implementation with federal funds (for example, public housing and urban renewal), the state legislature and executive branch also retain a role; they have the legal prerogative to permit local participation in the federal program and to define conditions under which participation may occur.[4]

The combination of a viable federal structure, localist political values, and the sharing of responsibilities for major domestic services means that administrators at every level of government deal continuously with officials at other levels of government. A crazy quilt of communications connects administrators with members of executive, legislative, and judicial branches from local, state, and national governments. Federal administrators must contend with decisions—or anticipated decisions—of administrators, executives, legislators, and judges of each state and local government involved with the programs of their agencies. Federal administrators may hear from state and local officials directly or through federal legislators or interest groups that serve as intermediaries. For state and local administrators, intergovernmental relations may take the form of requests, demands, or appeals sent to federal agencies or to the federal legislature, executive, or judiciary. In many respects, state administrators have a similar relationship to local agencies that federal administrators have to state or local agencies—as providers of funds, information, advice, and program standards. Figure 13-1 depicts in outline form the principal actors and flows of communication that may affect administrative units at any level of the federal structure.

---

[2] See A. de Tocqueville, *Democracy in America* (New York: Vintage, 1959), p. 282.

[3] M. Grodzins, "American Political Parties and the American System," *Western Political Quarterly,* 13 (December 1960): 974–998.

[4] E. C. Banfield and M. Grodzins, *Government and Housing in Metropolitan Areas* (New York: McGraw-Hill, 1958).

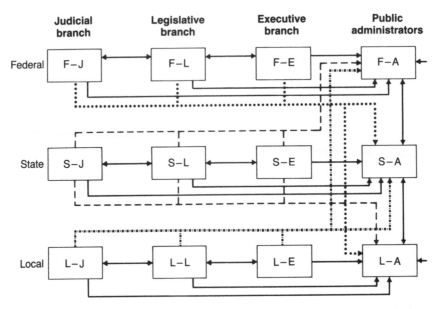

Figure 13-1 Intergovernmental Communications That Impinge on Administrators. [SOURCE: Ira Sharkansky, *Public Administration: Policy-Making in Government Agencies* (Chicago: Rand McNally, 1978).]

It depicts vertical intergovernmental relationships between officials of national, state, or local governments. (Noted later are horizontal intergovernmental relations between officials of different states or different localities.)

Much of intergovernmental relations occurs between administrators of different governments and is routine in nature. State educators, for example, deal mostly with the U.S. Department of Education and local superintendents. When the administrators seek altered statutes or funds from Congress, they deal with members of committees or congressional staffs that specialize in education. This is not to say that the exchanges of requests, instructions, money, and technical assistance between governments do not pass without political disputes. Governors and mayors often feel dominated by program administrators and confined to a ceremonial role in which they have little control over what happens. Not only do they object to their lack of control over intergovernmental programs, but they also feel that budgetary commitments to intergovernmental programs limit their overall control of state or local resources.[5] State and local chief executives charge that

---

[5]See D. H. Haider, *When Governments Come to Washington: Governors, Mayors, and Intergovernmental Lobbying* (New York: Free Press, 1974); and K. C. Olson, "The States, Governors, and Policy Management: Changing the Equilibrium of the Federal System," *Public Administration Review*, 35 (December 1975): 764–770.

their own budgets for education, for example, are pulled inexorably into those programs that receive federal aid. No matter how much they may want to reduce the resources taken from their own taxpayers, or allocate resources to other programs, the elected officials cannot counter the arguments of administrators that state and local money spent on federally aided programs will bring in additional dollars from Washington, D.C.

FEDERAL AID

Of all the forms of relations among federal, state, and local administrators, grants-in-aid have attracted more attention than others. This attention is warranted, insofar as grants probably account for the greatest tangible resources in intergovernmental relations. However, grants are not the only cause for intergovernmental relations. There are other kinds of financial assistance and nonfinancial relations: federal loans, guarantees of loans contracted from normal financial sources, shared taxes, tax credits, and the feature that permits deductions of state and local taxes from federally taxable income. Federal agencies also provide training and other technical assistance for state and local personnel.

Grants-in-Aid

In 1979, federal aid amounted to $82 billion, or 25 percent of state and local expenditures. Federal grants-in-aid were the typical form of assistance until 1972. Grants-in-aid have several distinct features, each of which has implications for administrators.[6] Grants support a specific state or local program rather than providing general support of state or local activities. Grants typically require that recipient agencies submit detailed applications for the funds, provide some of their own resources to support the aided activities, and administer the programs according to prescribed standards. The specific nature of federal grants-in-aid and the requirements that come along with the money are frequent sources of conflict between federal, state, and local administrators. It is said that federal inducements lead recipients to undertake activities that are not in their best interests and that many requirements are inconsistent with state or local problems.

Federal grants-in-aid are older than the Constitution, although they have reached great heights only since the 1930s. Throughout the late eighteenth and most of the nineteenth century, grants came in the form of land. About 230 million acres passed from the federal government to the states in the

---

[6]See D. S. Wright, *Understanding Intergovernmental Relations* (North Scituate, Mass.: Duxbury, 1978).

There is no such thing as a free lunch. Federal grants to state and local governments cost money to taxpayers. Here is an indication of how much the residents of each state receive, compared to how much they pay.

Table 13-1   Federal Grants-in-Aid to State and Local Governments and Estimated Federal Tax Burden for Federal Grants, Fiscal Year 1979

| State | In millions of dollars | | Tax burden per dollar of aid | |
	Grants[a]	Estimated tax burden for grants[b]	Amount	State rank
Alabama	$1,341.9	$1,037.4	$ .77	35
Alaska	379.9	231.4	.61	47
Arizona	795.5	790.1	.99	24
Arkansas	839.4	550.6	.66	43
California	8,165.4	9,265.1	1.13	12
Colorado	915.3	1,013.5	1.11	15
Connecticut	1,074.6	1,396.5	1.30	4
Delaware	232.4	239.4	1.03	22
District of Columbia	905.1	311.2	.34	51
Florida	2,392.9	3,056.4	1.28	6
Georgia	2,176.2	1,508.3	.69	42
Hawaii	407.7	351.1	.86	31
Idaho	315.4	263.4	.83	32
Illinois	3,781.5	4,915.8	1.30	4
Indiana	1,390.8	1,955.2	1.41	1
Iowa	877.1	1,053.4	1.20	7
Kansas	720.7	853.9	1.18	8
Kentucky	1,340.9	1,021.5	.76	38
Louisiana	1,509.3	1,229.0	.81	33
Maine	503.1	295.3	.59	48
Maryland	1,600.1	1,699.8	1.06	20
Massachusetts	2,725.5	2,090.8	.77	35
Michigan	3,565.4	3,726.8	1.05	21
Minnesota	1,512.0	1,484.3	.98	26
Mississippi	1,035.5	550.6	.53	50
Missouri	1,509.1	1,643.9	1.09	16

[a]Excludes shared revenues and payments in lieu of taxes; includes general revenue sharing and trust fund aids.
[b]The total tax burden for grants is assumed to equal grant payments.

SOURCE: *Monthly Tax Features,* 24 (April, 1980). Reprinted with permission of Tax Foundation, Incorporated.

Table 13-1 (continued)

State	In millions of dollars		Tax burden per dollar of aid	
	Grants[a]	Estimated tax burden for grants[b]	Amount	State rank
Montana	$ 406.4	$ 255.4	$ .63	45
Nebraska	473.3	542.7	1.15	11
Nevada	263.7	311.2	1.18	8
New Hampshire	291.6	311.2	1.07	18
New Jersey	2,715.4	3,144.2	1.16	10
New Mexico	535.4	351.1	.66	43
New York	8,870.3	6,703.4	.76	38
North Carolina	1,785.7	1,604.0	.90	28
North Dakota	292.5	207.5	.71	41
Ohio	3,070.1	4,022.1	1.31	3
Oklahoma	945.7	933.7	.99	24
Oregon	877.1	949.7	1.08	17
Pennsylvania	4,096.5	4,205.6	1.03	22
Rhode Island	412.2	319.2	.77	35
South Carolina	983.9	798.0	.81	33
South Dakota	311.4	191.5	.62	46
Tennessee	1,442.3	1,292.8	.90	28
Texas	3,588.2	4,883.9	1.36	2
Utah	433.0	383.1	.88	30
Vermont	241.3	135.7	.56	49
Virginia	1,715.6	1,843.4	1.07	18
Washington	1,381.3	1,556.2	1.13	12
West Virginia	770.1	550.6	.72	40
Wisconsin	1,723.4	1,588.1	.92	27
Wyoming	163.5	183.6	1.12	14
Total	$79,802.6	$79,802.6	$1.00	—

nineteenth century. For example, each new state received a grant for the support of primary education as it was admitted to the Union. Also, the "land-grant" colleges of many states trace their origin to the Morrill Acts of 1862 and 1890. The states were expected to sell or lease the land, and use proceeds to support educational programs. As the supply of public land dwindled in the late nineteenth century, the emphasis shifted to money grants. The first regular and continuing money grant began in 1887 for the support of agricultural experiment stations.

The grants-in-aid programs enacted during each decade of the twentieth century have represented in microcosm the contemporary orientations of American governments. Until World War I, the grants emphasized agriculture and other rural problems. Typical of that period were the Smith–Lever Act of 1914, which established cooperative agricultural extension programs; the Smith–Hughes Act of 1917, which established a program for supporting vocational education (with heavy emphasis in agriculture and home economics); and the Federal Aid Highway Act, which authorized the secretary of agriculture to cooperate with state highway departments in the construction of rural roads. This act was supposed to "get the farmer out of the mud."

In the 1920s, the Harding–Coolidge–Hoover reliance on private enterprise made itself felt. No authorizations were made for new programs. The 1930s emphasized programs to lighten the hardships of the Depression. New programs offered welfare payments for the aged, the blind, and dependent children; health services for mothers and children; employment security; and public housing. Some agricultural programs were also begun during the 1930s to cope with economic problems: surplus commodity distribution and soil conservation.

The period of World War II did not invite new domestic activities. The total funds provided to states and localities decreased from $2.4 billion in 1940 to $800 million in 1946. With the continuing mobilization of the Cold War, federal aid was made part of the defense effort—for example, the Interstate and *Defense* Highway Act of 1952 and the *Defense* Education Act of 1957. It is debatable how important highway and educational activities were to the defense effort; probably, they were merely made more attractive to Congress by being identified as such.

In the 1960s and 1970s, the program emphases of new grant programs were poverty, urban affairs, education, and environmental protection. The Elementary and Secondary Education Act of 1965 pushed educational grants from $610 million in 1965 to $2.5 billion in 1968.

Changes in program emphases testify to the flexibility of federal grants-in-aid. Policy-makers in the national government can adjust the kinds of activities that receive funds. Depending on the assessment of need and performance, the funds appropriated for each program can be increased in small or large amounts, can be passed over with no increase, or can be decreased. Each program can receive additional features that reflect newly

Table 13-2 Federal Grants-in-Aid in Relation to State–Local Receipts from Own Sources, Total Federal Outlays, and Gross National Product, 1955–1981

Fiscal year[a]	Amount (in billions of dollars)	Percent increase	As a percentage of		
			State–local receipts from own source[b]	Total federal outlays	Gross national product
1955	$ 3.2	4.9%	11.8%	4.7%	0.8%
1956	3.7	15.6	12.3	5.3	0.9
1957	4.0	8.1	12.1	5.3	0.9
1958	4.9	22.5	14.0	6.0	1.1
1959	6.5	32.7	17.2	7.0	1.4
1960	7.0	7.7	16.8	7.6	1.4
1961	7.1	1.4	15.8	7.3	1.4
1962	7.9	11.3	16.2	7.4	1.4
1963	8.6	8.9	16.5	7.8	1.5
1964	10.1	17.4	17.9	8.6	1.6
1965	10.9	7.9	17.7	9.2	1.7
1966	13.0	19.3	19.3	9.6	1.8
1967	15.2	16.9	20.6	9.6	2.0
1968	18.6	22.4	22.4	10.4	2.2
1969	20.3	9.1	21.6	11.0	2.2
1970	24.0	18.2	22.9	12.2	2.5
1971	28.1	17.1	24.1	13.3	2.8
1972	34.4	22.4	26.1	14.8	3.1
1973	41.8	21.5	28.5	16.9	3.4
1974	43.4	3.8	27.3	16.1	3.2
1975	49.8	14.7	29.1	15.3	3.4
1976	59.1	18.7	31.1	16.1	3.6
1977	68.4	15.7	31.0	17.0	3.7
1978	77.9	13.9	31.7	17.3	3.8
1979	82.9	6.4	30.9	16.8	3.6
1980[c]	89.8	8.3	30.5	15.8	3.5
1981[c]	91.1	1.4	28.3	14.9	3.2

[a]For 1955–1976, years ending June 30; 1977–1981 years ending September 30.
[b]As defined in the national income accounts.
[c]Estimate.

SOURCE: U.S. Advisory Commission on Intergovernmental Relations staff computations.

apparent service problems. For each feature, the matching formula can be adjusted to make the component more or less attractive to potential recipients, thereby affecting the speed of adoption. When members of Congress are especially anxious to have all states take immediate advantage of a new program, they set the federal–state matching formula at an irresistible level.

And in order to elicit cooperation on individual components of a program, new bonus offers of aid are extended in exchange for compliance with special regulations. When the interstate highway program was first enacted in 1953, the federal–state matching formula was set at 90–10, meaning that state highway departments would receive $.90 worth of federal highway money for each $.10 of their own money. By not taking immediate advantage of the program, a state would lose a considerable amount of its citizens' federal tax money that would pay for highways in *other* states. After the program was under way for several years, Congress added other features (for example, billboard controls) and auxiliary grants for state compliance. Moreover, the legislature has adjusted the flow of highway grants to changes in the economy. Allocations have been speeded up during periods of unemployment and slowed down at other times to curb inflation. Presidents have also slowed the allocation of highway funds in order to elicit cooperation from Congress on other programs.

Every cabinet department of the federal government provides some grants-in-aid to state and local governments. Even such nondomestic units as the Department of Defense and the Department of State offer grants-in-aid to state governments for the National Guard and international cultural affairs.

The mechanics of federal aid differ in the ways of offering some discretion to state or local recipients. Most restrictive are the *project grants,* which require federal approval of state or local applications on a project-by-project basis. They differ from *formula grants* that provide funds to state or local agencies according to a formula established by Congress or the administration. Under a formula grant, decisions on individual projects are left to state or local agencies. There are also *bloc grants.* Bloc grants finance a broad function of government (health and crime control are examples) and allow recipient agencies to decide their own program priorities.

Revenue Sharing

Revenue sharing has been the most important change in federal aid during recent decades. It began in 1972 with annual grants of $2.6 billion to the states. Two-thirds of the funds were for local governments. By 1980 the annual revenue-sharing allocations to state and local governments were some $6.9 billion. The allotments to individual states and localities reflect various criteria: revenue increases according to the size of the population, the efforts of a recipient government to tax its population, and poverty as reflected by income per capita.

Revenue sharing differs dramatically from traditional grants-in-aid by the lack of strings attached. Money flows to states and communities as a matter of right, without detailed applications. Recipients spend money at their discretion, subject only to the following restrictions:

State and local governments have extensive freedom in their use of revenue-sharing money. There are some patterns in how they choose to use it. Education gets the greatest share of state money received as revenue sharing. Local governments distribute their receipts more evenly among numerous programs, with police protection, highways, and fire protection receiving large shares.

Table 13-3 State and Local Use of Revenue Sharing, 1976–1977

Use	State governments		Local governments	
	Amount (in thousands of dollars)	Percent of total expenditure for function	Amount (in thousands of dollars)	Percent of total expenditure for function
Airports	$ 252	0.1%	$ 7,711	0.9%
Correction	54,322	1.9	112,330	6.9
Education	1,209,789	1.8	38,648	0.2
Finance and general administration	77,965	1.9	249,710	3.8
Fire protection	—	—	523,467	12.5
General public buildings	26,777	4.8	234,942	12.4
Health	207,742	5.4	268,990	9.8
Highways	130,257	0.7	668,767	7.2
Hospitals	48,942	0.6	89,550	1.3
Housing and urban renewal	249	0.1	17,378	0.9
Interest on general debt	52,500	1.1	3,311	0.1
Libraries	6,031	2.6	73,691	6.8
Natural resources	14,285	0.4	13,170	2.3
Parks and recreation	—	—	247,588	6.9
Police protection	1,297	0.1	941,512	10.5
Public welfare	47,593	0.1	118,106	0.8
Redemption of debt	2,319	0.1	87,895	1.0
Sanitation other than sewerage	—	—	292,096	11.5
Sewerage	—	—	78,781	1.5
Utility systems	—	—	79,281	0.6
All other	196,186	1.1	331,214	2.2
Total	$2,076,556	1.2%	$4,478,138	3.5%

—Represents zero or rounds to zero.

SOURCE: *Congressional Quarterly*, February 23, 1980.

1. State governments have no restrictions on their expenditures, but local governments must spend their allotments according to certain priorities: public safety, environmental protection (including sanitation), public transportation, health, recreation, libraries, social services for the poor and aged, financial administration, and "ordinary and necessary" capital expenditures.

2. Discrimination on the basis of race, color, national origin, or sex is not permitted in any program financed with these funds.

3. Revenue-sharing funds may not be used to match federal funds provided under other grant programs.

4. Construction workers paid with revenue-sharing funds must receive at least the wage prevailing on similar construction activity in the locality.

5. Recipient governments must publish plans and publicly account for the use of revenue-sharing funds.

While the lack of detailed controls on revenue sharing appeals to elected officials in state and local governments, this feature disturbs certain administrators and interest groups, who have no guarantee that the money will be spent on the programs that concern them. With grants-in-aid in contrast, program supporters can concentrate their efforts at the national level and count on state and local officials to carry out federal requirements.

The general idea of revenue sharing—with few controls on its use—was a topic of reform proposals for many years. Its actual enactments owed something to electoral politics in 1972. Deterioration of the international economic position of the United States and serious problems with domestic inflation and unemployment led the Nixon Administration to become active in national economic planning. Some of that planning was directed toward reforms in federal aid for state and local governments. The President's efforts to decentralize the administration of programs through revenue sharing reflected Republican calls for decentralization since the 1930s. Support for revenue sharing could not come from the White House alone. It required the backing of a Democratic Congress and a change in heart of then-Chairman Wilbur Mills of the House Ways and Means Committee. Mills had earlier spoken strongly in opposition to revenue sharing. His shift came early in the presidential campaign of 1972, when he may have been seeking some credit with local politicians as a potential Democratic nominee. Whatever his reasons, Mills was then a shrewd legislator, with special influence in the revenue field. Any explanation of revenue sharing must take account of his reasoning as well as the President's.

Other Aid

Grants-in-aid and revenue sharing are only two devices that federal agencies use to provide resources for state and local agencies. Federal loans, loan guarantees, tax credits, and the deductibility of state and local taxes from federally taxable income are additional aids. Some are mixed with grants-in-aid to provide different options within the same program. In the public housing program, for example, a federal guarantee for loans arranged in the private sector supports the bulk of project costs, while an outright grant pays for additional costs. Some programs make available a direct loan from the federal Treasury if a federal loan guarantee will not allow a recipient agency to obtain a commercial loan at a desirable interest rate. The unemployment compensation program combines a federal tax credit with a grant-in-aid. Employers are exempt for up to 90 percent of a federal payroll tax for the money they pay as state tax to support unemployment compensation; and an amount up to the remaining 10 percent of the federal tax is available to the state employment agency for administrative costs.[7]

Many taxpayers are not aware of the federal aid for state and local governments that is written into the income tax code. In computing income that is subject to federal taxation, amounts may be deducted that were paid as state or local income, sales, excise, or property tax. This provision lightens the burden of state or local taxes and may allow states and localities to levy higher taxes without encountering severe resistance. Moreover, any income received from interest on state or local government bonds is not subject to federal taxation. Not taxing interest permits state and local agencies to pay lower-than-commercial interest rates for the money they borrow.[8]

Several other federal programs provide indirect aid to state and local agencies. Providing federal benefits to institutions or to private citizens relieves states and localities of service demands that would otherwise come to them. In this category are federal grants, loans, or loan guarantees to institutions of higher education, both public and private. Many federal "research contracts" also provide financial aid to colleges and universities. They allow researchers to hire student assistants (and thereby subsidize the students' education) and support sophisticated research to enrich the intellectual climate and the educational offerings of these institutions. The federal social security program also alleviates demands on state and local authorities for welfare and health programs. "Social security" is the popular designation for a series of programs that provides insurance coverage for old-age pensions, disability, and hospital and physician charges.

The Advisory Commission on Intergovernmental Relations (ACIR) is a research agency of the federal government whose purpose is to provide

---

[7]See J. A. Maxwell, *Tax Credits and Intergovernmental Fiscal Relations* (Washington, D.C.: Brookings Institution, 1962).

[8]Tax deductibility lowers the burden of state and local taxes by excusing the taxpayer of that portion of federal income tax that would be due on the money paid out in state and local taxes. If the taxpayer is in an income bracket in which 25 percent of income is paid in federal income taxes, then the federal government pays, in effect, 25 percent of the taxpayers' state and local taxes. The no-tax feature applied to the income on state and local government bonds makes these bonds more attractive to investors than are the bonds of private firms, and they permit state and local agencies to borrow money at lower-than-commercial rates of interest.

Reform at one level of government prompts reforms elsewhere. The U.S. Civil Service Reform Act of 1978 prompted many state government actions.

Table 13-4 Governments in 32 States Are Pursuing Civil Service Reform Programs in the Following Areas

State	Senior executive service	Merit pay	Labor relations	Performance appraisal system	Decentralization of personnel functions	Protection for "whistle blowers"	Veterans' preference and benefits
Alabama							
Alaska							
American Samoa							
Arizona			•				
Arkansas		•	•				
California			•	•			•
Colorado	•			•	•	•	
Connecticut	•	•		•	•	•	
Delaware						•	
District of Columbia							
Florida	•		•	•	•		
Georgia	•			•			
Guam							
Hawaii		•		•		•	•
Idaho		•				•	•
Illinois		•		•			
Indiana			•				
Iowa	•						
Kansas				•		•	
Kentucky					•	•	
Louisiana		•		•			
Maine		•		•			
Maryland					•		•
Massachusetts	•	•		•			•

Michigan
Minnesota
Mississippi
Missouri
Montana
Nebraska
Nevada
New Hampshire
New Jersey
New Mexico
New York
North Carolina
North Dakota
Ohio
Oklahoma
Oregon
Pennsylvania
Puerto Rico
Rhode Island
South Carolina
South Dakota
Tennessee
Trust Territory
Utah
Vermont
Virginia
Virgin Islands
Washington
West Virginia
Wisconsin
Wyoming

SOURCE: U.S. Office of Personnel Management, *Civil Service Reform: A Report on the First Year* (Washington, D.C.: U.S. Government Printing Office, 1980).

[303]

information and technical assistance to state and local governments and to facilitate the administration of federal programs in a way that is most helpful to states and localities. The commission includes representatives of national, state, and local governments, plus other members representing the public. A professional staff does detailed analyses and prepares recommendations for review by the commissioners.

Growth in Financial Aid

There is no disputing the fact that financial aid has grown over the years, but the appearance of growth varies with the techniques used to measure it. During the 1900–1981 period, the sheer magnitude of federal contributions increased by more than 30 times: from $3 million annually to $91 billion. However, these figures do not correct for obvious changes in the value of the dollar, the number of people who are served by federally aided programs, the pool of economic resources from which federal aid is taken, and the level of state and local government activities that federal aid recipients support with their own funds. When these corrections are made, the magnitude of recent increases appears more temperate. There was a marked increase during the Depression, a fall in magnitude during World War II, and an increase since World War II. This growth appears almost shocking when viewed in raw dollar amounts, but corrections for other economic, social, and governmental happenings place the growth in perspective. The role of federal grants in state and local affairs has expanded, both absolutely and relative to state and local revenues. However, administrative agencies in state and local government still receive the bulk of their financial resources from their own sources.[9] In some years, including 1978–1981, federal aid has not kept up with the increasing cost of goods and services.

STATE AID

State aid to local authorities includes many of the mechanisms found in federal aid to state and local governments. However, state aid emphasizes revenue sharing and bloc grants more than grants-in-aid for specified programs. A fixed portion of taxes that are "shared" revert to the local government in whose jurisdiction they are collected. Bloc grants and shared taxes provide more freedom to local governments than do grants-in-aid. Funds

---

[9]See I. Sharkansky, *The Maligned States: Policy Accomplishments, Problems, and Opportunities* (New York: McGraw-Hill, 1978), Chapters 5 and 7.

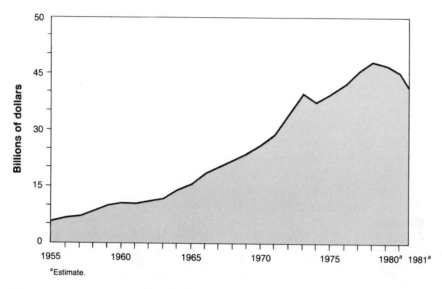

Figure 13-2 Federal Aid in Constant 1972 Dollars, 1955–1981. In the three years before 1981, federal aid to state and local governments declined in relation to the cost of goods and services. [SOURCE: U.S. Advisory Commission on Intergovernmental Relations.]

are not awarded for specified projects or in response to detailed applications, but go automatically to local governments on the basis of certain criteria, and may be used for any program within a generalized function (education, roads, and streets) or for the support of any governmental activity. State aid is generally "free" and does not require matching state funds with a certain proportion of locally raised revenues. Local governments receive much of their state aid with few application procedures and few limitations on expenditures.

The concept of state aid is necessarily loose due to the wide variety of programs and techniques in the 50 state governments. In many states, the aid rendered to local governments is only a small portion of the services state governments provide to local residents. State governments vary in the services they provide directly and the kinds they leave to local authorities. In the field of education, for example, some state governments pay the entire cost of public junior colleges, while other governments only provide supporting funds to county or municipal governments. In public welfare, some state governments pay for all aid not covered by federal grants, while other states share costs with local governments. The most complete record of state involvement in the support of public services shows the percentage of total state and local government revenues raised or spent at the state level. Table 13-6 shows this record for each state during 1977.

Federal aid has grown tremendously. Between 1969 and 1977, it has grown overall from about 19 percent to about 26 percent of state–local expenditures. It has grown more in some fields than in others. In some—like social insurance distribution—it has actually declined as a percentage of state–local expenditures.

Table 13-5   Federal Aid as Percent of State–Local Expenditures, 1969 and 1977

Use	1969	1977
Education	10%	10%
Highways	28	27
Public welfare	52	56
Health and hospitals	8	10
Natural resources	12	19
Housing and urban renewal	48	85
Air transportation	16	29
Social insurance administration	92	90
Other	6	33
Total	17%	27%

SOURCE: *National Journal,* January 19, 1980. Reprinted with permission.

There is considerable variation in the revenue that state governments raise for themselves and local governments. The nationwide average is 57.5 percent of total state and local taxes raised by the state government. However, the range extends from over 80 percent in Alaska, Delaware, and New Mexico to less than 50 percent in Colorado, New York, South Dakota, New Jersey, and New Hampshire. As noted in Chapter 12, the low-income states have a tendency to rely heavily on state-collected revenues. This tendency is evident in the heavy reliance on state revenues in Alabama, Arkansas, Kentucky, Mississippi, North Carolina, and West Virginia.

FEDERAL AND STATE AID TO CITIES

Although cities have no constitutional standing in the American federal system, they still have political clout. A striking demonstration of their power appears in the efforts of national and state governments to direct massive aid to the cities, especially to the largest cities, which seem to have the greatest needs. Table 13-7 shows the weight of intergovernmental assistance in city budgets. In cities with the largest populations (at least 500,000), 47.5 percent of the expenditures come initially from Washington, D.C., and state capitals. For all other cities, the percentage is only 35.6. With the advent of many new federal social programs in 1964–1965, the largest cities' per capita receipts of intergovernmental aid have grown by 595 percent, while those of other cities have grown by 517 percent.

Table 13-6 State Government Percentages of State and Local Revenues, 1977

State	Percent	State	Percent
Alabama	75.0%	Montana	53.6%
Alaska	82.8	Nebraska	50.7
Arizona	61.1	Nevada	58.3
Arkansas	75.8	New Hampshire	38.1
California	52.8	New Jersey	45.5
Colorado	49.9	New Mexico	80.4
Connecticut	53.0	New York	47.9
Delaware	81.0	North Carolina	72.8
Florida	61.7	North Dakota	66.6
Georgia	62.0	Ohio	52.1
Hawaii	78.6	Oklahoma	67.7
Idaho	67.1	Oregon	51.6
Illinois	55.0	Pennsylvania	61.6
Indiana	62.2	Rhode Island	59.2
Iowa	60.0	South Carolina	75.2
Kansas	57.3	South Dakota	46.1
Kentucky	75.0	Tennessee	63.1
Louisiana	68.9	Texas	58.1
Maine	65.6	Utah	64.2
Maryland	57.6	Vermont	58.7
Massachusetts	50.7	Virginia	59.2
Michigan	60.4	Washington	69.9
Minnesota	69.0	West Virginia	78.1
Mississippi	76.9	Wisconsin	67.5
Missouri	54.7	Wyoming	58.1

SOURCE: U.S. Bureau of the Census, *State Government Finances in 1978* (Washington, D.C.: U.S. Government Printing Office, 1979).

State governments are changing their constitutions and statutes to permit local authorities more flexibility in raising their own revenues. Historically, localities have been limited to the tax on real property. This tax has suffered from political hostility; from its failure to tap the economic resources of individuals who work and shop in the central city, but who reside in the suburbs; from a "regressive" rate structure that puts greater burdens on low-income taxpayers than upper-income taxpayers;[10] and often from

---

[10] The regressive tax structure also prevents local property taxes from operating like the state and national progressive income taxes, which increase in productivity faster than inflation as the inflation moves individuals into brackets in which they pay a higher percentage of their income as taxes.

Table 13-7   Large Cities' Receipt of State and Federal Aid, 1964–1978

	Cities of at least 500,000	All other cities
Combined state and federal aid as percentage of city expenditures		
1977–1978	47.5%	35.6%
1974–1975	50.8	37.1
1964–1965	24.0	18.1
Per capita receipt of aid		
1977–1978	$404.48	$116.64
1974–1975	362.25	93.79
1964–1965	58.20	18.90

SOURCE: U.S. Bureau of the Census, *City Government Finances in 1977–78, . . . 1974–75*, and *. . . 1964–65* (Washington, D.C.: U.S. Government Printing Office, 1980, 1976, and 1966).

arbitrary and anachronistic assessments of property value. As of 1978, local governments in 27 states collected a sales tax, and localities in 10 states collected an income tax. Agencies of most states try to improve the administration of local property taxes. They typically compare market values (as determined by actual sales) and local property assessments. The sales-assessment ratios serve to equalize the distribution of those state aids that go to local governments on the basis of property values and to identify local areas that need additional attention from tax assessors. This procedure minimizes tax competition between local governments and keeps assessments reasonably equivalent across the state for properties of similar values.

State governments have also increased their own expenditures in metropolitan areas. Investments are made in state clinics and hospitals, parks, intraurban expressways, and state universities located in urban areas. Most states have a department of local affairs that integrates the distribution of state financial aid to local governments. Some departments offer sizable state supplements to such federal urban programs as public housing, mass transit, urban renewal, and worker training.

HORIZONTAL RELATIONS

The presence of 50 state governments and over 70,000 local governments provides numerous opportunities for horizontal relationships among administrators at the same level. The formats for horizontal relations include:

1. *Compacts* and *federations* between different states and localities that permit the joint administration of public services.
2. Agreements to share information or technical assistance.
3. Reciprocal legislation that permits the citizens of one jurisdiction to receive certain services within another jurisdiction.
4. The membership of government officials in organizations that seek to develop solutions for common problems.

Officials in administrative agencies and legislative and executive branches usually take the lead in formulating intergovernmental arrangements. On occasion, however, the action of aroused citizens imposes intergovernmental pacts on officials who are reluctant to surrender their autonomy. The most frequent settings for horizontal relationships between administrative units are in metropolitan areas, where there are a high density of people and an obvious need for the interdependence of local governments. Some public services can be provided with greater efficiency when they are administered on an areawide basis. If the service units are sufficiently large, they can employ a variety of specialists needed for complete and competent service. A large tax base can support diverse collections for such services as libraries, zoos, and museums in central locations, with smaller collections in branch units. In the case of pollution control, wind and water currents do not respect political boundaries. An enforcement agency must have access to violators throughout the area. Likewise in the case of slum control. If a blighted area can spread across a street to another jurisdiction with an inadequate housing code, then one community's slum program will have limited success. Police and fire departments have arranged for reciprocal rights of pursuit, assistance in apprehending fugitives, and assistance in dealing with major fires. Without these protections, criminals might evade the law simply by crossing a street, or a community might suffer major fire loss while its neighbor's equipment stands idle.

Rural areas also require horizontal intergovernmental relations. Rivers or lakes that serve as the boundaries between different states may join their governments to the problems of water supply and pollution. The Mississippi River system (with the Ohio and Missouri as major tributaries) flows through or between 19 states! The Great Lakes wash the shores of eight states and present additional problems by lying alongside the Canadian border. Because Canada, like the United States, has a federal structure, Ontario provincial officials, as well as Canadian federal officials, take part in negotiations. Pollution control requires the cooperation of governments on either side of a stream, as well as those upstream and downstream. Too often, the sewage from an upstream location enters the water supply of its downstream neighbors. The problems of water use also involve diversions by one state or community that another state or community desires for its own use. The Great Lakes states have charged that Chicago's diversion of water from Lake Michigan into the Chicago River (and eventually to the Mississippi) lowers shorelines around the lakes and causes much damage and inconvenience to recreational and port facilities. On the Colorado River, conflicts over diversions for irrigation have prompted interstate compacts that portion out the water to Colorado, Arizona, Nevada, and California.

The contacts arranged by administrators of different states or localities to resolve their common problems are often informal and designed merely to inform them of one another's activities. However, some devices are very detailed and involve formal commitments from several state or local governments, and from the national or a foreign government as well.

Several devices attempt to cope with the problems of governmental coordination within metropolitan areas. The most complete are *federations* or *consolidations*. These terms imply general-purpose governments that provide a full range of services throughout the urban area. In some places, however, these entities handle only some local government functions. In Dade County, Florida, for example, the metropolitan government leaves numerous functions to municipalities and the county. "Special districts" provide services to extensive areas across the boundaries of several municipalities. Districts offer elementary and secondary education, water and sewerage, refuse collection, police and fire protection, parks, mass transportation, and libraries. With the multiplication of special districts, they become part of the metropolitan problem of confused jurisdictions. Each district may have its own borders that are not coterminous with those of other districts; one district may include several municipalities and parts of other municipalities or the rural fringe, and may overlap only partly with the territory covered by another kind of district. Where districts have proliferated, they can provide individual services on an economical basis, but they do not reduce the confusion or inequities that arise from numerous separate jurisdictions. Many citizens do not know which districts include their own residences, much less how they can influence policies within their districts.[11]

Where a metropolitan area spills over into more than one state, it may be necessary to formalize intergovernmental agreements as *interstate compacts*. These compacts must be defined in legislation acceptable to the officials of each state and to the U.S. Congress. The Port of New York Authority is one such compact. It is an agreement between New York and New Jersey that defines the legal authority and financial procedures for developing and maintaining transportation facilities in the New York City area. The Port Authority owns bridges, tunnels, airports, highways, and port facilities. It raises money by selling bonds that it pays off with tolls and other revenues earned by its facilities.

Some intergovernmental agreements commit administrators to share

---

[11]A. H. Walsh, *The Public's Business: The Politics and Practices of Government Corporations* (Cambridge, Mass.: MIT Press, 1978).

information used for enforcement programs. Tax officials of different states and the federal government share information about individuals who move from one state to another or about business firms that operate in many states. Returns filed by an individual or a business for state and federal taxes can be checked for consistency, and an audit performed by one agency may produce information useful to another.

The organizations of government officials are important media for horizontal relations among state or local governments. These organizations bring their members together for periodic meetings and sometimes provide staff services that compile information and write position papers on topics of common interest. Some attain national publicity. The U.S. Conference of Mayors includes the chief executives of most large cities, and the Governors' Conference includes all of the state chief executives. Other organizations exist for such administrative specialties as budgeting and personnel administration. Each of the service fields also has professional associations that facilitate contacts among administrative personnel from all levels of government and academic specialists from universities. Such organizations provide channels that smooth relations between neighboring jurisdictions. They also facilitate administrators' job mobility from one state or locality to another. When administrators face an unfamiliar situation, they can often contact colleagues in neighboring jurisdictions to see if they have worked out a policy to deal with similar situations. Two organizations publish collections of data that are widely used by state and local administrators to see how their activities compare with those across the country: The International City Managers' Association publishes *The Municipal Year Book* and the Council of State Governments publishes the *Book of the States*.

INTERGOVERNMENTAL INTEREST GROUPS

Organizations of elected officials and administrators are important for intergovernmental communications, and also act as interest groups that present the demands of administrators to other government officials. Along with the large annual increases in federal aid for state and local governments that marked the 1960s and 1970s, the organizations of state and local officials increased their staffs and the scope of their activities. The staffs and budgets of the U.S. Conference of Mayors and the National League of Cities went from 15 employees and $200,000 in 1954 to 200 employees and $7 million in 1973; the Washington office of the National Governors' Conference went from 5 professionals and $260,000 in 1967 to 12 professionals and $400,000 in 1972; the National Association of Counties increased its budget from $18,000 to over $1 million between 1957 and 1972.[12] These

---

[12]Haider, op. cit.

representatives of states and localities are labeled *public interest groups*; perhaps their acronym PIGS indicates as well their overall success in obtaining federal money.

The competition *between* the PIGS is as much a feature of the Washington scene as is their coordinated pursuit of resources. The differences between large and small municipalities, central cities and suburbs, assures some conflict between the U.S. Conference of Mayors, representing the largest cities, and the more broadly based National League of Cities. Partisan differences add their spices to the pot. In some years, Republicans have taken a leading role in the National Governors' Conference, while Democrats have dominated the U.S. Conference of Mayors. Each of these groups has been influential in the White House. Big-city programs had center stage during the Johnson Administration, while the states came back stronger during the Nixon years.

THE POTPOURRI OF RELATIONS

It is misleading to describe vertical and horizontal relations among administrative agencies as if to imply that these relations are clearly one type or another. Relations among administrators of different governments evolve from concrete problems that affect several jurisdictons, and therefore horizontal and vertical relations are often combined. Triangular relationships may also develop: two local governments are involved with a single federal or state agency, or two federal or state agencies are involved with a single local government. Neighboring localities may develop a joint project under the prodding of a federal grant. Or an integrated set of local programs may receive support from different federal grants offered by distinct agencies. Beyond this level of complexity, a variety of "polyangular" relationships may evolve among a number of federal, state, or local agencies that have a common interest in a particular problem.

It is also an oversimplification to assume that the involvement of a "superior" level of administration permits that organization to control its "subordinate" associates. A study of intergovernmental relations in a rural Indiana county found that several federal programs in the hands of local commissions were operated with substantial discretion. They were extensions of the federal administrative organization, but their mixture of local considerations with federal standards confound any simple equation of federal involvement with federal control.[13] These units included the Selective Service Board, the Welfare Board, the County Agricultural Stabilization

---

[13]D. St. Angelo, "Formal and Routine Local Control of National Programs," *Southwestern Social Science Quarterly*, 47 (March 1966): 416–427.

and Conservation Committee, and the Civil Defense Board. They were responsible for selecting young men for the armed services; deciding on applications for welfare assistance; distributing crop allotments and payments for conservation activities; establishing emergency procedures, and securing federal grants for fire fighting and hospital equipment. Indeed, a criticism of the military draft as it operated until the late stages of the Vietnam War was its provisions for local discretion. Members of local boards were able to excuse potential inductees for the pursuit of higher education, work in occupations of importance to the local economy, or because they were conscientious objectors to war. However, studies found that these provisions were used arbitrarily. The studies contributed to a reform that sharply lessened the discretion of local personnel.[14]

A SPACE-AGE CASE OF INTERGOVERNMENTAL RELATIONS

During the era of massive investment in the Cape Canaveral space facilities, east-central Florida experienced a vast expansion of intergovernmental relations. Between 1950 and 1966, the population of Brevard County increased from 23,600 to 221,000. The economy shifted from one based on citrus, cattle, truck crops, fishing, and forestry to one based almost exclusively on the space program. At the end of 1965, the air force, NASA, or their contractors employed about 37 percent of the area's labor force. A brief survey of the most prominent interactions provides a rich illustration of the diverse ways in which the administrative agencies of separate governments can come together to make demands on one another or to provide one another with benefits. During the boom, the following goals motivated intergovernmental relations:[15]

1. An agency's desire to make life more convenient and agreeable for its burgeoning work force.

2. An agency's concern that projects begun by other units would affect its own program.

3. An agency's desire to support its own projects with the resources controlled by other governments.

4. An agency's desire to protect its constituents' interests from being disturbed by the projects of other governments.

---

[14]J. W. Davis, Jr., and K. M. Dolbeare, *Little Groups of Neighbors: The Selective Service System* (Chicago: Markham, 1968).

[15]I. Sharkansky, "Intergovernmental Relations in Brevard County, Florida" (report to Urban Research Institute of Florida State University, 1966).

BOX 13-1   ACIR's Poll of Major Intergovernmental Events of Past 20 Years

In order to more accurately identify and review the key intergovernmental events and trends between 1959 and 1979, a poll of ACIR professional staff members was conducted in the fall of 1979. Two rounds of surveys were undertaken. The first asked for a list of the ten most significant intergovernmental events during the past 20 years and the reasons why each item was chosen. The second round listed these responses in three clusters—intergovernmental events, trends, and societal events—and called for a ranking of the most important ones in each category. The survey results were then reviewed and discussed by ACIR's management staff.

Listed below are the intergovernmental events that were ranked highest by the staff. . . .

While the poll was neither scientific in technique nor necessarily representative of the views of the wide range of participants in intergovernmental relations, we hope it will serve as a point of reference for—and perhaps stimulant to—others who attempt to assess federalism in transition.

1. Passage of General Revenue Sharing and Five Bloc Grants

   Most frequently cited item by the staff, primarily due to the fact that these enactments put into place a tripartite system of federal aid that gave states and localities added discretion over how federal dollars could be spent.

2. Enactment of Civil Rights/ Voting Rights Legislation

   Facilitated the expression of minority political clout, especially in central cities.

3. *Baker* v. *Carr*

   A landmark Supreme Court decision calling for "one man, one vote" in state legislatures that brought to an end rural domination of many state legislatures and led to the modernization that occurred there throughout the 1970s.

4. Passage of California's Proposition 13

   Was the most dramatic expression of citizen dissatisfaction with government and led to considerable activity in cutting taxes and establishing spending and taxing limits in cities and states across the country and a rethinking of the roles of the various levels of government. Was also significant in that such a major tax policy was the result of citizen initiative—successfully bypassing representative government.

5. Economic Opportunity Act/ War on Poverty	Heralded the major acceleration of federal domestic assistance, providing substantial federal dollars to inner cities while largely bypassing state and local government.
6. National Environmental Policy Act (NEPA)	Led to federal preemption of the air/water quality field and served as a forerunner to other national-level actions in the regulatory area that threatened the "balance" of federalism.
7. *Serrano* v. *Priest*	A California Supreme Court decision that reaffirmed the prinicple of equity in funding/service delivery and brought about significant reorganization of school finance systems.
8. New York City Fiscal Crisis	Capped the awareness of the intergovernmental effects of suburbanization and the intergovernmental responsibilities toward central cities and urban areas.
9. School Desegregation Court Cases: *Green* v. *New Kent County School Board, Swann* v. *Charlotte-Mecklenburg Board of Education, Milliken* v. *Bradley*	While *Brown* v. *Board of Education* was the first such case in the early 1950s, the past two decades saw cases that in combination laid the basis for HEW school desegregation initiatives that have powerfully affected and sometimes damaged numerous central cities.
10. Peaking of Federal Aid	After years of skyrocketing federal aid increases, the last year of the decade brought a turnaround and an apparent peaking of the massive aid increases. The impact on state and local governments which have grown accustomed to substantial federal aid "fixes" may well be enormous.
11. Passage of Medicare/ Medicaid	Represents another major expansion of governmental activity involving all three levels of government and significantly expanding social programs to the elderly and poor.

SOURCE: U.S. Advisory Commission on Intergovernmental Relations, *Intergovernmental Perspective*, 6 (Winter 1980).

5. Agency administrators' desires to build rapport with other units of government.
6. Agency personnel recognition that they had surplus resources valuable to other units of government.

NASA officials prominently played the role of a large employer concerned about the convenience of its employees. The agency wanted community amenities that would help it, and its contractors, to recruit personnel to the area. NASA also wanted convenient travel facilities to ensure that its employees could arrive at work promptly and in good spirits. It had a special interest in travel problems. The main NASA facilities were separated from the mainland by a wide estuary. Because the facilities were spread north and south over 50 miles, it was necessary to provide numerous roads, causeways, and bridges between each major work site and the communities that housed the workers. NASA's Office of Community Services surveyed the travel habits of its employees and those of other federal agencies and contractors, and provided the data to state, county, and municipal officials and to the U.S. Bureau of Public Roads.

The choice of specific locations for causeways and bridges involved the U.S. Army Corps of Engineers. That agency showed the second motivation for intergovernmenal relations. In this case, the corps had to review the designs of causeways and bridges to see that they did not interfere with navigation in the intracoastal waterway and in other streams in the Cape Canaveral area.

The question of money generated much activity. Displaying the third motivation for intergovernmental relations, several administrators sought the financial resources of other agencies for road and bridge improvements. The county road department requested extra funds from the state road board. In their turn, state officials argued that federal agencies should pay more than their usual portion for Brevard County road improvements because of the federally induced traffic. Federal agencies did accept some additional financial responsibility, but they hedged against filling state demands, arguing that the economic benefits of the space program would compensate for state road expenditures.

Together, state and county administrators approached federal officials in the pursuit of extra federal aid. During March 1965, a member of the state road board said that a delegation led by Governor Burns would meet with Florida senators and representatives and would try for an audience with President Johnson. This meeting did not occur, but during April, state officials met with Vice-President Humphrey during his visit to Orlando for the purpose of honoring astronaut John Young. Vice-President Humphrey then arranged a Washington, D.C., meeting between the governor, members of the state road board, the chairman of the Brevard County Commission, both Florida senators, the secretary of the air force (which operates Patrick Air Force Base in the Cape area), and the director and associate director of NASA's Kennedy Space Center. Out of this meeting came a state–federal agreement about the division of costs for certain roads and bridges, an indication that NASA and the air force would be willing to request a budget allocation for roads based on military needs, and plans for the submission of a supplementary appropriations bill in Congress.

The Orlando meeting with Vice-President Humphrey produced an incident that showed some of the tensions that can accompany intergovernmental relations. Local officials and allied newspaper editors dramatized a blunder in intergovernmental courtesy that displays the fourth motivation for intergovernmental relations (protecting one's constituents from another government's projects). The incident occurred as the meeting began. A security guard could not find the name of the Brevard County Commission chairman on the list of invited guests and insisted that he leave. Local officials and editors viewed the exclusion as depriving Brevard County of a representative at the discussion that might have long-range effects on the county. The *Titusville Star Advocate* in Brevard County quoted a local official as saying: "Brevard County is the ninth most populous county in Florida. ... I feel Brevard County is due an apology for [the commissioner's] ouster from that important meeting." The commissioner later came to see an advantage in his exclusion from the meeting. In the Vice-President's embarrassment and apology that followed, the commissioner found that other governments were more cooperative than he had originally expected.

Decisions concerning roads and bridges provide other examples of intergovernmental relations that were motivated by officials' desires to protect their constituents. The Bureau of Sports Fisheries of the U.S. Department of the Interior analyzed the design and location of bridges and causeways with respect to their impact on the health of marine life and recreational opportunities. Municipal authorities opposed the choice of certain locations for new roads and bridges because of their likely impact on local restaurants, motels, and retail shops. Authorities operating existing toll bridges opposed the development of competing toll-free facilities.

NASA's decision to create a Visitors Information Center produced another flurry of intergovernmental relations. The center promised to become the major tourist attraction in the area. A survey by the U.S. National Parks Service predicted that 3.2 million persons would visit the center annually. Reacting to this prediction, one county editor wrote:

> Three million people will eat a lot of meals in Brevard County. Many of them will want a place to stay overnight. They will want to buy souvenirs, visit our beaches, perhaps stay over long enough to fish or relax in our fine year-around climate.

Their cars will need fuel and probably some repairs and maintenance. They may even want to look around with an eye to choosing a retirement home or looking for a job. . . .

We'd better be ready to render the services they demand and will be willing to pay for.[16]

Communities closest to the Visitors Center would glean the most business from tourists. Also, the center's exact location would determine which routes the national automobile clubs and oil companies would recommend for tourists. If a town did not have convenient access to the center, it would lose tourist business. Before NASA made a decision about the center's location, several chambers of commerce urged it for their areas. Three communities offered free land for the center; one offered a vacant supermarket as a suitable building.

To avoid the honky-tonkism that would surround a location on a public highway (few major roads in the county were free of strip development), NASA decided to build the center inside its reservation, with a federally controlled road between it and a major highway. Although this decision did not escape harsh criticism from community newspapers, NASA tried to minimize the controversy. During the course of public presentations, NASA asserted that it would not compete with the private tourist industry. As a way to support local eateries, the Visitors Center would limit its refreshment stands to snack, rather than lunch or picnic, facilities. In order to keep all important communities on the tourist routes, NASA would make the center accessible from various parts of the county. To accomplish this, NASA would allow the state road board to build additional highways through its reservation.

While intergovernmental competition and conflict were prominent in the relationships generated by road and bridge development and by NASA's Visitors Information Center, most intergovernmental relations in Brevard County appeared amicable. NASA and the air force tried to promote rapport with state and local governments. At the national level, NASA worked to establish a subregional office of another federal agency (the Department of Housing and Urban Development) in Brevard County. The subregional office was not a usual component of HUD's organization. Rather, it was the department's effort to help area communities cope with their rapid growth. NASA's involvement came partly from its desire to have good working relations with local governments, and partly from the hope that improved community facilities would help it recruit and hold employees. HUD's subregional office provided advice and technical assistance to local authorities who wished to apply for federal grants. Its staff listed and described the

---

[16]*Orlando Sentinel* (Brevard County edition), June 5, 1965.

programs of HUD and other federal departments and explained the criteria that federal officials were likely to consider when they reviewed local applications for grants. Somewhat in the manner of traveling sales representatives, HUD personnel called upon local authorities in order to acquaint them with new or changing programs.

The air force channeled many of its intergovernmental relations through the Civilian–Military Council at Patrick Air Force Base. Thus, base commanders and public relations officers were able to meet with local government officials, the clergy, retail business executives, and real estate agents. Formal meetings of this group were typically short and uneventful, but the accompanying social hour eased discussions of mutual concern and joint activities. Once each year the members spent several days together—partly at federal expense—visiting other air force installations throughout the United States. Members claim this extended period in close contact allowed them to understand each other's views more clearly and to comprehend the constraints that influenced each other's operations. Several instances of intergovernmental cooperation could be traced to the friendships that developed out of the council's meetings. A public relations officer for the air force cited the council's program as an explanation for the immediate response that he once received from the county road department in response to his call for assistance. During the Cuban missile crisis, it was necessary to close the main highway that ran alongside the airstrip. Within a few minutes of the official's telephone request, the county had a road grader on the scene to smooth a dirt road detour, and police officers arrived to block the highway and redirect traffic.

Many administrators tell stories about the exchange of favors between agencies. Some of the tales reflect high-level decisions to build intergovernmental rapport. However, lower-level employees also exchange favors for less complex motives. They do so when they are predisposed to cooperation, and when they have a surplus commodity that can benefit another agency in the area. These exchanges have not been significant in terms of money or working hours, but they make relations tolerable for the members of different units. Patrick Air Force Base loaned personnel and vehicles without charge to help a school construction project that had fallen behind schedule. County personnel and equipment—using materials donated by local businesses—helped to construct a swimming pool for noncommissioned officers. The county donated materials for a refreshment stand on the air force's Little League field. NASA and the air force donated obsolete missiles to local authorities for display purposes, and they allowed local government personnel to attend in-service training courses provided for federal employees. On one occasion, Patrick Air Force Base rescued a local government from embarrassment at the hands of another federal agency. When the Federal Aviation Agency would not allow a new airport to begin operations on the day of its formal opening because its tower operator lacked the proper credentials, the air force offered one of its tower operators.

There is no simple pattern of intergovernmental relations. No formal rules prescribe in clear terms how administrators of one government should deal with officials of another unit. Furthermore, each major occurrence of intergovernmental relations is not one event. It is a series of meetings, telephone conversations, memoranda, and informal or formal accords. At times, a government's decisions may influence another government even when no real contact has been made. An administrator of one unit may base a decision on anticipations of the likely actions that will be taken by officials of other units. If the officials of different units have obtained sufficient knowledge of each other's modes of action, their anticipations may lead to actions that differ little from what would occur with formal communications.

SUMMARY

Administrators from all levels of government seek to affect the decisions of administrators at other levels. Various kinds of intergovernmental aid join the resources of federal, state, and local governments in the support of all major domestic services. People at each level of government feel the impact of decisions that flow from other levels.

There are numerous forms of intergovernmental relations. Many involve financial assistance, and even those that are not overtly financial have economic importance for the participants: grants-in-aid, shared taxes, revenue-sharing tax credits, federal income tax provisions that allow deductions for state and local taxes and the exclusion of income earned on state or local government bonds, the direct provision of services from one government to the citizens of another, technical assistance, and informal ties between personal friends in different agencies and between members of administrators' professional societies. It is not feasible to estimate the economic value of all these relations to the providers or to the recipients. The resources involved in federal grants and state aid to localities are considerable. Federal aid to states and localities amounted to $69 billion in 1978 and state aid to localities was about $65 billion.

Growth in the magnitude of intergovernmental financial assistance has been impressive since World War II, although any report of growth is partly a function of the measurements that are used. The kinds of programs added during each decade of the twentieth century indicate that intergovernmental relations grow according to prevailing policy concerns. Recent programs in the fields of education and urban affairs, for example, reflect the preoccupation with those areas of policy that began during the 1960s and 1970s.

Not all intergovernmental relationships are vertical. Horizontal contacts occur among different states and localities. These arrangements do not emphasize financial aid, but they often have great economic significance for each of the participants. There are numerous kinds of metropolitan cooperation, interstate compacts, reciprocal agreements for the provision of services and enforcement programs, and informal links on the basis of personal friendships and contacts made through the organizations of government officials. It is often misleading to identify the type of intergovernmental relationship that prevails at any time or place. Multiple relationships evolve among different governmental units as their officials or clients perceive common interests. Individual problems may generate both vertical and horizontal relations among several units.

14

Laws, Rules, and the Regulatory Agencies

Laws and rules are the formal stuff that define how administrators should work in their organizations and deal with the public. For example, the U.S. Internal Revenue Service (IRS) adheres to laws enacted by Congress and rulings issued within the guidelines laid down by Congress and the courts. Federal laws and rules are made public in the U.S. statutes, formal decisions of various federal courts, and, for rules issued by the IRS and other agencies, in the *Federal Register*. Various commercial publishers compile and organize the official tax material for the convenience of taxpayers, attorneys, accountants, and other professional tax advisers who wish to figure out what they or their clients can use to their advantage in dealing with the IRS. It is not always clear how the IRS or the courts will interpret a taxpayer's own case with respect to the many laws and rules, but much public information is available about taxpayers' entitlements.

Formal laws and rules provide the basis for action, but their strength lies in administrative practices. While an obvious law of the land is not to cheat on taxes, the IRS deals with millions of returns each year and must by necessity develop some way of determining which returns to examine. The IRS possesses the resources needed to audit only a small percentage closely. It chooses which returns to audit according to analyses of previous returns. The IRS has identified the kinds of returns likely to show important errors. The agency programs its computers to identify those taxpayers who are probably in error—such as those claiming an unusually high percentage of total income as business expenses or charitable contributions. The IRS keeps secret the specific criteria used to identify taxpayer returns for audit.

Knowing this information would be valuable to some tax advisers, because it would tell them what their clients could get away with. For example, if a claim of $5,500 for charitable deductions at a certain level of gross income would invite an audit, the taxpayer might be advised to claim deductions of $5,300. Some tax advisers have figured out where the IRS draws the lines for audits, and have supplied this information to their clients.

How can the agency combat this violation of their secrets? One method is to require taxpayers to list the name of the lawyer, accountant, or other adviser who helped them prepare their tax return. Along with all the other information obtainable by computer analysis, the IRS has access to the names of tax advisers. Those whose clients have a high incidence of returns warranting scrutiny are more likely than other advisers to have their clients audited.

This chapter focuses on the laws and rules that govern the activities of administrators. As the IRS case illustrates, however, we should not underestimate the importance of unpublicized administrative procedures. Laws, rules, and procedures define what administrators *can do,* what they *should do,* and what they *must not do.* Laws and rules pertain both to the activities that take place within administrative agencies and to the activities directed at citizens and organizations outside of government. The key questions in this chapter are:

What are the laws and rules?
Who gets what?

TERMINOLOGY

In dealing with laws and rules that govern the behavior of administrators, we must enter a language thicket where terminology is crucial but generally haphazard. In most places, a decision is an agency's determination of how it will act in a particular case. In the Treasury Department, however, a decision is a general rule. According to the U.S. Administrative Procedures Act, an order is a judicial-type decision issued by an administrative body. Often, however, an order is a general regulation. A directive likewise can be a general regulation, or rule, or particular decision.

Although the ways in which terminology varies are often whimsical, terminology can be crucial. If you are charged formally with violating an order of an administrative agency, your lawyer might find that this agency can issue only directives. What the administrator termed an order may therefore have no standing in your case. Aware of the chaos engendered by loosely defined terms, Congress tried to standardize the language used in government in the Administrative Procedures Act (APA), but dared not insist on a government-wide editing of administrators' dictionaries. The terms employed in the APA have legal force only within the confines of that act.[1]

WHAT ARE REGULATORY AGENCIES?

Regulatory agencies are traditionally the focus of lawyers, politicians, and political scientists who are concerned with administrative laws and rules. These agencies are empowered by Congress to determine what various citizens and organizations may or may not do, to grant licenses or privileges to perform certain functions, and to proceed against violators of laws and rules.

The Interstate Commerce Commission is the granddaddy of regulatory agencies. It began in 1887 to set interstate freight rates and the prices of railroad tickets, to indicate which companies could operate between various points, and to set conditions of service. The Federal Trade Commission regulates product safety, the Securities and Exchange Commission controls the practices of stock exchanges, the Federal Communications Commission regulates radio and television broadcasting, and the Nuclear Regulatory Commission licenses nuclear facilities. These are the major federal independent regulatory commissions. Typically, they are headed by several commissioners, appointed by the President for fixed terms, with members of one political party allowed no more than a simple majority of each commission. The commission proclaims general rules and makes decisions in individual cases under statutory guidelines laid down by Congress. In reality, the commissioners oversee sizable staffs of professional analysts, investigators, and hearing officers, who do much of the actual spadework for the commissioners' actions. Individual commissioners may take an active role in some decisions. They may be personally attracted to cases with major policy import, or their involvement may be sought by individuals with a stake in a certain case, by members of Congress, or by the executive branch.

Other regulatory agencies within cabinet departments lack the structure of the independent regulatory commissions. Nevertheless, they also make rules, apply these rules to specific cases of regulation, and hear appeals from dissatisfied firms. One influential unit that makes and implements regulatory rules—but does not have the peculiar structure of a commission—is the Food and Drug Administration. It is headed by a single administrator, who is appointed (and is subject to removal) by the President. The FDA regulates the manufacture, advertising, and distribution of food, drugs, and cosmetics, and it determines which commodities or practices

---

[1]B. Schwartz, *Administrative Law* (Boston: Little, Brown, 1976).

should be removed from the market. There is no clear explanation for the trappings of the independent commissions being given to some regulatory units, while others, such as the Food and Drug Administration, are indistinguishable from companion agencies within cabinet departments. Perhaps some political contexts lend themselves to the development of elaborate safeguards against presidential dominance of a regulatory body—along the lines of the independent regulatory commission—while others permit regulation by a standard type of agency.

Administrative laws and rules are administered by the independent regulatory commissions and other agencies with regulatory functions. A less traditional but rapidly developing focus of administrative laws and rules is on the group of agencies that do not control so much as they serve us. For example, the Social Security Administration, the Department of Education, the Veterans Administration, and the National Parks Service provide pensions, medical insurance, educational assistance, recreational facilities, and a host of other programs to support, uplift, and entertain. They, too, are governed by laws and rules, with many of the rules coming from their own officials. Such laws and rules determine *Who gets what?* from the enormous goodies of the modern welfare state. Clients concerned with receiving at least their share of the pie must be aware of the laws and rules that govern these service agencies.

Regulatory Powers

Agencies possess different kinds of regulatory powers:

1. *Licensing.* Determining which companies or individuals can take part in the economic activities within the agency's jurisdiction. For example, determining who can operate an airline or a television station, and which among the licensed airlines or trucking companies can operate a daily service between Topeka and New Orleans.

2. *Setting rates.* Governing the amount that can be charged by companies falling within agency jurisdiction for such products or services as electricity, airline tickets, or hauling goods in trains or trucks.

3. *Controlling the practices of certain bodies.* For example, determining how the airlines must treat passengers with reserved places who are "bumped" from overbooked flights; or how interstate moving companies must estimate charges, weigh materials being shipped, and deal with the complaints from customers.

The rules that agencies issue with respect to these regulatory powers carry a confusing variety of names. Individuals having business with the

Independent regulatory commissions are only part of the scene. Other units perform regulatory functions from within conventional departments and agencies.

Table 14-1 The Regulatory Establishment Gets Bigger and Bigger (in millions of dollars, fiscal years), 1970 and 1980

Agency (in order of creation)	1970	1980
1824 Army Corps of Engineers	$ 2	$ 40
1836 Patent and Trademark Office, Commerce Department	49	96
1863 Comptroller of the Currency	32	190
1871 Bureau of Fisheries (became Fish and Wildlife Service in 1940)	NA	20
1887 Interstate Commerce Commission	27	80
1903 Antitrust Division	9	47
1913 Federal Reserve Board	3	11
1914 Federal Trade Commission	20	68
1915 Coast Guard	57	368
1916 Tariff Commission (became International Trade Commission in 1975)	4	15
1922 Commodity Exchange Authority, Agriculture Department (became Commodity Futures Trading Commission in 1974)	—	16
1927 Customs Service	20	116
1930 Federal Power Commission (became Federal Energy Regulatory Commission in 1977)	18	70
1931 Food and Drug Administration	68	317
1932 Federal Home Loan Bank Board	21	21
1933 Employment Standards Administration, Labor Department	NA	112
1933 Federal Deposit Insurance Corporation	39	122
1934 Federal Communications Commission	24	71
1934 Securities and Exchange Commission	22	68
1935 National Labor Relations Board	38	107
1936 Maritime Administration, Commerce Department (regulatory functions were transferred to the Federal Maritime Commission in 1961)	4	11
1937 Consumer and Marketing Service, Agriculture Department (duties were transferred in 1972 to the Agricultural Marketing Service and the Animal and Plant Health Inspection Service; major regulatory duties were transferred from the latter to the Food Safety and Quality Service in 1977)	197	872
1938 Civil Aeronautics Board	48	102
1946 Atomic Energy Commission (regulatory functions were transferred to the Nuclear Regulatory Commission in 1975)	12	345
1948 Federal Aviation Agency (became Federal Aviation Administration in 1967)	NA	229

Table 14-1   (continued)

Agency (in order of creation)	1970	1980
1951 Renegotiation Board	4	7
1953 Foreign Agricultural Service, Department of Agriculture	NA	NA
1953 Small Business Administration	NA	NA
1961 Agricultural Stabilization and Conservation Service, Agriculture Department	66	80
1963 Labor–Management Services Administration, Labor Department	12	52
1964 Equal Employment Opportunity Commission	12	124
1966 Federal Highway Administration	NA	29
1966 Federal Railroad Administration	4	23
1969 Council on Environmental Quality	NA	3
1970 Cost Accounting Standards Board	NA	2
1970 Environmental Protection Agency	71	1,154
1970 National Credit Union Administration	7	17
1970 National Highway Traffic Safety Administration	32	132
1970 Occupational Safety and Health Review Commission	—	7
1971 Farm Credit Administration	4	12
1972 Bureau of Alcohol, Tobacco and Firearms, Treasury Department	NA	137
1972 Consumer Product Safety Commission	—	41
1972 Domestic and International Business Administration, Commerce Department (now the Industry and Trade Administration)	—	9
1973 Drug Enforcement Administration	NA	14
1973 Federal Energy Administration (became Economic Regulatory Administration in 1977)	—	156
1973 Mine Enforcement and Safety Administration, Interior Department (became Mine Safety and Health Administration of the Labor Department in 1977)	NA	126
1973 Occupational Safety and Health Administration	—	173
1974 Council on Wage and Price Stability	—	6
1975 Federal Election Commission	—	9
1975 National Transportaton Safety Board	5	16
1976 Federal Grain Inspection Service, Department of Agriculture	—	25
1977 Office of Consumer Affairs and Regulatory Functions, Housing and Urban Development Department	—	21
1977 Office of Surface Mining Reclamation and Enforcement, Interior Department	—	148

SOURCE: Center for the Study of American Business, Washington University.

agencies must learn the vocabulary for each one. For this general discussion, however, it is important only to know that there are:

Substantive rules, which determine what an agency can do.

Procedural rules, which determine how an agency must exercise its powers.

Substantive rules may define the requirements for receiving an agency license—what it takes by way of equipment, training, and working capital to provide certain trucking or airline services; or what rules must be followed by the airlines or trucking companies in dealing with their customers. Procedural rules govern the activities of the agencies. They set the schedules for filing applications and for appealing adverse decisions of the agency. They may require agency personnel to advertise certain events—like the opening of competition for a new trucking route—and to permit public hearings in advance of making decisions.

Explicit rules for substance and procedure are crucial for the clients of regulatory agencies. They clarify what clients can receive and how they can apply for receiving it. These rules also provide standards for judging agency activities. If clients feel injured by arbitrary action on the part of agency administrators, they can cite the administrators for failing to abide by the rules. The first appeal of agency action is likely to be within the agency itself, in front of specially designated appeals officers. If clients remain unsatisfied by an agency's internal procedures, they may be able to appeal its decision in court.

In their practices, regulatory agencies appear to be somewhat like courts. They resemble the courts in their concern for judicial-like rituals of impartial officers who judge individual cases, take sworn testimony, and allow the subjects of their decisions to be represented by legal counsel. However, they differ from the courts in that the judges in conventional courtrooms are not expert in the substance of the cases brought before them. They are chosen for their skills in judicial procedure and their judicial temperament in being able to monitor the presentations of adversaries. Regulatory agencies, in contrast, must have substantive expertise in the issues at hand. An agency is likely to be a party to a case, making decisions that advance its programs to achieve certain standards in the regulated industry. Furthermore, the agencies are not passive. Unlike the courts, agencies do not wait for outsiders to bring cases to them. The regulatory agencies monitor activities within their jurisdictions, and pursue cases actively, in keeping with their legislative mandates. They may go after an alleged violator of their rules, bring charges, and judge guilt or innocence after hearing the defense offered by the citizen or business firm.

Like Congress, the regulatory agencies proclaim rules. Indeed, they greatly outdo Congress as a source of regulatory verbiage. The *Federal Reg-*

ister, which reports agency rules and other announcements on a daily basis, contained over 75,000 pages in a recent year. The *Code of Federal Regulations,* which codifies rules by subject matter, is well over 100 volumes and 90,000 pages. Like Congress, the regulatory agencies issue their rules after giving affected parties an opportunity to be heard. Like Congress, most regulatory agencies go beyond the official record of testimony, taking their inspiration from a wide range of public and private sources. To be legal, the rules issued by a regulatory agency must remain within the standards delegated to the agency by the acts of Congress. However, Congress has been generous in giving the agencies a long leash, and the courts have acceded to congressional practice. The Federal Communications Commission, for example, can issue its rules according to the vague standard of "public convenience, interest, or necessity." The FCC can justify its rules for station licensing or its control over programming according to the agency's interpretation of this loose formulation. Congress has authorized the Interstate Commerce Commission to set rates that are "just and reasonable," and it has authorized the Federal Trade Commission to regulate against "unfair methods of competition." The Securities and Exchange Commission has an equally broad mandate to maintain "fair and orderly" markets, assure "just and equitable principles of trade," and guard against "unreasonable rates of commission."

Judicial Review

Congress and the courts may have given a long leash to the regulatory agencies, but there is a leash. Parties who consider themselves aggrieved by agency action—or inaction—can bring their cases to the courts. Before addressing the substance of each case, however, the court must determine whether it will accept the matter. To determine this, the court will ask:

1. Do the statutes permit judicial review of the administrative action in the kind of case at issue?
2. Is the case being brought by a proper party (plaintiff)?
3. Is the case being brought against a proper defendant?
4. Is the timing of the case proper?
5. Is the agency action being challenged ready for review; in other words, has the agency made its final decision?
6. Have the proper forms of appeal been taken?

A negative answer to any of these queries will disqualify a case for judicial review. A court can focus its review of agency actions on procedural or substantive issues. As the basis of its decision, a court can rely on the laws

Another view of government regulation—according to the number of administrative judges employed by various agencies.

Table 14-2 Where the Judges Are and What They Do

Department/Agency	Prime function	Number
Agriculture	Disciplinary proceedings against stockyard owners, produce dealers, brokers, and commission merchants	5
Bureau of Alcohol, Tobacco and Firearms (Treasury)	Permits to import, sell, or distill alcoholic beverages	1
Civil Aeronautics Board	Airline route and rate applications, foreign permits, and mergers	17
Coast Guard (Transportation)	Misconduct, negligence, and incompetence; narcotics cases	16
Commodity Futures Trading Commission	Suspension or revocation of broker registration	4
Consumer Product Safety Commission	Violations of laws protecting the public from hazardous products	1
Drug Enforcement Administration (Treasury)	Suspension or revocation of controlled substance registration	1
Environmental Protection Agency	Permits to discharge pollutants into navigable waters; pesticide registration	6
Federal Communications Commission	Licensing of radio, TV, cable, and common carriers	14
Federal Energy Regulatory Commission	Natural gas pipeline construction, abandonment, curtailment, and rates; electric rates	23
Federal Labor Relations Authority	Federal employee labor relations	4
Federal Maritime Commission	Investigation and suspension of proposed rates; complaint proceedings for reparations	7
Federal Mine Safety and Health Review Commission	Violations of miner health and safety	12
Federal Trade Commission	False or misleading advertising; restraint of trade	12

Agency	Description	Number
Food and Drug Administration (Health, Education and Welfare)	New drug applications; food standards, color additives	1
Housing and Urban Development	Lack of full disclosure in interstate land sales	1
Interior	Coal mine health and safety violations, mining claims, and grazing rights	8
International Trade Commission	Import law violations	2
Interstate Commerce Commission	Complaints, investigations, and applications in the regulation of railroads, motor carriers, and water carriers	61
Labor	Unfair labor practices; longshoremen compensation claims, and rates in government contracts	49
Maritime Administration (Commerce)	Merchant marine operating differential subsidies; adequacy of U.S. flag service	3
Merit Systems Protection Board	Appeals from disciplinary proceedings against employees of the federal government	1
National Labor Relations Board	Unfair labor practices cases	98
National Transportation Safety Board	Challenges to denial, suspension, or revocation of Federal Aviation Administration certification	6
Nuclear Regulatory Commission	Construction permit safety reviews	1
Occupational Safety and Health Review Commission	Employer health and safety violations	47
Postal Rate Commission	Changes in mail classification and rates	1
Postal Service	False representation to obtain money through the mail; second-class mail privileges	2
Securities and Exchange Commission	Denial, suspension, or revocation of broker-dealer and investment adviser registration	8
Social Security Administration (Health, Education and Welfare)	Disability insurance and black lung benefits	660
Total		1,072

SOURCE: *National Journal*, July 28, 1979. Reprinted with permission.

[331]

There are several ways to depict growth in federal regulation. These indicators—number of agencies, money spent, and outputs in volume—all show growth in the 1970s.

Table 14-3 Federal Regulation Growth, 1970–1979

Year	Major regulatory agencies		Agency spending (millions)		Pages in *Federal Register*	Pages in *Code of Federal Regulations*
	Economic	Social	Economic	Social		
1970	8	12	$166.1	$1,449.3	20,036	54,105
1971	8	15	196.8	1,882.2	25,447	54,487
1972	8	15	246.3	2,247.5	28,924	61,035
1973	8	18	198.7	2,773.7	35,592	64,852
1974	9	18	304.3	3,860.1	42,422	69,270
1975	10	18	427.6	4,251.4	60,221	72,200
1976	10	18	489.8	5,028.3	57,072	73,149
1977	10	18	544.8	6,383.7	65,603	83,700
1978	10	18	512.5	7,225.4	61,261	88,562
1979	10	18	608.6	7,576.1	77,497	93,000[a]
Percent increase (1970– 1979)	25%	50%	266%	423%	287%	72%

[a]Estimate.

SOURCE: American Enterprise Institute for Public Policy Research.

passed by Congress, the rules set by the agency that is the target of the court case, or on the common-law practice of equity relief.

The use of judicial review is a controversial topic in the field of regulation. Statutory language that restricts judicial review puts great weight on the actions of the regulatory agencies themselves. If the statutes permit wide latitude of judicial review, however, then the regulatory agencies may be rendered little more than processing stations of individual cases on their way to final determination in the courts. Also, where the courts take a great deal upon themselves, the contribution of the agency's substantive experts to the regulatory process can be rendered insignificant. In this situation, the courts will be congested, and delays in individual cases will be endemic.

Industries that fear administrative controls seek statutory language that facilitates judicial review of agency decision. They can then fight adverse rulings through all the stages of appeal within an agency, then try to win favorable judgments in the courts. Even if their actions fail, filing appeals and suits delays giving in to the government.

WHO GETS WHAT?

The details of laws, rules, and regulatory and judicial decisions determine precisely *Who gets what?* from the cornucopia of government agencies. Individual citizens and business firms, politicians, journalists and other analysts, and officials of the agencies themselves devote much time and energy to musing about the effects of agency decisions. *Who gets what?* can be answered in particular terms: Did one airline or another receive permission to fly a new route? Was it the winning airline's friend in the White House or the quality of its formal presentaton that produced the victory? Did a taxpayer win a favorable ruling from the IRS or the tax court? *Who gets what?* must also be asked in terms of economic and political groups: Does business win more times than consumers in the decisions of the regulatory agencies? Does political favoritism win over the merits of cases? The quantity of resources at stake makes these questions important topics of political commentary.

A prominent theme in the writing about regulatory agencies is that the industries being regulated are the most assiduous and most successful in affecting agency rules and decisions. In short, it is claimed that cozy relationships and outright illegalities tilt decisions in the direction of the industries that are regulated. The results are said to be substantial profit for business coupled with high costs or poor services to consumers.

Nader's Raiders

Champions of the Public Interest

Ralph Nader is the preeminent muckraker in the field of government regulation. Nader first became prominent when his book, *Unsafe at Any Speed,* exposed the mechanical dangers inherent in automobiles. His book was a major stimulus for the enactment of federal auto safety regulations and for the demise of the Chevrolet Corvair. With the income from that book, his popular lectures, and personal appearances, Nader founded the Center for the Study of Responsive Laws. The center sponsors investigations into a wide range of regulatory activities. Among its major studies have been those dealing with the Food and Drug Administration, the Interstate Commerce Commission, the Federal Trade Commission, the National Air Pollution Control Administration, and the Antitrust Division of the Justice Department.[2]

---

[2]See E. F. Cox, R. C. Fellmeth, and J. E. Schulz, *Nader's Raiders* (New York: Grove, 1969); J. C. Esposito, *Vanishing Air* (New York: Grossman, 1970); J. S. Turner, *The Chemical Feast* (New York: Grossman, 1970); R. Fellmeth, *The Interstate Commerce Omission* (New York: Grossman, 1970); and M. J. Green, *The Closed Enterprise System* (New York: Bantam, 1972).

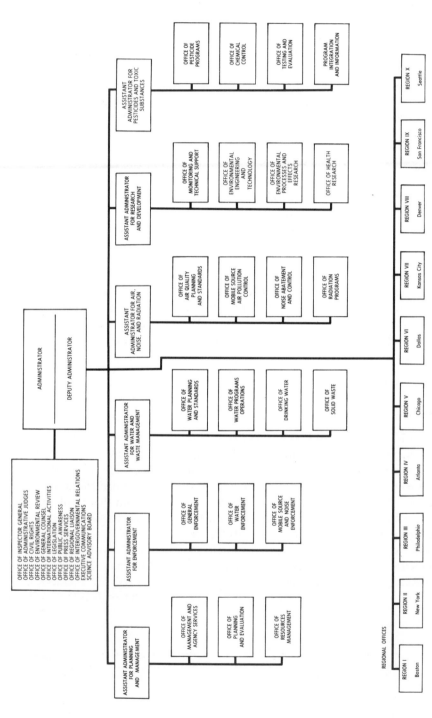

Figure 14-1 Environmental Protection Agency. The chart of a regulatory agency, identifying its programs, structure, and locations of regional offices. [SOURCE: *United States Government Manual, 1980–1981* (Washington, D.C.: U.S. Government Printing Office, 1980).]

Nader operates in the grand tradition of American muckrakers. His books provide one horrible example after another, pointing to the failure of regulation to protect the public from ill-conceived products and services, and demonstrating irresponsible actions by officials of private corporations and government agencies. The books clarify some complex details of regulatory statutes and the technical considerations that must go into policies for transportation, air pollution, food safety, and drug effectiveness.

The work of Nader and his associates is a good example of private interests that probe and criticize public administration, and it provides a great deal of information about the regulatory process. Like the work of other committed reformers, however, Nader's material emphasizes the sensational and negative. It lacks a sophisticated concern for how bad regulation actually is. It does not compare the incidence of regulatory failure to the incidence of success. Nor does it access the benefits from improved regulation in relation to the costs of improved surveillance. However, the findings of Nader and his colleagues are communicated with a force that is missing from the reports of academic political scientists. Nader writes with the conviction that publicity is the necessary first step to a sweeping reform. Nader himself is a frequent witness at congressional hearings. Some of the most vivid writing describes obvious failures in regulatory policies: the FDA's permission for the unrestricted use of cyclamates and monosodium glutamate long after serious research had questioned their dangers; the plight of families who believed that the ICC would assure a smooth move of furniture from one state to another; the ICC's cooperation in the decline of railroad passenger service; and the ICC's failure to protect motorists from unsafe trucks.

Many of the books put out by the Nader group bog down in stodgy and confusing details. Nevertheless, Nader helps to capture public interest with his catchy phrases and captivating prefaces. He began one book about monopoly regulation by referring to "crime in the suites." "Corporate socialism" is his term for cozy relations between government and business. He asserts that the tactics of nineteenth-century robber barons (flamboyantly acquisitive and morally corrupt business tycoons) have been written into public policy by present-day regulatory commissions.[3]

Nader's touch also appears in the titles of books and chapters: *Unsafe At Any Speed,* about automobile safety; *The Chemical Feast,* about the Food and Drug Administration; *The Closed Enterprise System,* about antitrust enforcement; *The Interstate Commerce Omission,* about the Interstate Commerce Commission; and *Vanishing Air,* about antipollution enforcement. Also these witticisms: "AT&T: The Phony Monopoly," "Defense Procurement: 'Everyone Feeds at the Trough,'" and "Drug Procurement: High on Profits."[4]

---

[3]Green, op. cit., p. vii; and M. J. Green, ed., *The Monopoly Makers* (New York: Grossman, 1973), pp. ix–xi.
[4]Green, ed., *The Monopoly Makers.*

Some Findings

The studies of "Nader's Raiders" should not surprise professional political scientists. Several years ago, Marver Bernstein described the life cycle of a regulatory agency.[5] In the early stage of its life, there is enthusiasm about new statutes and about the impending end of antisocial industrial practices. Gradually, this euphoria is replaced by the recognition that a regulatory agency is a guardian, as well as an antagonist, of a regulated industry. A Nader study of utility regulation found that U.S. and state government agencies routinely allow company claims of expenses to boost the cost of doing business, on top of which the agencies permit a specified profit. Company expenses are not adequately monitored for frivolous items, enormous salaries for management, a lack of concern for increasing worker productivity, and endless and expensive litigation and hearings before the regulatory agencies, such as the utility companies' efforts to gain higher rates. These unmonitored expenses are passed automatically onto consumers in the form of higher bills for telephones, gas, water, and electricity. One study estimates that the annual economic waste from government regulation in the transportation and communications sectors to be in the range of $16.02–$24.2 billion.[6]

Items that seem to be trivial can represent a great deal of money. Like the amount of peanuts, as opposed to vegetable oils, required by the FDA to be in each batch of peanut butter. The profit seemed enough for the peanut butter industry to seek delay after delay—almost 12 years' worth— in an effort to move the FDA's proposal of 95 percent peanuts down to 87 percent peanuts.[7]

Nader and his group have been useful in pointing to the resource problems of regulatory agencies. They remind us of the lessons from Chapters 7 and 8: that money and people are important in the running of government, and that laws and rules cannot be enforced without them. The study of antitrust enforcement ridiculed the budget of the Justice Department's Antitrust Division ($11.4 million for 1972) and its professional staff (354 lawyers, economists, and statisticians). These resources seem piddling in comparison with those of the opposition. The antitrust budget was only one-twentieth of what Proctor and Gamble spent on advertising. The 354 professional personnel seem hardly enough people to police a trillion-dollar economy where 245 firms had assets of over $1 billion.[8]

---

[5]M. H. Bernstein, *Regulating Business by Independent Commissions* (Princeton, N.J.: Princeton University Press, 1955).

[6]Green, ed., *The Monopoly Makers,* p. 24.

[7]M. J. Green, *The Other Government; The Unseen Power of Washington Lawyers* (New York: Norton, 1978), p. 138.

[8]Green, *The Closed Enterprise System,* pp. 122–123.

In several studies the Nader group alleged problems in the quality of personnel available to regulatory agencies. The study of antitrust enforcement used terms like "deadwood" and "appalling" in reference to some members of the Justice Department's legal staff, and considered its economists to be low in competence.[9] The study of the Federal Trade Commission found that personnel recruiters were inclined to hire the graduates of mediocre law schools and, even among this group, failed to make offers to the best applicants.[10]

One theme in Nader's reports is that regulatory agencies look for no evil, and consequently find none. The report on the FDA stated that the agency was uncomfortable with scientific information that upset its policies. The FDA dismissed one noted consultant who persisted in making negative reports about some pesticides that the agency had decided to approve. The regulatory agencies concentrate on trivial violations of the statutes in order to create an impressive record of enforcement while at the same time they ignore significant violations that would require intensive investigations and raise political complications. One pollution control agency, for example, conceded that auto emissions accounted for 60 percent of urban air pollution, at a time when it spent less than 3 percent of its budget on this problem.

Another prominent theme deals with the vulnerability of regulatory agencies to political pressures. Coalitions of industry and labor have proved more skillful in shaping policy than taxpayers or consumers. The Maritime Commission is more concerned with subsidizing the shipping industry than regulating it. The commission accepts virtually all industry-arranged rates to be charged shippers. It underwrites the costs of building ships in American yards to the extent of 39 percent. A total of $400 million per year "goes largely to underwrite the inefficient American shipyard worker, who is one-half as productive as his foreign counterpart."[11] Subsidies for American vessels pay for about 70 percent of each ship's labor costs, and offer no incentive either to management or to labor to hold down wages or to boost productivity.

In writing about the ICC's failures to regulate safety in the trucking industry, Nader's associates pointed to collusion between shippers, truckers, and drivers wherein each works in the common direction of evading regulation. The shippers and truckers want rapid, low-cost delivery of goods, while the drivers want the extra overtime pay they can get only by violating the maximum number of driving hours permitted and by using dangerous stimulants to keep awake through the extra working hours. The incentives for mutual support of rule evasion are substantial.

---

[9]Ibid., pp. 125–126.

[10]Cox et al., op. cit., pp. 140–161, 226–228.

[11]Green, ed., *The Monopoly Makers*, p. 105.

BOX 14-1   What the FTC Is Proposing

Although the Federal Trade Commission (FTC) has proposed few rules recently, several are scheduled to take effect soon and a number of others are close to being issued in final form.

On Oct. 21, a rule regulating the sale of franchises is scheduled to become effective. On Nov. 30, a rule on the sale of home insulation materials is to go into effect. And on Jan. 1, a rule dealing with vocational schools is scheduled to become effective.

In addition, the commission is expected to issue about five final rules in the next six months—including one regulating funeral homes—and another five in the following six months—including rules regulating the sale of used cars, over-the-counter drugs, and hearing aids.

Following is a list of the commission's 17 pending rule-making procedures:

Credit practices. The FTC seeks to reform consumer sales contracts by prohibiting clauses such as a waiver of the opportunity to be heard in the event of suit.

Holder-in-due course. The amendment to an existing rule would expand the rights of consumers who purchase goods on credit.

Care labeling. The amendment to a current rule will require that care instructions be provided on a permanent label on home furnishings such as upholstered furniture.

Funeral practices. The rule will require that funeral homes itemize their prices and refrain from practices such as requiring caskets for cremation.

Used cars. One proposal under consideration would require that used car dealers inspect the cars and disclose their condition prior to sale.

Hearing aids. The proposal would allow purchasers to cancel sales within 30 days.

Food advertising. A proposed rule would require that when food energy claims are made, the advertiser state that such energy comes from calories.

What would Nader and his associates do about government regulators? They know that statutory reform is not enough. An insipid administration, or one that cooperates with the "regulated" industry, will defeat any prospect of achieving success through new laws alone. Nader expresses some faith in the value of an alert citizenry, intense leadership, and public exposure of administrative shortcomings. At times, however, he calls for a more sweeping reform of the economic and political systems.

The main reason why citizens have no impact on the corporations which they support and which affect their lives and health is that the large corporate

Over-the-counter drugs. The proposal would prohibit advertising claims not allowed in labeling under Food and Drug Administration (FDA) regulations.

Protein supplements. The proposal would require disclosure in advertising and labeling that protein supplement products are usually unnecessary.

Appliance labeling. The rule will require major household appliances to be accompanied with labeling information about energy use.

Health spas. Under the proposal, purchasers of health spa memberships could cancel contracts and receive refunds within specified periods.

Mobile homes. The proposal would ensure that warranty obligations on mobile homes be fairly honored.

Over-the-counter antacids. No specific proposal has been made. The issue is whether and how FDA-mandated warnings for labeling should be disclosed in advertising.

Cellular plastics. The proposal would require that manufacturers test their products and disclose in promotional materials any unreasonable combustion hazards revealed by the tests.

Children's advertising. The FTC staff has suggested various ways to regulate television advertising of highly sugared foods to children, including a ban on all television advertising directed at children.

Games of chance. The amendment to an existing rule would require a 30-day break between games of chance run by grocery stores and gasoline stations.

Standards and certification. The proposal would regulate the way private product standards are developed and make certifiers responsible for the truthfulness of their certifications.

SOURCE: *National Journal,* October 13, 1979. Reprinted with permission.

polluter refuses to be held accountable to the public. . . . because their wealth buys legal and scientific apologists, because they are generally bigger and more powerful than government agencies making half-hearted attempts at confrontation, and because they can direct consumer choices away from environmental issues. . . .

So long as the crucial decisions remain with a small group of mammoth corporations, there is little reason to expect anything but further deterioration.[12]

---

[12]Fellmeth, op. cit., pp. 299–302.

To Regulate or Not to Regulate?

In their work on antitrust and some other economic regulations, Nader and his group have expressed support for deregulation. To them, no controls are better than the kinds currently engineered for the benefits of industry and labor, at the expense of consumers and taxpayers. However, they continue to support some forms of regulation:[13]

1. *Safety regulations,* including those concerning food and drug safety, airline safety, auto crashworthiness, flammable fabrics, occupational health and safety, and radiation levels. Marketplace competition does not offer adequate protection against these hazards.

2. *Enabling regulations,* which seek to establish the preconditions for enterprise and employment. These preconditions include programs to control discrimination, to provide for unemployment compensation, and to disclose corporate and product information for the benefit of investors and consumers.

The Carter Administration pursued a policy of deregulation in several fields affected by regulatory commissions. Airlines were given more freedom to choose their own routes and ticket prices: railroads were allowed more readily to drop unprofitable routes; and some measures were taken to restrain the workplace inspections of the Occupational Safety and Health Administration and the product controls exercised by the Federal Trade Commission. What is greater freedom in deregulation as seen from one perspective, however, may be greater dangers as seen from another perspective.

We owe a great deal to the sharp pen, the distinctive viewpoints, and the tireless research of Ralph Nader and his associates. They have done much to increase awareness of specific shortcomings in government regulation, and have alerted us to the general problem that regulatory policy may benefit some economic groups at the expense of others. In all fairness, however, the regulatory picture is not a simple one. Even the books of Nader and his associates concede some instances of tough and successful regulation.

Other Students of Regulation

Other analysts find greater complexity in government regulation. Erwin Krasnow and Lawrence Longley published a study of broadcast regulation that emphasizes the numerous participants in the regulatory game, and the mutual accommodations that take place among different interests. Krasnow

---

[13]Green, ed., *The Monopoly Makers,* pp. xiii, xiv, 7n.

The Occupational Safety and Health Administration (OSHA) has been the target of much criticism. It has been said to be a prime example of all that is bad about excessive government regulation. Here are some remedies that have been proposed.

BOX 14-2   Key Features of the OSHA Bill

Employers with safe workplaces would be exempt from regularly scheduled safety inspections by the Occupational Safety and Health Administration (OSHA) under legislation (S 2153, HR 6539) before Congress.

An employer would be exempt if none of its workers were killed in an occupational accident in a year and if none missed two or more workdays as a result of an accident. The information would be verified by state workers compensation data.

But if the data were not available from the state, an employer could file an affidavit with OSHA stating that none of its workers were killed in an occupational accident during a year and that no more than a specified number of workers suffered injuries resulting in lost workdays. The precise number would depend on the size of the work force.

Employers with 350 to 649 employees, for example, would be exempted if no more than nine workers sustained injuries causing lost workdays in a year; employers with 650 to 999 employees could have no more than 20. These numbers are lower than the national average injury rate of 4 out of every 100 employees. Employers who file false affidavits would be subject to penalty provisions now in the law: a maximum $10,000 fine and six months in prison.

OSHA would still be able to conduct safety inspections at exempt workplaces under some circumstances—to investigate a worker's death, for example, or to determine if an employer has taken steps to correct a previously cited hazard.

While the law generally requires OSHA to investigate written complaints from workers indicating the existence of unsafe conditions, the bill would require the agency to give employers the opportunity to make corrections.

No inspection would be necessary where an employer assures OSHA that no hazard exists or that it has been corrected. OSHA may still conduct an investigation, however, if it has reasonable grounds to believe a hazard exists despite an employer's assurance.

Employers with safe workplaces would be exempt from penalties for their first violations of the law if they establish employee safety committees and consultation programs to improve safety and health conditions.

The bill would not relieve employers from complying with the law and would not exempt them from OSHA health inspections.

SOURCE: *National Journal*, March 15, 1980. Reprinted with permission.

is general counsel of the National Association of Broadcasters, an industry group, and Longley is a professor of political science at Lawrence University. The authors describe a scene in which conflict occurs not only between industry on the one side and consumers on the other, but between different industrial groups.[14] One issue pitted FM against AM radio broadcasters. Another dealt with conflict between VHF and UHF television stations. A third saw the manufacturers of citizen's-band radios going against commercial television and radio stations. Krasnow and Longley describe the various actions, outside of the formal law and rules, that can be taken to affect regulation, such as appealing to public opinion and congressional allies. While different sides in disputes are unequal in their strengths, Krasnow and Longley see no participants as being strong enough to dominate regulation in a consistent or rigid fashion. As a result, it may be feasible to change policy only in small or incremental steps. Accommodation and an effort to build consensus are the tendencies these authors see in decisions of the Federal Communications Commission.

Cynthia Enloe has taken a cross-national look at regulation in the field of environmental protection. She writes that the quality of an agency's legal mandate is important for successful regulation. However, laws must not be so demanding as to discourage achievement of their objectives. The U.S. Environmental Protection Agency, for example, was given the task of achieving an unreasonably high standard of air quality in an unreasonably short period of time. The result was that certain targets were not achieved, and some were formally reduced. As a consequence, the agency acquired the reputation of being only a paper tiger. An agency's budget must match its legal mandate, and its top administrators must have the personal stature and political skills to fend off attacks from hostile pressure groups, legislators, and other agencies. Good luck also helps. Environmental units in the United States suffered from adverse changes in the economic environment. The fuel crisis, inflation, and the unemployment of the 1974–1976 period weakened the appeal of programs conceived in the rosier economic period of the late 1960s, when it was felt that factories could be ordered to burn natural gas or low-sulfur oil, or to install expensive pollution-control devices without substantially threatening the high levels of employment.[15]

SUMMARY

It is no easy task to find patterns in the rules followed by administrative agencies. There exists a thicket of terminology that differs in meaning from one agency to another. Some regulations come in the form of rules, deci-

---

[14]E. G. Krasnow and L. D. Longley, *The Politics of Broadcast Regulation* (New York: St. Martin's, 1978).

[15]C. H. Enloe, *The Politics of Pollution in a Comparative Perspective: Ecology and Power in Four Nations* (New York: Longman, 1975).

sions, opinions, and judgments; some are derived directly from statutes enacted by the legislature. Other direction comes from the agencies, and is promulgated by guidelines laid down by the legislature or the courts. Some regulations define the procedures to be followed by agency personnel and the clients who appear before them. Others deal in the substance of agency policy.

Who gets what? is a key question used in evaluating administrative rules. Ralph Nader is widely recognized for his view that regulatory agencies tilt toward business. He and his colleagues describe agency decisions that seem to fly in the face of the standards received from the legislature. They show the skimpy nature of resources allocated to the agencies, and the timidity with which they have pursued the public interest. In contrast to the Nader writings, however, are others who see a more complex picture. One study of the Federal Communications Commission focuses on the influences that impinge on its decisions and the frequency of conflict among business interests. A study of regulation in the field of environmental protection found that the quality of regulation varies from one setting to another. Regulation seems to depend on the nature of legal mandates, the resources provided, and simply good or bad luck in the severity of the problems being faced.

15

On the Margins
of Government

Modern government defies definition. It grows, while at the same time it seems to do less. Government's own officials will not—or cannot—report the true size of the budget or work force. Because officials do not say exactly how much money there is or how many employees there are, policy-makers have problems in controlling government and observers have problems in describing it. Thus, academic specialists in public administration and political science suffer from confusion about the very things that are central to their careers.[1]

Officials get more done, while they themselves do less by assigning activities to bodies that are not, strictly speaking, part of government. Just how this happens depends on the conditions within each country. The national government of the United States has, in certain respects, actually shrunk in size during the period between 1955 and 1976. Its number of employees declined from 146 to 134 per 10,000 population. Yet no one could claim that the national government did less in 1976 than in 1955. It shrank because Washington transferred new activities and some old, established programs to state and local governments. It assigned others to special authorities and to private firms and foundations operating as contractors for government agencies. This chapter deals with those contractors that operate on the margins of American government.

---

[1]This chapter relies on I. Sharkansky, "Policy-Making and Service Delivery on the Margins of Government: The case of Contractors," *Public Administration Review*, 40 (March–April 1980); and I. Sharkansky, *Wither the State? Politics and Public Enterprise in Three Countries* (Chatham, N.J.: Chatham, 1979).

It has been estimated that more people work for private firms that are under contract to the U.S. government than work for the government directly. A more precise estimate dealing with the former Department of Health, Education and Welfare—one of the most active civilian users of government contractors—is that 750,000 people worked under contract to HEW, while only 157,000 were employees. In 1976, 80,000 federal employees worked to oversee the administration of contracting.[2] The Department of Defense arranged some 10.4 *million* contracts in one year for a total of $46 billion.[3] The most recent catalog of U.S. government contractors seems to have been assembled in 1948—by a contractor. More recently, contractors have conducted courses for federal employees on how to arrange and supervise contracts.[4]

There have long been people who work on the margins of government. Now that these margins have grown larger than core departments, however, they warrant renewed attention. Because they are largely self-governing, bodies on the margins threaten certain political theories with obsolescence. Elections, legislatures, chief executives, and government departments have limited importance if governments isolate much of what they do from traditional devices of political control.

A pessimist could point to the margins of government as disasters in the making. The label "beltway bandits" for consulting firms located on the periphery of Washington, D.C., suggests that contractors are more concerned with helping themselves than with helping government. Yet the picture is not altogether clear. There are problems of management and accountability, to be sure, but it is not clear that the result of expanding activities on the margins of government is any better or worse than expanding activities in the core departments of government. The disaster seems more to be one of information. Professional observers of the government—journalists, academics, and policy-makers—have remained preoccupied with classical topics of elections, legislatures, executives, and the official civil service, when, in fact, much of the action is elsewhere.

Some years ago, Fred Riggs used the term *formalism* with respect to the governmental bodies of developing countries.[5] To him, the elections, legislatures, presidents, and prime ministers of Asia, Africa, and Latin America are patterned after the forms observed in Europe and North America, except that they do not perform like the originals. Often they mask dicta-

---

[2]J. D. Hanrahan, *Government for Sale: Contracting-Out the New Patronage* (Washington, D.C.: American Federation of State, County, and Municipal Employees, 1977), p. 217.

[3]Ibid., p. 218.

[4]U.S. House of Representatives, Committee on Post Office and Civil Service, *Contracting Out of Jobs and Services* (Washington, D.C.: U.S. Government Printing Office, 1977), p. 31.

[5]F. W. Riggs, *Administration in Developing Countries: The Theory of Prismatic Society* (Boston: Houghton Mifflin, 1964).

torships or corruption in the clothing of western democracies. (See Chapter 12.) When the concept of formalism is applied to the United States, a key question is:

> *How many public activities are left to the control of elections and representative government?*

A related question is:

> *If much of government's work is done by nongovernmental bodies, what controls can government place on them?*

THE CONTRACTORS, THE CONTRACTS

Organizations large and small, well known and obscure, sell their products and services to government. Individuals also contract for work. Among the various types of contractors are:

1. Major corporations that are household names (such as Westinghouse and Lockheed) that contract not only to sell the hardware that has made them well-known, but also for such services as vocational training or serving food in the cafeterias for government employees.
2. Firms of lawyers, certified public accountants, and specialists in public administration, or individuals in these fields, that offer policy analysis, program evaluation, advice on program management and the drafting of legislation and regulation.
3. Voluntary organizations, such as churches or charities, that offer their services to clients of government programs for vocational training, counseling, workshops, and halfway houses (for criminal offenders, drug or alcohol treatment, and the mentally ill).
4. Private clinics that seek to serve the clients of Medicare and Medicaid.

The functions of government contracts range from the pedestrian to the profound:

1. Janitorial and security services for government buildings.
2. Cafeteria service for government employees.
3. Design, construction, installation, operation, and service of equipment, facilities, and supplies (ranging from paper clips to office buildings, from rifles to ICBMs).

4. Problem analysis and definition—determining just what is wrong and what government can do to fix it.

5. Program design—drafting legislation, writing administrative manuals.

6. Services delivery—such as operating health clinics, halfway houses, counseling services, and job training courses.

7. Selecting personnel to manage or work in government departments.

8. Program monitoring and evaluation—determining just what a government agency or another contractor is doing, and whether it is doing a good job.

In short, officers contract out virtually any work that the government can do with its own personnel. An exception is the actual approval of public policy, which is reserved, constitutionally, to members of the executive, legislative, and judicial branches. However, the constitutional branches do contract for the supply of information and advice, with an eye to the decisions they will need to make.

WHY CONTRACT?

The reasons behind contracting can be elusive. To the question *Why should government contract out what it may otherwise do in-house?* the answers may be:

1. To abide by requirements to freeze the size of the civil service, even while adding programs or enlarging services that are already offered.

2. To purchase services more inexpensively than if they were done by government employees; contractors may pay lower wages and, avoid the fringe benefits required for government employees.

3. To weaken the power of government employee unions by giving work to contractors.

4. To evade civil service regulations of various sorts, such as veterans' preference, maximum salary rules, a prohibition against paying moving expenses to new employees, or affirmative action procedures. The contractor is responsible for staffing, and may be limited only by a total amount that can be spent on personnel.

5. To provide for certain personnel attributes—like specialization or length of service—not available from regular employees. The Department of Defense contracts for certain persons to maintain scrutiny over complex inventory programs, which is a function not expected from uniformed personnel, who rotate frequently between tasks and places.

BOX 15-1   Private Firms Help Fill Information Gap

In terms of dollars, general revenue sharing is one of the largest federal grant-in-aid programs. Yearly it dispenses $6.9 billion to approximately 39,000 units of state and local government.

Yet the entire Treasury Department Office of Revenue Sharing (ORS), which administers the program, employs only about 150 people, from secretaries to administrators. It has no regional or local offices.

This is, of course, what Congress had in mind when it established the program—the centerpiece of the Nixon administration's "New Federalism"—in 1972. Take a big chunk of money, the theory went, give it to the states and local governments, and let them deal with the details.

There's a Washington fable that when Congress enacted revenue sharing, it was designed so that the whole program could be run by a computer and a bookkeeper. And today, the reality is not far from that.

The limited size of the revenue sharing bureaucracy creates complications, however, for many of the government units that participate in the program.

Filling out the forms, complying with all the reporting and legal requirements, and understanding the regulations are a difficult business. This is especially true for the 70 percent of participating governments that have populations of less than 2,500 and lack the financial infrastructure to handle federal funds.

PRIVATE ENTERPRISE STEPS IN

Thus private enterprise has stepped in to offer aid to cities, towns, counties, and states that want both to do it right and to get the most they can from the revenue sharing program.

Two Washington-based private companies—the Advisory Center on General Revenue Sharing, an arm of Government Information Services, and Revenue Sharing Advisory Service Inc.—offer local and state governments seminars, monthly newsletters, and handbooks on the latest in general revenue sharing.

The director of the Advisory Center, Jeffrey H. Schiff, was at one time the manager of Intergovernmental Relations in the Office of Revenue Sharing.

Revenue Sharing Advisory Service Inc. was founded by Dick Thompson, who was legislative liaison for the National League of Cities when the original Revenue Sharing Act was signed into law. He has been replaced as executive director by Robert H. Koch, who has handled revenue sharing funds at the local level.

Both firms hold one-day revenue sharing seminars around the country, but their approaches differ.

Schiff says that his seminars are specifically geared to provide technical assistance, explain existing regulations, and provide updates on new provisions.

The Revenue Sharing Advisory Service, on the other hand, tries to focus on a specific element of the revenue sharing program in its seminars. This spring the topic will be the non-discrimination provisions of the law.

And while Schiff actually conducts the Advisory Center's seminars, the Revenue Sharing Advisory Service brings in experts to speak at its seminars.

The fee is $65 for subscribers to the Advisory Center's monthly newsletter, "Shared Revenues Report," and $75 for non-subscribers. For the registration fee participants get not only the seminar, but also a copy of the "General Revenue Sharing and Anti-Recession Aid Resource Book," coffee, rolls, and luncheon.

The Revenue Sharing Advisory Service usually charges $45–$50 for its seminars. It also publishes a newsletter called "Revenue Sharing Bulletin," which has 5,100 subscribers and costs $35 a year, and a looseleaf reference book, updated monthly, called the "Revenue Sharing Handbook." The handbook, which has about 5,000 subscribers, costs local governments $55 a year and states and private companies $75.

The Revenue Sharing Advisory Service also offers a tape series on auditing procedures. Under the 1976 Revenue Sharing Act, communities that receive more than $25,000 a year must submit an independent audit at least once every three years—11,000 governments are affected by the provision.

The tape series explains how to meet all the auditing requirements. Once the participant has listened to the tapes, he takes an examination and mails it to Washington. If he passes, the Advisory Service sends him a small "graduation" certificate.

The best part for local governments is that all of these services can be legitimately paid for with revenue sharing funds.

NOT IN COMPETITION

Koch says that Revenue Sharing Advisory Service is not "in competition with the government." Instead, the company tries to look at all of the agencies involved in revenue sharing, not only the ORS, but the Labor Department, the Census Bureau, and others. "We draw all of that together in one source so that the governments have easy access to the information they need."

The Advisory Service has a technical inquiry service too, but Koch says it tells clients that its advice is not the final answer and often refers them to the ORS.

Why do such organizations exist? Schiff says many small governments "operate in a vacuum" and many have never had to deal with the federal government before. They need someone they can talk to "one to one," someone with whom they can discuss their area's particular problems. The Office of Revenue Sharing, with a staff of less than 150, just is not big enough to do the work.

SOURCE: *Congressional Quarterly,* February 23, 1980.

6. To reward certain persons for favors rendered in the past by giving them contracts.

7. To provide certain programs experimentally, without risking continuation beyond a certain date that can be fixed in a contract.

8. To avoid borrowing money and to save on the cost of building in the short term. Government may lease a new building for an extended period of time; the contractor borrows for the construction of the building, and includes an amount for mortgage payments in the annual rental fee.

What is troubling is the common thread that runs through several of these reasons to contract: *to evade* formal requirements imposed on the conventional departments of government. Why not remove these offending constraints, like freezes on the size of the civil service, the power of unions, veterans' preference, or the disinclination of policy-makers to borrow in the government's name for building construction? One explanation is political feasibility. Each of these constraints is firmly imbedded in the expectations of many elected officials. It is easier to evade them than to face the task of eliminating them overtly. Another explanation is that American policy-makers believe in free enterprise. They think that private contractors work more efficiently and effectively than civil servants. One more explanation is that existing administrative units are already too great in number and too large for effective control by elected officials. In other words, popular demands for government activities are so great that the government cannot manage directly all that it is compelled to undertake.

Recently, political commentators have emphasized the growth in contracting. Many attribute this to the spurt in social programs begun during the Johnson Administration's War on Poverty. A great deal of contracting is prompted by federal aid, which has climbed sharply. Aid programs grew by 356 percent between 1965 and 1975, 130 percent faster than total government revenues. Because federal money is "soft money"—subject to cuts or curtailment by Washington—states and localities are loath to expand their permanent staffs for federally funded programs.

Claims about the newness of contracting must be viewed with caution. President George Washington's complaints about the contractors who supplied military hardware preceded those of Senator William Proxmire's by almost 200 years. In 1961, the Government Employees Council of the AFL–CIO noted that it was "gravely concerned over the growing practice in the Federal service, to contract to private interests, certain governmental services and functions that have historically been performed by civil service employees."[6] At about the same time, an interagency committee of the U.S.

---

[6]Government Employees Council, AFL–CIO, "Presentation of the Government Employees Council, AFL–CIO to the Executive Branch in Reference to Bureau of the Budget Bulletin 60–2," Washington, D.C., 1962.

government raised some basic issues about how to control contractors. In a report to the President, it expressed concern about the capacity of government officials to oversee contractors adequately and to maintain control over basic policies. In response to this report, a spokesperson for contractors raised the issue of excessive control by government agencies over their contractors.[7] Thus, the issues of contractor control versus autonomy have been well defined for some years.

CONTROVERSIES ABOUT CONTRACTING

Contracting does not proceed quietly. It has warm supporters and intense opponents. Stories abound of wonderful successes and horrible failures, each one mingled with simple ideology, myth, and personal stakes. At one extreme are right-wing reformers who react negatively to symbols of government and politics. They allege that creativity, hard work, and efficiency are to be found in the private sector. At the other extreme are left-wing reformers—like Ralph Nader's Center for the Study of Responsive Laws—and organized civil servants. These groups resist contracting out jobs to the private sector. Two book titles convey their spirit: Nader's center-supported *Shadow Government: The Government's Multi-Billion-Dollar Giveaway of Its Decision-Making Powers to Private Management Consultants, "Experts," and Think Tanks*,[8] and the American Federation of State, County, and Municipal Employees' *Government for Sale: Contracting-Out the New Patronage*.[9]

The Urban Institute asked a series of questions about the benefits and problems associated with contracting by local governments. The report deals with several issues relevant to the evaluation of contracting out versus providing services in house: cost, flexibility, competitiveness, and the quality of management and services. In its conclusions the report concedes the lack of sufficient information to answer its questions in a satisfactory manner.[10] There is no doubt that both managerial control and political accountability are strained by the autonomy of contractors. However, these strains have advantages as well as disadvantages.

Flexibility

Flexibility is a common feature of contracting. Policy-makers can select just the kind of contract that seems suitable to their needs, and fine-tune details

---

[7] M. D. Reagan, *Politics, Economics and the General Welfare* (Chicago: Scott, Foresman, 1965), Chapter 5.

[8] D. Guttman and B. Willner, *The Shadow Government: The Government's Multi-Billion-Dollar Giveaway of Its Decision-Making Powers to Private Management Consultants, "Experts," and Think Tanks* (New York: Pantheon, 1976).

[9] Hanrahan, op. cit.

[10] D. D. Fisk, H. Kiesling, and T. Muller, *Private Provision of Public Services: An Overview* (Washington, D.C.: Urban Institute, 1978).

of organizational structure, goals, and personnel. From the consumer's side, especially in large cities, multiple providers of a service are usually within reach.[11] This great variety may be incoherent to all but experts. Policy-makers and consumers need help in sorting through the options. The variety of available contractual services hinders evaluating programs according to common or clear standards.

Contractors can be innovative in ways not likely to survive in a government office. One Wisconsin department contracted for services to high school dropouts prone to delinquency. The services included counseling, training in basic skills, and work discipline. Among the qualifications that one contractor asked of potential counselors was:

> in order to facilitate an effective working relationship with ex-offenders, the applicant should have some experience in confinement in a county jail or state correctional institution (although this is not required).[12]

Government offices may have greater trouble recruiting former convicts, either because of political constraints or state laws that bar felons from the civil service.

The assessment of contracting must compare the opportunities for doing good that result from its inherent flexibility with the opportunities for doing bad with the same flexibility. Many cases are close to the boundaries of good and bad. One state government engaged in a nationwide search for a new division chief. In the early spring it selected a person from another region with a national reputation in the field at issue. The job was to begin on July 1. The candidate wanted the job, but found it awkward to wait several months to begin work and receive a salary. Also, there was the matter of not being allowed moving expenses. Writing a contract helped to solve these problems. The candidate accepted a consultant's contract until July 1, at a level of compensation sufficient to cover some of the costs of relocating. In this case, a contract allowed a state government to make its position more attractive to a candidate who was selected on the basis of stiff professional criteria. Personal favors were not at stake. However, a special deal was made outside the usual procedures and pay scale of civil service.

Flexible procedures for arranging contracts permit abuse. The General Accounting Office estimates that 85 percent of defense contracts and 71 percent of civilian contracts in sample years were not advertised and bid competitively.[13] Instead, agency personnel identify a contractor they consider appropriate, and proceed to negotiate an agreemeet. Key administra-

---

[11]S. V. Ostrom, *The Intellectual Crisis in American Public Administration* (University: University of Alabama Press, 1974).

[12]Sharkansky, "Policy-Making and Service Delivery on the Margins of Government."

[13]Guttman and Willner, op. cit., p. 26.

tors and elected office holders have plenty of opportunities to steer contracts to friends, family members, party supporters, or firms allied with organized crime that threaten retribution if contracts do not come their way.

Critics charge that contracting does not offer all the flexibility that its boosters claim. It is seldom easy to shift from one contractor to another. New firms may not want to bid for a community's trash pickup, even when the local authorities signal their dissatisfaction with an existing contractor. Garbage companies require a great deal of expensive equipment, plus a site for solid waste disposal. Contractors may use the old gimmick of the "introductory offer" to win a contract. Then they boost prices when a community has committed itself and closed the door to other options. A critic of contracting reports that residents of Seattle found that their charges for contracted trash collection increased by 98 percent from 1974 to 1976.[14]

The Quality of Services

Quality and efficiency are not automatic attributes of contracting. Some claims of reduced costs are simply the products of reduced services. Trash pickup twice a week by a private contractor will be less expensive than pickup three times a week by the city's department of sanitation. A memo from the nursing director of a state institution for the retarded complained about a contractor's laundry service in the most homely terms:

> Their work on the whole is almost totally unacceptable. I'm sure most of us as private citizens wouldn't tolerate for one minute sending our laundry out and getting it back like this without complaining and demanding immediate remedial action. . . .
>
> Many of the items sent to the laundry are never returned. . . . Laundry received on the cottage is often not for that cottage and must be resorted. It isn't at all unusual to find laundry from such places as Lake Geneva Bunny Club, Marriott Inn, Holiday Inn, etc. Laundry comes back wet and mildewy—smelly.[15]

Conflict of Interest and Corruption

Conflict of interest is an occasional companion of contracting. At times the conflict is blatant and criminal. Vice-President Spiro Agnew is the most prominent of many officials who have lost their positions, paid fines, or served time in jail for receiving bribes, kickbacks, or other improper favors

---

[14]Hanrahan, op. cit., p. 69.

[15]Sharkansky, "Policy-Making and Service Delivery on the Margins of Government."

from contractors. Of the 1,000 or so federal, state, and local officials con-
victed of felonies between 1970 and 1976, a high proportion of their crimes
concerned contracts between government agencies and private firms.[16]

Some contracting is made suspect by cozy dealing. Contractors work both
for a government agency and for business firms that are subsidized or regulated by the agency. Peat, Marwick, Mitchell and Company, a large accounting and management consulting firm, was simultaneously a contractor for
the U.S. Department of Transportation (DOT) and Penn Central. DOT
asked the contractor to help account for Metroliner costs when the government subsidized Penn Central's operation of the train. Later, Penn Central's
bankruptcy was the subject of investigations by the Securities and Exchange
Commission and Congress. Part of the inquiry focused on misleading
reports about Penn Central's financial condition. According to Wright Pat-
man, Chairman of the House Banking and Currency Committee:

> Information in the Committee's possession shows that this policy of "doctor-
> ing" the financial statements was done at the direction of top Penn Central
> officials. These documents further indicate that Peat, Marwick, Mitchell and
> Co. played a substantial role in these successful attempts to misinform the
> investing public.[17]

At times, one government steals from another with the help of contracting. State governments have learned to write contracts from one state
agency to another in order to make it look as if one of them is spending
real money for services. The supposed expenditures are reported to Washington as the state's contribution to a federal–state program, which draws
federal aid on a matching basis. With this gimmick, the state of Illinois
boosted its receipts of social service grants by almost twice the national
average between 1971 and 1973, and caused a bureaucratic furor that
reached the President's desk. Illinois also taught New York State how to do
it, and New York increased its federal receipts even more than Illinois.[18]

Contracting with Voluntary Agencies

Government contracting with voluntary social service agencies raises its own
variety of issues. A voluntary social service agency is one that is supported
by private contributions. It may be associated with a religious body (e.g.,
Catholic Charities) or be secular in its nature (e.g., United Way). Both religious and secular social service agencies become less than voluntary, how-

---

[16] Ibid., pp. 3–4.

[17] Guttman and Willner, op. cit., pp. 55–56, 120, 151.

[18] M. Derthick, *Uncontrollable Spending for Social Services Grants* (Washington, D.C.: Brookings Institution,
1975).

ever, as they receive substantial funding from government sources. Government expenditures for a group of child-care programs grew by 650 percent between 1950 and 1970, while comparable growth financed by the voluntary sector was only 200 percent.[19] Much of the increase in government spending funnels through voluntary agencies, and makes them leading social service contractors in local communities.

Voluntary agencies associated with each of the major religious denominations have gone heavily into government contracting. One study of Jewish-sponsored social service agencies shows an increase from $27 million to $561 million in government contracts during the 1962–1973 period. Government payments went from 11 to 51 percent of the total income received by these agencies. A study of United Way agencies in the San Francisco area found a doubling in government's purchase of certain social services in 1970–1975.[20] Of the $145 million that New York City spent on daycare, homemakers' services, and foster care in 1969, $108 million (75 percent) went to voluntary organizations. In 1968, Pennsylvania allocated 88 percent of its spending for certain child-care programs to voluntary agencies.[21]

Some observers applaud the diversity in social service delivery that is achieved by contracting with voluntary agencies. Clients are freed from depending on government agencies that monopolize service programs, and the clients may benefit from competition between service providers.[22] Other observers focus on the dilemmas created by:[23]

1. Problems of coordination among separate agencies that deal in similar services in the same community.
2. Challenges to the autonomy of voluntary agencies via mechanisms of government control.
3. Lack of public control over the programs administered by voluntary agencies.
4. Dilution of the benefits derived from voluntarism in social services, as agencies and their contributors come to rely on government contracts for the bulk of their funds.

---

[19] E. L. Brilliant, "Private or Public: A Model of Ambiguities," *Social Service Review*, 47 (September 1973): 384–396.

[20] N. Gilbert, "The Transformation of Social Services," *Social Service Review*, 51 (December 1977): 624–641.

[21] E. P. Cole, "Voluntary Agencies in the Purchase of Care and Services," in I. R. Winogrond, ed., *Purchase of Care and Services in the Health and Welfare Fields* (Milwaukee: University of Wisconsin School of Social Welfare, 1970).

[22] P. N. Reid, "Reforming the Social Services Monopoly," *Social Work*, 17 (November 1972): 44–54.

[23] Brilliant, op. cit.; R. M. Kramer, "Voluntary Agencies and the Use of Public Funds: Some Policy Issues," *Social Service Review*, 40 (November 1966): 15–26; and G. Manser, "Further Thoughts on Purchase of Service," *Social Casework*, 55 (July 1974): 421–427.

5. Problems of church–state separation, felt both by secular interests toward social service agencies having a religious sponsorship and by the religious sponsors, who see the erosion of their traditional social service roles.

CONTROLLING THE MARGINS OF GOVERNMENT

The large number of diverse contracts and their origins at the working levels of agencies render them hard to control by legislatures or chief executives. When a committee of the Wisconsin legislature sought information on contracting, it was told that:

> it would take 3 to 5 months of searching to obtain the data . . . just for the Department of Natural Resources and Health and Social Services and the University of Wisconsin . . . it would involve searching through 1.5 million documents, and . . . [since] the documents . . . sought . . . [were] not available by category . . ., the data obtained would probably be incomplete, if it could be found at all.[24]

In response to the legislature's request, administrative departments made some effort to cull information on contracting for 1973–1978. The deputy secretary of the Department of Health and Social Services sent a memo to his division administrators that reflected something other than a burning desire to cooperate:

> The Legislative Joint Committee on Review of Administrative Rules has requested the Department to provide them with the information listed on the attached. After reviewing this, you will realize, I am certain, that this is an almost impossible task.
>
> In an attempt to reduce this task to more manageable proportions, we are going to provide the Committee with a list of types of contracts we have in the Department, and hopefully convince them that representative samples of the different types would be sufficient. . . .[25]

A mixed bag of information came in response to this memo. Two divisions sent in handwritten lists of contracts. One listed a random sample of voucher payments, including only the voucher number and the amount of payment, with no reference to the kind of service being purchased or the name of the contractor. Another sent a 10-page list of contractors' names with no indication of the nature of services being purchased.

Federal controls over contractors are also thin. While there is an abundance of control agencies and regulations, weaknesses appear at the working levels. Each control agency usually takes a narrow view of its responsi-

---

[24]Sharkansky, "Policy-Making and Service Delivery on the Margins of Government."
[25]Ibid.

bilities, and is usually willing to overlook obvious problems as long as they can be defined as being outside the agency's province. The Office of Personnel Management and the Merit System Protection Board each has a role in certain matters dealing with government employees affected by contracting, but neither one has delved into the effect of the government work force being reduced because of contracting. Moreover, neither does any systematic checking on the contracting done by agencies. Each waits for agency requests or for a complaint filed by an employee who alleges improper treatment.[26] The General Accounting Office has a long record of "oversight" dealing with defense contractors and other firms that sell equipment to government agencies, or that do public works construction under contract. However, the GAO has only recently shown interest in the newer topic of social service contracting.[27]

Contractors help to confound government control by seeking to enhance their access to government. The crudest of their techniques can result in disgrace and incarceration for government officials on the take. Also of interest are subtle payoffs, where the beneficiaries appear to be receiving nothing more than an honor. Some prominent nonprofit bodies, such as the United Way, and church and ethnic welfare agencies, choose their boards of directors from government officials who make decisions about contracts. This kind of action can look innocent, at least at first glance. However, charities and other prestigious bodies have become important government contractors. In 1978, the Wisconsin Department of Health and Social Services appointed a citizens' committee to oversee a survey of its contracting. Either through innocence or guile, the foxes were chosen to count the chickens—most members of the original committee were officials of the nonprofit organizations that served as contractors.

The OMB's Influence on Contracting

The Office of Management and Budget has a limited responsibility to check comparative cost figures for contracting out a service versus doing it in house. But this kind of estimating is only necessary for new activities. When asked about analyzing costs for established programs that are contracted out, an OMB executive said, "There is no requirement and no desire that any of these actions be reviewed by the Office of Management and Budget."[28]

---

[26]U.S. House of Representatives, op. cit., pp. 2–16.

[27]R. J. Woodrow, "Federal Grants and Contracts to Colleges and Universities" (Cambridge, Mass.: Sloan Commission on Government and Higher Education, 1977), mimeo.

[28]U.S. House of Representatives, op. cit., p. 22. A recent report that may portend a new interest of the GAO in social service contracting is *Social Research and Development of Limited Use to National Policymakers* (Washington, D.C.: General Accounting Office, 1977).

Government contracting is a live issue in Washington, D.C. The OMB's Circular A-76 has put the national government on a procontracting course since 1967. While the circular was modified in 1976–1978, its procontracting policy was not substantially altered: The OMB is to "continue to support the policy that the Government should rely on the private sector for goods and services. . . .[29] However, the procedures for figuring the comparative costs of contracting out and in-house activities have been made more precise, and greater concern is now shown for government employees who may be affected by contracting out.

One of the small points of the 1976–1978 review may have crucial impact. The issue was the cost of government retirement programs, to be used in assessing in-house versus contracted services. The true cost of government retirement is elusive. It depends on unknown future events, like inflation and the generosity of Congress to pensioners. Since both factors have been considerable in recent years, the cost of government pensions—and thereby the long-run cost of retaining government employees—can escalate *after* a decision is made to perform a service in house. The higher the cost figure assigned to government retirement costs, the more likely it is that a comparison will favor contracting out a service.

Between August 1976 and April 1978, the figure to be used for government retirement costs oscillated, responding to the pressure contest between contractors on the one side and government employees' unions on the other. In August 1976, President Ford's OMB announced that:

> New guidance . . . for calculating overhead costs of commercial and industrial activities of the federal government could result in substantially greater use of the private sector, and lower costs.[30]

What followed was an increase from 7 to 24.7 percent in the overhead factor for retirement benefits, which put an additional 17.7 cents on each federal payroll dollar when comparing prices with private contractors.

The OMB's position shifted in the Carter Administration, at least for awhile. By June 1977, the OMB's language showed more awareness of government employees' interests, and its calculations dropped from 24.7 to 14.1 percent of payroll for retirement costs. By November 1977, the OMB's figure moved up to 20.4 percent of payroll for retirement costs. While the result appeared to be from compromise, the OMB tried to legitimize the percentage by naming other involved agencies:

---

[29]U.S. Office of Management and Budget, "Statement by the Honorable Lester A. Fettig, Administrator for Federal Procurement Policy, Office of Management and Budget, Before the Subcommittee on Research and Development of the House Armed Services Committee, April 10, 1978," mimeo.

[30]U.S. Office of Management and Budget, Circular of August 24, 1976, mimeo.

This factor was produced by the Civil Service Commission's actuarial model, as modified and validated by the General Accounting Office, using current economic assumptions supplied by the Council of Economic Advisers.[31]

PROSPECTS FOR REFORM

The contracting experiences of American governments should not be viewed in isolation. Contracting reflects the general proliferation of activities in modern governments beyond conventional departments or ministries. Whether the margins of a government are populated with contractors, special authorities, or government-owned companies, the common denominator is operational autonomy outside the conventional orbit of the legislature, executive branch, or core departments of government.

Can the officers of government put their house in order? The question requires a consideration of the basic reasons for putting activities on the margins. One reason is government's incapacity to handle all the activities demanded by citizens and promulgated by politicians. Other reasons for putting programs on the margins reveal some measure of indifference or guile: Politicians respond to some demands out of political necessity, without caring how the programs develop. If a quasi-governmental body handles the new program, the politician has little risk or responsibility for the outcome. If the program goes sour, the autonomy of its administrators allows the government and its political leaders to avoid blame. Politicians also put programs on governmental margins to keep their expenses off the government's budget or to keep their employees off the civil service list. Politicians can thereby add programs without explicitly violating official demands to limit the growth of government. Programs that operate on the margins are vulnerable to patronage demands from the politicians who create them: to hire someone from outside the formal controls of the civil service commission or to provide a service to a constituent whose case might not survive the scrutiny of a government office. It is difficult to assign clear or simple motives to decisions to put programs on the margins of government; assuredly, there are a variety of reasons for doing so. Whatever these motives are, they stand in the way of any general reform for bringing programs from the margins more clearly into the orbit of governmental control. It may not be so much a question of the government's inability to put its house in order as it is a lack of desire to give up the benefits received from having institutions on the margins that perform numerous important functions without close governmental control.

---

[31] U.S. Office of Management and Budget, "Statement by the Honorable Lester A. Fettig."

The essence of being a politician is to bear contrary pressures: to serve the people *and* to keep taxes low, plus minimize government employment; to hire managers who can work quickly *and* to respect the procedures for clearing major decisions with key government officers, no matter how long the delay; to accept demands that the government hire people according to strict rules that respect traits of competence, ethnicity, sex, or veteran status *and* to allow some bodies to hire whom they want. A typical way out of such conflicts is to create an ambiguous situation. The bodies on the margins of government provide ideal conditions for ambiguity. The margins are *of* but not *in* the government; as such, they satisfy some of the contrary demands that are part of the political process.

As for the dilemma of autonomy and accountability, policy-makers may require a greater capacity to comprehend and control contractors. However, they should not pursue the virtues of central control so thoroughly that they override the virtues of contracting. Neither should policy-makers so overload government officials with such a mass of control tasks that their "oversight" activities must become routine and indiscriminate.

SUMMARY

Government contracting has become a major way to carry out government programs. Contracts are awarded beyond the conventional areas of providing equipment and supplies or constructing public works. Contracting now appears extensively in the design, delivery, and evaluation of social services.

Contractors command special attention for two reasons. First, they do a great deal of government's work, but are outside the conventional concepts of government departments. For this reason, they require some rethinking of the importance attributed to elections, legislatures, and the chief executive. Second, because contractors operate on the margins of government, they tend to escape established procedures for supervision and control. A great deal of government's resources and responsibilities have been transferred to nongovernmental bodies. Policy-makers should create new devices to bring them more information about these bodies, but without losing the advantages of their autonomy.

16

The Client's Perspective

Administration is inevitable; without it, government would not exist. Administration is also the citizen's most frequent contact with public affairs. As the delivery point of policy, administration is, for most of us, the essence of government. How citizens view administration depends, to an extent, on their roles in relation to public administration: as students or teachers of the subject, as occasional or full-time employees of administrative agencies, or as clients of programs administered by government departments or related bodies. The primary concerns of previous chapters have been those of students, teachers, and employees of public administration. In this chapter, the emphasis is on the roles of clients. The key question is:

> *How do clients get the most of what they deserve from administrative agencies?*

This question implies others, such as:

> *How do clients determine what they deserve?*
> *How do clients get their benefits with minimal expenditures of money, time, and exasperation?*

FRUSTRATIONS

No fail-safe methods exist for clients to get the results they want from government agencies. The range of public administration is broad. Its nature varies from one place to another, from one agency to another, from one project to another. The issues of this chapter are chosen with an eye to "worst-case analysis." For the well-established programs that work routinely, clients usually do not need much help. In fact, survey research finds that people have a generally high level of regard for public services. Complaints are directed more against agencies that seek to regulate than to serve—there are more complaints against tax authorities than against social service units. Also, complaints are expressed most often by the young, the poor, and minorities.[1]

Confusion

For clients—and even for many government officials—government is a maze. Countless government agencies and quasi-governmental units are involved in the myriad government programs. Individuals have to locate and deal with numerous administrative bodies. Units and programs develop piecemeal. Without a pervasive guiding hand, the boundaries between different programs overlap. Some clients have a choice of service providers. At times there are gaps between programs, with no program able to provide a needed service.

Imagine yourself as a young adult who is: poor, without a job, and with inadequate skills; in need of training, emotional counseling, and perhaps medical care; without housing that provides the space, quiet, and cleanliness that encourages good health and a stable life. You may be eligible for temporary monetary help until you find work, a job or skills training program, therapeutic and medical aid, food stamps, and housing benefits. If you asked for help from government, you would face a bewildering collection of departments and authorities, plus private bodies working for government under contract. National, state, and local funds and regulations would all be involved in your aid. To find your way through this maze, you would need to know the rules—a formidable task, since eligibility requirements differ with each requested benefit.

Most people who need the services of agencies are likely to be vulnerable to government action and not shrewd in finding their own way. As a result, numerous citizens visit the wrong offices, and must search elsewhere. Many clients never learn the extent of the benefits for which they are eligible. This unfortunate situation is due, in part, to interagency hostility; employees in one agency often refuse to cooperate with employees of another agency—and the clients are the ones to suffer. Clients would profit from having a single office hear their problems and refer them to the appropriate service bureaus. However, few communities have provided such a resource to cover

---

[1]D. Katz, B. Gutek, R. L. Kahn, and E. Barton, *Bureaucratic Encounters: A Pilot Study in the Evaluation of Government Services* (Ann Arbor: University of Michigan Survey Research Center, 1975).

the scope of social services. Numerous agencies do have outreach programs designed to make clients aware of benefits; even these programs, however, tend to advertise only one agency's benefits, thus furthering clients' confusion. For example, a brochure describing the ways to obtain food stamps may not inform clients about similar eligibility requirements for housing and medical care.

Self-Centeredness

Much in the behavior of administrative organizations resembles the selfishness of small children. Someone searching for a slogan to summarize the attitudes of some administrators could select "Me first," "Beggar thy neighbor," or "That's your problem." The self-centered character of government agencies work to strengthen the lack of clarity in organization and procedure just discussed. Administrators usually take a proprietary view of their programs. The autonomy and growth of an administrator's activities are usually considered more important than integrating them into the larger organization or coordinating them carefully with other governmental bodies.

Agencies compete in seeking funds, and budgets depend on the number of clients served. As a result, they may not refer clients to another agency, even when their own organization does not provide the service requested. "No, we do not provide that kind of program. . . . No, we don't know who does." University professors may be as guilty of this as clerks behind a counter. Departments depend on student enrollments. Cooperating with another department in program development depends on the question *What's in it for us?* Fear of a disadvantage in enrollment may deter joint endeavors. Personal antagonisms often intensify organizational rivalries. Units with huge budgets and highly trained professionals may deal with each other no more smoothly than petty merchants in adjoining shops: grumbling as they encounter one another, and refusing to refer customers to one another.

Changing Conditions

What we learn here and now about public administration may not help us in some other place and time. Conditions vary from one country to another, from one region or locality to another, and from one period of time to another. More-developed versus less-developed economies mark the clearest differences between administrative activities. The details of laws and regulations operate within the larger frameworks of economics, culture, and taxation.

The overall policies of programs change, but to a large extent they remain the same. Most change occurs incrementally. Time creeps ahead with much of today looking like yesterday. Although incrementalism is a dominant form of policy-making, change does occur. Small changes may accumulate into major ones. Occasional massive changes may remake the character of an agency or the services it provides to clients. Key personalities can bring about distinctive changes, creating new agencies or setting an existing agency on a new course. For individual clients, however, the street-level bureaucrats remain all-important. No matter what the general picture looks like—or even what the laws and rules are—individual police officers, welfare clerks, and school teachers still have the ability to dish out basic benefits or miseries.

SUGGESTIONS

The problems that lead to frustration when dealing with government bodies are chronic: agencies created under our complex system are bound to retain some of their incoherent nature; a competitive environment such as ours can only encourage the self-centered pursuit of agency growth; and in this vast land and changing political climate, regional differences and the potential for many policy changes must be expected. In other words, there are no simple cures to some of the major patterns in public administration that can cause client frustration.

The best ways to avoid problems with public administrative policies are to be rich, healthy, self-sufficient, and smart, thus for the most part avoiding being clients at all! The client who has the most enviable position with respect to a government agency is one who can choose to engage it or to avoid it—to submit one's case now or wait for more opportune circumstances. The person who does not need the services of, or who can ignore or defer contact with, an agency is in the best position. Even a benefit-providing agency imposes entanglement along with its benefits; the cost of "free" services can be high in terms of time and frustration. Although few people can avoid relying on public services or can shun other contacts with government, those who possess the advantages of wealth, health, independence, and intelligence have the most capacity to deal effectively with government administration.

Strategy

The nature of one's case affects the strategy that is best to follow. Three principal strategies are:

1. If you want something from an agency, make your case seem routine.

2. If you want to avoid something from an agency, make your case seem unique.
3. Be willing to compromise.

Assume that most agencies offering benefits will distribute them more readily to clients who appear to fit the criteria set forth in their agency manuals. Knowing the manual is the key! Clients who want to qualify for benefits should make their cases look as routine as possible. It also helps to know an agency's informal traits, such as which personnel are likely to make which interpretations of vague rules.

Clients who want to avoid penalties being imposed on them by an agency should make their cases look as complicated as possible, so that they do not quite fit the situations agency manuals cover. It is harder to be accused of breaking the rules when the rules don't fit the case. Clients who contemplate encounters with the Internal Revenue Service, Occupational Safety and Health Administration, or a parole office would be helped by having access to the manuals written for agency employees detailing how they should treat clients. Unofficial manuals written for the clients of these agencies are sometimes available.

The optimum posture to take with an agency is difficult to ascertain, and therefore to achieve. At some point in the negotiations with an agency, it is usually a good idea to be willing to compromise. Waiting for a better deal may not be worth the inevitable delays, red tape, consumption of time—and consequent frustration. The client who is not satisfied with a reasonable but imperfect solution may even end up the loser. For example, if a client demands more benefits or fewer penalties, an administrator may inspect a case more closely, resulting in the discovery of an error in awarding previous benefits or calculating penalties. The difference is as likely to move against as in favor of the client.

Getting Through the Maze

The concept of maze smartness cannot be defined exactly, but the university is a good place to acquire it. The details of degree requirements, examinations, and the various standards of individual professors offer appropriate training for the mazes of the outside world. In personal conversations, Norton Long has described the university as a microcosm of the larger society, with the principal task of teaching maze smartness. A student who emerges from the maze of higher education with a degree is ready for life amid other organizations.

Education is only one of a university's products. In many institutions the instructional staff includes only a minority of its employees. Other programs offer income support, health care, job placement, housing, police protection, and entertainment. Each program contributes to the pattern of the maze. It may be no simpler to qualify for a scholarship or to deal with the housing office than to decipher an instructor's grading criteria.

Like other organizations, a university makes some demands on its clients that appear sensible and makes others that appear silly. Also, no university is like another. Some describe their academic requirements in great detail, specifying a large number of particular courses to be completed: swimming, state history and politics, English composition, three years of a foreign language, and so on. Others make only general demands: 120 semester credits overall, with a distribution of courses to include something of the student's choice in the humanities, the social sciences, and the natural sciences. Some private institutions require a certain number of chapel visits each term. Some are strict about the separation of males and females in dormitories or the use of drugs and alcohol. Others take no official interest in these matters.

Knowing the Rules

What to do in the face of an administrative maze? Learn its rules, then figure out the easiest way to reach your goals. This advice is easier said than done. Knowing what your goals are may present a problem. Many students enter college without a clear sense of their own desires, just as many clients approach government agencies without knowing exactly why they have come. Knowing yourself, as well as knowing what services an agency offers, comes with experience. First encounters with an organization may provide clients with an opportunity to learn what benefits it offers and how its programs meet their interests. At a certain point, however, clients should define their goals as clearly as possible. Too long a time spent just in learning about opportunities may turn from purposive experience to a waste of time.

There is no precise timetable for learning about an organization. Complex bodies, like universities, may surprise their most experienced clients and staff with new information. As personal goals become clearer, however, there can be a more directed pursuit of what the organization has to offer, along with a higher probability of satisfying needs.

Learning an organization's rules may present some problems. Remember that formal rules are likely to be written into the university catalog (or an agency manual). There will probably be many rules, and some confusion as to which of the seemingly overlapping or contradictory provisions apply in any one case. Then there are the informal norms and practices. The staff may generally view certain rules as obsolete, without bothering to remove them formally. There are also the whims of individual staff members. Some are generous, while others are stingy with their time and with the resources of the organization. Some professors grade easily while others are tough graders. Similarly, in a welfare office, some clerks will dole out the government's money one dollar at a time, while others will seek a way through the rules—or even ignore the rules—in order to help a client. Just as some physicians in a government clinic will refer a patient to a specialist at the first sign of complications, others will refuse to see the need. Some personnel play favorites among their clients on the basis of sex, race, and social class.

If it is difficult to learn the formal rules of an organization, it is even more difficult to chart its informal practices. The nuances of individual staff members can be vital, but especially hard to describe in a systematic fashion. Nonetheless, a perceptive client may benefit from the principle of *precedent.* Because government organizations are constrained by law or politics to treat clients equally, one client can demand—and often receive— similar benefits that were given to another client in more or less the same circumstances. Knowing what precedents exist may require having an "ear to the ground" to know what other clients have demanded and received. Information of this kind can help to cut through an organization's rules. Learning what an organization *does* may be simpler and more effective than learning what it *should* do.

Aggressive Self-Interest

Knowing the rules is only one component of maze smartness. Another is adopting an aggressive style of dealing with organizations. Passive clients depend heavily on others to diagnose their needs and to deliver services to them. Often the demands on an organization are so great that passive clients suffer delay and incomplete services. Clients must show a certain level of aggressiveness in defining their needs and insisting on their satisfaction, up to the level that is consistent with an organization's procedures. Active self-interest is not a prescription for unrestrained selfishness or a lack of concern for other clients. The ancient Hebrew sage Hillel said it best:

If I am not for myself, who is for me?
And if I am only for myself, what am I?

Just how actively clients should pursue their own interests requires a detailed assessment of conditions. Some cultures reward more vivid displays of aggression than others. While a calculated display of temper—shouting and pounding the counter—would produce effective service in some settings, it might bring the police elsewhere. Often the key is to get the attention of a staff member with the capacity to recognize and satisfy your demands. If the counter clerk can do that, fine. It is best to avoid intruding into the realm of higher officials if subordinates are acting satisfactorily. Superiors unnecessarily brought into a case might only see a problem, and disturb what might have been adequate service rendered in routine fashion.

When the routines do not work properly, however, it is time to seek the attention of staff with more clout. Often a simple request to see the office manager will be adequate. As a general rule, the client's profile should be as low as possible. If administrators feel they are being harassed, they can strike back. Their weapons include delay and misplaced files. When clients are being denied proper attention, then some assertiveness is appropriate. If the case is a good one, it pays to risk some degree of harassment from the staff. Important here is the *calculation* between probable costs and gain. Unless clients cherish a squabble for its own sake or for the higher principles involved, it is better to accept less than a full measure of service than to enter into a major confrontation for the likelihood of a small gain.

CLIENT SERVICES

The Ombudsman

The office of ombudsman has appeared in several states and localities, and is popular with citizens and administrators alike, because of its intermediary role. The ombudsman listens to the problems of citizens who feel deprived of benefits or claim they are unfairly trapped by regulations. Departments generally have their own procedures for reviewing cases when citizens appeal decisions. Sometimes, however, these procedures themselves may fail to satisfy claimants, or their complexity may discourage citizens from using them. The ombudsman is available to try to solve simple appeals from the public. He or she is responsible for sorting out the merits of a complaint and trying to set things right. Typically, the ombudsman is a person of public prominence and status, and has a staff to help with the details. Usually the ombudsman is appointed for an extended term. Thus, the appointee can enjoy the respect of administrators while being independent of the agencies that are subject to review.

The powers of ombudsman vary from place to place. Generally, they are unable to *order* a change in administrative decisions, but must rely on persuasion and the threat of adverse publicity. In order to avoid being swamped by crank or repetitious complaints, the ombudsman usually has discretion over the cases to be pursued. At times, the proposed creation of an ombudsman has rankled administrators, who fear the annoyance of additional reviews or a threat to their independence. However, agency heads usually come to welcome the ombudsman as an additional device to monitor their subordinates. The ombudsman's findings typically go first to agency heads, and most often are satisfied by agency compliance. Sometimes an inquiry about an individual case leads an agency to reconsider the merits of a more general matter, resulting in a change of policy for a large number of individuals.

One-Stop Shop

One weakness of the ombudsman approach is in its fixing of bad decisions. Many citizens have problems that began *prior* to bad decisions. They do not know where to turn in the face of numerous service providers, especially if their needs do not fit squarely into the orbit of one provider. For this kind of problem, a multiple-service referral agency (what Australians call a "one-stop stop") is the answer. A one-stop shop can be widely advertised and easy for clients to locate, and can be staffed by personnel who can clarify an incoherent maze of agencies.

Outreach

The purpose of outreach activities is to make potential clients aware of programs. Agencies advertise what they have to offer. However, few efforts are made to advertise widely the full range of social services that is available. Recall that social services have developed separately, with no one responsible for meshing different programs into a coherent whole or seeking to match clients with the programs appropriate to their needs. Outreach has met resistance by those who fear that program costs will escalate if they are actually extended to all who might qualify. Critics of outreach also feel that potential clients should be able to identify their own needs and take the first steps to arrange services.

Private Agents

Perhaps only a private agent—who works for a fee—will render advice that truly is in the client's interest. In the tax field, for example, lawyers and tax advisers sell information that they feel is more client-serving than the free advice offered by the Internal Revenue Service.

The model of the private tax adviser may spread to other sectors of public service. Storefront agencies could specialize in clusters of service that bridge the activities of several agencies in their locales. They could sell advice about which agencies a client should visit and in which sequence, fill out the forms, and accompany clients through the official maze. Payment for such services could come either directly from the clients or from referral chits given out by the service agencies.

The payment of such agents will raise questions of exploitation and corruption. Undoubtedly, some needy clients will pay more in agent fees than seems appropriate. Also, some clerks in social service programs will undoubtedly accept favors in order to expedite cases brought in by certain private agents. Similar problems occur in relations between tax offices and citizens who employ attorneys or other intermediaries. Someone must worry about appropriate procedures of control for this new kind of client's agent in the social service field. The government may have to police these agents, just as they must police lawyers and tax advisers. It is to be hoped that the controls will not be so oppressive as to curtail the benefits that private agents can offer to their clients. These inevitable problems are not reasons enough for avoiding this kind of reform. In the future, clients may have to take some steps—and some chances—to promote their own best interest.

SUMMARY

This book has mainly talked to those who are involved with public administration as students, teachers, or employers. This last chapter discusses clients' relations to public administration.

Administrative offices can be confusing if clients approach them not knowing what they want or what the agencies can do for them. No guidebook is available to tell clients which departments to apply to for benefits or to make complaints. Besides confusion, clients may run into hostility—one agency may be unwilling to help another, and certain agencies may even have a reputation for being contentious with the clients they supposedly serve. Conditions can be different in each agency office; policies and attitudes may differ from branch to branch.

To have the least frustrating and most successful experiences is to learn how to get through the administrative maze. It is best to learn as much as possible about an agency before approaching it with a problem. What are the rules—both formal and informal? What decisions have administrators made about similar cases? What is the ambience of the local office, the basic attitude toward clients? This kind of information helps clients to judge how best to press their cases.

Clients should base their approach on the nature of their cases. If they want benefits, they should present their problems in such a way that they conform with the rules. If they want to avoid penalties, they should make their situations as atypical as possible. While it is important to be aggressive when necessary, it is also important to know when to compromise.

Some channels are available to help solve clients' complaints: the ombudsman, who acts as an intermediary; the multiple-service referral agency, which can sort out the facets of a case; and the private agent, who can represent a client in agency dealings, for a fee. Outreach programs can also be helpful for their educational value and their obvious desire to obtain clients.

There is no magic formula that clients can use to deal with public agencies; they must learn to assess each situation with sensitivity and care.

Suggestions
for Further Reading

CHAPTER 1

Argyris, C. *Understanding Organizational Behavior.* Homewood, Ill.: Dorsey, 1960.

Barnard, C. *Functions of the Executive.* Cambridge, Mass.: Harvard University Press, 1938.

Marini, F., ed. *Toward a New Public Administration.* San Francisco: Chandler, 1971.

Ostrom, V. *The Intellectual Crisis in American Public Administration.* University: University of Alabama Press, 1974.

Sharkansky, I., ed. *Policy Analysis in Political Science.* Chicago: Markham, 1970.

Simon, H. *Administrative Behavior: A Study of Decision-Making Processes in Administrative Organizations,* 3d ed. New York: Free Press, 1976.

Wade, L. L., and R. L. Curry. *A Logic of Public Policy: Aspects of Political Economy.* Belmont, Calif.: Wadsworth, 1970.

Whyte, W. H. *The Organization Man.* New York: Simon & Schuster, 1957.

CHAPTER 2

Blau, P. M., and W. R. Scott. *Formal Organizations.* San Francisco: Chandler, 1962.

Davis, K. C. *Discretionary Justice: A Preliminary Inquiry.* Urbana: University of Illinois Press, 1971.

Gerth, H. H., and C. W. Mills, trans. *From Max Weber: Essays in Sociology.* New York: Oxford University Press, 1946.

Karl, B. *Executive Reorganization and Reform in the New Deal.* Cambridge, Mass.: Harvard University Press, 1963.

Lindblom, C. E. *The Policy-Making Process*. Englewood Cliffs, N.J.: Prentice-Hall, 1978.

March, J. G., and H. A. Simon. *Organizations*. New York: Wiley, 1958.

Michels, R. *Political Parties*. New York: Free Press, 1962.

Redford, E. S. *Democracy in the Administrative State*. New York: Oxford University Press, 1969.

Seidman, H. *Politics, Position and Power: The Dynamics of Federal Organization*. New York: Oxford University Press, 1980.

Sharkansky, I. *Wither the State? Politics and Public Enterprise in Three Countries*. Chatham, N.J.: Chatham, 1979.

Thompson, V. A. *Modern Organization: A General Theory*. New York: Knopf, 1964.

Wilensky, H. L. *Organizational Intelligence: Knowledge and Policy in Government and Industry*. New York: Basic Books, 1967.

CHAPTER 3

Banfield, E. C. *The Unheavenly City Revisited*. Boston: Little, Brown, 1974.

Bauer, R., ed. *Social Indicators*. Cambridge, Mass.: MIT Press, 1966.

Bernstein, M. *Regulating Business by Independent Commissions*. Princeton, N.J.: Princeton University Press, 1955.

Boyer, W. W. *Bureaucracy on Trial: Policy-Making by Government Agencies*. Indianapolis: Bobbs-Merrill, 1964.

Burns, J. M. *The Deadlock of Democracy: Four-Party Politics in America*. Englewood Cliffs, N.J.: Spectrum, 1963.

Cole, R. L. *Citizen Participation and the Urban Policy Process*. Lexington, Mass.: Heath, 1974.

Dahl, R. A. *A Preface to Democratic Theory*. Chicago: University of Chicago Press, 1956.

Edelman, M. *The Symbolic Uses of Politics*. Urbana: University of Illinois Press, 1964.

Ladd, E. C., Jr. *Where Have All the Voters Gone? The Fracturing of America's Political Parties*. New York: Norton, 1978.

Milbrath, L. W. *The Washington Lobbyists*. Chicago: Rand McNally, 1963.

Nie, N. H., S. Verba, and J. R. Petrocik. *The Changing American Voter*. Cambridge, Mass.: Harvard University Press, 1976.

Selznick, P. *TVA and the Grass Roots*. Berkeley: University of California Press, 1949.

Yates, D. *Neighborhood Democracy*. Lexington, Mass.: Heath, 1973.

CHAPTER 4

Brown, R. E. *The GAO: Untapped Source of Congressional Power*. Knoxville: University of Tennessee Press, 1970.

Dodd, L. C., and R. L. Schott. *Congress and the Administrative State*. New York: Wiley, 1979.

Fiorina, M. P. *Congress: Keystone of the Washington Establishment.* New Haven: Yale University Press, 1977.

Fisher, L. *Presidential Spending Power.* Princeton, N.J.: Princeton University Press, 1975.

Haider, D. H. *When Governments Come to Washington: Governors, Mayors, and Intergovernmental Lobbying.* New York: Free Press, 1974.

Heller, W. W. *New Dimensions of Political Economy.* New York: Norton, 1967.

Neustadt, R. *Presidential Power: The Politics of Leadership.* New York: Wiley, 1976.

Pfiffner, J. P. *The President, the Budget, and Congress: Impoundment and the 1974 Budget Act.* Boulder: Westview, 1979.

Ripley, R., and G. A. Franklin. *Congress, the Bureaucracy and Public Policy.* Homewood, Ill.: Dorsey, 1980.

Rossiter, C. *The American Presidency.* New York: Signet, 1966.

Zeigler, H. *The Political Life of American Teachers.* Englewood Cliffs, N.J.: Prentice-Hall, 1967.

CHAPTER 5

Dean, J. *Blind Ambition: The White House Years* New York: Simon & Schuster, 1976.

Keyt, V. O., Jr. *The Administration of Federal Grants to the States.* Chicago: Public Administration Service, 1939.

Krislov, S. *Representative Bureaucracy.* Englewood Cliffs, N.J.: Prentice-Hall, 1974.

Mosher, F. C. *Democracy and the Public Service.* New York: Oxford University Press, 1968.

Nachmias, D., ed. *The Practice of Policy Evaluation.* New York: St. Martin's, 1980.

Pitkin, H. *The Concept of Representation.* Berkeley: University of California Press, 1976.

Rawls, J. *A Theory of Justice.* Cambridge, Mass.: Belknap, 1971.

CHAPTER 6

Argyris, C. *Integrating the Individual and the Organization.* New York: Wiley, 1964.

Blake, R. R., and J. Mouton. *The Managerial Grid.* Houston: Gulf, 1964.

Crozier, M. *The Bureaucratic Phenomenon.* Chicago: University of Chicago Press, 1964.

Etzioni, A. *Modern Organizations.* Englewood Cliffs, N.J.: Prentice-Hall, 1964.

Golembiewski, R. T. *Men, Management, and Morality: Toward a New Organizational Ethic.* New York: McGraw-Hill, 1965.

Gulick, L. H., et al. *Papers on the Science of Administration.* New York: Institute of Public Administration, 1937.

Homans, G. *The Hunan Group.* New York: Harcourt, Brace, 1950.

Kaufman, H. *Administrative Feedback: Monitoring Subordinates' Behavior.* Washington, D.C.: Brookings Institution, 1973.

Maslow, A. A. *Motivation and Personality.* New York: Harper, 1970.

Stogdill, R. M. *Handbook of Leadership: A Survey of Theory and Research*. New York: Free Press, 1974.

Taylor, F. *Scientific Management*. New York: Harper, 1911.

CHAPTER 7

Anton, T. J. *The Politics of State Expenditures in Illinois*. Urbana: University of Illinois Press, 1966.

Fenno, R. F., Jr. *The Power of the Purse: Appropriation Politics in Congress*. Boston: Little, Brown, 1966.

Hitch, C. J. *Decision-Making for Defense*. Berkeley: University of California Press, 1965.

Ippolito, D. S. *The Budget and National Politics*. San Francisco: W. H. Freeman and Company, 1978.

Kramer, F. A., ed. *Contemporary Approaches to Public Budgeting*. Cambridge, Mass.: Winthrop, 1979.

Manley, J. F. *The Politics of Finance: The House Committee on Ways and Means*. Boston: Little, Brown, 1970.

Pierce, L. C. *The Politics of Fiscal Policy Formation*. Pacific Palisades, Calif.: Goodyear, 1971.

Schilling, W. R., et al. *Strategy, Politics, and Defense Budgets*. New York: Columbia University Press, 1962.

Wildavsky, A. *The Politics of the Budgetary Process*. Boston: Little, Brown, 1979.

CHAPTER 8

Gawthrop, L. C. *Bureaucratic Behavior in the Executive Branch: An Analysis of Organizational Change*. New York: Free Press, 1969.

Heclo, H. *Government of Strangers*. Washington, D.C.: Brookings Institution, 1977.

Mann, D. E. *The Assistant Secretaries: Problems and Processes of Appointment*. Washington, D.C.: Brookings Institution, 1965.

Nigro, F. A., and L. G. Nigro. *The New Public Personnel Administration*. Itasca, Ill.: Peacock, 1976.

O'Neil, R. *The Rights of Government Employees: The Basic ACLU Guide to a Government Employee's Rights*. New York: Avon, 1978.

Stahl, O. G. *Public Personnel Administration*. New York: Harper, 1976.

Warner, W. L., et al. *The American Federal Executive*. New Haven: Yale University Press, 1963.

CHAPTER 9

Coleman, J. S. *Equality of Educational Opportunity*. Washington, D.C.: U.S. Government Printing Office, 1966.

Dorfman, R., ed. *Measuring Benefits of Government Investments.* Washington, D.C.: Brookings Institution, 1965.

Hatry, H. P., and D. M. Fisk. *Improving Productivity and Productivity Measurement in Local Government.* Washington, D.C.: National Commission on Productivity, 1971.

Meltsner, A. *Policy Analysis in the Bureaucracy.* Berkeley: University of California Press, 1976.

Suchman, E. A. *Evaluative Research: Principles and Practice in Public Service and Social Action Programs.* New York: Russell Sage, 1967.

Weiss, C. H. *Evalution Research: Methods of Assessing Program Effectiveness.* Englewood Cliffs, N.J.: Prentice-Hall, 1972.

Wholey, J. S., et al. *Federal Evaluation Policy.* Washington, D.C.: Urban Institute, 1970.

CHAPTER 10

Braybrooke, D., and C. E. Lindblom. *A Strategy of Decision.* New York: Free Press, 1963.

Crecine, J. P. *Government Problem-Solving: A Computer Simulation of Municipal Budgeting.* Chicago: Rand McNally, 1969.

Deutsch, K. W. *The Nerves of Government.* New York: Free Press, 1963.

Downs A. *Inside Bureaucracy.* Boston: Little, Brown, 1967.

Dror, Y. *Public Policymaking Reexamined.* San Francisco: Chandler, 1967.

Enloe, C. H. *The Politics of Pollution in a Comparative Perspective: Ecology and Power in Four Nations.* New York: Longman, 1975.

Gore, W. J. *Administrative Decision-Making: A Heuristic Model.* New York: Wiley, 1964.

Kaufman, H., *Red Tape: Its Origins, Uses, and Abuses.* Washington, D.C.: Brookings Institution, 1977.

Logsdon, J. M. *The Decision to Go to the Moon: Project Apollo and the National Interest.* Cambridge, Mass.: MIT Press, 1970.

Lyden, F. J., and E. G. Miller. *Planning-Programming-Budgeting: A Systems Approach to Management.* Chicago: Markham, 1968.

March, J. G., ed. *Handbook of Organizations.* Chicago: Rand McNally, 1965.

Sharkansky, I. *The Routines of Politics.* New York: Van Nostrand, 1970.

CHAPTER 11

Bardach, E. *The Implementation Game: What Happens After a Bill Becomes a Law.* Cambridge, Mass.: MIT Press, 1977.

Derthick, M. *New Towns in-Town: Why a Federal Program Failed.* Washington, D.C.: Urban Institute, 1972.

Edwards, G. C., III. *Implementing Public Policy.* Washington, D.C.: Congressional Quarterly, 1980.

Moynihan, D. P. *Maximum Feasible Misunderstanding: Community Action in the War on Poverty.* New York: Free Press, 1970.

Pressman, J. L., and A. Wildavsky. *Implementation.* Berkeley: University of California Press, 1973.

Sindler, A. P., ed. *American Political Institutions and Public Policy.* Boston: Little, Brown, 1969.

Sowell, T. *Race and Economics.* New York: Longman, 1975.

CHAPTER 12

Adelman, I., and C. T. Morris. *Society, Politics, and Economic Development.* Baltimore: Johns Hopkins University Press, 1967.

Armstrong, J. A. *The European Administrative Elite.* Princeton, N.J.: Princeton University Press, 1973.

Dye, T. R. *Politics, Economics, and the Public: Policy Outcomes in the American States.* Chicago: Rand McNally, 1966.

Gant, G. F. *Development Administration: Concepts, Goals, Methods.* Madison: University of Wisconsin Press, 1979.

Heady, F. *Public Administration: A Comparative Perspective.* New York: Dekker, 1979.

Radian, A. *Resource Mobilization in Poor Countries: Implementing Tax Policies.* New Brunswick, N.J.: Transaction, 1980.

Riggs, F. W. *Administration in Developing Countries: The Theory of Prismatic Society.* Boston: Houghton Mifflin, 1964.

Sharkansky, I. *The United States: A Study of a Developing Country.* New York: Longman, 1975.

CHAPTER 13

Beer, S. H., and R. E. Barringer, eds. *The State and the Poor.* Cambridge, Mass.: Winthrop, 1970.

Davis, J. W., Jr., and K. M. Dolbeare. *Little Groups of Neighbors: The Selective Service System.* Chicago: Markham, 1968.

Derthick, M. *The Influence of Federal Grants.* Cambridge, Mass.: Harvard University Press, 1970.

Elazar, D. *American Federalism:* New York: Crowell, 1976.

Sharkansky, I. *The Maligned States: Policy Accomplishments, Problems, and Opportunities.* New York: McGraw-Hill, 1978.

Walsh, A. H. *The Public's Business: The Politics and Practices of Government Corporations.* Cambridge, Mass.: MIT Press, 1978.

Wright, D. W. *Understanding Intergovernmental Relations.* North Scituate, Mass.: Duxbury, 1978.

CHAPTER 14

Cox, E. F., R. C. Fellmeth, and J. E. Schulz. *Nader's Raiders.* New York: Grove, 1969.

Esposito, J. C. *Vanishing Air.* New York: Grossman, 1970.

Fellmeth, R. *The Interstate Commerce Omission.* New York: Grossman, 1970.

Green, M. J. *The Closed Enterprise System.* New York: Bantam, 1972.

————, ed. *The Monopoly Makers.* New York: Grossman, 1973.

————, ed. *The Other Government: The Unseen Power of Washington Lawyers.* New York: Norton, 1978.

Krasnow, E. G., and L. D. Longley. *The Politics of Broadcast Regulation.* New York: St. Martin's, 1978.

Schwartz, B. *Administrative Law.* Boston: Little, Brown, 1976.

Turner, J. S. *The Chemical Feast.* New York: Grossman, 1970.

CHAPTER 15

Derthick, M. *Uncontrollable Spending for Social Services Grants.* Washington, D.C.: Brookings Institution, 1975.

Fisk, D. D., H. Kiesling, and T. Muller. *Private Provision of Public Services: An Overview.* Washington, D.C.: Urban Institute, 1978.

Guttman, D., and B. Willner. *The Shadow Government: The Government's Multi-Billion-Dollar Giveaway of Its Decision-Making Powers to Private Management Consultants, "Experts," and Think Tanks.* New York: Pantheon, 1976.

Hague, D. C., W. J. M. MacKenzie, and A. Barker. *Public Policy and Private Interests.* London: Macmillan, 1975.

Hanrahan, J. D. *Government for Sale: Contracting-Out the New Patronage.* Washington, D.C.: American Federation of State, County, and Municipal Employees, 1977.

Smith, B. L. R., ed. *The New Political Economy: The Public Use of the Private Sector.* New York: Halsted, 1975.

CHAPTER 16

Aberbach, J. D., and J. L. Walker. *Race in the City: Political Trust and Public Policy in the New Urban System.* Boston: Little, Brown, 1973.

Alford, R. R. *Bureaucracy and Participation: Political Cultures in Four Wisconsin Cities.* Chicago: Rand McNally, 1969.

Devine, D. J. *The Attentive Public: Polyarchal Democracy.* Chicago: Rand McNally, 1970.

Fowler, F. J., Jr. *Citizen Attitudes Toward Local Government Services and Taxes.* Cambridge, Mass.: Ballinger, 1974.

Gilmour, R. S., and R. B. Lamb. *Political Alienation in Contemporary America.* New York: St. Martin's, 1975.

Katz, D., B. Gutek, R. L. Kahn, and E. Barton. *Bureaucratic Encounters: A Pilot Study in the Evaluation of Government Services.* Ann Arbor: University of Michigan Survey Research Center, 1975.

Lipsky, M. *Protest in City Politics: Rent Strikes, Housing and the Power of the Poor.* Chicago: Rand McNally, 1970.

Lowi, T. J. *The End of Liberalism.* New York: Norton, 1979.

Index

379